# Oracle SQL*Plus

*The Definitive Guide*

# Oracle SQL*Plus
## *The Definitive Guide*

Jonathan Gennick

**O'REILLY®**

*Beijing · Cambridge · Farnham · Köln · Paris · Sebastopol · Taipei · Tokyo*

**Oracle SQL\*Plus: The Definitive Guide**
by Jonathan Gennick

Published by O'Reilly & Associates, Inc. 101 Morris Street, Sebastopol, CA 95472.

**Editor:** Deborah Russell

**Production Editor:** Ellie Fountain Maden

**Printing History:**

| | |
|---|---|
| March 1999: | First Edition. |

ISBN: 1-56592-578-5                                                                      [2/00]
[M]

*I dedicate this book to my wife Donna, who, in spite of all my crazy dreams and ambitions, continues to stand with me.*

—Jonathan Gennick

# Table of Contents

# *Preface*

Every day, computer professionals the world over wake up, travel to the office, sit down in front of a computer, and begin another day working with that database called Oracle. Programmers write queries and stored procedures. Database administrators monitor performance, make database changes, and perform other maintenance tasks. Operations people may need to back up or recover a database. Analysts may need to explore the structure of a database to answer the question "What's out there?" Testers may work on developing and loading test data. A wide variety of people perform a wide variety of tasks, yet the vast majority of them are likely to have one thing in common—SQL*Plus.

SQL*Plus is the command-line interface to the Oracle database. It's a client-server application that allows you to enter and execute SQL statements and PL/SQL blocks. One of the most common uses for SQL*Plus is as an ad hoc query tool. You type in a SELECT statement, execute it, and see what results come back from the database. Programmers do this all the time when developing queries and when experimenting with Oracle's built-in functions. Database administrators sometimes issue queries against Oracle's data dictionary tables in order to see what objects are "out there" in the database.

One important capability of SQL*Plus is its ability to format and paginate query results. You can enter a SELECT statement, execute it, and have the results formatted so you can print them and produce a credible-looking report. SQL*Plus implements a full range of formatting commands that allow you to add page headers and footers to your reports. There are also commands that allow you to format the data displayed in the report. You can control column headings, number formats, and column widths.

Another important capability of SQL*Plus, and one you should take advantage of if you don't already, is its ability to run predefined SQL script files. A script file is analogous to a DOS BAT file, and is simply a text file that contains commands to execute. These commands may be SQL statements, PL/SQL code blocks, or SQL*Plus commands. Scripts may be used to automate frequently-performed tasks. One of the easiest things to do is to write a script to generate a report. You do this by placing all the formatting commands and the SELECT query for the report into the script file. Then whenever you want the report, you just execute the script. In addition to producing printed reports, scripts may also be used to automate routine tasks such as creating a new user, or they may be used to display data on the screen. You might, for example, write a script to display constraint definitions for a table, or perhaps to list the system privileges granted to one of your users.

SQL*Plus is also frequently used as a tool for loading stored code, such as a stored procedure, into the database. Years ago it used to be that SQL*Plus was just about the only tool that could be used to load and compile a stored procedure, trigger, or package. That situation has changed somewhat with the arrival of new GUI-based tools, but many people still rely on the old workhorse SQL*Plus for this purpose.

A sometimes overlooked capability of SQL*Plus is its use as a data extraction tool. If you've been around Oracle for a while, you are no doubt familiar with SQL*Loader. SQL*Loader is Oracle's general-purpose data load utility. Using it, you can read data from a flat file and load it into one or more database tables. The strange thing is that Oracle does not have a corresponding SQL*Unloader utility. When people want to extract data from Oracle into a flat file, such as a comma-delimited file, they often get frustrated when looking for a utility to do the job. SQL*Plus, it turns out, is a viable choice for the task. It's a relatively simple matter to spool the results of a query to a file. It doesn't take much extra work to format that output so that it is comma- or tab-delimited.

Finally, SQL*Plus gives you a reliable way to propagate database structure changes when you need to make the same change to more than one database. If you have a table change that needs to be made on several similar databases, you can write a SQL*Plus script to do the job. This script can easily be executed against each database, saving you the trouble of making the same change several times over. This is a great convenience if you deal with clients in a variety of locations, because you can send the script out to each client, where it can be executed by the staff against the database.

To many people, SQL*Plus, with its command-line interface, must seem increasingly like an anachronism. Graphical user interfaces are prevalent everywhere, and often it seems as if computer users have forgotten how to do anything but point and click with a mouse. You might ask, then, "Why bother to learn SQL*Plus? Why bother with an ancient command-line utility?" These are fair questions.

I have come to lean heavily on SQL*Plus because it is always there, and it always works. In my work as a consultant, I frequently visit clients and work with databases on a variety of platforms. Some sites have Enterprise Manager installed. Some do not. Some Unix sites lean more heavily on the GUI version of Server Manager, and others actually do most of their work at the command line. One thing I can always count on, no matter where I go, is that SQL*Plus will be available. Not only is SQL*Plus available on the database administrator's PC, it is often available on user PCs as well. No matter which machine I use at a client site, I can almost always count on this venerable utility being available, and because I know it well, I can immediately be productive.

Scripting and batch processing are two other reasons I use SQL*Plus. Following proper procedures is important, and SQL*Plus allows me to encapsulate the commands necessary to add a new database user into one script, so each time I create a new user it is done consistently.

Finally, one more reason I use SQL*Plus is speed. I type very fast, and I type very accurately. Wonderful as many of the modern GUI applications are, I can often perform a task more quickly using SQL*Plus. This is not always true, but it is true often enough, especially when you consider the time it takes to load and start a GUI interface such as Enterprise Manager versus the time it takes to load and start SQL*Plus.

## *Why I Wrote This Book*

My motivation for writing this book stems from my early experiences learning about the Oracle database. Oracle's documentation tends to be very narrowly focused, each manual discussing only those things strictly related to the product being written about, and the manual for SQL*Plus is no exception. Oracle's manual will tell you about SQL*Plus, but only about SQL*Plus. There is little information on how to use SQL*Plus in conjunction with other Oracle products such as PL/SQL or SQL*Loader. There is also little information on using SQL*Plus to perform common tasks like viewing a constraint definition or extracting data.

I remember clearly the frustration of working with three manuals spread out in front of me: the SQL manual, the SQL*Plus manual, and the PL/SQL manual. I remember the frustration of frequently picking up the wrong manual because I didn't understand clearly the relationship between these three products. Was DESCRIBE a SQL command? How could I use a SQL*Plus variable in a PL/SQL script?

Even when I knew that something could be done with SQL*Plus, I frequently didn't find clear direction in the Oracle manuals. The first time I wrote a script to extract data to a file, I spent quite a bit of time flipping back and forth in the manual and experimenting with various commands before I finally got the results I wanted. Things became even more complicated when I began to write scripts and batch jobs with SQL*Plus. Suddenly I found myself wanting to branch, and even to loop, from a SQL*Plus script. SQL*Plus doesn't officially provide this functionality, but there are some tricks you can put to good use.

Finally, this is the book I want to give my clients and coworkers when they ask me how-to questions. Next time I'm asked how to get data out of Oracle and into a comma-delimited file, I'll just refer them to Chapter 5. When I'm asked about formatting a report, I'll refer them to Chapter 3, and when I'm asked how to write an IF statement in SQL*Plus, I'll refer them to Chapter 7. Each of these chapters presents a solution to its respective problem, and leads you step by step through the process of implementing that solution.

# Objectives of This Book

The single, driving objective of this book is to help you squeeze every last possible ounce of productivity and usefulness out of SQL*Plus. If you read this book cover to cover, at the end you will have learned:

- Methodical approaches to common tasks such as generating a report and extracting data to a flat file

- How to enter and edit commands in the SQL*Plus environment, with and without an external editor

- How to write simple scripts using SQL*Plus

- How to prompt for user input and use that input in SQL commands, PL/SQL blocks, and SQL*Plus commands

- How to stretch the limits of what you can do in a SQL*Plus script by implementing pseudo-IF statements, and by using one script to generate another

- How the Product User Profile, an Oracle security feature, works with SQL*Plus

- How to customize your SQL*Plus environment

- How you can use SQL*Plus to view the definitions for database objects such as views, tables, constraints, triggers, indexes, and synonyms

- How to use SQL*Plus as a tuning aid to maximize the performance of your SQL queries

An additional objective of this book is to serve as a ready reference you can pull out when faced with a common task. If you need to generate a report, open to the chapter on reports and follow the steps. Need to extract data? Open to the chapter on data extraction, and again just follow the steps. Every effort has been made to organize the information topically, so that all the information you need to accomplish a specific task is in one chapter. Where feasible, step-by-step instructions are provided so you don't need to wade through a lot of theory in order to accomplish something.

# *Structure of This Book*

This book is divided into eleven chapters and two appendixes. The chapters are task-oriented and show you how you can use SQL*Plus to perform common tasks such as printing a report, or extracting data to a file. The appendixes contain reference material, such as a list of all SQL*Plus commands.

Chapter 1, *Introduction to SQL*Plus*, goes into more detail about what SQL*Plus really is and why you should master it. It gives you a taste of the many different tasks SQL*Plus can be used for. A short history of SQL*Plus is included, as well as a description of the database used for many of the examples in this book, particularly the reporting examples.

Chapter 2, *Interacting with SQL*Plus*, shows you how to start SQL*Plus, enter, execute, and edit commands. This is basic information you need to know.

Chapter 3, *Generating Reports with SQL*Plus*, explains the reporting features of SQL*Plus, and also presents a step-by-step method for creating a report that has worked very well for me.

Chapter 4, *Writing SQL*Plus Scripts*, explains the basic scripting capabilities of SQL*Plus. Primarily, this chapter shows how SQL*Plus substitution variables work, and how you can use them to your advantage. In addition, it covers the subject of getting input from a user, and shows you how to control the output the user sees as the script is executed.

Chapter 5, *Extracting and Loading Data*, shows how you can use SQL*Plus to extract data from an Oracle database and place it into a text file suitable for loading into another program such as a spreadsheet. This text file may be delimited, by commas, for example, or it may consist of fixed-width columns. The chapter ends with an example showing how SQL*Loader may be used to load that same data into another Oracle database.

Chapter 6, *Exploring Your Database*, shows how you can query Oracle's data dictionary tables in order to see the structure of commonly-used database objects, such as tables and indexes.

Chapter 7, *Advanced Scripting*, builds on Chapter 4, but covers some advanced, and sometimes unusual, scripting techniques. This chapter introduces bind variables, and explains how they are different from user variables. This chapter also shows some creative techniques you can use to add some limited branching, and even some looping, to your SQL*Plus scripts.

Chapter 8, *Tuning and Timing*, presents the SQL*Plus features that support the tuning of SQL statements. Also covered in this chapter is Oracle's EXPLAIN PLAN command, which lets you get a look at the execution strategy that the Oracle optimizer will use for any given SQL statement.

Chapter 9, *The Product User Profile*, introduces a security feature that a database administrator can use to limit what a user can do with SQL*Plus. The product user profile allows you to turn off specific SQL and SQL*Plus commands for one user or a group of users. It can also be used to limit a user's access to certain roles while connected via SQL*Plus.

Chapter 10, *Administration with SQL*Plus*, covers the new administrative commands that have been added to SQL*Plus beginning with version 8.1 (available with Oracle8i). These commands are the same ones that the Server Manager product implements. They have been added to SQL*Plus in preparation for Server Manager's demise.

Chapter 11, *Customizing Your SQL*Plus Environment*, shows a number of ways in which you may customize your SQL*Plus environment. The site and user profiles are explained, as well as several registry settings that affect users on Windows 95, 98, and NT.

Appendix A, *SQL*Plus Command Reference*, contains syntax diagrams for all SQL*Plus commands.

Appendix B, *SQL*Plus Format Elements*, describes the various format elements that may be used to build up format strings to be used with commands, such as COLUMN and ACCEPT, that format output or accept user input.

## *Audience*

I like to think there is something in this book for everyone: programmers, database administrators, and other technically inclined Oracle users. If you work with Oracle on a daily basis, and if you use SQL*Plus in your work, then you need to know what's in this book. If you are someone just learning Oracle, this book will provide you with a good understanding of SQL*Plus, how it fits into the Oracle environment, and how you can use it productively. You know, if you've read this far, that SQL*Plus is a multifaceted product, and can be used for a wide variety of tasks. You can benefit by learning to get the most out of the tools you work with on a daily basis.

# *Obtaining the Scripts and Sample Data*

Many examples from the book, as well as SQL*Plus scripts to load the data used for the examples, can be downloaded from O'Reilly's web site at *http://www.oreilly.com/catalog/orsqplus*.

To load the data, download the file named *SAMPLE_DATA.ZIP*, unzip the files, and follow the instructions given in Chapter 1.

# *Conventions Used in This Book*

The following conventions are used in this book:

*Italic*
> Used for filenames, directory names, URLs, and occasional emphasis.

`Constant width`
> Used for code examples.

**`Constant width bold`**
> Used in examples that show interaction between SQL*Plus and a user. Commands typed by the user are shown in bold, while output from SQL*Plus is shown in normal text.

*`Constant width italic`*
> In some code examples, indicates an element (e.g., a filename) you supply.

*UPPERCASE*
> In code examples, indicates PL/SQL keywords. In text, indicates PL/SQL keywords, table names, and column names.

*lowercase*
> In code examples, indicates user-defined items such as variables, parameters, etc.

*Punctuation*
> In code examples, enter exactly as shown.

*Indentation*
> In code examples, helps to show structure (but is not required).

--   In code examples, a double hyphen begins a single-line comment, which extends to the end of a line.

*/* and */*
> In code examples, these characters delimit a multiline comment, which can extend from one line to another.

.    In code examples and related discussions, a dot qualifies a reference by separating an object name from a component name. In this book, dot notation is most often used in fully-qualified column names, which you will see written as *table_name.field_name*. The dot separates the table name from the column name.

< > In syntax descriptions, angle brackets enclose the name of a syntactic element.

[ ]   In syntax descriptions, square brackets enclose optional items.

{ }   In syntax descriptions, curly brackets enclose a set of items from which you must choose only one.

|    In syntax descriptions, a vertical bar separates the items enclosed in curly brackets, as in {VARCHAR2 | DATE | NUMBER}.

---

Indicates a tip, suggestion, or general note. For example, we'll tell you if you need to use a particular Oracle version or if an operation requires certain privileges.

---

---

Indicates a warning or caution. For example, we'll tell you if Oracle does not behave as you'd expect or if a particular operation has a negative impact on performance.

---

# Which Platform and Version?

SQL*Plus changes frequently. Each new version brings with it new commands, and new options to use with old commands. Most of the examples in this book use SQL*Plus 8.0. A few use SQL*Plus 2.3, and the ones in Chapter 10, *Administration with SQL*Plus*, use Oracle8i and SQL*Plus 8.1. You should be able to apply the information in this book to any reasonably current version of the product. If you have any doubts about whether or not a command will work with the specific version of SQL*Plus you are using, check the *SQL*Plus User's Guide and Reference* manual for that version.

A note is in order on operating systems. Throughout the book, references are made to the "Windows" operating system. Whenever you see the term "Windows" used, please understand it to mean Windows NT, Windows 95, Windows 3.1, Windows 3.11, Windows 98, or whatever other flavor of Windows might exist.

# How to Contact Us

We have tested and verified the information in this book to the best of our ability, but you may find that features have changed (or even that we have made mistakes!). Please let us know about any errors you find, as well as your suggestions for future editions, by writing to:

O'Reilly & Associates, Inc.
101 Morris Street
Sebastopol, CA 95472
1-800-998-9938 (in the U.S. or Canada)
1-707-829-0515 (international/local)
1-707-829-0104 (FAX)

You can also send us messages electronically. To be put on the mailing list or request a catalog, send email to:

*info@oreilly.com*

To ask technical questions or comment on the book, send email to:

*bookquestions@oreilly.com*

We have a web site for the book, where we'll list examples, errata, and any plans for future editions. You can access this page at:

*http://www.oreilly.com/catalog/orsqplus/*

For more information about this book and others, see the O'Reilly web site:

*http://www.oreilly.com*

# Acknowledgments

The first book that I ever wrote consumed so much energy that I promised myself, and my family, that I would never write another. That promise lasted about two months, when I became consumed with the idea of writing the book you are now reading. I owe a lot to my wife Donna, who understands my drive to write, and who bears a lot more of the load than she should have to while I hole up in my office and work. This book has been my excuse for avoiding just about every household chore imaginable, yet Donna has been very supportive during the endeavor.

My children have also contributed to the development of this book. If nothing else, they burst into my office on a daily basis to distract me, and to remind me that there are more important things in life than typing on a computer all day. They have also contributed time that I might otherwise have spent with them. My three-year-old son Jeff has grown up watching me write, and must think that all daddies come with a laptop computer attached. To my daughter Jenny, I want to say that I have enjoyed all our late-night excursions together to the local book-store. I'm glad to see that you have developed the same love for books that I have. You may not always believe it, but you are my pride and joy. I see a lot of myself in you, and I'm glad you ended up as *my* daughter.

My profound thanks also go out to John-Paul Navarro and David Dreyer, who read each chapter as it was written. David Dreyer is an independent consultant resid-ing near Detroit, Michigan, and specializes in PowerBuilder and Oracle develop-ment. Dave is one of the most cerebral programmers that I know. Always calm and thoughtful, Dave has added a great deal to this book with his insightful com-ments. John-Paul Navarro is a systems administrator for Argonne National Labora-tories in Argonne, Illinois. John-Paul and I go way back both as friends and col-leagues, and I have no end of respect for his technical abilities. He was always willing to discuss technical issues that came up during the writing of this book, and for that I am in his debt.

Thanks to Alison Holloway, product manager for SQL*Plus. "Home" for Alison, and SQL*Plus, too, in case you ever wondered, is in Melbourne, Australia. Alison helped dig up background information and history on SQL*Plus. She provided information on new features being added to SQL*Plus for the upcoming Oracle8i release, and also provided me with an early look at the documentation. Without her help, Chapter 10 would not exist. In addition to all her other help, Alison did a technical review of the entire book after it was written.

Kirk Bradley, Ken Jacobs, Jay Rossiter, and Richard Rendell, all of Oracle Corpora-tion, provided the historical information about SQL*Plus in Chapter 1. It's always nice to know something of the tools one works with besides just the raw techni-cal details of how they are used. SQL*Plus has been around a long time, and Kirk, Ken, and Richard have provided some interesting historical tidbits.

A number of technical reviewers read and commented on the final manuscript. These include David Kaufman of TUSC, Dave Kreines, Eric Givler, Alison Hollo-way, and John-Paul Navarro. I am grateful to each of these people for giving me an unbiased view of the manuscript, pointing out errors, and providing sugges-tions on ways to improve the clarity of the text. This book is the better for their efforts.

Howard Vanderstow and Paul Cheney, both database administrators with the State of Michigan's Office of Technology Resources, provided some welcome assistance in generating the examples for the HELP command in Chapter 2. They also helped me research the location and structure of the database table containing the help text used by SQL*Plus.

I owe a great debt to Brian Gill, who encouraged me when I had the initial idea for this book. Without him, this project might never have gotten off the ground. Thanks also to my agent, David Rogelberg of Studio B, who helped me keep up with the business end of this project, and who also manages that wonderfully interesting email list that serves so well to distract me from my real work.

Several O'Reilly & Associates people contributed to this book in various ways. To Debby Russell of O'Reilly & Associates, and the editor of this book, I say: "thanks for all the red ink!" Debby is a great editor to work with. She had a lot of good ideas for organizing this book. She was very understanding when I fell behind schedule. She was very encouraging, always drawing attention to things I did well.

Edie Freedman designed the cover, and is responsible for that wonderful looking moving leaf insect on the front. Steve Abrams helped in various ways during the development of the book. Many thanks! Rob Romano did a great job with the figures. Ellie Maden pulled everything together and saw this book through the production process.

1

# Introduction to SQL\*Plus

SQL\*Plus is the command-line interface to the Oracle database. Its fundamental reason for existence is to allow you to enter and execute ad hoc SQL statements and PL/SQL code blocks. This chapter explains what SQL\*Plus is, how it relates to other Oracle tools (as well as the database), and why you should master it. At the end of the chapter I'll introduce you to the sample data, which is used for many of the examples in this book. If you like, you can load that data into your database and test out each example as you go through this book.

## What Is SQL\*Plus?

SQL\*Plus is essentially an interactive query tool, with some scripting capabilities. It is a non-GUI, character-based tool that has been around since the dawn of the Oracle age. Using SQL\*Plus, you can enter an SQL statement, such as a SELECT query, and view the results. You can also execute Data Definition Language (DDL) commands that allow you to maintain and modify your database. You can even enter and execute PL/SQL code. In spite of SQL\*Plus's age and lack of "flash," it is a workhorse tool used day in and day out by database administrators, developers, and yes, even end users. As a database administrator, it is my tool of choice for managing the databases under my care. I use it to peek under the hood—to explore the physical implementation of my database, and to create and manage users, tables, and tablespaces. In my role as a developer, SQL\*Plus is the first tool that I fire up when I need to develop a query. In spite of all the fancy, GUI-based SQL generators contained in products such as PowerBuilder, Clear Access, and Crystal Reports, I still find it quicker and easier to build up and test a complex query in SQL\*Plus before transferring it to whatever development tool I am using.

## Uses for SQL*Plus

Originally developed simply as a way to enter queries and see results, SQL*Plus has been enhanced with scripting and formatting capabilities, and can now be used for many different purposes. The basic functionality is very simple. With SQL*Plus, you can do the following:

- Issue a SELECT query and view the results

- Insert, update, and delete data from database tables

- Submit PL/SQL blocks to the Oracle server for execution

- Issue DDL commands, such as those used to create, alter, or drop database objects such as tables, indexes, and users

- Execute SQL*Plus script files

- Write output to a file

- Execute procedures and functions that are stored in a database

While they might not seem like much, these things are the building blocks you can use to perform a variety of useful functions. Consider the ability to enter a SELECT statement and view the results. The following example shows how to do this using SQL*Plus:

```
SQL> SELECT employee_id, employee_name, employee_billing_rate
  2    FROM employee;

EMPLOYEE_ID EMPLOYEE_NAME                              EMPLOYEE_BILLING_RATE
----------- ----------------------------------------- ---------------------
        101 Jonathan Gennick                                            169
        102 Jenny Gennick                                               135
        104 Jeff Gennick                                                 99
        105 Horace Walker                                               121
        107 Bohdan Khmelnytsky                                           45
        108 Pavlo Chubynsky                                             220
        110 Ivan Mazepa                                                  84
        111 Taras Shevchenko                                            100
        112 Hermon Goche                                                 70
        113 Jacob Marley                                                300

10 rows selected.
```

Combine this capability with SQL*Plus's formatting abilities and you can turn the above query into a very credible looking report, complete with page titles, page numbers, column titles, and nicely formatted output. That report might look something like this:

```
Employee Listing           Page  1

                           Billing
   Emp ID Name                Rate
   ------- -------------------- ---------
       101 Jonathan Gennick        169
       102 Jenny Gennick           135
       104 Jeff Gennick             99
       105 Horace Walker           121
       107 Bohdan Khmelnytsky       45
       108 Pavlo Chubynsky         220
       110 Ivan Mazepa              84
       111 Taras Shevchenko        100
       112 Hermon Goche             70
       113 Jacob Marley            300
```

Another twist on the same theme is to format the output so you get a comma-delimited list of values. That output could look like this:

```
101,"Jonathan Gennick",169
102,"Jenny Gennick",135
104,"Jeff Gennick",99
105,"Horace Walker",121
107,"Bohdan Khmelnytsky",45
108,"Pavlo Chubynsky",220
110,"Ivan Mazepa",84
111,"Taras Shevchenko",100
112,"Hermon Goche",70
113,"Jacob Marley",300
```

Using the SQL\*Plus SPOOL command, you could write this output to a file, and later load it into a program such as Microsoft Excel for further manipulation. It's a small leap from executing only queries to executing any other SQL statement. In fact, SQL\*Plus will let you execute any valid SQL statement, and is frequently used during database maintenance tasks. Creating a new user for example, can be accomplished by the following statement:

```
CREATE USER ashley IDENTIFIED BY some_password;
```

Of course, it's rare that you would only issue one command when you add a new user. Usually you want to assign a default tablespace and a quota on that tablespace. You may also want to grant the privileges needed to connect to the database. Whenever you have a task that requires a sequence of commands to be executed, you can simplify things by taking advantage of SQL\*Plus's scripting capabilities. The following commands, when placed in a script file, allow you to add a new user with just one command:

```
CREATE USER &&1 IDENTIFIED BY &&2
   DEFAULT TABLESPACE USER_DATA
   TEMPORARY TABLESPACE TEMPORARY_DATA
   QUOTA UNLIMITED ON TEMPORARY_DATA
   QUOTA &&3.m ON USER_DATA;

GRANT CONNECT TO &&1;
```

Assuming you named the file *CREATE_USER.SQL*, you could then issue the following command from SQL*Plus whenever you needed to add a user to your database:

```
@CREATE_USER username password quota
```

The following example shows how this works, by creating a user named ASHLEY, with a password of JUSTIN, and a quota of 10 megabytes in the USER_DATA tablespace:

```
SQL> @CREATE_USER ashley justin 10
old   1: CREATE USER &&1 IDENTIFIED BY &&2
new   1: CREATE USER ashley IDENTIFIED BY justin
old   5:    QUOTA &&3.m ON USER_DATA
new   5:    QUOTA 10m ON USER_DATA

User created.

old   1: GRANT CONNECT TO &&1
new   1: GRANT CONNECT TO ashley

Grant succeeded.
```

The output you see is SQL*Plus showing you the before and after version of each line containing a substitution variable. You will read more about substitution variables, and the subject of scripting, in Chapter 4, *Writing SQL\*Plus Scripts.*

To write really complicated scripts, you can take advantage of Oracle's built-in procedural language, PL/SQL. The following example shows how a PL/SQL block can be executed using SQL*Plus:

```
SQL> SET SERVEROUTPUT ON
SQL> BEGIN
  2      DBMS_OUTPUT.PUT_LINE('Hello World!');
  3  END;
  4  /
Hello World!
```

Once you know how to use SQL*Plus to perform the basic functions just described, you can leverage them to do the things described in this book. This includes:

- Producing reports with SQL*Plus

- Writing scripts that can be executed with SQL*Plus

- Using SQL*Plus to extract data to a text file

- Examining the structure of your database by querying the data dictionary tables

- Tuning queries using the EXPLAIN PLAN command

There are chapters in this book covering each of the above topics in detail. A lot can be accomplished with SQL*Plus. This book will show you how.

## SQL*Plus's Relation to SQL, PL/SQL and the Oracle Database

SQL*Plus is often used in conjunction with two other products, both of which have the letters "SQL" in their names. The first is SQL itself. Without a doubt, the most common use of SQL*Plus is to submit SQL statements to the database for execution. The second product is Oracle's PL/SQL procedural language. Table 1-1 gives a short summary of each of these three products.

*Table 1-1. The Three SQLs: SQL, PL/SQL, and SQL\*Plus*

| Product | Description |
|---------|-------------|
| SQL | SQL, which stands for Structured Query Language, is an ANSI (and ISO) standard language used for querying, modifying, and managing relational databases. It is used to insert, delete, update, and retrieve data. |
| PL/SQL | PL/SQL is a proprietary procedural language developed by Oracle as an extension to SQL. Like SQL, it also executes inside the database. It was created as a tool for coding business rules and procedures at the database level. |
| SQL*Plus | SQL*Plus is an Oracle-developed tool that allows you to interactively enter and execute SQL commands and PL/SQL blocks. |

Because these three products all have "SQL" as part of their names, people occasionally get confused about the relationship between them and about which commands get executed where. SQL*Plus does have its own set of commands it recognizes and executes, but any SQL queries, DDL commands, and PL/SQL blocks are sent to the database server for execution. Figure 1-1 illustrates this relationship.

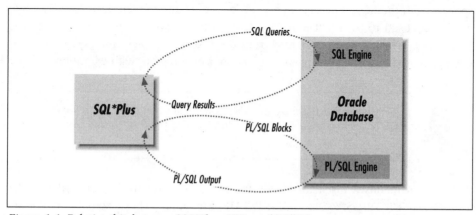

*Figure 1-1. Relationship between SQL\*Plus, SQL, and PL/SQL*

Think of SQL\*Plus as kind of a middleman, standing between you and Oracle, and helping you to communicate with your database. You type in a SQL query, SQL\*Plus takes it and sends it to the database, the database returns the results to SQL\*Plus, and SQL\*Plus displays those results in a format you can understand.

# *History of SQL\*Plus*

SQL\*Plus has been around for a long time, pretty much since the beginning of Oracle. In fact, the original author was Bruce Scott. Any DBA will recognize the name Scott. It lives on, immortalized as the owner of the demo tables that are installed with every version of Oracle. The original purpose of SQL\*Plus can be summed up in the succinct words of Kirk Bradley, another early author of SQL\*Plus, who told me, "We needed a way to enter statements into the database and get results."

This is still arguably the major reason most people use SQL\*Plus today, over fifteen years after it was originally written. SQL\*Plus certainly satisfies a compelling, and enduring, need.

The original name of the product was not SQL\*Plus. The original name was UFI, which stands for User Friendly Interface. This name has its roots in one of the first relational database systems ever developed, IBM's System R. System R was the product of a research effort by IBM. Some of IBM's documents referred to the command-line interface as the User Friendly Interface, and that name was adopted by Oracle for their interactive SQL utility.

One of the more interesting uses Oracle had for UFI was as a tool to produce their documentation. The DOCUMENT command, now considered obsolete, was used for this purpose. Script files were created that contained the manual text, interspersed with the SQL statements needed for the examples. The DOCUMENT command was used to set off the manual text so that it would just be copied to the output file. When these scripts were run, the text was copied, the SQL statements were executed, and the result was documentation complete with examples.

 UFI was used extensively in Oracle's internal testing and QA efforts. SQL\*Plus still plays a significant role in Oracle's testing, even today.

SQL\*Plus maintains a fascinating relic from the old days in the form of the SET TRIMOUT, SET TRIMSPOOL, and SET TAB commands. These commands control the printing of trailing spaces and the use of tabs to format columnar output. To understand why these commands even exist, you have to realize that when

SQL*Plus first made its appearance, people thought a dial-up speed of 1200 bps was *fast*. If you had a lot of whitespace in your report, you spent a lot of time watching spaces print across your screen. In that environment, trimming spaces and using tabs to format columns provided a huge gain in throughput. Today, with our 10-megabit-per-second LAN connections and our 56kb modems, we hardly give this a thought.

During the mid-1980s, Oracle experimented with efforts to add procedural capabilities to UFI. The result of this effort was AUFI, which stood for Advanced User Friendly Interface. AUFI implemented such things as IF statements and looping constructs, and was demonstrated publicly at an International Oracle User Group meeting in 1986 by Ken Jacobs, who is now the Vice-President of Data Server Product Management for Oracle. In spite of the public demos, whether or not to actually release AUFI as a shipping product was the subject of some debate within Oracle. Trying to layer a procedural language on top of the existing UFI command set was proving very difficult. It was made even more difficult by the need to maintain full backward compatibility so that existing scripts written by Oracle's clients would not suddenly break when those clients upgraded. Because of these issues, the code to support the procedural enhancements became very complex and somewhat unreliable. The issues of reliability and complexity led to Oracle's ultimate decision to kill the product, so AUFI never actually shipped. With the later advent of PL/SQL, procedural logic was supported within the database, and efforts to support a procedural scripting language were then seen as unnecessary. The name AUFI lives on in the name of the temporary file created when you use the SQL*Plus EDIT command. That file is named *AFIEDT.BUF*. Even today, AFI is the prefix used for all the source code.

With the release of Oracle 5.0 in 1985, the name of the product was changed to SQL*Plus. The changes since then have been mostly evolutionary. Each new release brings with it a few new commands and a few new options on existing commands. Some commands have been made obsolete, but many of these obsolete commands are still supported for purposes of backward compatibility.

The most recent changes to SQL*Plus have been the addition of support for commands such as STARTUP, SHUTDOWN, and RECOVER, which were previously only available in Server Manager. SQL*Plus is now the primary command-line interface to the Oracle database. Even SQL Worksheet, Enterprise Manager's ad-hoc query tool, makes use of SQL*Plus to execute the commands that you enter. Oracle's future plans for the product don't call for anything revolutionary, just a steady stream of enhancements in order to keep up with each new release of Oracle. It's just possible that SQL*Plus will be around for another fifteen years.

# *Why Master SQL\*Plus?*

SQL*Plus is a universal constant in the Oracle world. Every installation I have ever seen has this tool installed. For that reason alone it is worth learning. Even if you prefer to use other tools, such as Enterprise Manager or Clear Access, you may not always have them available. In my work as a consultant I frequently visit clients to help them with Oracle. Some clients use GUI-based query tools, some don't. Some clients use Oracle Enterprise Manager, some don't. The one universal constant I can count on is the availability of SQL*Plus. The last thing I want is to be at a client site needing to look up something mundane such as an index definition, and not be able to do it because I'm not familiar with their tools. SQL*Plus is always there.

If you are a database administrator, SQL*Plus is undoubtedly a tool you already use on a daily basis. Anything you use that often is worth learning and learning well. You undoubtedly use SQL*Plus to query Oracle's data dictionary tables in order to understand the structure of your database. SQL*Plus can be used to automate that task. Sometimes it's difficult to remember the specific data dictionary tables you need to join together in order to get the information you want. With SQL*Plus, you can figure this out once and encapsulate that query into a script. Next time you need the same information, you won't have all the stress of trying to remember how to get it, and you won't have to waste time rereading the manuals in order to relearn how to get it.

SQL*Plus is also very useful for automating some routine DBA tasks. I have several SQL*Plus scripts (a *script* is a file of SQL statements and SQL*Plus commands) that produce reports on users and the database and object privileges these users have. I use these scripts to run periodic security audits on our database. I have scripts that report on tablespace usage, to help me keep on top of free space or the lack thereof. I also have scripts that run nightly to perform various maintenance tasks.

If you are a developer, you can use SQL*Plus to build up queries, to quickly develop ad-hoc reports, and to explore the data in your database. You can also use SQL*Plus to create and debug stored procedures, stored functions, packages, and object types. If you have queries that aren't performing well, you may be able to find out why by using Oracle's EXPLAIN PLAN command from SQL*Plus. EXPLAIN PLAN will tell you the execution strategy chosen by the optimizer for the query. Chapter 8, *Tuning and Timing*, talks more about this.

Many modern GUI development tools, such as PowerBuilder, for example, provide GUI-based query generators. These typically let you drag and drop tables into your query and then draw lines between fields joining those tables together. This drag-and-drop functionality may be great for a simple query that just joins a few tables, but I find that it quickly becomes cumbersome as the query grows in complexity. It's not unusual, when developing reports, to have queries that are a page or more long. Sometimes these queries consist of several SELECT statements unioned together, each query having one or more subqueries. When developing one of those mega-queries, I'll take SQL*Plus and a good editor over a GUI query tool any day of the week. Why? Because with an editor I can keep bits and pieces of the query lying around. Using Windows copy and paste, I can pull out a subquery and execute it independently without losing track of the larger query I am trying to build. I can easily comment out part of a WHERE clause when debugging a query and then uncomment it later.

If you are developing stored procedures, functions, packages, or Oracle object types using PL/SQL, then SQL*Plus may be the only tool you have for creating those in the database. Other tools, such as Oracle's Procedure Builder and Platinum Technology's SQL Station, are on the market, but not everyone will have a license to use those. In addition, third-party tools in particular may be slightly behind the curve when it comes to keeping up with Oracle releases. I suspect it took awhile for the third-party vendors to catch up when Oracle8, with its new object types, was released.

Almost anything that you want to do with an Oracle database can be done using SQL*Plus. You can write scripts to automate routine maintenance tasks, report on the state of your database, or generate ad-hoc reports for end users. You can execute queries to explore your database, and you can use SQL*Plus to create and manage any schema or database object. Because of its universal availability, you will be able to perform these functions anywhere you go. If you manage an Oracle database or develop software to run against an Oracle database, you will greatly improve your productivity by mastering this tool.

# Creating and Loading the Sample Tables

Many of the examples in this book, particularly the reporting examples, have been developed against a sample time-tracking database. It's a fairly simplistic database, containing only three tables, but it's enough to illustrate everything I talk about in this book. You may or may not wish to create this database for yourself. Creating the database will allow you to try all the examples in this book exactly as they are shown. If you choose not to create and load the sample database, at least familiarize yourself with the data model. Also glance at the sample data itself, which is reproduced later in this section. If you have looked at the model and at the data, you shouldn't have any trouble following and understanding the examples in this book.

## The Data Model

Figure 1-2 shows an Entity Relationship Diagram, or ERD, for the sample database.

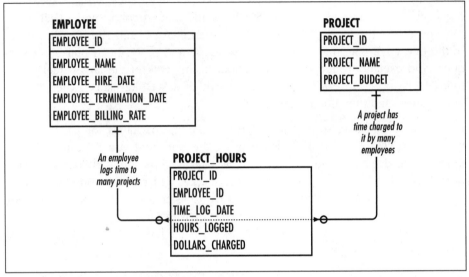

*Figure 1-2. The sample database*

As you can see from the ERD, there are only three entities: EMPLOYEE, PROJECT, and PROJECT_HOURS. Table 1-2 gives a brief description of each entity.

*Table 1-2. Entity Descriptions*

| Entity Name | Description |
| --- | --- |
| EMPLOYEE | Contains one record for each employee. This record contains the employee's name, hire date, termination date, and billing rate. The primary key is an arbitrary employee ID number. The termination date for current employees is set to NULL. |
| PROJECT | Contains one record for each project that an employee may work on. Contains the project name and budget. The primary key is an arbitrary project ID number. |
| PROJECT_HOURS | Each time an employee logs time to a project, a record is generated in this table. The record contains the number of hours charged against the project as well as the total dollar amount charged. The dollar amount charged is calculated at the time the record is created because an employee's billing rate may fluctuate over time. The primary key is a combination key made up of an employee ID, a project ID, and the date. |

The number of employees and projects is fairly small. However, there is a fairly large amount of data in the PROJECT_HOURS table to allow for the generation of multiple page reports, which are needed to demonstrate pagination, page headings, page footings, and summarization.

## The Tables

This section shows the column descriptions, including column datatypes and lengths, for each of the three sample tables. This is the same information you would get using SQL*Plus's DESCRIBE command.

### The EMPLOYEE table

```
Name                               Null?     Type
---------------------------------- --------- ----
EMPLOYEE_ID                        NOT NULL  NUMBER
EMPLOYEE_NAME                                VARCHAR2(40)
EMPLOYEE_HIRE_DATE                           DATE
EMPLOYEE_TERMINATION_DATE                    DATE
EMPLOYEE_BILLING_RATE                        NUMBER
```

### The PROJECT table

```
Name                               Null?     Type
---------------------------------- --------- ----
PROJECT_ID                         NOT NULL  NUMBER
PROJECT_NAME                                 VARCHAR2(40)
PROJECT_BUDGET                               NUMBER
```

### The PROJECT_HOURS table

```
Name                               Null?     Type
---------------------------------- --------- ----
PROJECT_ID                         NOT NULL  NUMBER
EMPLOYEE_ID                        NOT NULL  NUMBER
TIME_LOG_DATE                      NOT NULL  DATE
HOURS_LOGGED                                 NUMBER
DOLLARS_CHARGED                              NUMBER
```

## The Data

This section shows the data contained in the three sample tables.

### The EMPLOYEE table

```
 ID Name                   Hire Date     Term Date       Billing Rate
---- --------------------- ------------- --------------- ------------
 101 Jonathan Gennick      15-Nov-1961   Still Employed        169.00
 102 Jenny Gennick         16-Sep-1964   05-May-1998           135.00
 104 Jeff Gennick          29-Dec-1987   01-Apr-1998            99.00
 105 Horace Walker         15-Jun-1998   Still Employed        121.00
 107 Bohdan Khmelnytsky    02-Jan-1998   Still Employed         45.00
 108 Pavlo Chubynsky       01-Mar-1994   15-Nov-1998           220.00
 110 Ivan Mazepa           04-Apr-1998   30-Sep-1998            84.00
```

```
111  Taras Shevchenko    23-Aug-1976  Still Employed     100.00
112  Hermon Goche        15-Nov-1961  04-Apr-1998         70.00
113  Jacob Marley        03-Mar-1998  31-Oct-1998        300.00
```

## The PROJECT table

```
  ID Project Name                            Budget
----- ------------------------------  ---------------
 1001 Corporate Web Site                 1,912,000.00
 1002 Year 2000 Fixes                  999,998,000.00
 1003 Accounting System Implementation    897,000.00
 1004 Data Warehouse Maintenance          294,000.00
 1005 TCP/IP Implementation               415,000.00
```

## The PROJECT_HOURS table

The PROJECT_HOURS table contains the following information, repeated for each employee.

```
Proj ID Emp ID Log Date     Hours Charged Amt Charged
------- ------ ------------ ------------- -----------
   1001    101 01-Jan-1998           1.00      169.00
   1003    101 01-Jan-1998           3.00      507.00
   1005    101 01-Jan-1998           5.00      845.00
   1002    101 01-Feb-1998           7.00    1,183.00
   1004    101 01-Feb-1998           1.00      169.00
   1001    101 01-Mar-1998           3.00      507.00
   1003    101 01-Mar-1998           5.00      845.00
   1005    101 01-Mar-1998           7.00    1,183.00
   1002    101 01-Apr-1998           1.00      169.00
   1004    101 01-Apr-1998           3.00      507.00
   1001    101 01-May-1998           5.00      845.00
   1003    101 01-May-1998           7.00    1,183.00
   1005    101 01-May-1998           1.00      169.00
   1002    101 01-Jun-1998           3.00      507.00
   1004    101 01-Jun-1998           5.00      845.00
   1001    101 01-Jul-1998           7.00    1,183.00
   1003    101 01-Jul-1998           1.00      169.00
   1005    101 01-Jul-1998           3.00      507.00
   1002    101 01-Aug-1998           5.00      845.00
   1004    101 01-Aug-1998           7.00    1,183.00
   1001    101 01-Sep-1998           1.00      169.00
   1003    101 01-Sep-1998           3.00      507.00
   1005    101 01-Sep-1998           5.00      845.00
   1002    101 01-Oct-1998           7.00    1,183.00
   1004    101 01-Oct-1998           1.00      169.00
   1001    101 01-Nov-1998           3.00      507.00
   1003    101 01-Nov-1998           5.00      845.00
   1005    101 01-Nov-1998           7.00    1,183.00
   1002    101 01-Dec-1998           1.00      169.00
   1004    101 01-Dec-1998           3.00      507.00
```

The detail is actually the same for each employee. They all work the same hours on all projects. There are enough PROJECT_HOURS records to produce some reasonable summary reports, as you will see in Chapter 3, *Generating Reports with SQL\*Plus*.

## Loading the Sample Data

In order to load the sample data you will need an Oracle userid and password. If you are accessing a remote database, often the case for people using Windows, you will also need a connect string. If you are using Oracle Personal Edition (formerly Personal Oracle), then the connect string is not needed to connect to your local database. You must have the necessary privileges and quotas to create tables in the database you are using. Specifically, you must have the following system privileges:

```
CREATE SESSION
ALTER SESSION
CREATE TABLE
CREATE VIEW
CREATE TRIGGER
CREATE PROCEDURE
CREATE SYNONYM
CREATE SEQUENCE
CREATE TYPE (Oracle8 only)
```

Your database administrator can help you with any of these items. Once you have a username and password and have been granted the necessary privileges, you can create the sample tables and data by following these four steps:

1. Download and unzip the script files.

2. Start SQL\*Plus.

3. Log into your Oracle database.

4. Run the *BLD_DB.SQL* script file.

The screenshots in the remainder of this section show you how things would look if you were creating the sample tables and data using SQL\*Plus in a Windows 95 or NT environment. Under other operating systems, such as Unix, everything would look much the same, except that SQL\*Plus may not have its own window and the userid/password prompts may not be in a dialog box.

If you are new to SQL\*Plus and are completely uncertain how to start it in your particular environment, you should first read the section titled "Starting SQL\*Plus" in Chapter 2, *Interacting with SQL\*Plus*. Once you know how to start SQL\*Plus, you can come back here and run the script to create the sample tables and fill them with data.

### Step 1: Download and unzip the script files

The SQL scripts to create the tables and data used for the examples in this book can be downloaded from O'Reilly & Associates' web site. See the Preface for more information.

The scripts are stored in a ZIP file named *BLD_DB.ZIP*. Download this file, and extract the contents into a directory on your hard disk. If you do not have an unzip utility, you may download *BLD_DB.EXE* instead. *BLD_DB.EXE* is a self-extracting ZIP file. Just run it, the scripts will be extracted, and you won't need a separate unzip utility.

### Step 2: Start SQL\*Plus

When you first start SQL\*Plus in a Windows environment, you will see a SQL\*Plus window open. You will also immediately be prompted for a userid, a password, and a host string. Your screen should look like the one shown in Figure 1-3.

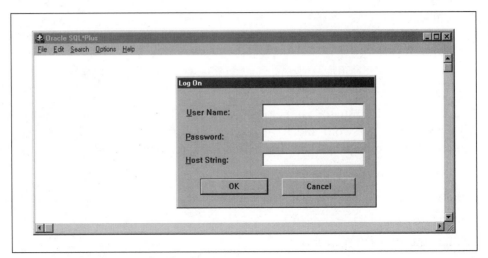

*Figure 1-3. SQL\*Plus immediately after startup*

On a Unix system, you won't see a dialog box like that shown in Figure 1-3. Instead you will simply see a userid prompt.

### Step 3: Log into your Oracle database

Type your userid, password, and host string into the three dialog box fields. If you are using Oracle Personal Edition, you typically leave the host string field blank. Once the correct information is entered, click the OK button. If you are using a Unix system, answer the username prompt by typing in your username and pressing ENTER. Answer the password prompt in the same way. Once logged in, you should see a screen similar to that shown in Figure 1-4.

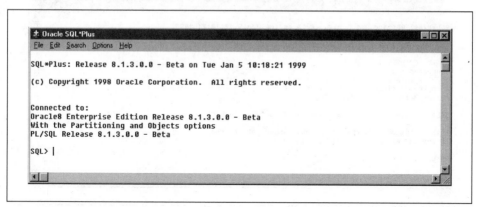

```
✦ Oracle SQL*Plus                                          _ □ ✕
File  Edit  Search  Options  Help

SQL*Plus: Release 8.1.3.0.0 - Beta on Tue Jan 5 10:18:21 1999

(c) Copyright 1998 Oracle Corporation.  All rights reserved.


Connected to:
Oracle8 Enterprise Edition Release 8.1.3.0.0 - Beta
With the Partitioning and Objects options
PL/SQL Release 8.1.3.0.0 - Beta

SQL> |
```

*Figure 1-4. SQL*Plus after a successful login*

The opening screen shows the SQL*Plus version, some copyright information, and some Oracle database version information. The exact version numbers and options you see may vary from those shown in Figure 1-4.

### Step 4: Run the BLD_DB.SQL script file

The next and final step is to run the *BLD_DB.SQL* script file, which is one of the files in the ZIP archive you downloaded in step 1. To do that, simply use the @ command as shown below:

```
SQL> @c:\...\bld_db
```

You need to specify the full directory path to this file.

After you type in the above command and press ENTER, your SQL*Plus screen should look like the one shown in Figure 1-5.

The first thing the script does is confirm that you really do want to load the sample data. Go ahead and answer with a Y, or with an N if you've changed your mind about loading the data.

You must answer the script questions with either a Y or an N. Your reply is not case-sensitive, so a lowercase response is fine. Input validation is minimal, but it is there. If you give an invalid response, an error message will be displayed and the script will stop. You will then need to restart the script, using the START command as shown earlier, and answer correctly.

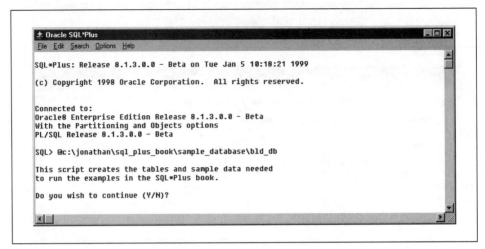

*Figure 1-5. After the BLD_DB script is started*

If you've answered Y to the question about continuing, the next thing you will see is another prompt asking if you want to first drop the sample tables. This is shown in Figure 1-6.

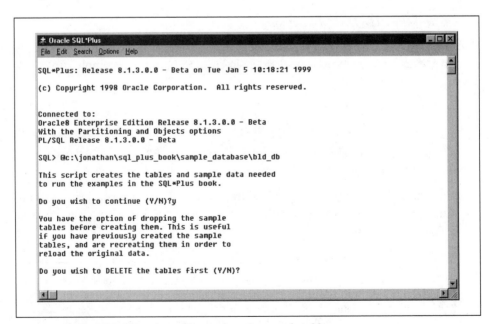

*Figure 1-6. The BLD_DB script asking to drop the sample tables*

This option to first drop the sample tables is convenient if you have loaded them before and wish to quickly reload them. If this is your first time running this script, you should answer this question with an N. If you have loaded the tables previously, and you know that they exist now, then you should answer with a Y.

Now you can just sit back and watch. The next thing the script does is create the sample tables. Following that it inserts data into each table. Figure 1-7 shows the progress messages being displayed on the screen while all this is occurring.

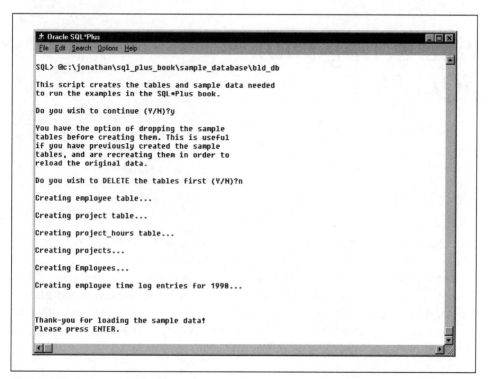

*Figure 1-7. Progress messages from the BLD_DB script*

The entire load process should take less than a minute. When the load is complete, you will be asked to press ENTER one final time. After doing that, you can use the EXIT command to exit SQL*Plus.

Now that you have loaded the sample data, you can proceed with the book and try out the examples as you go.

# 2

# Interacting with SQL*Plus

This chapter shows you the rudiments of interacting with SQL*Plus. The first part of this chapter shows how to start SQL*Plus and connect to a database. You will then read about a few basic SQL*Plus commands you can use to get started. Following that are some examples showing how to enter SQL statements and PL/SQL blocks. The remainder of the chapter focuses on editing your SQL and PL/SQL. There is extensive coverage of the built-in line-editing commands, and you will also see how you can work with an external editor such as Windows' Notepad.

## Starting SQL*Plus

How you start SQL*Plus varies somewhat between operating systems, and also depends on whether you are operating in a GUI environment such as Windows NT or a command-line environment such as DOS or Unix. Generally speaking though, if you are using a command-line operating system, you use the *SQLPLUS* command. On case-sensitive operating systems, such as Unix, the command must be entered in lowercase as *sqlplus*. If you are using Windows, or another GUI-based operating system, you click or double-click on an icon.

### Command-Line Versus GUI Versions

There are two variations of SQL*Plus, command-line and GUI. The command-line implementation was the original, and is the one shipped with Oracle for Unix, VMS, and other command-line operating systems. A command-line version even ships with the Windows client software, in case you want to invoke SQL*Plus from a DOS prompt. For Microsoft Windows, Oracle has also developed a GUI implementation, which wraps the SQL*Plus command-line environment in a standard window complete with scrollbars, drop-down menus, a close box, and other GUI adornments.

At first glance, the GUI version doesn't appear to add anything extra, because it only implements a simple, scrolling window into which you type commands. But there are some advantages to using it. The GUI version implements cut and paste functionality, allows you to size the window any way you want, and implements a scrollback buffer so you never have to worry about your query results scrolling off the top of the screen. If you are running under Windows, I highly recommend using the GUI version. Once you get used to using SQL*Plus with a 1000-line scrollback buffer and a large vertical window size, you won't want to go back.

## Operating System Authentication

Before talking about how to start SQL*Plus, it's important to understand how you authenticate yourself to Oracle in order to connect to a database. There are two options here:

1. You log in with a database-specific username and password.

2. Oracle authenticates you based on your operating system username, trusting that the operating system has properly authenticated you. This is known as *operating system authentication.*

Not all environments support operating system authentication, but in many cases the DBA is free to choose that as an option when creating a user. The logon-related examples in this chapter focus on the first situation, where you need a specific Oracle username/password, because that is most commonly the case. There are notes, where appropriate, to explain how to connect to your database if you are using operating system authentication.

## Starting the GUI Version

To start the GUI version, first find the icon. Figure 2-1 shows the SQL*Plus icon for SQL*Plus version 8. It looks like a blue disk drive topped with a yellow plus sign.

*Figure 2-1. The SQL*Plus icon*

You'll find the SQL*Plus icon in a program group under the Start menu. On Windows 95, this group is named "Oracle for Windows 95". Look at Figure 2-2 to see the Windows 95 Start menu expanded to show the SQL*Plus icon.

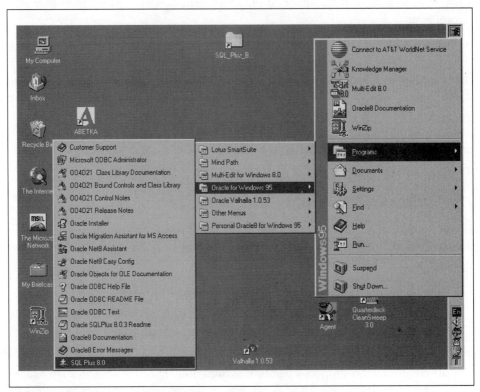

*Figure 2-2. Windows 95 Start menu expanded to show the SQL\*Plus icon*

The Windows NT implementation is the same, except that the program group is named "Oracle for Windows NT." Select the SQL*Plus entry from the Start menu, and SQL*Plus will start.

### Logging into a database

After starting SQL*Plus, your next step is to log into the database. Simply enter your database username, password, and host string into the dialog box and click OK. Figure 2-3 shows how this will look.

The host string tells SQL*Plus which database to connect to, and is sometimes referred to as a connect string. In Figure 2-3, the host string is "dev", probably indicating a development database. Your DBA should give you the correct host string to use if you are connecting to a remote database. You don't need one if you are connecting to the default database on your local machine.

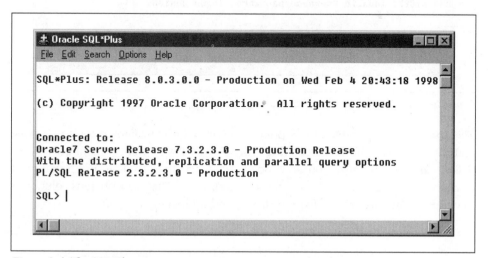

Figure 2-3. *SQL\*Plus logon dialog box*

Be very careful to enter the correct information in the logon dialog box. If you make a mistake, SQL*Plus will reprompt you for your username and password, but not for the connect string. This is annoying when you are trying to connect to a remote database. See the later section, "Making a mistake on the logon dialog."

After you have successfully logged into your database, the SQL*Plus screen will look much like that shown in Figure 2-4.

```
Oracle SQL*Plus                                          _ □ X
File  Edit  Search  Options  Help

SQL*Plus: Release 8.0.3.0.0 - Production on Wed Feb 4 20:43:18 1998

(c) Copyright 1997 Oracle Corporation.  All rights reserved.


Connected to:
Oracle7 Server Release 7.3.2.3.0 - Production Release
With the distributed, replication and parallel query options
PL/SQL Release 2.3.2.3.0 - Production

SQL> |
```

Figure 2-4. *The SQL\*Plus screen*

Notice that SQL*Plus displays some potentially useful information for you now that you have connected to the database. The first few lines of the display show the specific SQL*Plus version and the copyright information. After that, you are given some information about the database to which you just connected. SQL*Plus will display the specific database version, list any options that may be installed, and then show the specific PL/SQL version that is supported.

From here you can go on to enter commands, run SQL queries, execute PL/SQL blocks, generate reports, run script files, and generally do anything else you might need to do with your database.

### Making a mistake on the logon dialog

One mildly annoying thing about the GUI version of SQL*Plus is the way it reacts if you make a mistake typing your username, password, and connect string into the logon dialog. You would expect it to give you an error message and then redisplay the logon dialog so you can enter the correct information, but SQL*Plus does not do that. Instead, when you make a mistake, SQL*Plus uses line-mode prompts to ask you for the correct information Figure 2-5 shows how this looks.

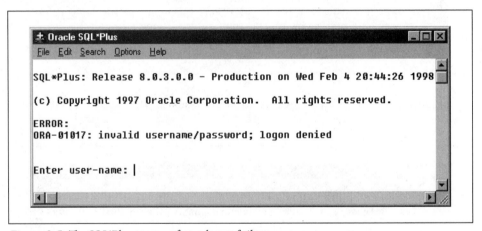

*Figure 2-5. The SQL\*Plus screen after a logon failure*

The annoying thing is that at this point you will only be prompted for a username and password, not the connect string. This is okay if you want to connect to your default database, because you don't need a connect string for that. But if you want to connect to a remote database, you have a problem.The most obvious solution is to exit SQL*Plus (use File → Exit), restart it, and try logging in again.

Beginning with SQL*Plus version 8.0.4, Oracle has corrected this behavior. If you make a mistake on the login, you will get the dialog box again.

The other solution to this problem is to enter your username, password, and connect string all in response to the username prompt. For example:

```
Enter user-name: jonathan/mypass@dev
```

Oracle will parse out all three pieces of information, and you won't need to restart SQL*Plus in order to get the logon dialog back. If you don't want your password to display, enter your username first, and the rest of the information at the password prompt. Here's how that would look:

```
Enter user-name: jonathan
Enter password: mypass@dev
```

The ability to respond to a logon prompt with multiple pieces of information is not documented well in the Oracle manuals, but it sure does come in handy. The rule is that at any prompt, you can also supply all the fields that subsequent prompts would ask for.

### Missing the Product User Profile

SQL*Plus implements a security feature known as the *product user profile*. Sometimes database administrators neglect to create the tables and views that support this feature. Consequently, SQL*Plus users will occasionally see an error message such as the following when connecting to a database:

```
Error accessing PRODUCT_USER_PROFILE
Warning:  Product user profile information not loaded!
You may need to run PUPBLD.SQL as SYSTEM
```

Alarming as it sounds, this message is nothing to worry about. Nothing is wrong with your database, and all SQL*Plus commands will work as normal. This is only telling you that the product user profile security feature has not been implemented at your site. Chapter 9, *The Product User Profile*, describes this feature in detail, and also shows how your database administrator can easily create the necessary tables to make this message go away. If you don't know who your database administrator is, or you can't persuade him to create the profile table, don't worry about it. Just ignore the message, and do whatever you need to do.

## Starting the Command-Line Version

To start the command-line version, you simply use the *SQLPLUS* command. The following example shows how this looks from a DOS command prompt:

```
C:\>SQLPLUS

SQL*Plus: Release 8.0.3.0.0 - Production on Sun Jan 25 10:12:55 1998

(c) Copyright 1997 Oracle Corporation.  All rights reserved.

Enter user-name:
```

SQL*Plus will start by prompting you for a username and password.

> You may need to use a command like *PLUS80* or *PLUS23*, where the
> last two digits represent the specific version of Oracle client soft-
> ware you have installed.

The above command is fine if you want to connect to the default Oracle database
or if you want to be prompted for your username and password. To connect to a
remote database, you must supply a connect string as part of your login. One way
is to put your login information on the command line, as shown in this example:

```
C:\ORAWIN95\BIN>PLUS80 system/munising@oak

SQL*Plus: Release 8.0.4.0.0 - Production on Sat Oct 31 21:36:14 1998

(c) Copyright 1997 Oracle Corporation.  All rights reserved.


Connected to:
Oracle7 Server Release 7.3.4.0.0 - Production
With the distributed, replication, parallel query and Spatial Data options
PL/SQL Release 2.3.4.0.0 - Production

SQL>
```

The two examples just shown represent the most common ways to start SQL\*Plus,
especially if you're going to be using it interactively, as you will be for the examples in this chapter. There are some other options and variations on the SQL\*Plus
command which are useful when you are executing SQL\*Plus script files. These
are described next.

## Command-Line Options

Regardless of whether you are starting the GUI or the command-line version of
SQL\*Plus, there are some options you may want to be aware of. You've already
seen how you can pass your username and password on the command line. In
addition to that, there are options to start SQL\*Plus without connecting to a database, to start it in a *silent* mode, and to invoke a script file.

> The option to start SQL\*Plus without connecting to a database
> becomes especially important beginning with version 8.1, which
> ships with Oracle8i. That version of SQL\*Plus implements several
> administrative commands, such as STARTUP and SHUTDOWN, that
> used to be available only in Server Manager. Using these commands
> requires you to connect in an administrative mode, such as SYS-
> DBA, and you can't do that from the command line. See Chapter 10,
> *Administration with SQL\*Plus*, for more information on this.

The complete syntax for the SQLPLUS command is as follows:

```
SQLPLUS [[-SILENT] [username[/password][@connect]|/|/NOLOG]
        [@scriptfile [arg1 arg2 arg3...]]]|-|-?
```

where:

*SQLPLUS*

Is the command to use when invoking SQL*Plus. On a Unix system, this will be lowercase *sqlplus*. From Windows or MS-DOS, you may need to use *PLUS80* or *PLUS80W.* Beginning with release 8.1, the command under Windows or from a DOS prompt will always be *SQLPLUS.*

*-S[ILENT]*

Tells SQL*Plus to run in silent mode. No startup messages, such as the copyright message, will be displayed. No command prompt will be displayed, and no commands will be echoed to the screen. This is useful if you are invoking SQL*Plus from within some other program, and you want to do it transparently. Normally you would use this option in conjunction with invoking a script file.

*username*

Is your database username.

*password*

Is your database password.

*connect*

Is the connect string, or host string, telling SQL*Plus the database to which you want to connect.

/       Use a forward slash instead of your username, password, and connect string when you want to connect to a local database using operating system authentication.

*/NOLOG*

Tells SQL*Plus not to connect you to any database at all. You will get a SQL> prompt, but you must issue a CONNECT command before you can do much else.

*scriptfile*

Is the name of a SQL*Plus script file you want to run. SQL*Plus will start up, execute the file, and then exit.

*arg1 agr2 arg3*

Are optional command-line arguments to pass to your script. You can have as many as your script requires. Arguments are separated from each other by at least one space.

–       Causes SQL*Plus to display a short summary of the SQLPLUS syntax.

–?      Causes SQL*Plus to display version and copyright information.

The following examples show the use of the - and -? options:

```
C:\WINDOWS>PLUS80 -
Usage: SQLPLUS [<option>] [<user>[/<password>] [@<host>]]
               [@<startfile> [<parm1>] [<parm2>] ...]
where <option> ::= { -s | -? }
-s for silent mode and -? to obtain version number

C:\WINDOWS>PLUS80 -?

SQL*Plus: Release 8.0.4.0.0 - Production on Sun Nov 1 12:14:29 1998

(c) Copyright 1997 Oracle Corporation.  All rights reserved.

C:\WINDOWS>
```

Information on running script files from SQL\*Plus can be found later in this chapter in the section titled "Executing a Script," and also in Chapter 4, *Writing SQL\*Plus Scripts.*

# Some Basic SQL\*Plus Commands

Now that you know how to start SQL\*Plus, it's time to learn a few basic commands. This section will show you how to exit SQL\*Plus, how to switch your database connection to another database, how to get help, and how to view a database table definition.

 All SQL\*Plus commands are case-insensitive; you may enter them using either lowercase or uppercase. In this book, commands are shown in uppercase to make them stand out better in the examples. Be aware, however, that when a filename is used as an argument to a command, it may or may not be case-sensitive, depending on the specific operating system you are using. For example, under Windows NT, filenames are not case-sensitive, but under Unix, they are.

## EXIT

A good place to start, since you've just seen how to start SQL\*Plus, might be with the EXIT command. The EXIT command terminates your SQL\*Plus session, and either closes the SQL\*Plus window (GUI version) or returns you to the operating system prompt. Used in its simplest form, the EXIT command looks like this:

```
SQL> EXIT
Disconnected from Personal Oracle8 Release 8.0.3.0.0 - Production
With the Partitioning option
PL/SQL Release 8.0.3.0.0 - Production
```

There are some optional arguments to the EXIT command, which may be used to return success or failure values to the operating system. These are useful when running scripts in batch mode, and are described fully in Chapter 7, *Advanced Scripting.*

## PASSWORD

The PASSWORD command allows you to change your database password.

 The PASSWORD command was introduced beginning with SQL\*Plus version 8. In prior versions, you need to use the ALTER USER command to change a password. To change other people's passwords, you need the ALTER USER system privilege.

The syntax for the PASSWORD command is:

```
PASSWORD [username]
```

where:

*PASSW[ORD]*

May be abbreviated to PASSW.

*username*

Is the user whose password you want to change. Usually only database administrators (DBAs) can change passwords for other users. You do not need to supply a username if you are changing your own password.

Here is an example showing how the PASSWORD command is used:

```
SQL> PASSWORD
Changing password for JONATHAN
Old password: *******
New password: *******
Retype new password: *******
Password changed
```

If you are running a version of SQL\*Plus prior to version 8, the PASSWORD command will not be available. Instead, use the ALTER USER command to change your password. Here's how:

```
SQL> ALTER USER jonathan IDENTIFIED BY wonker;
```

As you can see, the PASSWORD command has the advantage of not showing the new password on the screen.

# HELP

The HELP command is used to get help on SQL statements, SQL\*Plus commands, and PL/SQL commands.

---

 SQL\*Plus 8.1, released with Oracle8i, provides help only on SQL\*Plus commands. This is because there wasn't time for Oracle to update the help text to cover all the new functionality in SQL and PL/SQL in time for the 8i release. Subsequent versions of SQL\*Plus should reenable SQL and PL/SQL help.

---

The syntax for HELP is:

    HELP [topic]

where:

*HELP*

> May not be abbreviated.

*topic*

> Is the help topic you want to read about. Most SQL commands, SQL\*Plus commands and PL/SQL statements are valid help topics. There are others as well. Entering HELP MENU will get you a complete list of valid topics.

Help is not available on all implementations. The Windows versions of SQL\*Plus simply don't implement the feature. Under Unix, the HELP command will work only if your DBA has installed that feature in the database. You will know SQL\*Plus help has not been installed if you enter the HELP command and get the results shown in this example:

    SQL> **HELP**
    HELP not accessible.

SQL\*Plus reads help text from a database table named HELP, owned by the user SYSTEM. You will get the "HELP not accessible" message if that table does not exist, or if SQL\*Plus cannot select from it because of some other problem. Assuming the help feature has been installed, you can get a list of the various help topics available by using the HELP MENU command.

---

 Beginning with version 8.1 of SQL\*Plus, you need to use HELP INDEX instead of HELP MENU.

---

Here's an example of how HELP MENU can be used to get a list of help topics:

```
SQL> HELP MENU
```

```
                                 Menu

    SQL TOPICS        PL/SQL TOPICS      FUNCTIONS          SQL*PLUS TOPICS
    --------------    ----------------   ---------------    ---------------
    alias             attributes         1 row number       help
    comments          blocks             1 row char         commands
    conditions        commands           conversion         old commands
    data dictionary   cursors            date functions     overview
    ...
```

The HELP command is not available from the Windows versions of SQL\*Plus. If you are running in a Windows 95 or NT environment, you will need to refer to the appropriate Oracle manuals for information on SQL\*Plus, SQL, and PL/SQL commands. These manuals are available on the distribution CD-ROM, and, beginning with version 7.3.3, are in HTML format.

After identifying a topic of interest, you can get further help by using that topic name as an argument to the HELP command. Here is the information HELP gives you about the DESCRIBE command:

```
SQL> HELP DESCRIBE
```

```
                            DESCRIBE

    DESC[RIBE] {[user.]table[@database_link_name] [column] |
    [user.] object[.subobject]}

    DESCRIBE lists the column definitions for a table, view, or synonym,
    or the specifications for a function, procedure, package, or
    package contents.
    ...
```

Entering HELP without an argument will get you help on using HELP.

If you are running under Windows NT or 95, Oracle prefers to point you to the manual set included on the distribution CD-ROM. The HELP command itself will still work; however, you will get the dialog box shown in Figure 2-6, which points you to the documentation on the CD-ROM.

On most Oracle distribution CD-ROMs, you can get to the HTML documentation by opening a file named *INDEX.HTM* in the *DOC* directory.

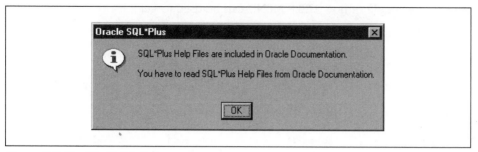

*Figure 2-6. The "No Help" dialog*

## DESCRIBE

The DESCRIBE command lists the column definitions for a database table. It can also be used to view procedure, function, package, and object definitions. If you have created and loaded the sample tables described in Chapter 1, *Introduction to SQL\*Plus*, you can use the DESCRIBE command to view their column definitions. The following example shows how DESCRIBE is used to list the columns in the EMPLOYEE table:

```
SQL> DESCRIBE employee
 Name                             Null?    Type
 -------------------------------- -------- ----
 EMPLOYEE_ID                      NOT NULL NUMBER
 EMPLOYEE_NAME                             VARCHAR2(40)
 EMPLOYEE_HIRE_DATE                        DATE
 EMPLOYEE_TERMINATION_DATE                 DATE
 EMPLOYEE_BILLING_RATE                     NUMBER
```

As you can see, the command lists three things for each column in the table:

- The column's name

- The column's datatype, and length if applicable

- Whether or not the column can be null

See Chapter 6, *Exploring Your Database*, for more information about DESCRIBE, including examples of its use against procedures, functions, packages, synonyms, and object types.

## CONNECT

The CONNECT command lets you log into your database as a different user, or log into a completely different database. It's useful if you develop against, or manage, more than one database, because you can quickly switch between them when you need to. It's also quite common for a developer or DBA to have multiple user-names on one database, with each being used for a different purpose. A DBA might log in as SYSTEM in order to create users and manage tablespaces, but might choose to log in with a less privileged username when running reports.

The complete syntax for CONNECT is:

```
CONNECT [username[/password][@connect]|/|] [AS {SYSOPER|SYSDBA}]|[INTERNAL]
```

where:

*CONN[ECT]*
> May be abbreviated CONN.

*username*
> Is your database username.

*password*
> Is your database password.

*connect*
> Is the connect string, or host string, telling SQL\*Plus the database to which you want to connect.

/  Use a forward slash instead of your username, password, and connect string when you want to connect to a local database using operating system authentication.

*AS*  Tells SQL\*Plus that you are connecting in an administrative role.

*SYSOPER*
> Tells SQL\*Plus that you are connecting as an operator.

*SYSDBA*
> Tells SQL\*Plus that you are connecting as a database administrator.

*INTERNAL*
> Tells SQL\*Plus that you want to connect internally.

Everything beginning with the keyword AS applies when you are using SQL\*Plus for database administration tasks. Chapter 10 is devoted to that subject, and explains the use of the SYSOPER, SYSDBA, and INTERNAL keywords.

The simplest way to use the CONNECT command is to use it by itself, with no arguments, as shown here:

```
SQL> CONNECT
Enter user-name: jonathan
Enter password: *******
Connected.
```

In the case above, SQL\*Plus prompted for *both* a username and a password. Notice, too, that the password characters were echoed back as asterisks. This prevents anyone from looking over your shoulder as you type and stealing your password. SQL*Plus did not prompt for a connect string, and won't, either, so using the above method only allows you to connect to your default database.

Another form of the CONNECT command allows you to specify the username, password, and connect string all on one line. This is the version I use most frequently as I switch back and forth between databases that I manage. For example:

```
SQL> CONNECT system/driveway@plum
Connected.
```

If you are security conscious (you should be) and happen to have someone looking over your shoulder, you may omit the password and let SQL*Plus prompt you for it. The advantage here is that the password characters will be echoed to the screen as asterisks. For example:

```
SQL> CONNECT system@oak
Enter password:*******
Connected.
```

 In at least one version of SQL*Plus version 8.0.4, there is a bug that keeps this from working. You can enter CONNECT with the username as an argument, then enter the password when prompted, but SQL*Plus won't pass the correct information to the database.

Go ahead and try the CONNECT command a few times, trying the variations shown above. If you only have one username you can use, try reconnecting as yourself just to get the hang of it.

## *DISCONNECT*

The DISCONNECT command is one I rarely use. It's the analog of the CONNECT command, and simply disconnects you from the Oracle database while leaving you in SQL*Plus. The syntax is very simple, and looks like this:

```
DISCONNECT
```

where:

*DISC[ONNECT]*
   May be abbreviated to DISC.

Here is an example of the DISCONNECT command being used:

```
SQL> DISCONNECT
Disconnected from Personal Oracle8 Release 8.0.3.0.0 - Production
With the Partitioning option
```

```
PL/SQL Release 8.0.3.0.0 - Production
SQL>
```

Any pending transactions are committed before you are disconnected from Oracle. At this point you have three choices:

1. Reconnect to Oracle using the CONNECT command.

2. Exit SQL*Plus.

3. Execute SQL*Plus commands that do not require a database connection. The SET command, for example, does not require you to be connected.

DISCONNECT is useful if you want to leave a SQL*Plus session open for a long period of time, but do not wish to tie up a database connection.

# Running SQL Queries

Using SQL*Plus, you can execute any SQL query or command that you desire. This includes data manipulation commands such as INSERT, UPDATE, DELETE, and SELECT. This also includes data definition commands such as CREATE TABLE, CREATE INDEX, CREATE USER, etc. Essentially, you can execute any command listed in the Oracle SQL reference manual.

Here is an example of a simple SELECT statement against the PROJECT table:

```
SQL> SELECT *  /* All Columns */
  2    FROM project;

PROJECT_ID PROJECT_NAME                            PROJECT_BUDGET
---------- --------------------------------------- --------------
      1001 Corporate Web Site                            1912000
      1002 Year 2000 Fixes                             999998000
      1003 Accounting System Implementation              897000
      1004 Data Warehouse Maintenance                    294000
      1005 TCP/IP Implementation                         415000
```

Look again at the SELECT query shown above. Notice that the statement spans more than one line. Notice that it contains an embedded comment. Notice that it ends with a semicolon. All of these things are important because they illustrate the following rules for entering SQL statements:

- SQL statements may span multiple lines.

- Line breaks may occur anywhere SQL allows whitespace, but blank lines are not allowed.

- Comments, delimited by /*...*/, may be embedded anywhere whitespace is allowed. A comment entered this way may span multiple lines.

- SQL statements must be terminated in one of three ways:

  — The statement may end with a trailing semicolon.

  — The statement may end with a forward slash character, but the forward slash must be on a line by itself and it must be in column 1 of that line.

  — The statement may end with a blank line, in which case it will be stored in the *SQL buffer* rather than be executed immediately.

Pay close attention to the three ways to terminate a SQL statement. The reason you have to worry about this at all is because they can span multiple lines, and when you press ENTER for a new line, SQL\*Plus needs some way of knowing whether you are done with the statement or whether you just want to continue it on another line. Until you enter a semicolon, a forward slash, or a blank line, SQL\*Plus assumes that you are continuing your statement from one line to the next.

---

 SQL\*Plus 8.1, which ships with Oracle8i, implements a feature allowing you to include blank lines in SQL queries. For compatibility reasons, this feature is not enabled by default. You can turn it on by issuing the command SET SQLBLANKLINES ON.

---

I usually recommend terminating SQL statements with semicolons, because I think that's the simplest and cleanest-looking method. The SELECT statement above shows a semicolon at the end of the line, but if you forget and hit ENTER too quickly, you can also put it on the next line by itself. For example:

```
SQL> INSERT INTO project
  2    /* all columns */
  3  (project_id, project_name, project_budget)
  5    VALUES (1006,'Mainframe Upgrade',456789)
  6  ;

1 row created.
```

You may also use the forward slash character to terminate a SQL statement, but remember that it must be on a line by itself and must be the first and only character on that line. Here is an example:

```
SQL> UPDATE project
  2    SET project_budget = 1000000
  3  WHERE project_id = 1006
  4  /

1 row updated.
```

You will read more about the forward slash character later in this chapter because it's also used to execute the SQL statement, or PL/SQL block, currently in the SQL buffer.

The final option for terminating an SQL statement is to simply press ENTER on a blank line. There is a catch to this method, though. Here's an example:

```
SQL> DELETE
  2     FROM project
  3     WHERE project_id = 1006
  4
SQL>
```

Look carefully at the preceding example. Notice that nothing happened! You typed in the DELETE command, pressed ENTER on a blank line, got back another SQL> prompt, but SQL*Plus said nothing about deleting the row that you just asked to delete. Why? Because when you terminate an SQL query with a blank line, SQL*Plus stores that command in an internal buffer but does not execute it. You'll read more about this later in this chapter in the section titled "The SQL Buffer." For now, though, if you haven't entered any other commands after the DELETE statement shown above, just type a forward slash on a line by itself and press ENTER.

```
SQL> /

1 row deleted.
```

Now the DELETE statement has been executed, and the row deleted. The forward slash tells SQL*Plus to execute the SQL command most recently entered.

If you have been following along with SQL*Plus, and entering the examples while reading this section, you've probably noticed a couple of things. First, it's a pain when you make a mistake. Second, it's even worse when that mistake is on a previous line. If you were using the GUI version of SQL*Plus, you may have even tried to arrow up to correct a mistyped line. Well, don't waste your time—you can't do that. However, SQL*Plus does have some built-in line-editing capabilities, and it can also call the text editor of your choice. You'll read about these options in just a bit, after the next section on executing PL/SQL blocks.

# *Working with PL/SQL*

PL/SQL is a programming language developed by Oracle as an extension to SQL in order to allow procedural logic to be implemented at the database level. PL/SQL is used to write stored procedures, stored functions, and triggers, and, beginning with Oracle8, to define object types. It can also be used to simply write a block of procedural code for the database to execute. SQL*Plus was originally one of the only front-ends that could be used to send PL/SQL code to the database, and even today it is still one of the most widely used.

This section explains the mechanics of entering and executing PL/SQL code with SQL\*Plus. You'll learn what PL/SQL mode is, and you'll learn the differences between entering a PL/SQL block and a SQL query.

If you are unfamiliar with PL/SQL, you may want to pick up a copy of Steven Feuerstein and Bill Pribyl's book, *Oracle PL/SQL Programming*, second edition (O'Reilly & Associates, 1997). PL/SQL opens up a world of possibilities. You'll want to take advantage of it if you are doing serious work with Oracle.

## What Is a PL/SQL Block?

The PL/SQL *block* is the fundamental unit of PL/SQL programming. The term block refers to a program unit that contains some or all of the following elements:

- Variable and subprogram declarations
- Procedural code, which may include nested PL/SQL blocks
- An error handler

Here is an example of a reasonably simple, but complete, PL/SQL block:

```
DECLARE
    X   VARCHAR2(12) := 'Hello World!';
BEGIN
    DBMS_OUTPUT.PUT_LINE(X);
EXCEPTION
WHEN OTHERS THEN
    DBMS_OUTPUT.PUT_LINE('An error occurred.');
END;
```

This code contains all the elements of a PL/SQL block, and is one implementation of the traditional "Hello World!" program. Using SQL\*Plus, you can send it to the database for execution.

## Executing a PL/SQL Block

To execute a PL/SQL block, you type it into SQL\*Plus and terminate it with a forward slash. The forward slash tells SQL\*Plus that you are done entering the block and to send it to the database for execution. Here's how it would look to enter and execute the code shown previously:

```
SQL> DECLARE
  2    X VARCHAR2(12) := 'Hello World!';
  3  BEGIN
  4    DBMS_OUTPUT.PUT_LINE(X);
  5  EXCEPTION
  6  WHEN OTHERS THEN
```

```
7    DBMS_OUTPUT.PUT_LINE('An error occurred.');
8    END;
9    /
```

PL/SQL procedure successfully completed.

### *Where's the output?*

Now you may be wondering why there was no output from the code block in the previous section. After all, the code does contain a call to the PUT_LINE procedure that sure looks as if it ought to display something.

In fact, the code did generate some output. You just didn't see it. Remember from Chapter 1 that SQL*Plus itself does not execute PL/SQL code. It just sends that code to the database server, which executes the code for you. The Oracle database server doesn't have any way to directly display the output for you to see. Instead, any output from PL/SQL code is buffered by the server for later retrieval by the application that executed it, in this case SQL*Plus.

By default, SQL*Plus does not retrieve PL/SQL output from the server. You have to tell it to retrieve the output if you want to see it. The command for that is:

```
SET SERVEROUTPUT ON
```

If you enter the above command, followed by the same PL/SQL block that you entered earlier, your output will look like this:

```
SQL> SET SERVEROUTPUT ON
SQL> DECLARE
2      X VARCHAR2(12) := 'Hello World!';
3    BEGIN
4    DBMS_OUTPUT.PUT_LINE(X);
5    EXCEPTION
6    WHEN OTHERS THEN
7    DBMS_OUTPUT.PUT_LINE('An error occurred.');
8    END;
9    /
Hello World!

PL/SQL procedure successfully completed.
```

This time around, you do see the output from the block. The SERVEROUTPUT setting "sticks" for the duration of your SQL*Plus session, so you don't have to keep turning it on each time you execute another block. There are some other parameters to the SET SERVEROUTPUT command that affect formatting and the output buffer size. The SIZE parameter lets you increase the buffer size from the default of 2000 bytes, something you should do if you expect to display a lot of information from PL/SQL. The FORMAT parameter lets you control whether, and how, long lines of output are wrapped when they are displayed. The following example shows how you can turn server output on, allow for a maximum of 1,000,000 bytes to be displayed, and word-wrap any long lines.

```
SET SERVEROUTPUT ON SIZE 1000000 FORMAT WORD_WRAPPED
```

Prior to version 8 of SQL*Plus, the SIZE and FORMAT parameters did not exist. To increase the buffer size, you had to make a call to DBMS_OUTPUT.ENABLE. You can read about this in Chapter 11, *Customizing Your SQL\*Plus Environment*, under the section titled "The SET Command."

### Rules for entering PL/SQL blocks

When you begin entering a PL/SQL block, SQL*Plus switches to what is called *PL/ SQL mode*. It knows to do this by watching for the keywords BEGIN and DECLARE, either of which may start a PL/SQL block. Once in PL/SQL mode, you can pretty much type anything you please. SQL*Plus simply buffers everything you type until you terminate PL/SQL mode by typing one of the termination characters—either a forward slash or a period on a line by itself. Parsing and syntax checking of your PL/SQL code is done by the database server, not by SQL*Plus, and doesn't happen until after you have completely entered and terminated the block.

 The following SQL commands also put you into PL/SQL mode: CREATE PROCEDURE, CREATE FUNCTION, CREATE TRIGGER, CREATE PACKAGE, CREATE PACKAGE BODY, and CREATE TYPE. That's because these commands allow you to define stored objects based on PL/SQL code.

The rules for entering a PL/SQL block are as follows:

- The first word of a PL/SQL block must be BEGIN, DECLARE, CREATE PROCEDURE, CREATE FUNCTION, CREATE TRIGGER, CREATE PACKAGE, or CREATE TYPE. Lowercase is OK; PL/SQL is not case-sensitive.

- PL/SQL blocks may span multiple lines.

- Line breaks may occur anywhere you can legally enter whitespace.

- Comments, delimited by /*...*/, may be embedded anywhere whitespace is allowed. These commands may span multiple lines.

- A double hyphen (--) makes everything after it on the same line a comment.

- Blank lines are allowed in a PL/SQL block, but SQL*Plus filters them out.

- Entry of a PL/SQL block must be terminated in one of two ways:

  — By use of the forward slash character. The forward slash must be on a line by itself, and must be in column 1 of that line. Using a forward slash tells SQL*Plus to execute the block you have just entered.

  — By use of a period. The period must be on a line by itself, and in the first position. Using a period causes the statement to be stored in the SQL buffer rather than being executed immediately.

Because blank lines are allowed within a block of code, they can't be used to terminate a block. That's where the period comes into play. Oracle needed to provide a way to enter a PL/SQL block into the buffer without executing it. Since a blank line can't be used for that purpose, as it can be with a SQL statement, Oracle decided to allow the period on a line by itself to serve this function.

Likewise, because a PL/SQL block may be made up of many statements, each of which itself ends with a semicolon, that character cannot reliably be used as a termination character. So to enter and execute a block, we are left with only the forward slash.

## *Executing a Single PL/SQL Command*

The SQL*Plus EXECUTE command may be used to execute a singe PL/SQL statement. The syntax is simply:

```
EXECUTE statement
```

where:

*EXEC[UTE]*
    May be abbreviated to EXEC.

*statement*
    Is the PL/SQL statement you want to execute.

EXECUTE is most helpful when you want to make a quick call to a PL/SQL function. In the following example, EXECUTE is used to make a call to DBMS_OUTPUT.ENABLE, in order to allow more than the default 2000 bytes of PL/SQL output to be displayed.

```
SQL> EXECUTE DBMS_OUTPUT.ENABLE(10000)
```

The value of 10,000 in this example tells Oracle to allow for up to 10,000 bytes of output to be displayed by the DBMS_OUTUT.PUT_LINE command procedure. The EXECUTE command is nothing more than a SQL*Plus shortcut. SQL*Plus takes whatever text you type after EXECUTE, adds a semicolon to the end, wraps the keywords BEGIN and END around it, and sends it to Oracle as just another PL/SQL block.

# The SQL Buffer

SQL\*Plus keeps a copy of the most recently entered SQL statement or PL/SQL block in an internal memory area known as the *SQL buffer*, often referred to simply as the *buffer*. The reason for this is simple. SQL\*Plus needs a place to store your statement or block until you are finished entering it. SQL\*Plus also provides you with the ability to edit the statement in the buffer. This can be a real convenience if you make a mistake halfway through typing a long, multiline query.

> SQL\*Plus buffers SQL statements and PL/SQL blocks, but not SQL\*Plus commands. For example, the DESCRIBE command would not be buffered, but a SELECT statement would be. To help make the distinction, it may help to think in terms of where the command is executed. If you enter something to be executed by the database server, then it is buffered. If it's a command local to SQL\*Plus, then it is not buffered.

SQL\*Plus provides two ways to edit the statement currently in the buffer. The first method is to use the set of line-editing commands built into SQL\*Plus. The second method is to use the EDIT command to invoke an operating system–specific text editor, such as Notepad in the Windows environment, or *vi* under Unix.

> If you are editing a statement in the buffer, be sure you don't forget yourself and execute any other SQL command. Even a simple SQL command like COMMIT will overwrite the buffer. Commands to SQL\*Plus, such as the editing commands, do not affect the buffer.

There are some other useful things you can do because of the buffer. If you have several similar SQL statements to execute, using the buffer can save you the effort of completely typing out each one. You may be able to enter the first statement, execute it, make a minor change, execute the new statement, and so on until you are done. SQL\*Plus also allows you to save and load the buffer to and from a text file, allowing you to store frequently executed statements for later use.

# Line Editing

The concept of line editing goes way back to the days when all many people had to work with were *dumb terminals* that didn't allow full-screen editing, and connection speeds were so slow that full-screen editing would have been very painful anyway. A good line editor will allow you to work productively at speeds as low as 300 bits per second. While this isn't much of a concern today, it accurately reflects the environment at the time SQL*Plus was first conceived.

The line-editing process in SQL*Plus follows these steps:

1. You enter a SQL statement or PL/SQL block, which SQL*Plus stores in the buffer.

2. You then list the contents of the buffer to the screen.

3. You enter SQL*Plus commands that tell SQL*Plus to make changes to the statement in the buffer.

4. You list the buffer again.

5. If you like what you see, you execute the statement; otherwise, you go back to step three and make some more changes.

I can remember that in my younger days my fellow programmers and I always took a great pride in the number of line-editing changes we could make and visualize in our heads before we had to break down and list our code again.

## *The Current Line*

When working with the line editor in SQL*Plus, it's important to understand the concept of the *current line*. Simply put, the current line is the one that you have most recently "touched." When you are entering a statement, the most recently entered line is the current line. Consider the following SQL statement for example:

```
SQL> SELECT employee_name, project_name
  2   FROM employee, project, project_hours
  3   WHERE employee.employee_id = project_hours.employee_id
  4     AND project_hours.project_id = project.project_id
  5   GROUP BY employee_name, project_name
  6
SQL>
```

The statement shown above is five lines long. Line 6 doesn't count, and is not added to the buffer, because that's where the blank line was used to terminate entry of the statement. In this case, the last line "touched" happens to be the last line entered, so line 5 is the current line.

Most line-editing commands, by default, operate on the current line. Some commands, such as LIST and DEL, allow you to specify a line number. When you specify a line number for a command, the command is executed, and that line then becomes the new current line. You'll see how this works as you read through the examples that follow.

## Line-Editing Commands

SQL\*Plus contains a number of useful line-editing commands, some of which have several variations. Most of these commands may be abbreviated to one letter. Table 2-1 describes each of these commands, and shows the abbreviations and variations for each one.

*Table 2-1. SQL\*Plus Line-Editing Commands*

| Command | Abbreviation | Variations | Description |
| --- | --- | --- | --- |
| APPEND | A | A *text* | Appends text to the end of the current line. |
| CHANGE | C | C /*from*/*to*/ | Scans the current line for the string *from*, and replaces the first occurrence of *from* with *to*. |
| | | C /*delete*/ | Deletes the first occurrence of *delete* from the current line. Think of this as changing *delete* to an empty string. |
| DEL | none | DEL | Deletes the current line. |
| | | DEL *linenum* | Deletes line number *linenum* from the buffer. |
| | | DEL *start end* | Deletes lines *start* through *end* from the buffer. |
| INPUT | I | I | Allows you to add one or more lines of text to the buffer. These lines are inserted into the buffer immediately following the current line. |
| | | I *text* | Adds just one line to the buffer, consisting of *text*, which is inserted immediately following the current line. |
| LIST | L | L | Displays the entire buffer on the screen for you to see. |
| | | L *linenum* | Lists a specific line number, and makes that line current. |
| | | L *start end* | Displays the specified range of lines, making the last line of that range current. |
| *linenum* | | | Lists that line number, making the line current. |
| CLEAR BUFFER | CL BUFF | CL BUFF | Clears the buffer. This deletes all the lines in one shot. |

Notice that two of the commands, LIST and DEL, allow you to specify a line number or a range of line numbers. For these two commands, there are two special keywords you can use in place of a number. These keywords are * and LAST, and have the meanings shown here:

*   An asterisk always refers to the current line.

*LAST*

The keyword LAST refers to the last line in the buffer.

You will see examples of how these elements are used as you read more about each of the commands.

### Getting a statement into the buffer

To put a SQL statement into the buffer, simply enter the statement and terminate it with a blank line, as shown here:

```
SQL> SELECT *
  2     FROM project
  3
```

The statement is actually inserted into the buffer one line at a time as you enter it. Pressing ENTER on a blank line tells SQL*Plus to leave it there without transmitting it to the server. PL/SQL blocks are entered the same way, except that you terminate them by entering a period on the last line. Following is an example of the shortest PL/SQL block one can write:

```
SQL> BEGIN
  2     NULL;
  3  END;
  4  .
```

Terminating the block with a period tells SQL*Plus not to send it to the database, but just to keep it in the buffer.

### LIST

The LIST command shows you the current contents of the buffer. It is fundamental to the use of the other line-editing commands. Use LIST to view your SQL statement as it currently exists, to see if any changes need to be made. Use LIST after making changes to be sure that they were made correctly.

Look at the following example, which shows a SQL statement being entered into SQL*Plus, and then shows the LIST command being used to display it again:

```
SQL> SELECT employee_name, time_log_name, project_name
  2     FROM employee, project
  3    WHERE employee.employee_num = time_log.employee_num
  4  HAVING employee_name = project_name
  5      AND time_log.project_num = project.project_num
  6    GROUP BY employee_name, project_name
  7
SQL> LIST
```

```
1  SELECT employee_name, time_log_name, project_name
2    FROM employee, project
3   WHERE employee.employee_num = time_log.employee_num
4  HAVING employee_name = project_name
5     AND time_log.project_num = project.project_num
6*  GROUP BY employee_name, project_name
```

Notice the asterisk marking line number 6. The asterisk indicates the current line, which LIST always sets to be the last line displayed. You can display just the current line by using LIST *, as in the following example:

```
SQL> LIST *
6*  GROUP BY employee_name, project_name
```

You can display one specific line by specifying the line number as an argument to the LIST command. The next example shows how to list line 3:

```
SQL> LIST 3
3*  WHERE employee.employee_num = time_log.employee_num
```

Notice the asterisk. By listing line 3 you have made it the current line for editing purposes.

The keyword LAST may be used to display the last line in the buffer. For example:

```
SQL> LIST LAST
6*  GROUP BY employee_name, project_name
```

You may also specify a range of lines to be displayed. This is done by specifying both the starting and ending lines as arguments to the LIST command. Either or both of these arguments may be the keyword LAST or *. The next example shows several different ways to display a range of lines using LIST.

```
SQL> LIST 1 3     List lines 1 through 3
1  SELECT employee_name, time_log_name, project_name
2    FROM employee, project
3*  WHERE employee.employee_num = time_log.employee_num   Line 3 is now current
SQL> LIST * LAST     List everything beginning from the current line
3   WHERE employee.employee_num = time_log.employee_num
4  HAVING employee_name = project_name
5     AND time_log.project_num = project.project_num
6*  GROUP BY employee_name, project_name   Line 6 is now current
SQL> LIST 4 *     List from line 4 through 6 (the current line)
4  HAVING employee_name = project_name
5     AND time_log.project_num = project.project_num
6*  GROUP BY employee_name, project_name
SQL> LIST * *     A one-line range, same effect as LIST *
6*  GROUP BY employee_name, project_name
SQL> LIST LAST LAST   A one-line range, same as LIST LAST
6*  GROUP BY employee_name, project_name
```

As a shortcut to using the LIST command, if there is just one line you are interested in, you can list it by entering the line number itself and then pressing

ENTER. This won't work for a range of lines, but it will work for just one. Here's an example:

```
SQL> 3
   3*  WHERE employee.employee_num = time_log.employee_num
```

On a six-line statement, you might wonder why you would ever bother to list just one line or a range of lines. Remember, though, that line speeds were very slow when SQL*Plus was first developed. In addition, SQL statements and PL/SQL blocks are often much longer than six lines. Listing a range allows you to focus on one area at a time while you fix it.

Keep the above SQL statement in the buffer as you read on about the rest of the line-editing commands. It has several mistakes that will be fixed using the other commands.

## APPEND

The APPEND command is used to add text onto the end of a line. It works on the current line, so you must first decide which line you want to change and then make that line current. Use the LIST command to review the SQL statement currently in the buffer:

```
SQL> L
   1  SELECT employee_name, time_log_name, project_name
   2    FROM employee, project
   3   WHERE employee.employee_id = time_log.employee_id
   4  HAVING employee_name = project_name
   5     AND time_log.project_id = project.project_id
   6* GROUP BY employee_name, project_name
```

I really intended this SELECT statement to join all three sample tables, but if you look at line 2, you will see that I forgot to include the PROJECT_HOURS table. This can easily be corrected by first making line 2 the current line, and then using the APPEND command to add the third table to the join. The first step is to LIST line 2 in order to make it current:

```
SQL> L 2
   2*    FROM employee, project
```

Now that line 2 is the current line, the APPEND command may be used to add PROJECT_HOURS to the join:

```
SQL> A , project_hours
   2*    FROM employee, project, project_hours
```

Notice that APPEND took all the text following the command, appended it to the current line, then redisplayed that line to show the results of the edit. Now the SELECT statement in the buffer joins all three tables.

## *CHANGE*

The CHANGE command searches the current line for a specified string and replaces that string with another. CHANGE only replaces the first occurrence it finds, so if you need to change multiple occurrences of a string in the same line, you will need to execute the same CHANGE command several times. CHANGE may also be used to simply delete text from a line.

List the contents of the buffer again. Your output should match that shown below:

```
SQL> L
  1   SELECT employee_name, time_log_name, project_name
  2     FROM employee, project, project_hours
  3    WHERE employee.employee_num = time_log.employee_num
  4   HAVING employee_name = project_name
  5      AND time_log.project_num = project.project_num
  6*  GROUP BY employee_name, project_name
```

Notice that line 1 references a column that does not exist. In just a bit you will see how to remove that column reference with the CHANGE command. Next, notice that the WHERE clause has three mistakes: the table name TIME_LOG is used instead of PROJECT_HOURS, and employee_num is used twice when it really should be employee_id. The CHANGE command can be used to fix all these problems. To start with, here's how to change TIME_LOG to PROJECT_HOURS:

```
SQL> L 3
  3*   WHERE employee.employee_num = time_log.employee_num
SQL> C /time_log/project_hours/
  3*   WHERE employee.employee_num = project_hours.employee_num
```

In the above example, the LIST command is first used to make line 3 the current line. Then the CHANGE command, abbreviated to C, is used to change the table name. After the edit is complete, the line is automatically redisplayed so you can see the effects of the change.

Next, the employee_num field name needs to be corrected. It should be employee_id. Remember, CHANGE only does one substitution at a time. Since there are two occurrences of employee_num that need to be changed, CHANGE will have to be executed twice. The following example shows this:

```
SQL> L 3
  3*   WHERE employee.employee_num = project_hours.employee_num
SQL> C /employee_num/employee_id/
  3*   WHERE employee.employee_id = project_hours.employee_num
SQL> C /employee_num/employee_id/
  3*   WHERE employee.employee_id = project_hours.employee_id
```

Notice that the CHANGE command searched the current line from left to right. The leftmost occurrence of employee_num was the first to be changed. Notice also that the CHANGE command had to be retyped each time. SQL*Plus does not have any command recall capability.

Now that line 3 is fixed up, take another look at line 1. This time, omit the L command, and just type the line number in order to list the line:

```
SQL> 1
  1* SELECT employee_name, time_log_name, project_name
```

Line 1 contains a bad column name, which needs to be deleted. A variation of the CHANGE command, where you don't supply any replacement text, is used to do this. The following example shows how:

```
SQL> C /time_log_name,//
  1* SELECT employee_name,  project_name
```

At first glance, the use of the CHANGE command to delete text may not seem very intuitive. It may help to think in terms of searching for a string, in this case for "time_log_name," and replacing it with nothing.

With the CHANGE command, you can use delimiters other than the forward slash character. You just need to be consistent within the command. SQL*Plus interprets the first nonspace character following the CHANGE command as the delimiter character. The following commands, for example, are all equivalent:

```
C /FRUB/FROM/
C *FRUB*FROM*
C XFRUBXFROMX
```

The only time you would ever need to use a delimiter other than / is if you needed to include a / as part of the text to be searched for or replaced. You also have the option of leaving off the trailing delimiter, so long as you aren't trying to include trailing spaces in your substitution string. The following two commands are equivalent:

```
C /FRUB/FROM/
C /FRUB/FROM
```

However, if your substitution strings contain spaces, you do need to include the trailing delimiter. The following two commands will *not* produce equivalent results:

```
C / FRUB / FROM /
C / FRUB / FROM
```

It's probably easiest to be in the habit of including the trailing delimiter all the time. You'll make fewer mistakes that way.

### DEL

The DEL command is used to erase one or more lines from the buffer. Used by itself, it erases the current line. You may also specify a line, or a range of lines, as arguments to the DEL command. Unlike the other line-editing commands, DEL cannot be abbreviated. This is perhaps a safety measure to keep you from accidentally deleting a line.

---

> Be careful that you do not spell out the command as DELETE instead of DEL. SQL\*Plus will interpret DELETE as a new SQL command, and will place it in the buffer in place of the command that you are editing.

---

List the buffer. If you have been following along through all the line-editing examples, you should see the following output:

```
SQL> L
  1   SELECT employee_name, project_name
  2     FROM employee, project, project_hours
  3    WHERE employee.employee_id = project_hours.employee_id
  4   HAVING employee_name = project_name
  5      AND time_log.project_num = project.project_num
  6*   GROUP BY employee_name, project_name
```

Line 4, with its HAVING clause, is completely spurious. It can be erased by using the DEL command as follows:

```
SQL> DEL 4
SQL> L *
  4*      AND time_log.project_num = project.project_num
```

SQL\*Plus doesn't echo anything back at you, but line 4 has been erased. Notice that L * was used following the delete to list the current line, which is now line 4. Why line 4? Because 4 was the number of the line most recently "touched" by an editing command. In this case, the original line 4 was erased, what was line 5 became line 4, and the new line 4 becomes current.

The DEL command may also be used to erase a range of lines. As with LIST, the keywords LAST and * may be used to specify the last line in the buffer and the current line, respectively. The next example shows how to erase lines 3 through the current line. Remember that line 4 is current.

```
SQL> DEL 3 *
SQL> L *
  3*  GROUP BY employee_name, project_name
```

Because line 4 was current, the DEL command just shown erased lines 3 and 4. The new current line would ordinarily still be line 4, because that was the last line number "touched" (erased), but in this case, because only three lines are left in the buffer, the last line becomes current.

## INPUT

The INPUT command is used to insert one or more lines of text into the buffer. The INPUT command with a text argument allows you to insert only one line, which is placed into the buffer following the current line. The INPUT command with no arguments puts you into a multiline input mode where you can type as many lines as desired, ending with a blank line. These lines are also inserted into the buffer following the current line.

List the buffer again. You can see that we have done serious damage to our SELECT statement by deleting the entire WHERE clause.

```
SQL> L
  1   SELECT employee_name,  project_name
  2     FROM employee, project, project_hours
  3*  GROUP BY employee_name, project_name
```

The statement listed above is actually syntactically correct and would execute. However, it would simply return all possible combinations of employees and projects. The original intent was to list each employee together with all projects to which the employee actually charged hours. In order to do that, the WHERE clause deleted earlier needs to be put back in. The following example shows how to insert the first line of the WHERE clause by using INSERT with a text argument:

```
SQL> L 2      Make line 2 current, so we can insert after it
  2*    FROM employee, project, project_hours
SQL> I WHERE employee.employee_id = project_hours.employee_id
SQL> L
  1   SELECT employee_name,  project_name
  2     FROM employee, project, project_hours
  3   WHERE employee.employee_id = project_hours.employee_id
  4*  GROUP BY employee_name, project_name
```

An easier alternative, when you have several lines to insert, would be to use the INPUT command with no arguments. This throws you into input mode, where you can type as many lines as you like. Pressing a blank line exits input mode, terminating entry. Here's how to put in the second line of the WHERE clause using this method:

```
SQL> L 3      Make line 3 current, so new lines follow it
  3* WHERE employee.employee_id = project_hours.employee_id
SQL> I        Enter input mode and type the new line
  4i    AND time_log.project_num = project.project_num
  5i
SQL> L
  1   SELECT employee_name,  project_name
  2     FROM employee, project, project_hours
```

```
3  WHERE employee.employee_id = project_hours.employee_id
4    AND time_log.project_num = project.project_num
5* GROUP BY employee_name, project_name
```

The LIST command was used to make line 3 current, so that new lines will be inserted after it. Then the INPUT command was used by itself to enter input mode, and a new line was entered to be added to the WHERE clause. Notice that the prompt included an "i" following the line number, to remind you that you were inserting lines into an existing statement.

If you are picky about formatting, use the second form of the INPUT command shown above. That will let you enter leading spaces in order to make things line up nicely. INSERT text will trim off leading spaces before text is inserted.

To add lines at the end of a buffer, first do a LIST or a LIST LAST to make the last line current. Then use the INPUT command to put yourself into input mode. Any lines you type will be appended onto the end of the buffer.

---

There is no way to insert a line prior to the first line in the buffer. That's because inserted lines *follow* the current line, and there is no line prior to line 1 that you could make current. If you do need to insert a line prior to the first line, insert it as line 2, then retype the first line as line 3, and finally delete the original first line.

---

### Retyping a line

Using the line editor, you can completely replace a line in the buffer by entering the desired line number followed by a new version of the line. Assume that you have the following SELECT statement in the buffer:

```
SQL> L
  1    SELECT employee_name,  project_name
  2      FROM employee, project, project_hours
  3     WHERE employee.employee_id = project_hours.employee_id
  4       AND time_log.project_num = project.project_num
  5*  GROUP BY employee_name, project_name
```

With respect to the sample tables used for this book, you can see that line 4 has several mistakes. There is no TIME_LOG table, and the primary key for a project is project_id, not project_num. The CHANGE command could be used to correct these items, but you might find it faster and easier just to retype the entire line. Here's how you can do that:

```
SQL> 4     AND project_hours.project_id = project.project_id
SQL> L
  1    SELECT employee_name,  project_name
  2      FROM employee, project, project_hours
  3     WHERE employee.employee_id = project_hours.employee_id
```

```
    4      AND project_hours.project_id = project.project_id
    5*     GROUP BY employee_name, project_name
```

Notice that line 4 has been replaced by the text that was typed after the numeral 4 on the first line of this example. You can replace any line in this way. If you want to preserve the indenting, you can insert extra spaces following the line number.

# Executing the Statement in the Buffer

Once you get a statement into the buffer and have edited it the way you want it, the next step is to execute that statement. That can be done with one of the following two methods:

1. Type a forward slash on a line by itself, then press ENTER.

2. Use the RUN command, which may be abbreviated to R.

The only difference between using RUN and / is that the RUN command lists the contents of the buffer before executing it, while the / command simply executes the command without relisting it. Assume that you have the SQL statement shown next in the buffer, which you will if you have followed through all the examples in this chapter.

```
SQL> L
    1     SELECT employee_name,  project_name
    2       FROM employee, project, project_hours
    3      WHERE employee.employee_id = project_hours.employee_id
    4      AND project_hours.project_id = project.project_id
    5*     GROUP BY employee_name, project_name
```

Here is how you would run it using the / command:

```
SQL> /

EMPLOYEE_NAME                           PROJECT_NAME
------------------------------------    --------------------------------
Bohdan Khmelnytsky                      Accounting System Implementation
Bohdan Khmelnytsky                      Corporate Web Site
Bohdan Khmelnytsky                      Data Warehouse Maintenance
Bohdan Khmelnytsky                      TCP/IP Implementation
Bohdan Khmelnytsky                      Year 2000 Fixes
    ...
```

Now, here is how you would execute it using the RUN command, which in the following example is abbreviated to R:

```
SQL> R
    1     SELECT employee_name,  project_name
    2       FROM employee, project, project_hours
```

```
   3      WHERE employee.employee_id = project_hours.employee_id
   4      AND project_hours.project_id = project.project_id
   5*     GROUP BY employee_name, project_name


EMPLOYEE_NAME                          PROJECT_NAME
-------------------------------------  --------------------------------------
Bohdan Khmelnytsky                     Accounting System Implementation
Bohdan Khmelnytsky                     Corporate Web Site
Bohdan Khmelnytsky                     Data Warehouse Maintenance
Bohdan Khmelnytsky                     TCP/IP Implementation
Bohdan Khmelnytsky                     Year 2000 Fixes
 ...
```

Notice this time that the SQL statement in the buffer was first displayed on the
screen, and then executed. I almost always use the forward slash to execute commands, but RUN is useful if you are printing an ad-hoc report, or sending the
query results to a file, and wish to have a copy of the SQL statement included for
future reference.

## If Your Statement Has an Error

If a SQL statement fails to execute, SQL\*Plus does three things. It makes the line
containing the error current, displays that line for you to edit, and displays the
error message returned by Oracle. Look at the following example of a SQL SELECT
statement with a invalid column name:

```
SQL> SELECT employee_name
  2    FROM project;
SELECT employee_name
       *
ERROR at line 1:
ORA-00904: invalid column name
```

SQL\*Plus displays the error returned by Oracle, which tells you that your column
name is bad. The offending line is displayed, and an asterisk points to the incorrect column name. You can quickly edit that line, change employee_name to
project_name, and re-execute the command as follows:

```
SQL> C /employee_name/project_name/
  1* SELECT project_name
SQL> /

PROJECT_NAME
--------------------------------------
Corporate Web Site
Year 2000 Fixes
Accounting System Implementation
Data Warehouse Maintenance
TCP/IP Implementation
```

This is a very convenient feature if you have entered a long command and have only made one or two small mistakes.

 When debugging SQL statements (or PL/SQL blocks), don't get too hung up on where Oracle thinks the error is. When SQL*Plus displays an error line with an asterisk under it, that asterisk is pointing to where Oracle was looking when the problem was detected. Depending on the nature of the error, you may need to look elsewhere in your statement. Getting the table name wrong, for example, may lead to spurious invalid column errors. The error in the example just shown could also have been corrected by changing the table name from PROJECT to EMPLOYEE. Know what results you are after, and be prepared to look beyond the specific error message that you get from Oracle.

If you are trying to create a stored object, such as a stored procedure, you will need to use the SHOW ERRORS command to see where any errors lie. Here is an example:

```
SQL> CREATE PROCEDURE example1 AS
  2   BEGIN
  3     bad_statement;
  4   END;
  5   /

Warning: Procedure created with compilation errors.

SQL> SHOW ERRORS
Errors for PROCEDURE EXAMPLE1:

LINE/COL ERROR
-------- --------------------------------------------------------
3/3      PLS-00201: identifier 'BAD_STATEMENT' must be declared
3/3      PL/SQL: Statement ignored
```

The reason for this difference is that when you compile code for a stored object, such as a procedure or function, Oracle parses all the code, and reports all the errors it finds. This is quite convenient, because if you have a large code block, you certainly don't want to have to find and correct errors one at a time.

## Doing It Again

Three other things worth knowing about the RUN (or /) command are:

- Unless an error occurs, the current line is not changed.
- Executing a command does not remove it from the buffer.
- Executing a SQL*Plus command also leaves the buffer intact.

These three features make it easy to rerun an SQL statement either as it stands or with minor changes. Take a look at the following example, which displays the name for employee number 107:

```
SQL> SELECT employee_name
  2    FROM employee
  3    WHERE employee_id = 107;

EMPLOYEE_NAME
----------------------------------------
Bohdan Khmelnytsky
```

A quick change to line 3 will let you see the name for employee ID 110:

```
SQL> 3
  3*   WHERE employee_id = 107
SQL> c /107/110
  3*   WHERE employee_id = 110
SQL> /

EMPLOYEE_NAME
----------------------------------------
Ivan Mazepa
```

At this point, line 3 is still current. Since no error occurred, SQL\*Plus had no reason to change it, so it's even easier to look at the name for employee number 111:

```
SQL> c /110/111
  3*   WHERE employee_id = 111
SQL> /

EMPLOYEE_NAME
----------------------------------------
Taras Shevchenko
```

Sometimes it makes sense to execute the same statement over and over again, without making any changes to it. A SELECT statement that queried one of the V$ tables, perhaps V$SESSION, to get a list of current users, would be a good example of this. INSERT statements are often repeatedly executed in order to generate small amounts of test data.

## *Saving and Retrieving the Buffer*

SQL\*Plus allows you to save the contents of the buffer to a file and to read that file back again. If you have built up a long and complicated SQL statement, you can save it for reuse later, and save yourself the bother of figuring it all out again. Two commands, GET and SAVE, are provided for this purpose.

# SAVE

The SAVE command allows you to save the current contents of the buffer to a file. Here is the syntax for SAVE:

```
SAVE filename [CREATE|REPLACE|APPEND]
```

where:

*SAV[E]*

May be abbreviated SAV.

*filename*

Is the name of the file to which you want to save the buffer. The default extension is *.SQL*, but you may specify another if you like.

*CRE[ATE]*

Tells SQL*Plus that you want to create a new file. The save will fail if the file you've specified already exists. This is the default behavior.

*REPLACE*

Tells SQL*Plus to save the buffer to the file specified, regardless of whether or not that file already exists. If the file does exist, it will be overwritten.

*APPEND*

Tells SQL*Plus to add the contents of the buffer to an existing file.

The following example shows the SAVE command being used to save the contents of a rather long SQL query to a file. First the query is entered into the buffer without being executed; then the SAVE command is used to write the buffer to a file.

```
SQL>    SELECT employee_name,  project_name
  2       FROM employee, project, project_hours
  3      WHERE employee.employee_id = project_hours.employee_id
  4        AND project_hours.project_id = project.project_id
  5        AND employee_billing_rate in (
  6              SELECT MAX(employee_billing_rate)
  7                FROM employee
  8              )
  9      GROUP BY employee_name, project_name
 10
SQL> SAVE C:\A\HIGHEST_BILLED_EMP_PROJECTS
Created file C:\A\HIGHEST_BILLED_EMP_PROJECTS
```

The SAVE command shown above created a *new* file, with the default extension of *.SQL*, and saved the contents of the buffer to that file. SQL*Plus also terminated the statement in the buffer with a trailing forward slash on a line by itself, so the resulting output file looks like this:

```
SELECT employee_name,  project_name
    FROM employee, project, project_hours
```

```
    WHERE employee.employee_id = project_hours.employee_id
      AND project_hours.project_id = project.project_id
      AND employee_billing_rate in (
            SELECT MAX(employee_billing_rate)
              FROM employee
              )
    GROUP BY employee_name, project_name
  /
```

SQL\*Plus will not automatically replace an existing file. Had the file already existed, and had we wanted to replace it, the REPLACE option would have been needed on the SAVE command. For example:

```
SAVE C:\A\HIGHEST_BILLED_EMP_PROJECTS REPLACE
```

The APPEND option adds the contents of the buffer onto the end of an existing file. If you append multiple statements to a file, you won't be able to load that file back into the buffer and execute those commands. However, you will be able to execute the file using the START command.

 Try to use descriptive filenames when saving your SQL statements. You want the filename to jog your memory later when you need to retrieve that statement. The query shown above returns a list of projects worked on by the employee (or employees) with the highest billing rate; thus the filename of *HIGHEST_BILLED_EMP_ PROJECTS* seemed appropriate. The length of a filename is governed by what your operating system allows.

## GET

The GET command is the opposite of SAVE. It retrieves the contents of a file to the buffer. Here is the syntax:

```
GET filename [LIST|NOLIST]
```

where:

*GET*

May not be abbreviated.

*filename*

Is the name of the file containing the text you want to load into the buffer. The default extension is *.SQL*, but you may specify another if you like.

*LIS[T]*

May be abbreviated to LIS, and tells SQL\*Plus to list the contents of the buffer after loading the file.

*NOL[IST]*

> May be abbreviated to NOL, and tells SQL*Plus to load the file without listing it for you to see.

The following example shows how to retrieve the SQL statement that was saved in the previous section:

```
SQL> GET C:\A\HIGHEST_BILLED_EMP_PROJECTS
  1    SELECT employee_name,  project_name
  2      FROM employee, project, project_hours
  3     WHERE employee.employee_id = project_hours.employee_id
  4       AND project_hours.project_id = project.project_id
  5       AND employee_billing_rate in (
  6             SELECT MAX(employee_billing_rate)
  7               FROM employee
  8             )
  9*   GROUP BY employee_name, project_name
```

Notice that the GET command automatically displays the contents of the retrieved file for you to see. This allows you to confirm that you have loaded the correct statement. Once the statement has been loaded into the buffer, you may execute it using either RUN or /, or you may use any of the editing commands to change it.

---

The GET command will load *any* text file into the buffer. You can even load your *AUTOEXEC.BAT* file (for Windows users) into the buffer, edit it, and save it again. This might be a useful thing to know if you are ever really hard up for an editor.

---

While SQL*Plus will let you load any text file into the buffer, be aware that you cannot execute the buffer unless it contains exactly *one* SQL statement or *one* PL/SQL block. To be safe, the text file should terminate the statement (or block) with a forward slash on a line by itself. See the previous section on the SAVE command for an example of this.

# *The EDIT Command*

You don't like line editing? SQL*Plus does not have a built-in full-screen editor, but it does have the EDIT command. The SQL*Plus EDIT command allows you to invoke the text editor of your choice to use in editing SQL statements. The specific editor invoked depends on the operating system, and on whether or not you've changed the default. The default editor under Windows NT/95 is Notepad, while under Unix it is *vi*. You may, however, configure SQL*Plus to use another editor of your choice. Do this by defining the user variable named _EDITOR to point to executable of the editor you want to use.

## *Invoking the Editor*

You invoke the editor with the EDIT command. The syntax looks like this:

```
ED[IT] [filename]
```

where:

*ED[IT]*

May be abbreviated ED.

*filename*

Is an optional argument indicating a specific file you want to edit. The default extension is *.SQL*, but you may supply a different extension if you like.

The typical use of the EDIT command is to edit a statement currently contained in the buffer. The following example shows a query being entered and the editor being invoked:

```
SQL> SELECT project_name
  2      FROM projects
  3   WHERE project_id in (
  4            SELECT DISTINCT project_id
  5              FROM project_hours)
  6
SQL> EDIT
Wrote file afiedt.buf
```

Upon entering the EDIT command, the contents of the buffer are written to a file named *AFIEDT.BUF*, and the editor is invoked. Figure 2-7 shows what your screen would now look like on a Windows 95 or NT system. On Unix systems, the filename is lowercase, and will be *afiedt.buf.*

The filename *AFIEDT.BUF* is simply a work file used by SQL\*Plus to hold your command while it is being edited. The name is a throwback to the very early days of SQL\*Plus when it was briefly known as AUFI, which stood for Advanced User Friendly Interface.

SQL\*Plus will not invoke the editor if the buffer is empty; instead you will see the message shown below:

```
SQL> EDIT
Nothing to save.
```

If you have an empty buffer and wish to enter a new query, you must type something, perhaps just the first line, into SQL\*Plus before using the EDIT command.

Another use for the EDIT command is to edit an existing text file. You can edit any text file you like, whether it contains a query or not. The following EDIT command for example, lets you edit your Unix Korn shell profile:

```
EDIT .profile
```

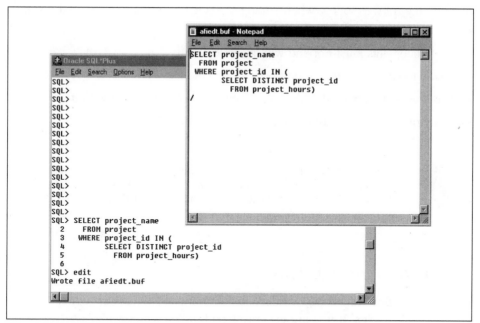

*Figure 2-7. Results of the EDIT command under Windows 95/NT*

When you edit a file in this way, the contents of the file are *not* loaded into the buffer. This is just a convenient way for you to edit a file without having to exit SQL*Plus first.

## Formatting Your Command

Take another look at Figure 2-7. Pay attention to the way in which the SQL statement is terminated. Notice that there is no trailing semicolon. Notice also that the statement is terminated by a forward slash on a line by itself. When you edit the statement in the editor, do not attempt to terminate it with a semicolon. Semicolons only work as terminators when you are executing a script file, or when you are typing a SQL statement in from the command prompt. Adding a semicolon to the end of a statement being edited with the EDIT command will result in an invalid character error when you try and execute it. The easiest thing to do is to leave the statement as it is, terminated by a forward slash on a line by itself. Strictly speaking, though, the forward slash is optional, and may be omitted.

Although SQL statements do not require a trailing semicolon, a PL/SQL block does. That's because the trailing semicolon is part of the PL/SQL syntax, but not part of the SQL syntax.

Here are the rules to follow when editing the SQL buffer with an external text editor:

- SQL statements must not end with a semicolon.
- PL/SQL blocks do need to end with a semicolon.
- Optionally, terminate the file with a forward slash on a line by itself.
- Only one SQL statement or PL/SQL block is allowed.

> Watch the semicolons. I'm so used to using a semicolon at the end of my SQL statements that I sometimes include one when editing the buffer like this. Don't make that same mistake, because your SQL statement won't run and you will need to edit it again.

## Getting Back to SQL\*Plus

Once you are finished editing your statement, you need to exit the editor in order to return to SQL\*Plus. If you are using Notepad under Windows NT or 95, you do this by going to the File menu and choosing Exit.

> Be sure to save the file before leaving the editor! In order for SQL\*Plus to see your changes, they must be written back to the work file. Most editors, including Notepad, will remind you to save your changes before you exit, but *vi* will not. You should explicitly save your changes unless you want to throw them away.

When you exit the editor, control returns to SQL\*Plus. The contents of the work file are loaded into the buffer and displayed on the screen for you to see. You may then execute your revised statement by using either the RUN command or the / command.

> The work file (*AFIEDT.BUF*) is not deleted. Its contents remain undisturbed until your next use of the EDIT command.

# Executing a Script

Most of this chapter has focused on what you need to know in order to enter a command directly into SQL*Plus and have it executed. Another option available to you is to have SQL*Plus execute a script. A script is simply a text file that contains one or more statements to execute. When SQL*Plus executes a script, the commands or statements in the file are executed just as if you had typed them in directly from the keyboard. A script file can contain any combination of valid SQL*Plus commands, SQL statements, or PL/SQL blocks.

The START command is used to execute a script. Here is the syntax to use:

```
START filename [arg1 arg2 arg3...]
```

where:

*STA[RT]*

> May be abbreviated to STA.

*filename*

> Is the name of the script file you want to execute. The default extension is *.SQL.*

*arg1 arg2 arg3*

> Represent any command-line arguments you want to pass to the script file. These are delimited by spaces, and you may specify as many as are needed by the script. Arguments containing spaces should be enclosed in either single or double quotes.

Let's say you had a file named *DESCRIBE_ALL.SQL*, and it contained the following SQL*Plus commands:

```
DESCRIBE employee
DESCRIBE project
DESCRIBE project_hours
```

You could execute this file with the START command as shown here:

```
SQL> START C:\JONATHAN\SQL_PLUS_BOOK\XB_CH_2\DESCRIBE_ALL
 Name                                 Null?    Type
 ------------------------------------ -------- ----
 EMPLOYEE_ID                          NOT NULL NUMBER
 EMPLOYEE_NAME                                 VARCHAR2(40)
 EMPLOYEE_HIRE_DATE                            DATE
 EMPLOYEE_TERMINATION_DATE                     DATE
 EMPLOYEE_BILLING_RATE                         NUMBER

 Name                                 Null?    Type
 ------------------------------------ -------- ----
 PROJECT_ID                           NOT NULL NUMBER
 PROJECT_NAME                                  VARCHAR2(40)
```

```
PROJECT_BUDGET                                   NUMBER

Name                               Null?    Type
------------------------------     --------  ----
PROJECT_ID                         NOT NULL NUMBER
EMPLOYEE_ID                        NOT NULL NUMBER
TIME_LOG_DATE                      NOT NULL DATE
HOURS_LOGGED                                NUMBER
DOLLARS_CHARGED                             NUMBER
```

In the previous example, SQL*Plus has executed all three DESCRIBE commands contained in the *DESCRIBE_ALL.SQL* file. The output of each command is sent to the screen, but by default SQL*Plus does not echo the individual commands to the screen.

More commonly, the @ command is used instead of the START command. Both commands do exactly the same thing, but @ is much shorter to type.

You can do a lot with command files. They are handy for running reports, extracting data, creating new database users, or performing any other complex task that you need to repeat on a periodic basis. Much of this book centers around the concept of writing SQL*Plus scripts to automate these types of routine tasks. You will begin to see scripts used beginning in Chapter 3, *Generating Reports with SQL\*Plus*, where you will learn how to write scripts to take advantage of SQL*Plus's reporting functionality. Chapter 4 delves into the subject of scripting even more deeply.

## *The Working Directory*

Whenever you work with files in SQL*Plus, it's important to understand the concept of a working directory. The *working directory* is simply the directory that is used whenever you specify a filename without also including a path. The working directory is also where SQL*Plus writes temporary files, such as the *AFIEDT. BUF* file created when you invoke the EDIT command.

If you work under an operating system like Unix, you are already familiar with the concept of a current working directory. You also very likely know how to move between directories, and are familiar with commands such as *pwd* that tell you what your current directory is. The working directory simply happens to be whatever directory you are in when you invoke SQL*Plus.

Users of the Microsoft Windows operating system tend to be a bit insulated from the concept of a current directory. SQL*Plus is typically invoked under Windows by clicking an icon, and the user often does not think of himself as being "in" any particular directory when this is done. In spite of this, some directory will be current when you run SQL*Plus under Windows. Take a look at Figure 2-8. It shows the properties for the SQL*Plus menu item under Windows 95.

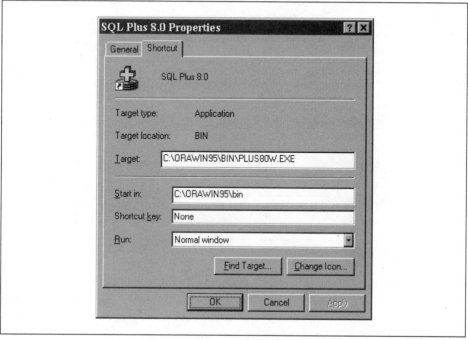

*Figure 2-8. The SQL*Plus shortcut properties under Windows 95*

Notice the *Start in* setting shown in Figure 2-8. It's set to the *C:\ORAWIN95\BIN* directory, the same directory in which the executable sits. This is the default setting used when installing Oracle on any version of Windows. The implication is that whenever you run SQL*Plus under Windows and use the SAVE command without specifying a path for the file, the file will be created in the Oracle *BIN* directory. The same is true when you use the SPOOL command to send report output to a file. If you don't specify a path, the report output will go to the *BIN* directory. Also, when you use the EDIT command, the *AFIEDT.BUF* temporary file will be created in this directory.

It's best, if you are using SQL*Plus under Windows, always to specify a path when you save a query, or report output, to a file. If you save a file, and later can't seem to find it, the Oracle *BIN* directory is the first place you should look.

You can change the default directory if you like. One way would be to edit the shortcut properties and change the *Start in* setting to some other directory. This would be a permanent change, and is probably more trouble than it is worth. Another, more useful, technique is to use the File → Open dialog to navigate to the directory you want to be current, and then press the Cancel button. Figure 2-9 shows this dialog in preparation for making the *C:\JONATHAN\SQL_SCRIPTS* directory the current working directory.

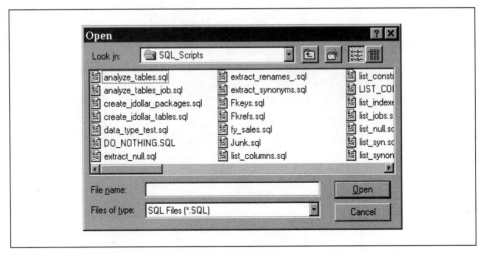

*Figure 2-9. The SQL\*Plus file open dialog*

Once you navigate to the directory you want as the current directory, you just press the Cancel button. It's not necessary to actually open a file. This use of the file open dialog is undocumented, but it's a very handy technique for quickly changing your working directory under Windows.

# 3

# *Generating Reports with SQL\*Plus*

SQL\*Plus is a very effective reporting tool. You can count on having SQL\*Plus available in any Oracle environment, and it gets the job done well with a minimum of fuss. This chapter shows you how to leverage the power of SQL\*Plus to produce reports, and presents a report development methodology that works well in most situations.

## *Following a Methodology*

Designing a report is a development project, albeit a very small one. As with any development project, it helps to have a methodology, or sequence of steps, to follow that will lead you successfully through the process of designing a report with a minimum of fuss and backtracking. For example, when designing a report, it makes no sense to worry about formatting the data until you have first decided what data to include.

This chapter presents a micro-methodology for developing reports with SQL\*Plus that has worked very well for me. It divides the design process for a simple report into the following steps:

1. Formulate the query.

2. Format the columns.

3. Add page headers and footers.

4. Format the page.

5. Print it.

Dividing the design process into discrete, logical steps reduces both the amount and the complexity of the information you must keep in your head at any given time.

For more advanced reports, such as a master-detail report, there are some additional tasks you may want to perform. These include:

- Add page and line breaks

- Add totals and subtotals

Try to work through report design in a methodical manner. Often there is a temptation just to start typing in commands. Resist this temptation!

## Saving Your Work

Consider saving all the commands to produce a report in a script file. I can't remember ever producing an ad-hoc report that was truly generated just once. Often there are formatting issues I don't see until after the first printing. Other times a client will look at a report and immediately think of one or two things to add. By saving your work in a file, you will be prepared when the request for that same report, or one similar to it, comes again.

The only time I ever print a report by typing the commands interactively into SQL\*Plus is when the query is very simple and I don't care how the output is formatted. In such a case, if I'm in a hurry, I may simply spool off the output from a SELECT statement, print it, and live with the incorrect pagination, lack of titles, and lack of column formatting.

Saving your work in a file also protects you from simple mistakes and minor catastrophes. If you've typed 20 formatting commands into SQL\*Plus and your computer locks up, you've lost your work. You'll have to restart your computer and then attempt to remember all those commands. If you are working on a long SQL query, and that query exists only in the SQL buffer, a simple thing like typing COMMIT will clobber it—something I've done many times myself. Save yourself some work by saving your work in a file.

## Designing a Simple Report

The first part of this chapter will lead you through the five steps involved in generating a simple, columnar report. This report will be complete with page headings, page footings, and column headings. In addition, you will learn about several settings, controlled by the SET command, that are useful when printing and formatting reports.

## Step 1: Formulate the Query

The very first step to designing a report is to formulate the underlying SQL query. There is little point in doing anything else until you have done this. The remaining steps all involve formatting and presentation. If you haven't defined your data, there is no reason to worry about how to format it.

For this chapter, let's look at developing a report that answers the following questions:

- To what projects is each employee assigned?

- How many hours have been charged to each project?

- What is the cost of those hours?

One way to satisfy those requirements would be to develop a report based on the following query, which summarizes the hours and dollars charged by employee and project:

```
SELECT E.EMPLOYEE_NAME,
       P.PROJECT_NAME,
       SUM(PH.HOURS_LOGGED) ,
       SUM(PH.DOLLARS_CHARGED)
  FROM EMPLOYEE E,
       PROJECT P,
       PROJECT_HOURS PH
 WHERE E.EMPLOYEE_ID = PH.EMPLOYEE_ID
   AND P.PROJECT_ID = PH.PROJECT_ID
 GROUP BY E.EMPLOYEE_ID, E.EMPLOYEE_NAME,
          P.PROJECT_ID, P.PROJECT_NAME;
```

If you execute this query using SQL*Plus, here's what the output will look like:

```
EMPLOYEE_NAME                            PROJECT_NAME
---------------------------------------- ------------------------------------
SUM(PH.HOURS_LOGGED) SUM(PH.DOLLARS_CHARGED)
-------------------- -----------------------
Jonathan Gennick                         Corporate Web Site
                  20                     3380

Jonathan Gennick                         Year 2000 Fixes
                  24                     4056

Jonathan Gennick                         Accounting System Implementation
                  24                     4056
```

Looks pretty ugly, doesn't it? I wouldn't want to hand that to a client. It's a start, though. At least now you can see what the data looks like, and you know what you have to work with.

## Step 2: Format the Columns

Now that you have the data, you can begin to work through the formatting process. Look again at the listing produced in step 1. There are at least three things that can be done to improve the presentation of the data:

- Get each record to fit on just one line.

- Use better column headings.

- Format the numbers.

The first thing that probably leaped out at you was the need to avoid having report lines so long that they wrap around onto a second line and become difficult to read. This is often a result of SQL\*Plus allowing for the maximum width in each column. Another cause is that for calculated columns, the entire calculation is used for the column heading. That can result in some very long headings!

### The COLUMN command

The COLUMN command is used to format the data returned from a SELECT statement. In the next few sections, you will see how this command may be used to specify headings, widths, and display formats. The syntax for COLUMN looks like this:

```
COL[UMN] [column_name [ALI[AS] alias|
                       CLE[AR] |
                       FOLD_A[FTER] |
                       FOLD_B[EFORE] |
                       FOR[MAT] format_spec|
                       HEA[DING] heading_text|
                       JUS[TIFY] {LEFT|CENTER|CENTRE|RIGHT} |
                       LIKE source_column_name|
                       NEWL[INE] |
                       NEW_V[ALUE] user_variable|
                       NOPRI[NT] |
                       PRI[NT] |
                       NUL[L] null_text|
                       OLD_V[ALUE] user_variable|
                       ON|
                       OFF|
                       TRU[NCATED]...]]
                       WOR[D_WRAPPED] |
                       WRA[PPED] |
```

where:

*COL[UMN]*

May be abbreviated to COL. Issuing the COLUMN command with no parameters gets you a list of all current column formats.

*column_name*

> Is the name of the column that you are formatting. If it is a computed column, then the expression is the name. If your SELECT statement aliases the column, then you must use that alias here. Issuing the command COLUMN *column_name*, with no further parameters, causes SQL*Plus to display the current format for that column.

*ALI[AS] alias*

> May be abbreviated ALI. ALIAS allows you to specify an alternate name for this column that is meaningful to SQL*Plus. Do not confuse this with the column alias in a SELECT statement. This alias may be used in subsequent BREAK, COMPUTE, and COLUMN commands.

*CLE[AR]*

> May be abbreviated to CLE. CLEAR erases any format settings for the column in question. This puts you back to the way things were before any COLUMN commands were issued for the column.

*FOLD_A[FTER]*

> May be abbreviated to FOLD_A, and causes SQL*Plus to advance to a new line before displaying the next column. In other words, the output is wrapped after this column prints.

*FOLD_B[EFORE]*

> May be abbreviated to FOLD_B. This is the opposite of FOLD_AFTER, and causes SQL*Plus to wrap to a new line *before* this column is printed.

*FOR[MAT] format_spec*

> May be abbreviated to FOR, and allows you to control how the data for the column is displayed. For text fields, you can control the width. For numeric fields, you can control the width, placement of commas, placement of the dollar sign, and so on. See Appendix B, *SQL*Plus Format Elements*, for a list of format specification elements supported by SQL*Plus.

*HEA[DING] heading_text*

> May be abbreviated HEA, and allows you to define a heading for the column. The heading text displays at the top of each column, and is redisplayed every time a page break occurs. You should enclose the heading text in quotes, but you don't have to if the heading is a single word. Either single or double quotes may be used. If you need to include a quote as part of your heading, use two quote characters back to back.

*JUS[TIFY]*

> May be abbreviated JUS, and controls where the heading text prints relative to the column width. By default, headings for numeric fields print flush right, and headings for text fields print flush left. This parameter allows you to change

that behavior. You must follow this keyword with one of the following: LEFT, RIGHT, CENTER, or CENTRE. LEFT causes the heading to print flush left. RIGHT causes the heading to print flush right. CENTER and CENTRE cause the heading to print centered over the top of the column. Note that this parameter has no effect whatsoever on how the data for the column is displayed.

*LIKE source_column_name*

Causes the column to be defined with the same format attributes as another column. LIKE must be followed by a column name, and that column becomes the source column.

*NEWL[INE]*

May be abbreviated NEWL. This is the same as FOLD_BEFORE. It causes SQL\*Plus to wrap to a new line before the column is printed.

*NEW_V[ALUE] user_variable*

May be abbreviated NEW_V, and causes SQL\*Plus to keep a user variable updated with the current value of the column. The user variable is updated whenever the column value changes.

*NOPRI[NT]*

May be abbreviated NOPRI, and tells SQL\*Plus not to print the column. NOPRINT is sometimes used when you just want to get a column value into a user variable (see NEW_VALUE), but you don't want it displayed. This is often done when generating master/detail reports.

*PRI[NT]*

May be abbreviated to PRI, and is the opposite of NOPRINT. Use PRINT when you want to turn printing back on for a column.

*NUL[L] null_text*

May be abbreviated NUL, and allows you to specify text to be displayed when the column value is null. As with the heading text, this may optionally be enclosed in quotes.

*OLD_V[ALUE] user_variable*

This may be abbreviated to OLD_V, and must be followed by a user variable name. OLD_VALUE works like NEW_VALUE, except that when the column changes, the previous value is stored in a user variable. This is useful when you need to print a value in the page footer of a master/detail report.

*ON*

Causes SQL\*Plus to print the column using the format you have specified. This is the default behavior. You don't need to use ON unless you have previously used OFF.

*OFF*

> Disables the format settings for the column. SQL*Plus acts as if you had never issued any COLUMN commands for the column in question.

*TRU[NCATED]*

> May be abbreviated TRU, and causes the column text to be truncated to the width of the column. Longer values are not wrapped.

*WOR[D_WRAPPED]*

> May be abbreviated WOR. WORD_WRAPPED is similar to WRAPPED, but line breaks occur at word boundaries. Words that are longer than the column is wide will still be broken at the column boundary.

*WRA[PPED]*

> May be abbreviated WRA. WRAPPED affects the printing of values that are longer than the column is wide, and causes SQL*Plus to wrap those values to a new line as many times as necessary in order to print the entire value. Line breaks will occur exactly at the column boundary, even in the middle of a word.

Don't be intimidated by all these parameters. The most important and complex ones are described in this chapter, complete with examples. Multiple parameters may be specified with one COLUMN command. COLUMN commands are cumulative. Issuing two COLUMN commands for the same column, but using different parameters, is the same as issuing one command with all the parameters.

### Column headings

The COLUMN command with the HEADING clause may be used to specify column headings that are more understandable by an end user. COLUMN commands are issued prior to the SELECT statement you want them to affect. SQL*Plus stores the headings and uses them when the results from the SELECT statement are displayed. The following COLUMN commands define more readable headings for our report:

```
COLUMN employee_name HEADING 'Employee Name'
COLUMN project_name HEADING 'Project Name'
COLUMN SUM(PH.HOURS_LOGGED) HEADING 'Hours'
COLUMN SUM(PH.DOLLARS_CHARGED) HEADING 'Dollars|Charged'
```

Notice that you can refer to the calculated columns in the query by using the calculation as the name. While possible, it is cumbersome, to say the least, and requires you to keep the two copies of the calculation in sync. There is a better way. You can give each calculated column an alias and use that alias in the COLUMN commands. To give each column an alias, the changes to the query look like the following.

```
SUM(PH.HOURS_LOGGED) hours_logged ,
SUM(PH.DOLLARS_CHARGED) dollars_charged
```

The commands to format these two columns then become:

```
COLUMN hours_logged HEADING 'Hours'
COLUMN dollars_charged HEADING 'Dollars|Charged'
```

The heading for the dollars_charged column has a vertical bar separating the two words. This vertical bar tells SQL\*Plus to place the heading on two lines, and allows you to use two rather long words without the need for an excessive column width.

The vertical bar is the default heading separator character and may be changed with the SET HEADSEP command. See Chapter 11, *Customizing Your SQL\*Plus Environment*, for details.

### Column display formats

Next you can specify more readable display formats for the numeric columns by adding a FORMAT clause to the COLUMN commands as shown here:

```
COLUMN hours_logged HEADING 'Hours' FORMAT 9,999
COLUMN dollars_charged HEADING 'Dollars|Charged' FORMAT $999,999.99
```

Finally, you can use FORMAT to specify a shorter length for the employee_name and project_name columns. The database allows each of those columns to contain up to 40 characters, but a visual inspection of the output shows that the names are typically much shorter than that. The format clauses shown next make these columns each 20 characters wide:

```
COLUMN employee_name HEADING 'Employee Name' FORMAT A20 WORD_WRAPPED
COLUMN project_name HEADING 'Project Name' FORMAT A20 WORD_WRAPPED
```

Normally SQL\*Plus will wrap longer values onto a second line. The WORD_ WRAPPED keyword keeps SQL\*Plus from breaking a line in the middle of a word.

WRAPPED and TRUNCATE are both alternatives to WORD_ WRAPPED. WRAPPED allows a longer value to break in the middle of a word and wrap to the next line. TRUNCATE does what it says; it throws away characters longer than the format specification allows.

### Report output after formatting the columns

The script to produce the report now looks like this:

```
--Format the columns
COLUMN employee_name HEADING 'Employee Name' FORMAT A20 WORD_WRAPPED
COLUMN project_name HEADING 'Project Name' FORMAT A20 WORD_WRAPPED
COLUMN hours_logged HEADING 'Hours' FORMAT 9,999
COLUMN dollars_charged HEADING 'Dollars|Charged' FORMAT $999,999.99

--Execute the query to generate the report.
SELECT E.EMPLOYEE_NAME,
       P.PROJECT_NAME,
       SUM(PH.HOURS_LOGGED) hours_logged,
       SUM(PH.DOLLARS_CHARGED) dollars_charged
  FROM EMPLOYEE E,
       PROJECT P,
       PROJECT_HOURS PH
 WHERE E.EMPLOYEE_ID = PH.EMPLOYEE_ID
   AND P.PROJECT_ID = PH.PROJECT_ID
 GROUP BY E.EMPLOYEE_ID, E.EMPLOYEE_NAME,
          P.PROJECT_ID, P.PROJECT_NAME;
```

Here is what the output will look like:

```
                                                   Dollars
Employee Name         Project Name         Hours    Charged
--------------------  --------------------  ------  ------------
Jonathan Gennick      Corporate Web Site       20    $3,380.00
Jonathan Gennick      Year 2000 Fixes          24    $4,056.00
Jonathan Gennick      Accounting System        24    $4,056.00
                      Implementation

Jonathan Gennick      Data Warehouse           20    $3,380.00
                      Maintenance

Jonathan Gennick      TCP/IP                   28    $4,732.00
                      Implementation
```

This is a great improvement over step 1. The headings are more readable. The numbers, particularly the dollar amounts, are formatted better. Most records fit on one line, and when two lines are needed, the data is wrapped in a much more readable format.

Notice that a blank line has been inserted after every record with a project name that wraps to a second line. That blank line is a *record separator*, and it's added by SQL*Plus every time a wrapped column is output as part of a report. I suppose it is added to prevent confusion, because in some circumstances you might think that the line containing the wrapped column data really represented another record in the report. I usually turn it off; the command to do that is:

```
SET RECSEP OFF
```

The next step is to add page headers and footers to the report.

## Step 3: Add Page Headers and Footers

Page headers and footers may be added to your report through the use of the TTITLE and BTITLE commands. TTITLE and BTITLE stand for "top title" and "bottom title" respectively.

### The top title

The TTITLE command is used to define page headers. Here is the syntax:

```
TTI[TLE] [[OFF|ON]|
        COL x|
        S[KIP] x|
        TAB x|
        LE[FT]|
        CE[NTER]|
        R[IGHT]|
        BOLD|
        FOR[MAT] format_spec|
        text|
        variable...]
```

where:

*TTI[TLE]*

> May be abbreviated TTI. Issuing the TTITLE command with no parameters causes SQL\*Plus to display the current top title setting.

*OFF*

> Turns the page title off, but does not erase its definition. You can turn it back on again with ON.

*ON*

> Turns on printing of page titles. The default title, if you do not specify another, will be the current date, the page number, and all or part of the SELECT statement.

*COL x*

> Causes any title text following this parameter to print at the specified column position.

*S[KIP] x*

> May be abbreviated as S, and inserts the specified number of line breaks before printing any subsequent title text.

*TAB x*

> TAB is similar to COL, but moves you the specified number of columns relative to the current position. Negative numbers move you backwards. TAB has nothing whatsoever to do with tab characters.

*LE[FT]*

> May be abbreviated LE, and causes subsequent title text to be printed beginning at the leftmost column of the current title line.

*CE[NTER]*

> May be abbreviated CE, and causes subsequent title text to be centered within the current line. The LINESIZE setting controls the line width.

*R[IGHT]*

> May be abbreviated R, and causes subsequent title text to be printed flush right. The LINESIZE setting controls where SQL*Plus thinks the right end of the line is.

*BOLD*

> Makes your title "bold" by printing it three times. Only title text following the BOLD command is repeated on each line. There is not a NOBOLD parameter.

*FOR[MAT] format_spec*

> May be abbreviated to FOR, and allows you to control how subsequent numeric data in the title is displayed. The format elements you can use here are the same as for the COLUMN command, and are described in Appendix B. It is possible to specify a character format, such as A20, but that has no effect on subsequent character strings.

*text*

> Is any text you want to have in the title. To be safe, you should enclose this in quotes, but you don't have to as long as your title text doesn't include any keywords like BOLD or TAB that have meaning to TTITLE. Either single or double quotes may be used. If you need to include a quote as part of your text, use two quote characters back to back.

*variable*

> May be one of the system variables maintained by SQL*Plus. See Table 3-1, in the following section on bottom titles, for a list.

You should always begin a TTITLE command with a parameter such as LEFT or RIGHT, as opposed to text or a variable name. Failure to do this causes SQL*Plus to interpret the command as an old, now obsolete, form of TTITLE. The old form is still acceptable for compatibility reasons, but is greatly limited in what it can do.

TTITLE commands typically end up being a long string of parameters, interspersed with text, and they often span multiple lines. Let's say you wanted a page header that looked like this:

```
                    The Fictional Company


  I.S. Department              Project Hours and Dollars Report
  ============================================================
```

This heading is composed of the company name centered on the first line, two blank lines, a fourth line containing the department name and the report title, followed by a ruling line made up of equal-sign characters. You can begin to generate this heading with the following TTITLE command:

```
TTITLE CENTER 'The Fictional Company'
```

The keyword CENTER is referred to as a *printspec*, and tells SQL\*Plus to center the text that follows. To get the two blank lines into the title, add a SKIP printspec as follows:

```
TTITLE CENTER 'The Fictional Company' SKIP 3
```

SKIP 3 tells SQL\*Plus to skip forward three lines. This results in two blank lines and causes the next line to print on that third line. To generate the fourth line of the title, containing the department name and the report name, you again add on to the TTITLE command:

```
TTITLE CENTER 'The Fictional Company' SKIP 3 -
       LEFT 'I.S. Department' -
       RIGHT 'Project Hours and Dollars Report'
```

The text "I.S. Department" will print flush left because it follows the LEFT printspec, while the report title will print flush right because it follows the RIGHT printspec. Both strings will print on the same line because there is no intervening SKIP printspec. The last thing to do is to add the final ruling line composed of equal-sign characters, giving you this final version of the TTITLE command:

```
TTITLE CENTER 'The Fictional Company' SKIP 3 -
       LEFT 'I.S. Department' -
       RIGHT 'Project Hours and Dollars Report' SKIP 1 -
       LEFT '============================================================='
```

This is actually one very long command. The hyphens at the end of the first three lines are SQL\*Plus command continuation characters. There are 61 equals-sign characters in the last line of the title.

> You must use the SKIP printspec to advance to a new line. If you want to advance just one line, use SKIP 1. SQL\*Plus will not automatically advance for you. If you removed the two SKIP printspecs from the above TTITLE command, you would end up with a one-line title consisting entirely of equals signs.

### The bottom title

The BTITLE command works exactly the same way as TTITLE, except that it defines a footer to appear at the bottom of each page of the report. The syntax looks like this:

```
BTI[TLE]  [OFF|ON]|
          [COL x|
          S[KIP] x|
          TAB x|
          LE[FT]|
          CE[NTER]|
          R[IGHT]|
          BOLD|
          FOR[MAT] format_spec|
          text|
          variable...]
```

where:

*BTI[TLE]*

> May be abbreviated BTI. Issuing the BTITLE command with no parameters causes SQL*Plus to display the current bottom title setting.

*OFF*

> Turns the page footer off, but does not erase its definition. You can turn it back on again with ON.

*ON*

> Turns on printing of page footers. The default footer, if you do not specify another, will be the first part of the SELECT statement.

*COL x*

> Causes any footer text following this parameter to print at the specified column position.

*S[KIP] x*

> May be abbreviated as S, and inserts the specified number of line breaks before printing any subsequent footer text.

*TAB x*

> TAB is similar to COL, but moves you the specified number of columns relative to the current position. Negative numbers move you backwards. TAB has nothing whatsoever to do with tab characters.

*LE[FT]*

> May be abbreviated LE, and causes subsequent footer text to be printed beginning at the leftmost column of the current footer line.

*CE[NTER]*

> May be abbreviated CE, and causes subsequent footer text to be centered within the current line. The LINESIZE setting controls the line width.

*R[IGHT]*

> May be abbreviated R, and causes subsequent footer text to be printed flush right. The LINESIZE setting controls where SQL*Plus thinks the right end of the line is.

*BOLD*

Makes your footer "bold" by printing it three times. Only title text following the BOLD command is repeated on each line. There is not a NOBOLD parameter.

*FOR[MAT] format_spec*

May be abbreviated to FOR, and allows you to control how subsequent numeric data in the footer is displayed. The format elements you can use here are the same as for the COLUMN command, and are described in Appendix B. It is possible to specify a character format, such as A20, but that has no effect on subsequent character strings.

*text*

Is any text you want to have in the footer. To be safe, you should enclose this in quotes, but you don't have to as long as your title text doesn't include any keywords like BOLD or TAB that have meaning to BTITLE. Either single or double quotes may be used. If you need to include a quote as part of your text, use two quote characters back to back.

*variable*

May be one of the variables shown in Table 3-1.

As with TTITLE, you should always begin a BTITLE command with a parameter such as LEFT or RIGHT, as opposed to text or a variable name. If you wanted a footer composed of a ruling line and a page number, you could use the following BTITLE command:

```
BTITLE LEFT '===============================================================' -
       SKIP 1 -
       RIGHT 'Page ' FORMAT 999 SQL.PNO
```

This BTITLE command introduces two features that haven't been shown in previous examples. The first is the FORMAT parameter, which in this case specifies a numeric display format to use for all subsequent numeric values. The second is the use of the system variable SQL.PNO, which supplies the current page number. There are several values, maintained automatically by SQL\*Plus, that you can use in report headers and footers. These are shown in Table 3-1.

*Table 3-1. SQL\*Plus System Variables*

| System Variable | Value |
|---|---|
| SQL.PNO | The current page number |
| SQL.LNO | The current line number |
| SQL.RELEASE | The current Oracle release |
| SQL.SQLCODE | The error code returned by the most recent SQL query |
| SQL.USER | The Oracle username of the user running the report |

These values have meaning only to SQL*Plus, and can be used only when defining headers and footers. They cannot be used in SQL statements such as INSERT or SELECT.

## Setting the line width

One final point to bring up regarding page titles is that the printspecs LEFT, RIGHT, and CENTER all operate with respect to the current line width. The default line width, or *linesize* as it is called in SQL*Plus, is 80 characters. So by default, a centered heading will be centered over 80 characters. A flush right heading will have its last character printed in the 80th position. This presents a slight problem because this report, using the column specifications given in step 2, is only 61 characters wide. The result will be a heading that overhangs the right edge of the report by ten characters, and that won't appear centered over the data. You could choose to live with that, or you could add this command to the script:

```
SET LINESIZE 61
```

Setting the linesize tells SQL*Plus to format the headings within a 61-character line. It also tells SQL*Plus to either wrap or truncate any lines longer than 61 characters, but the column specifications in this report prevent anything like that from occurring.

The number of equal-sign characters in the ruling line must exactly match the linesize. Otherwise the ruling line will either be too short or too long. Either way it will look tacky.

## Report output with page titles

With the addition of the TTITLE, BTITLE, and SET LINESIZE commands, the script to generate the report will look like this:

```
--Set the linesize, which must match the number of equal signs used
--for the ruling lines in the headers and footers.
SET LINESIZE 61

--Setup page headings and footings
TTITLE CENTER 'The Fictional Company' SKIP 3 -
       LEFT 'I.S. Department' -
       RIGHT 'Project Hours and Dollars Report' SKIP 1 -
       LEFT '============================================================='

BTITLE LEFT '============================================================='
       SKIP 1 -
       RIGHT 'Page ' FORMAT 999 SQL.PNO
```

```
--Format the columns
COLUMN employee_name HEADING 'Employee Name' FORMAT A20 WORD_WRAPPED
COLUMN project_name HEADING 'Project Name' FORMAT A20 WORD_WRAPPED
COLUMN hours_logged HEADING 'Hours' FORMAT 9,999
COLUMN dollars_charged HEADING 'Dollars|Charged' FORMAT $999,999.99

--Execute the query to generate the report.
SELECT E.EMPLOYEE_NAME,
       P.PROJECT_NAME,
       SUM(PH.HOURS_LOGGED) hours_logged,
       SUM(PH.DOLLARS_CHARGED) dollars_charged
  FROM EMPLOYEE E,
       PROJECT P,
       PROJECT_HOURS PH
 WHERE E.EMPLOYEE_ID = PH.EMPLOYEE_ID
   AND P.PROJECT_ID = PH.PROJECT_ID
 GROUP BY E.EMPLOYEE_ID, E.EMPLOYEE_NAME,
          P.PROJECT_ID, P.PROJECT_NAME;
```

Executing this script will produce the following output:

```
                         The Fictional Company


I.S. Department                    Project Hours and Dollars Report
============================================================
                                                     Dollars
Employee Name        Project Name         Hours      Charged
--------------------  --------------------  ------  ------------
Jonathan Gennick     Corporate Web Site       20    $3,380.00
Jonathan Gennick     Year 2000 Fixes          24    $4,056.00
Jonathan Gennick     Accounting System        24    $4,056.00
                     Implementation

Jonathan Gennick     Data Warehouse           20    $3,380.00
                     Maintenance

Jonathan Gennick     TCP/IP                   28    $4,732.00
                     Implementation

Jenny Gennick        Corporate Web Site        9    $1,215.00
Jenny Gennick        Year 2000 Fixes           8    $1,080.00
============================================================
                                            Page     1
```

There are only a few things left to clean up before you can print this report; one obvious improvement is to fix the pagination in order to get more than 24 lines per page.

## *Step 4: Format the Page*

Most of the work to produce this report is behind you. Step 4 simply involves adjusting two SQL*Plus settings that control pagesize and pagination. These two settings are:

*pagesize*
> Controls the number of lines per page. SQL*Plus prints headings and advances to a new page every pagesize lines.

*newpage*
> Controls the size of the top margin, or tells SQL*Plus to use a formfeed character to advance to a new page.

The SET command is used to define values for each of these two settings. The values to use depend primarily on your output device, the paper size being used, and the font size being used. Since SQL*Plus is entirely character-oriented, these settings are defined in terms of lines. The first question to ask, then, is how many lines will your printer print on one page of paper.

### *How many lines on a page?*

Years ago, before the advent of laser printers with their multiplicity of typefaces, typestyles, and typesizes (i.e., fonts) this was an easy question to answer. The standard vertical spacing for printing was six lines per inch, with eight lines per inch occasionally being used. Thus, an 11-inch-high page would normally contain 66 lines. Most printers were pinfeed printers taking fanfold paper, and would allow you to print right up to the perforation, allowing you to use all 66 lines if you were determined to do so.

Today's printers are much more complicated, yet most will still print six lines per inch if you send them plain ASCII text. However (and this is important), many printers today will not allow you to print right up to the top and bottom edges of the paper. This is especially true of laser printers, which almost always leave a top and bottom margin. You may have to experiment a bit with your printer to find out how exactly how many lines you can print on one page.

---

 I usually duck this issue entirely by setting the pagesize to a safely low setting, usually below 60 lines, and setting newpage to zero, which causes SQL*Plus to use a formfeed character to advance to a new page. The examples in this chapter use this approach.

---

The other issue to consider is the font size you will be using to print the report. I usually just send reports to a printer as plain ASCII text, and that usually results in the use of a 12-point monospaced font, which prints at six lines per inch. Some-times however, I'll load the file containing a report into an editor, change the font size to something larger or smaller, and then print the report. If you do that, you'll need to experiment a bit to find out how many lines will fit on a page using the new font size.

### Setting the pagesize

You set the pagesize with the SQL\*Plus command SET PAGESIZE as follows:

```
SET PAGESIZE 55
```

This tells SQL\*Plus to print 55 lines per page. Those 55 lines include the header and footer lines, as well as the data. As it prints your report, SQL\*Plus keeps track of how many lines have been printed on the current page. SQL\*Plus also knows how many lines make up the page footer. When the number of remaining lines equals the number of lines in your footer, SQL\*Plus prints the footer and advances to the next page. How SQL\*Plus advances the page depends on the NEWPAGE setting.

### Setting the page advance

There are two methods SQL\*Plus can use to advance the printer to a new page. The first method, and the one used by default, is to print exactly the right number of lines needed to fill one page. Having done that, the next line printed will start on a new page. Using this method depends on knowing exactly how many lines you can fit on one page, and switching printers can sometimes cause your report to break. One laser printer, for example, may have a slightly larger top margin than another.

A more reliable method is to have SQL\*Plus advance the page using the formfeed character. The command to do this is:

```
SET NEWPAGE 0
```

The NEWPAGE setting tells SQL\*Plus how many lines to print in order to advance to a new page. The default value is 1. Setting it to 0 causes SQL\*Plus to output a formfeed character when it's time to advance the page.

 If you set NEWPAGE to 0, do not set PAGESIZE to exactly match the number of lines you can physically print on your printer. Doing that may cause your output to consist of alternating detail pages and blank pages. That's because filling the physical page will itself advance your printer to a new page. The subsequent formfeed advances the page again, resulting in a skipped page. Instead, set PAGESIZE to at least one line less than will fit on a physical page.

The examples in this chapter use a NEWPAGE setting of 0 and a PAGESIZE of 55 lines, so you can add these three lines to the script file:

```
--Setup pagesize parameters
SET NEWPAGE 0
SET PAGESIZE 55
```

I usually make these settings just prior to the TTITLE and BTITLE commands, but you are free to put them anywhere you like so long as they precede the SELECT statement that generates the report.

## Step 5: Print It!

Run the script file one more time and look at the output on the screen. If everything looks good, you are now ready to print. To print a report, you need to have SQL*Plus write the report to a file, and then print that file. When people speak of writing SQL*Plus output to a file, the term *spool* is often used as a verb. You are said to be *spooling* your output to a file. The SPOOL command is used for this purpose, and you will need to use it twice, once to turn spooling on and again to turn it off. The syntax for the SPOOL command looks like this:

```
SP[OOL] file_name|OFF|OUT
```

where:

*SP[OOL]*

May be abbreviated to SP.

*file_name*

Is the name of the file to which you want to write the report. The default extension depends on the operating system, and will be either LST or LIS. Under Windows 95 and NT, it's LST. A path may be specified as part of the filename.

*OFF*

Turns spooling off. You must have turned spooling on before you can turn it off.

*OUT*

Turns spooling off, and prints the file on the default printer. This option is not available in the Windows versions of SQL*Plus.

### Spooling to a file

To send report output to a file, put SPOOL commands immediately before and after the SQL query as shown here:

```
SPOOL C:\A\PROJ_HOURS_DOLLARS.LIS
SELECT E.EMPLOYEE_ID, E.EMPLOYEE_NAME,
...
SPOOL OFF
```

The first SPOOL command tells SQL*Plus to begin echoing all output to the specified file. After this command executes, everything you see on the screen is also echoed to this file. The second SPOOL command turns spooling off and closes the file.

There are two other commands you may wish to add to the script file before generating the report. The first is:

```
SET FEEDBACK OFF
```

Turning feedback off gets rid of both the "50 rows selected." and the "Commit complete." messages, which you may have noticed at the end of the report when you ran earlier versions of the script. The second command you may want to add is:

```
SET TERMOUT OFF
```

This command does what it says. It turns off output to the display (terminal output), but still allows the output to be written to a spool file. Your report will run several orders of magnitude faster if SQL*Plus doesn't have to deal with updating and scrolling the display. On my PC, the simple report used as an example in this chapter runs in 13 seconds with the display on, but takes less than 1 second with the display off. You should definitely use this option on any large report.

I usually put the above two settings immediately prior to the SPOOL command, then turn them back on again after spooling has been turned off. For example:

```
SET FEEDBACK OFF
SET TERMOUT OFF
SPOOL C:\A\PROJ_HOURS_DOLLARS.LIS
...
SPOOL OFF
COMMIT;
SET TERMOUT ON
SET FEEDBACK ON
```

Do make sure that you set TERMOUT off prior to spooling the output; otherwise the SET TERMOUT OFF command will appear in your spool file.

### The final script

After adding the SPOOL commands and the commands to turn feedback and terminal output off, the script file for the sample report looks like this:

```
--Setup pagesize parameters
SET NEWPAGE 0
SET PAGESIZE 55

--Set the linesize, which must match the number of equal signs used
--for the ruling lines in the headers and footers.
SET LINESIZE 61
```

```
--Set up page headings and footings
TTITLE CENTER 'The Fictional Company' SKIP 3 -
       LEFT 'I.S. Department' -
       RIGHT 'Project Hours and Dollars Report' SKIP 1 -
       LEFT '==============================================================='

BTITLE LEFT '===============================================================' -
       SKIP 1 -
       RIGHT 'Page ' FORMAT 999 SQL.PNO

--Format the columns
COLUMN employee_name HEADING 'Employee Name' FORMAT A20 WORD_WRAPPED
COLUMN project_name HEADING 'Project Name' FORMAT A20 WORD_WRAPPED
COLUMN hours_logged HEADING 'Hours' FORMAT 9,999
COLUMN dollars_charged HEADING 'Dollars|Charged' FORMAT $999,999.99

--Turn off feedback and set TERMOUT off to prevent the
--report being scrolled to the screen.
SET FEEDBACK OFF
SET TERMOUT OFF

--Execute the query to generate the report.
SPOOL C:\A\PROJ_HOURS_DOLLARS.LIS
SELECT E.EMPLOYEE_NAME,
       P.PROJECT_NAME,
       SUM(PH.HOURS_LOGGED) hours_logged,
       SUM(PH.DOLLARS_CHARGED) dollars_charged
  FROM EMPLOYEE E,
       PROJECT P,
       PROJECT_HOURS PH
 WHERE E.EMPLOYEE_ID = PH.EMPLOYEE_ID
   AND P.PROJECT_ID = PH.PROJECT_ID
 GROUP BY E.EMPLOYEE_ID, E.EMPLOYEE_NAME,
          P.PROJECT_ID, P.PROJECT_NAME;
COMMIT;
SPOOL OFF
SET TERMOUT ON
SET FEEDBACK ON
```

### Executing the report

If you've stored the script for the report in a text file, you can execute that file from the SQL*Plus prompt like this:

```
SQL> @c:\jonathan\sql_plus_book\xd_ch_4\04_query_1_step_5.sql
```

The @ character in front of a filename tells SQL*Plus to execute the commands contained in that file.

### Printing the file

After you run the script, the complete report will be in the *PROJ_HOURS_ DOLLARS.LIS* file. To print that file, you must use whatever print command is appropriate for your operating system. On a Windows 95 or NT machine, assuming that LPT1 was mapped to a printer, you could use the following DOS command:

```
C:\>COPY c:\a\proj_hours_dollars.lis LPT1:
```

A typical Unix print command would be:

```
lp proj_hours_dollars.lis
```

Another alternative is to load the file into a word processor such as Microsoft Word or Lotus Word Pro. These programs will interpret formfeeds as page breaks when importing a text file, so your intended pagination will be preserved. After you've imported the file, select all the text and mark it as Courier New 12pt. Then set the top and left margins to their minimum values—for laser printers, half-inch margins usually work well. Next, set the right and bottom margins to zero. Finally, print the report.

One final option, which, unfortunately, is not available in any Windows version of SQL\*Plus, is to use the SPOOL OUT command instead of SPOOL OFF. SPOOL OUT closes the spool file and then prints that file out to the default printer, saving you the extra step of manually printing it. For whatever reason, Oracle has chosen not to implement SPOOL OUT under Windows. It is, however, available under Unix.

## Advanced Report Formatting

You can add page breaks and line breaks to your reports with the BREAK command. BREAK is also commonly used to suppress repeating values in report columns. Take a look at the following script, which generates a detailed listing of all time charged to each project by each employee:

```
--Set up pagesize parameters
SET NEWPAGE 0
SET PAGESIZE 55

--Set the linesize, which must match the number of equals signs used
--for the ruling lines in the headers and footers.
SET LINESIZE 77

--Set up page headings and footings
TTITLE CENTER 'The Fictional Company' SKIP 3 -
      LEFT 'I.S. Department' -
      RIGHT 'Project Hours and Dollars Detail' SKIP 1 -
```

```
            LEFT '=======================================' -
                 '=================================' -
            SKIP 2

BTITLE LEFT '=======================================' -
            '=================================' -
            SKIP 1 -
            RIGHT 'Page ' FORMAT 999 SQL.PNO

--Format the columns
COLUMN employee_id HEADING 'Emp ID' FORMAT 9999
COLUMN employee_name HEADING 'Employee Name' FORMAT A16 WORD_WRAPPED
COLUMN project_id HEADING 'Proj ID' FORMAT 9999
COLUMN project_name HEADING 'Project Name' FORMAT A12 WORD_WRAPPED
COLUMN time_log_date HEADING 'Date' FORMAT A11
COLUMN hours_logged HEADING 'Hours' FORMAT 9,999
COLUMN dollars_charged HEADING 'Dollars|Charged' FORMAT $999,999.99

--Execute the query to generate the report.
SELECT E.EMPLOYEE_ID,
       E.EMPLOYEE_NAME,
       P.PROJECT_ID,
       P.PROJECT_NAME,
       TO_CHAR(PH.TIME_LOG_DATE,'dd-Mon-yyyy') time_log_date,
       PH.HOURS_LOGGED,
       PH.DOLLARS_CHARGED
  FROM EMPLOYEE E,
       PROJECT P,
       PROJECT_HOURS PH
 WHERE E.EMPLOYEE_ID = PH.EMPLOYEE_ID
   AND P.PROJECT_ID = PH.PROJECT_ID
ORDER BY E.EMPLOYEE_ID, P.PROJECT_ID, PH.TIME_LOG_DATE;
```

When you execute this script, here's what the output will look like:

```
                        The Fictional Company


I.S. Department                         Project Hours and Dollars Detail
=========================================================================


                                                               Dollars
Emp ID Employee Name    Proj ID Project Name    Date      Hours Charged
------ ---------------- ------- ---------------- ----------- ------ ---------
   101 Jonathan Gennick    1001 Corporate Web    01-Jan-1998     1   $169.00
                                Site

   101 Jonathan Gennick    1001 Corporate Web    01-Mar-1998     3   $507.00
                                Site

   101 Jonathan Gennick    1001 Corporate Web    01-May-1998     5   $845.00
                                Site

   101 Jonathan Gennick    1001 Corporate Web    01-Jul-1998     7 $1,183.00
                                Site
```

```
101 Jonathan Gennick     1001 Corporate Web    01-Sep-1998     1     $169.00
                              Site

101 Jonathan Gennick     1001 Corporate Web    01-Nov-1998     3     $507.00
                              Site

101 Jonathan Gennick     1002 Year 2000 Fixes  01-Feb-1998     7   $1,183.00
101 Jonathan Gennick     1002 Year 2000 Fixes  01-Apr-1998     1     $169.00
101 Jonathan Gennick     1002 Year 2000 Fixes  01-Jun-1998     3     $507.00
101 Jonathan Gennick     1002 Year 2000 Fixes  01-Aug-1998     5     $845.00
101 Jonathan Gennick     1002 Year 2000 Fixes  01-Oct-1998     7   $1,183.00
101 Jonathan Gennick     1002 Year 2000 Fixes  01-Dec-1998     1     $169.00
```

The first four columns repeat the same values over and over again. This makes the report a bit difficult to follow because you may not see when a value actually changes. Next, you will see how to suppress duplicate values in a column, making the report less repetitious. You will also see how to add page and line breaks to further improve readability. Finally, you will learn how to turn this report into a master/detail report that shows the employee information in the page header with the detail listed below it.

## *The BREAK Command*

The BREAK command is used to define page breaks and line breaks based on changing column values in a report. It controls whether or not duplicate values print in a column, and it controls the printing of computed values such as totals and subtotals.

The BREAK command looks like this:

```
BRE[AK] [ON {column_name|ROW|REPORT}
         [SKI[P] {lines_to_skip|PAGE}|
         NODUP[LICATES]|
         DUP[LICATES]...]
```

where:

*BRE[AK]*

May be abbreviated BRE. Issuing the BREAK command with no parameters causes SQL\*Plus to display the current break setting.

*column_name*

Specifies a report column to watch. When the value in the column changes, SQL\*Plus skips lines or pages as specified. SQL\*Plus also inhibits repeating, or duplicate, values from printing more than once unless the DUPLICATES keyword is used.

*ROW*

Causes SQL\*Plus to break on each row. You could double-space a report by using BREAK ON ROW SKIP 1.

*REPORT*

> Specifies a report-level break, and is used to cause SQL*Plus to print grand totals at the end of the report. SKIP PAGE will be ignored if it is specified as a report break action, but strangely enough, the other form of the SKIP parameter will work. You can skip lines on a report break.

*SKI[P] lines_to_skip*

> Tells SQL*Plus to skip the specified number of lines when a break occurs. SKIP may be abbreviated to SKI.

*SKI[P] PAGE*

> Tells SQL*Plus to advance to a new page when a break occurs.

*NODUP[LICATES]*

> Tells SQL*Plus to print a column's value only when it changes. By default, whenever you put a break on a column, you get this behavior. May be abbreviated NODUP.

*DUP[LICATES]*

> Forces SQL*Plus to print a column's value in every line on the report, regardless of whether or not the value is the same as that printed for the previous record. May be abbreviated as DUP.

SQL*Plus only allows one break setting to be in effect at any given time, but any number of ON clauses may be used in order to accommodate breaks on more than one column. Longer BREAK commands that define breaks on many columns end up looking like this:

```
BREAK ON column_name action ON column_name action -
     ON column_name action ON column_name action...
```

The hyphen on the end of the first line is the SQL*Plus continuation character, and allows you to improve readability by splitting long commands across several physical lines.

You should almost always sort or group your report by the same columns specified in the BREAK command, and the column orders should match.

## *Suppressing Duplicate Column Values*

To eliminate repeating values in a report column, use the BREAK command to specify the NODUPLICATES action for that column. For example, to eliminate duplicate values in the employee and project name columns, as well as the employee and project ID columns, you could issue this command:

```
BREAK ON employee_id NODUPLICATES ON employee_name NODUPLICATES
     ON project_id NODUPLICATES ON project_name NODUPLICATES
```

NODUPLICATES is the default action for BREAK and is almost never specified explicitly. Instead, the command just shown would usually be simplified to:

```
BREAK ON employee_id ON employee_name ON project_id ON project_name
```

Adding this BREAK command to the report script makes the output look like this:

```
                          The Fictional Company


I.S. Department                           Project Hours and Dollars Detail
==========================================================================


                                                              Dollars
Emp ID Employee Name    Proj ID Project Name   Date      Hours Charged
------ ---------------- ------- ---------------- ----------- ------ ---------
   101 Jonathan Gennick    1001 Corporate Web   01-Jan-1998     1   $169.00
                                Site

                                               01-Mar-1998     3   $507.00
                                               01-May-1998     5   $845.00
                                               01-Jul-1998     7 $1,183.00
                                               01-Sep-1998     1   $169.00
                                               01-Nov-1998     3   $507.00
                           1002 Year 2000 Fixes 01-Feb-1998    7 $1,183.00
                                               01-Apr-1998     1   $169.00
                                               01-Jun-1998     3   $507.00
                                               01-Aug-1998     5   $845.00
                                               01-Oct-1998     7 $1,183.00
                                               01-Dec-1998     1   $169.00
```

As you can see, this is a vast improvement over the previous version of the report. You can now easily spot changes in the employee and project columns.

---

 When using the BREAK command, your query should use an appropriate ORDER BY or GROUP BY clause to group related records together. It wouldn't make much sense to break on the employee_ name column if all records for one employee weren't grouped together. The query for this example sorts by employee_id and project_id. Because there is a one-to-one correlation between employee_id and employee_name, there is no need to specify both in the ORDER BY clause. The same holds true for project_id and project_name.

---

## Page and Line Breaks

To further aid readability, you might wish to start a new page when the employee name changes, and to leave one or two blank lines between the detail for each project. Having each employee start on a new page has the further benefit of allowing you to give each employee his section of the report. Perhaps you want him to double-check the hours he has reported. The SKIP action of the BREAK command can be used to accomplish both these objectives.

### Adding a page break

To have each employee's data start on a new page, add SKIP PAGE to the list of actions to be performed each time the employee changes. The resulting BREAK command looks like this:

```
BREAK ON employee_id SKIP PAGE NODUPLICATES -
      ON employee_name NODUPLICATES -
      ON project_id NODUPLICATES -
      ON project_name NODUPLICATES
```

Since both the employee ID and name columns change at the same time, the page break could have been defined on either column. In this case, the employee_id was chosen because it is the primary key for the table and can be depended on to be unique for each employee.

### Adding a line break

To add two blank lines between projects, use the SKIP 2 action. SKIP allows you to advance a specified number of lines each time a column's value changes. It takes one numeric argument specifying the number of lines to advance. Here's how the BREAK command looks with both the page and line breaks specified:

```
BREAK ON employee_id SKIP PAGE NODUPLICATES -
      ON employee_name NODUPLICATES -
      ON project_id SKIP 2 NODUPLICATES -
      ON project_name NODUPLICATES
```

### Report output with page and line breaks

When you run the report using this BREAK setting, the output will look like this:

```
                        The Fictional Company


I.S. Department                         Project Hours and Dollars Detail
========================================================================



                                                              Dollars
  Emp ID Employee Name    Proj ID Project Name   Date         Hours   Charged
  ------ ---------------- ------- -------------- -----------  ------ ---------
     101 Jonathan Gennick    1001 Corporate Web  01-Jan-1998      1   $169.00
                                  Site
```

```
                                        01-Mar-1998       3    $507.00
                                        01-May-1998       5    $845.00
                                        01-Jul-1998       7  $1,183.00
                                        01-Sep-1998       1    $169.00
                                        01-Nov-1998       3    $507.00


                    1002 Year 2000 Fixes  01-Feb-1998     7  $1,183.00
                                        01-Apr-1998       1    $169.00
                                        01-Jun-1998       3    $507.00
                                        01-Aug-1998       5    $845.00
                                        01-Oct-1998       7  $1,183.00
                                        01-Dec-1998       1    $169.00
  ...
                            The Fictional Company


  I.S. Department                          Project Hours and Dollars Detail
  ============================================================================

                                                                    Dollars
  Emp ID Employee Name    Proj ID Project Name    Date       Hours  Charged
  ------ ----------------  ------- ----------------  -----------  ------  ---------
     102 Jenny Gennick      1001 Corporate Web    01-Jan-1998      1    $135.00
                                 Site

                                                 01-Mar-1998       3    $405.00
                                                 01-May-1998       5    $675.00
```

As you can see, each change in employee starts a new page, and there are now two blank lines following each project.

---

 Sometimes column breaks and page breaks coincide. When that happens, SQL\*Plus will perform both sets of break actions, which can result in some pages that start with leading blank lines. In this example, if both a project and a page break occur simultaneously, SQL\*Plus will first advance to a new page, then print the two blank lines required for a project break. SQL\*Plus has not been designed to recognize that, because of the page break, the two blank lines are not needed.

---

When using BREAK to create page breaks and lines breaks, it is important that the column order specified in your BREAK command match the sort order (or grouping) used for the query. This is very important! Suppose you took the BREAK command just used and turned it around like this:

```
BREAK ON project_id SKIP 2 NODUPLICATES -
      ON project_name NODUPLICATES -
      ON employee_id SKIP PAGE NODUPLICATES -
```

```
ON employee_name NODUPLICATES
```

You would find that every change in project resulted in a skip to a new page. Why? Because when SQL*Plus executes a break action for a given column, it first executes the break actions for all columns to the right of it in the list. The reason it does that is because column breaks are also used to trigger the printing of totals and subtotals. If you were totaling up hours by project and employee, and the employee changed, it would be important to print the total hours for the employee's last project prior to printing the total hours for that employee.

## Master/Detail Formatting

With column breaks on both the employee columns and the project columns, the Project Hours and Dollars Detail report now contains quite a bit of whitespace. This is particularly true under the employee name column because that value changes so infrequently. This report is a good candidate for conversion to a master/detail style of report.

A *master/detail* report is one that displays the value of one record in a heading and then lists the detail from related records below that heading. The record shown in the heading is referred to as the master, and the records shown below that heading are referred to as detail records.

Only three additional steps are needed to convert this report from a plain columnar report to the master/detail style of report:

1. Retrieve the employee name and ID into *user variables*.
2. Modify the page heading to print the value of those variables.
3. Revise the report width and the width of the remaining fields.

User variables are text variables that can be used to hold values retrieved from the database or to hold values entered by a user. One use for user variables is to allow you to include report data as part of a page header or footer—just what we are going to do here. Chapter 4, *Writing SQL*Plus Scripts*, talks about using these variables to facilitate user interaction with your SQL*Plus scripts.

### Retrieve the employee information into user variables

Use the COLUMN command to get the value of the employee name and ID columns into user variables. Instead of specifying a display format for those columns, use the NEW_VALUE and NOPRINT clauses. For example:

```
COLUMN employee_id NEW_VALUE emp_id_var NOPRINT
COLUMN employee_name NEW_VALUE emp_name_var NOPRINT
```

The NEW_VALUE clause tells SQL*Plus to update a user variable with the new contents of the column each time a row is returned from the query. In this example, emp_name_var will be updated by SQL*Plus to contain the most recently retrieved employee name. Likewise, the emp_name_id variable will be updated with the employee ID. It is not necessary to declare these variables. Simply pick some names that make sense and use them. The NOPRINT clause is used to tell SQL*Plus not to include the employee name and ID columns in the report detail.

### Modify the page heading to print the employee name and ID

The next step is to modify the page header to include the employee information. That can be done using this updated TTITLE command:

```
TTITLE CENTER 'The Fictional Company' SKIP 3 -
       LEFT 'I.S. Department' -
       RIGHT 'Project Hours and Dollars Detail' SKIP 1 -
       LEFT '=============================================================' -
       SKIP 2 'Employee: ' FORMAT 9999 emp_id_var ' ' emp_name_var SKIP 3
```

The only change to the header is the addition of a fifth line—the bold line in the example. Here's how to interpret this line:

*SKIP 2*

Tells SQL*Plus to advance two lines after printing the ruling line of equal-sign characters. This effectively leaves *one* blank line before the employee ID and name are printed.

*'Employee: '*

This is a quoted literal, so SQL*Plus prints it just as it is shown. It serves to label the information that follows.

*FORMAT 9999*

Tells SQL*Plus to format any subsequent numeric values in a four-digit field with no leading zeros.

*emp_id_var*

Tells SQL*Plus to print the contents of this user variable, which contains the most recently retrieved employee ID number.

' ' Causes a space to print between the employee ID and name so the two fields don't run together.

*emp_name_var*

Tells SQL*Plus to print the contents of this user variable, which contains the most recently retrieved employee name.

It's usually not necessary to format a character field such as the employee name, but you do have that option. Specifying FORMAT A20 TRUNCATED, for example, will cause the employee name to print in a 20-character-wide field with any names longer than 20 characters being truncated.

### *Revisit the report width and the width of the remaining fields*

The employee_name and employee_id columns used a total of 22 characters. Since each column was followed by one blank space, eliminating them from the detail section of the report frees up 24 characters that may be usable elsewhere.

The one column that can benefit from a longer length is the project_name column. This column prints 12 characters wide on the report, but is defined in the database to hold up to 40. A quick look at the actual data shows that all but one project name is 26 characters or less, so let's increase it to 26 by changing its COLUMN command to:

```
COLUMN project_name HEADING 'Project Name' FORMAT A26 WORD_WRAPPED
```

The remaining 10 characters can be taken out of the linesize, which is currently 76, so the new linesize command becomes:

```
SET LINESIZE 66
```

By adjusting the linesize, you ensure that the right-justified portions of the page title line up with the right edge of the report. Remember to adjust the number of equal-signs in the TTITLE and BTITLE commands to match the linesize. The report output will now look like this:

```
                      The Fictional Company


I.S. Department                 Project Hours and Dollars Detail
================================================================

Employee:   101 Jonathan Gennick


                                                       Dollars
Proj ID Project Name             Date        Hours     Charged
------- ------------------------ ----------- ------ -----------
   1001 Corporate Web Site       01-Jan-1998      1     $169.00
                                 01-Mar-1998      3     $507.00
                                 01-May-1998      5     $845.00
                                 01-Jul-1998      7   $1,183.00
                                 01-Sep-1998      1     $169.00
                                 01-Nov-1998      3     $507.00
```

```
1002 Year 2000 Fixes          01-Feb-1998     7    $1,183.00
                              01-Apr-1998     1      $169.00
                              01-Jun-1998     3      $507.00
                              01-Aug-1998     5      $845.00
                              01-Oct-1998     7    $1,183.00
                              01-Dec-1998     1      $169.00
```

Here is the final version of the script, incorporating all the changes described in this section:

```
--Set up pagesize parameters
SET NEWPAGE 0
SET PAGESIZE 55
--Set the linesize, which must match the number of equals signs used
--for the ruling lines in the headers and footers.
SET LINESIZE 66

--Set up page headings and footings
TTITLE CENTER 'The Fictional Company' SKIP 3 -
       LEFT 'I.S. Department' -
       RIGHT 'Project Hours and Dollars Detail' SKIP 1 -
       LEFT '=========================================' -
            '==========================' -
       SKIP 2 'Employee: ' FORMAT 9999 emp_id_var ' ' emp_name_var SKIP 3

BTITLE LEFT '=========================================' -
            '==========================' -
       SKIP 1 -
       RIGHT 'Page ' FORMAT 999 SQL.PNO

--Format the columns
COLUMN employee_id NEW_VALUE emp_id_var NOPRINT
COLUMN employee_name NEW_VALUE emp_name_var NOPRINT
COLUMN project_id HEADING 'Proj ID' FORMAT 9999
COLUMN project_name HEADING 'Project Name' FORMAT A26 WORD_WRAPPED
COLUMN time_log_date HEADING 'Date' FORMAT A11
COLUMN hours_logged HEADING 'Hours' FORMAT 9,999
COLUMN dollars_charged HEADING 'Dollars|Charged' FORMAT $999,999.99

--Breaks and Computations
BREAK ON employee_id SKIP PAGE NODUPLICATES -
      ON employee_name NODUPLICATES -
      ON project_id SKIP 2 NODUPLICATES -
      ON project_name NODUPLICATES

--Execute the query to generate the report.
SELECT E.EMPLOYEE_ID,
       E.EMPLOYEE_NAME,
       P.PROJECT_ID,
       P.PROJECT_NAME,
       TO_CHAR(PH.TIME_LOG_DATE,'dd-Mon-yyyy') time_log_date,
       PH.HOURS_LOGGED,
       PH.DOLLARS_CHARGED
```

```
      FROM EMPLOYEE E,
           PROJECT P,
           PROJECT_HOURS PH
     WHERE E.EMPLOYEE_ID = PH.EMPLOYEE_ID
       AND P.PROJECT_ID = PH.PROJECT_ID
     ORDER BY E.EMPLOYEE_ID, P.PROJECT_ID, PH.TIME_LOG_DATE;
```

### Printing data in a page footer

You can print data as part of the page footer using the same method just shown for the page header. The only difference is that you would normally use the OLD_ VALUE clause with the COLUMN command rather than NEW_VALUE. That's because when SQL*Plus prints the footer, it has already read the next detail record from the database. Using NEW_VALUE for data in the footer would cause the footer to display information pertaining to the next page in the report—not something you would normally want to happen.

# Totals and Subtotals

SQL*Plus allows you to print totals and subtotals in a report. To do this, you use a combination of the BREAK command and one or more COMPUTE commands. This section continues where the previous section left off. It will show you how to modify the master/detail report created earlier so that it totals the hours and dollars by project and by employee. You will also see how to print grand totals for these columns at the end of the report.

## The COMPUTE Command

The COMPUTE command defines summary calculations needed in a report. You can use COMPUTE in conjunction with BREAK to calculate and print column totals, averages, minimum and maximum values, and so on. These calculations are performed by SQL*Plus as the report runs.

### Syntax of the COMPUTE command

The syntax for the COMPUTE command looks like this:

```
COMP[UTE] [{AVG|COU[NT]|MAX[IMUM]|MIN[IMUM]|
           NUM[BER]|STD|SUM|VAR[IANCE]}... [LABEL label_text]
           OF column_name...
           ON {group_column_name|ROW|REPORT}...]
```

where:

*COMP[UTE]*

May be abbreviated to COMP. Entering COMPUTE with no parameters causes SQL*Plus to list all currently defined computations.

*AVG*

Computes the average of all non-null values for a column. AVG only applies to columns of type NUMBER.

*COU[NT]*

Computes the total number of non-null values for a column. COUNT may be used with columns of any datatype, and may be abbreviated to COU.

*MAX[IMUM]*

Computes the maximum value returned for a column. MAXIMUM may be abbreviated as MAX, and applies to columns of type NUMBER, CHAR, VARCHAR2, NCHAR, and NVARCHAR2.

*MIN[IMUM]*

Computes the minimum value returned for a column. MINIMUM may be abbreviated as MIN, and applies to columns of type NUMBER, CHAR, VARCHAR2, NCHAR, and NVARCHAR2.

*NUM[BER]*

Similar to COUNT, but computes the number of all values, including nulls. This applies to columns of any datatype, and may be abbreviated to NUM.

*STD*

Computes the standard deviation of all non-null values for a column. STD applies only to columns of type NUMBER.

*SUM*

Computes the sum of all non-null values for a column. SUM applies only to columns of type NUMBER.

*VAR[IANCE]*

Computes the variance of all non-null values for a column. VARIANCE applies only to columns of type NUMBER, and may be abbreviated to VAR.

*LABEL label_text*

Allows you to specify a label for the computed value. If possible, this label will be printed to the left of the computed value. The label text may be enclosed in quotes, either single or double. To embed a quote within the label, when that label has been quoted, place two quote characters back to back.

*column_name*

Is the name of the column you are summarizing. If it is a computed column, then the expression is the name. If your SELECT statement aliases the column, then you must use that alias here.

*group_column_name*

> Causes SQL*Plus to restart the calculation every time this column changes. Typically, the report is sorted or grouped by this column, and then the computed value is printed once for each distinct value of the group column.

*ROW*

> Causes the computation to be performed once for each row returned by the query.

*REPORT*

> Causes the computation to be performed at the end of the report, and to include values from all rows. REPORT is used for grand totals.

The COMPUTE command is complex, and can be intimidating the first time you go to use it. In order to get any of the computed values to print, COMPUTE must be used in conjunction with the BREAK command. The next section will show you how this is done.

### Printing computed values

The COMPUTE command tells SQL*Plus what columns to summarize and over what range of records. That's all it does. By itself, it won't cause anything to print. In order to print the computed values, you must issue a BREAK command to define breaks on the same report elements used in your COMPUTE command. For example, if you total hours by project ID, then you need a project ID break in order to print that total.

### COMPUTE commands are cumulative

With the BREAK command, you have only one break setting, and each new BREAK command overwrites that setting with a new one. That's not the case with COMPUTE. Each defined computation is a separate entity, and COMPUTE commands do not overwrite each other. COMPUTE definitions also "stick" for the duration of a SQL*Plus session. A COMPUTE setting issued for one report may stick around to affect the printing of subsequent reports. SQL*Plus provides the CLEAR COMPUTES command to help you deal with this. CLEAR COMPUTES causes SQL*Plus to erase all computations so you can start over. If you are using COMPUTE in a report script, you may want to include a CLEAR COMPUTES command to avoid any possible contamination from previous reports that may have used COMPUTE.

## Printing Subtotals

The Project Hours and Dollars Detail report has two numeric columns showing the hours logged to a project together with the resulting dollar amount that was charged. You can easily see that it would be desirable to total these for each project and employee. The following five commands will accomplish this:

```
CLEAR COMPUTES
COMPUTE SUM LABEL 'Totals' OF hours_logged ON project_id
COMPUTE SUM LABEL 'Totals' OF dollars_charged ON project_id
COMPUTE SUM LABEL 'Totals' OF hours_logged ON employee_id
COMPUTE SUM LABEL 'Totals' OF dollars_charged ON employee_id
```

The first command simply clears any existing computations that may be defined. The next two commands summarize the hours and dollars by project. The last two commands do the same thing except that the totals are for the employee, and cover all projects to which an employee has charged hours. Here's how the output will look when you run the modified script:

```
                          The Fictional Company


I.S. Department                    Project Hours and Dollars Detail
==================================================================

Employee:   101 Jonathan Gennick


                                                      Dollars
Proj ID Project Name              Date        Hours   Charged
------- ------------------------ ----------- ------ ------------
   1001 Corporate Web Site        01-Jan-1998     1      $169.00
                                  01-Mar-1998     3      $507.00
                                  01-May-1998     5      $845.00
                                  01-Jul-1998     7    $1,183.00
                                  01-Sep-1998     1      $169.00
                                  01-Nov-1998     3      $507.00
****** ************************              ------ ------------
Totals                                          20    $3,380.00


   1002 Year 2000 Fixes           01-Feb-1998     7    $1,183.00
                                  01-Apr-1998     1      $169.00
                                  01-Jun-1998     3      $507.00
...
   1005 TCP/IP Implementation     01-Jan-1998     5      $845.00
                                  01-Mar-1998     7    $1,183.00
                                  01-May-1998     1      $169.00
                                  01-Jul-1998     3      $507.00
                                  01-Sep-1998     5      $845.00
                                  01-Nov-1998     7    $1,183.00
****** ************************              ------ ------------
Totals                                          28    $4,732.00


                                            ------ ------------
                                               116   $19,604.00
```

Notice that the label "Totals" appears in the project_id column. SQL*Plus always places the label you specify into the ON column of the COMPUTE command. The label will be formatted according to the rules specified in that column's COLUMN command.

 Only one label can be printed for project totals, though there are two COMPUTE commands. Had you specified two different labels, the first one would have taken precedence.

Why no label for the employee totals? Because this is a master/detail report, and the NOPRINT option has been used to suppress printing of the employee_name and employee_id columns. Normally, SQL*Plus would print the COMPUTE label in the employee_id column, but that can't be done if the column is not being printed. There is really nothing you can do if you aren't happy with this behavior. You either have to live with it or avoid master/detail reports.

The width of the label identifying the project totals is limited by the width of the project_id column, which simply won't hold a longer, more descriptive label such as "Project Totals." However, there are a couple of things you can do to make room for a longer label. The first and most obvious thing is simply to make the project_id column wider. Change the COLUMN command to widen the field from 7 to 14 digits:

```
COLUMN project_id HEADING 'Proj ID' FORMAT 99999999999999
```

Just be sure to bump up the linesize setting by the same amount, and also adjust the page headers and footers.

A less obvious approach would be to change the computations so the project totals are summarized for each project name rather than for each project ID. The resulting commands would be:

```
COMPUTE SUM LABEL 'Project Totals' OF hours_logged ON project_name
COMPUTE SUM LABEL 'Project Totals' OF dollars_charged ON project_name
```

The output would then look like this:

```
                                                               Dollars
Proj ID Project Name                  Date          Hours      Charged
------- ---------------------------   -----------   ------   -----------
   1001 Corporate Web Site            01-Jan-1998        1       $169.00
                                      01-Mar-1998        3       $507.00
                                      01-May-1998        5       $845.00
                                      01-Jul-1998        7     $1,183.00
                                      01-Sep-1998        1       $169.00
                                      01-Nov-1998        3       $507.00
        *************************                   ------   -----------
        Project Totals                                 20     $3,380.00
```

You now have room for a more descriptive label, and there is the added benefit that it looks better with the label indented closer to the printed totals.

## Print Grand Totals

The REPORT keyword is used to compute and print totals for an entire report. Use REPORT in the ON clause of a COMPUTE statement to define report-level computations. Use REPORT with the BREAK command to enable a report break that will cause the report-level computed values to print.

To print grand totals for the project_hours and dollars_charged columns, add the following two lines to the script file:

```
COMPUTE SUM LABEL 'Grand Totals' OF hours_logged ON REPORT
COMPUTE SUM LABEL 'Grand Totals' OF dollars_charged ON REPORT
```

Notice that instead of specifying a column in the ON clause, the keyword REPORT has been used. This tells SQL*Plus to sum the data over the entire report. Also notice that the LABEL clause has been used. Normally the label would print in the column specified in the ON clause. In cases like this where there is no ON column, SQL*Plus will place the labels in the first column of the report.

The next thing to do is to modify the BREAK command by adding a report break. Forget to do this and the report totals will not print. The final version of the BREAK command looks like this:

```
BREAK ON REPORT -
      ON employee_id SKIP PAGE NODUPLICATES -
      ON employee_name NODUPLICATES -
      ON project_id SKIP 2 NODUPLICATES -
      ON project_name NODUPLICATES
```

The REPORT break was added to the beginning of the BREAK command because it is the outermost break. The position doesn't really matter because SQL*Plus always makes the report break outermost, but I like to put it first anyway for the sake of clarity.

If you run the report now, the grand totals will be printed on a page by themselves at the end of the report. Here's how that output will look:

```
                        The Fictional Company


I.S. Department                         Project Hours and Dollars Detail
=====================================================================

Employee:    113 Jacob Marley
```

```
                                                      Dollars
       Proj ID Project Name           Date      Hours Charged
       ------- ------------------------- ----------- ------ ------------

                                                 ------ ------------
                                                 786  $110,779.00
```

Notice three things about how the report totals are printed. First, notice that they printed on a page by themselves. Next, notice that the page with the grand totals still shows an employee name in the page header. Finally, notice that the "Grand Totals" label did not print as expected in the first column. I'll explain all of these oddities next.

First the pagination issue. Before SQL*Plus executes a report break, it first executes all the other breaks. Execution begins with the innermost break and proceeds outwards until the report break actions are executed. In this example, SQL*Plus will skip two lines—the project break and the skip to a new page—the employee break, and then print the report totals. This is usually the behavior you want when printing a master/detail report. You may intend to give each employee his own section of the report so he can double-check his hours. Since the grand total doesn't really "belong" with any one employee, you don't want it on the pages you are giving out.

The last employee's name printed on the page header simply because it was the last value retrieved from the database. It would be nice if SQL*Plus were smart enough to make this value null or blank, but it isn't. The value in the header is refreshed only when a new value is read from the database, and in the case of a report break, that simply doesn't happen. This is only an issue on master/detail reports when you use variables to include report data in the header.

The final item to notice, and the only one you can do anything about, is the lack of a label for the grand total values. I did say that SQL*Plus puts the label for report-level calculations in the first column of the report. Contrary to what you might intuitively expect, SQL*Plus bases the first column on the SELECT statement, not on what is actually printed. When this report was converted to a master/detail report, printing of the first two columns was suppressed using the NOPRINT clause of the COLUMN command. No employee_id column, no "Grand Totals" label.

Since the employee_id and employee_name columns are not being printed, their position in the SELECT statement is irrelevant. You can move them to the end, making project_id the first column, widen the project_id column to hold 12 characters instead of 7, and the "Grand Totals" label will now print in the first column of the report.

The final listing, complete with the changes that allow the "Grand Totals" label to print, is shown next. To widen the project_id column to accommodate 12 characters, 5 extra leading spaces were inserted into the project_id column title. The linesize was also adjusted from 66 to 71, and 5 equal-sign characters were added to the ruling lines in the header and footer.

```
--Setup pagesize parameters
SET NEWPAGE 0
SET PAGESIZE 55

--Set the linesize, which must match the number of equal signs used
--for the ruling lines in the headers and footers.
SET LINESIZE 71

--Setup page headings and footings
TTITLE CENTER 'The Fictional Company' SKIP 3 -
       LEFT 'I.S. Department' -
       RIGHT 'Project Hours and Dollars Detail' SKIP 1 -
       LEFT '=======================================================' -
       SKIP 2 'Employee: ' FORMAT 9999 emp_id_var ' ' emp_name_var SKIP 3


BTITLE LEFT '=======================================================' -
       SKIP 1 -
       RIGHT 'Page ' FORMAT 999 SQL.PNO

--Format the columns
COLUMN employee_id NEW_VALUE emp_id_var NOPRINT
COLUMN employee_name NEW_VALUE emp_name_var NOPRINT
COLUMN project_id HEADING '     Proj ID' FORMAT 9999
COLUMN project_name HEADING 'Project Name' FORMAT A26 WORD_WRAPPED
COLUMN time_log_date HEADING 'Date' FORMAT A11
COLUMN hours_logged HEADING 'Hours' FORMAT 9,999
COLUMN dollars_charged HEADING 'Dollars|Charged' FORMAT $999,999.99

--Breaks and Computations
BREAK ON REPORT -
      ON employee_id SKIP PAGE NODUPLICATES -
      ON employee_name NODUPLICATES -
      ON project_id SKIP 2 NODUPLICATES -
      ON project_name NODUPLICATES
CLEAR COMPUTES
COMPUTE SUM LABEL 'Project Totals' OF hours_logged ON project_name
COMPUTE SUM LABEL 'Project Totals' OF dollars_charged ON project_name
COMPUTE SUM LABEL 'Totals' OF hours_logged ON employee_id
COMPUTE SUM LABEL 'Totals' OF dollars_charged ON employee_id
COMPUTE SUM LABEL 'Grand Totals' OF hours_logged ON REPORT
COMPUTE SUM LABEL 'Grand Totals' OF dollars_charged ON REPORT

--Execute the query to generate the report.
SELECT P.PROJECT_ID,
       P.PROJECT_NAME,
       TO_CHAR(PH.TIME_LOG_DATE,'dd-Mon-yyyy') time_log_date,
       PH.HOURS_LOGGED,
       PH.DOLLARS_CHARGED,
       E.EMPLOYEE_ID,
       E.EMPLOYEE_NAME
```

```
    FROM EMPLOYEE E,
         PROJECT P,
         PROJECT_HOURS PH
   WHERE E.EMPLOYEE_ID = PH.EMPLOYEE_ID
     AND P.PROJECT_ID = PH.PROJECT_ID
   ORDER BY E.EMPLOYEE_ID, P.PROJECT_ID, PH.TIME_LOG_DATE;
```

Here is the output produced by the final version of this script. Notice that the "Grand Totals" label does appear in the project_id column at the end of the report.

```
                      The Fictional Company


I.S. Department                    Project Hours and Dollars Detail
=======================================================================


Employee:   101 Jonathan Gennick


                                                           Dollars
       Proj ID Project Name          Date        Hours     Charged
       ------- -------------------   ----------- ------   -----------
          1001 Corporate Web Site    01-Jan-1998      1      $169.00
                                     01-Mar-1998      3      $507.00
                                     01-May-1998      5      $845.00
                                     01-Jul-1998      7    $1,183.00
                                     01-Sep-1998      1      $169.00
                                     01-Nov-1998      3      $507.00
                **************************           ------ -----------
                Project Totals                          20    $3,380.00
```

*...detail for several projects*

```
          1005 TCP/IP Implementation 01-Jan-1998      5      $845.00
                                     01-Mar-1998      7    $1,183.00
                                     01-May-1998      1      $169.00
                                     01-Jul-1998      3      $507.00
                                     01-Sep-1998      5      $845.00
                                     01-Nov-1998      7    $1,183.00
                **************************           ------ -----------
                Project Totals                          28    $4,732.00


  ************                                       ------ -----------
                                                        116   $19,604.00
```

*...several pages of output*

```
                      The Fictional Company


I.S. Department                    Project Hours and Dollars Detail
=======================================================================
```

```
Employee:    113 Jacob Marley


                                                           Dollars
            Proj ID Project Name              Date    Hours  Charged
        ------------ ------------------------- ----------- ------ ------------
                                                           ------ ------------
            Grand Totals                                   786  $110,779.00
```

When printing totals and grand totals, be sure that the summarized columns are wide enough to accommodate the final totals. None of the individual "Dollars Charged" values in this report required more than four digits to the left of the decimal, but the final total required six.

# Other Reporting Topics

In addition to what you've read so far in this chapter, there are several other techniques and topics worth discussing. One is a method for getting the current date into your page titles. Considering how easy it is to do page numbers, it's surprisingly difficult to do dates. Report headers and footers function similarly to page headers and footers, except that they print just once, at the beginning and end of a report.

If you find yourself printing reports only because you need to look at computed values such as group totals and report totals, you will want to read the section on summary reports that follows. You can save yourself a lot of network and other overhead by summarizing your data on the server instead of returning all the detail records and making SQL\*Plus do the work.

## Getting the Current Date into a Header

It's a very common practice to put the run date in the header of a report. It's such a common practice, in fact, that it's a wonder Oracle does not provide a convenient way to do it. Unlike the case with the page number, which SQL\*Plus conveniently maintains in the *SQL.PNO* user variable, the date is not so easily available. How then, do you display the date in the page header? The answer is to retrieve it from the database, put it into a user variable, and display that variable in the header.

You saw how to display the contents of a user variable in the header when the Project Hours and Dollars Detail report was converted to a master/detail style. You also saw how to use the COLUMN command to tell SQL\*Plus to continuously update the contents of a user variable with the value of a column in the query. Getting the system date to display in the header involves a little trick that takes advantage of this use of the COLUMN command. The trick is to execute a query that returns the current date, and use the NEW_VALUE clause of the COLUMN command to get that date into a user variable. That user variable sticks around for the duration of the session and can be used in a subsequent report.

### Getting the date from Oracle

The built-in SYSDATE function is used in the following example to return the current date from the database. Notice that the NEW_VALUE option of the COLUMN command is used to update the user variable report_date with the current value of SYSDATE as returned from the database.

```
COLUMN SYSDATE NEW_VALUE report_date
SELECT SYSDATE FROM DUAL;
```

SYSDATE is an Oracle built-in function that returns the current date and time. DUAL is a special Oracle table that always exists, always contains exactly one row, and always contains exactly one column. You could select SYSDATE from any other table, but DUAL works well because it returns only one row—all you need to set the date.

---

The date returned using this method is the date on the database server, not the client. If you are using a PC to access data on a remote database in a different time zone, the date returned may or may not match the local date. This depends on the time of day when the report is run and on the number of hours difference between the time zones.

---

### Formatting the date

You may find that the date format returned by SYSDATE is not what you would prefer. It depends on the setting of the NLS_DATE_FORMAT parameter, which can vary from one database to the next. You can use the ALTER SESSION command to specify a different format, for example:

```
ALTER SESSION SET NLS_DATE_FORMAT = 'DD-Mon-YYYY';
```

ALTER SESSION changes the format for the duration of the SQL*Plus session. Make sure you execute it prior to selecting SYSDATE from DUAL. Another alternative is to use the built-in TO_CHAR function to specify a format.

```
COLUMN current_date NEW_VALUE report_date
SELECT TO_CHAR(SYSDATE, 'DD-Mon-YYYY') current_date FROM DUAL;
```

A column alias of current_date was used in this example to give a usable name to the date column, one that could be used easily with the COLUMN command.

Consider using ALTER SESSION to format all dates in your report rather than using TO_CHAR to format each date column separately. This makes your SELECT statements easier to write, gives you one point at which to make changes, and helps to ensure consistency.

Table 3-2 shows some typical date format strings that may be used with Oracle's built-in TO_CHAR function or with the ALTER SESSION command.

*Table 3-2. Date Format Strings*

| Date Format String | Output |
|---|---|
| mm/dd/yy | 11/15/61 |
| dd-Mon-yyyy | 15-Nov-1961 |
| dd-mon-yyyy | 15-nov-1961 |
| Mon dd, yyyy hh:mm am | Nov 15, 1961 10:15 AM (or PM, depending on the time of day) |
| Month dd, yyyy | November 15, 1961 |

You may or may not care whether the output of the SELECT SYSDATE statement appears on the display, but you can suppress it by using the SET TERMOUT command to toggle the display output off and then back on again. Here's how to do that:

```
SET TERMOUT OFF
ALTER SESSION SET NLS_DATE_FORMAT = 'DD-Mon-YYYY';
COLUMN SYSDATE NEW_VALUE report_date
SELECT SYSDATE FROM DUAL;
SET TERMOUT ON
```

Finally, you need to add the date to either the report header or footer. Here's an example of how to do that using the BTITLE command from the Project Hours and Dollars Detail report:

```
BTITLE LEFT '===========================================================' -
       SKIP 1 -
       LEFT report_date -
       RIGHT 'Page ' FORMAT 999 SQL.PNO
```

The addition of "LEFT report_date" to this BTITLE command causes the date to print left-justified on the same line as the page number. When you execute the report, the page footer will look like this:

```
=======================================================================
22-Feb-1998                                                     Page    1
```

In addition to the system date, this technique may be used to retrieve any other value from the database for inclusion in a report.

# Report Headers and Footers

Report headers and footers work very much like page headers and footers, except that they print only once in a report. A report header prints at the beginning of the report, after the first page title, and before the first detail line. A report footer prints at the end of a report, after the last detail line, and before the final page footer. Figure 3-1 illustrates this by showing how the different types of headers and footers print relative to each other in a three-page report.

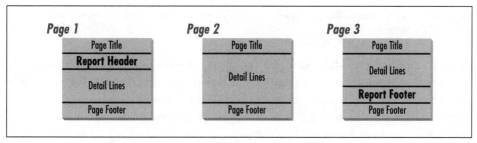

*Figure 3-1. Report headers and footers versus page headers and footers*

You define a report header using the REPHEADER command. The REPFOOTER command defines a report footer.

### REPHEADER and REPFOOTER command syntax

The syntax for the REPHEADER and REPFOOTER commands is the same. To define a report footer, simply use REPFOOTER in place of REPHEADER.

```
REPH[EADER]  [[OFF|ON]|
             COL x|
             S[KIP] x|
             TAB x|
             LE[FT]|
             CE[NTER]|
             R[IGHT]|
             BOLD|
             FOR[MAT] format_spec|
             text|
             variable...]
```

The parameters you can use with REPHEADER and REPFOOTER are the same as, and work the same way as, those used with the TTITLE command.

### An example

One use for a report header is to define a report title that prints just on the first page of a report, leaving only column titles at the top of all subsequent pages. A report footer can be used to mark the end of a report, so you know for sure

whether or not you have all the pages. Here, you will see an example showing
how these things can be done.

Recall that the Project Hours and Dollars Report, the first one shown in this chapter, used the following commands to define page headers and footers:

```
TTITLE CENTER 'The Fictional Company' SKIP 3 -
       LEFT 'I.S. Department' -
       RIGHT 'Project Hours and Dollars Report' SKIP 1 -
       LEFT '=================================================+++=============='

BTITLE LEFT '================================================================' -
       SKIP 1 -
       RIGHT 'Page ' FORMAT 999 SQL.PNO
```

The TTITLE command defined a title containing the name of the report, which in
this case was printed on each page of the report. By replacing TTITLE with REP-
HEADER, and adding a command to turn TTITLE off, the title containing the report
name will print just once. The following example shows how this is done, and
also defines a report footer:

```
TTITLE OFF
REPFOOTER CENTER '*** End of Hours and Dollars Report ***'
REPHEADER CENTER 'The Fictional Company' SKIP 3 -
       LEFT 'I.S. Department' -
       RIGHT 'Project Hours and Dollars Report' SKIP 1 -
       LEFT '==============================================================='

BTITLE LEFT '===============================================================' -
       SKIP 1 -
       RIGHT 'Page ' FORMAT 999 SQL.PNO
```

The report footer, defined with the REPFOOTER command, will print on the last
page, after the last detail record, to mark the end of the report. Here is what the
Project Hours and Dollars report looks like when you run it using the heading
commands shown in the previous example:

```
                         The Fictional Company


I.S. Department                   Project Hours and Dollars Report
=================================================================
                                                         Dollars
Employee Name         Project Name           Hours       Charged
--------------------  --------------------  ------  ------------
Jonathan Gennick      Corporate Web Site        20   $3,380.00
Jonathan Gennick      Year 2000 Fixes           24   $4,056.00
Jonathan Gennick      Accounting System         24   $4,056.00
...
Bohdan Khmelnytsky    Corporate Web Site        20     $900.00
=================================================================
                                                     Page     1
```

```
                                                      Dollars
     Employee Name          Project Name      Hours   Charged
     --------------------    ----------------  ------  ----------
     Bohdan Khmelnytsky      Year 2000 Fixes       24  $1,080.00
     Bohdan Khmelnytsky      Accounting System     24  $1,080.00
     ...
     Jacob Marley            TCP/IP                16  $4,800.00
                             Implementation

              *** End of Hours and Dollars Report ***
     ...
     =============================================================
                                              Page    3
```

As you can see, the report title printed only on the first page of the report. Subsequent pages began with the column titles. The report footer printed on the last page, following the last detail line. Keep in mind when working with report headers and footers that these report elements still print within the context of a page. Page titles and footers print on each page, regardless of whether a report header or footer also prints on that page. Had the above report included a page title (TTITLE), the page title would have printed on the first page, *prior* to the report header.

## Formatting Object Columns

Oracle8 introduced objects to Oracle's relational database world. Users of Oracle may now define object types, then use those object types as datatypes for columns in a relational table. The following example shows an object type named employee_type, and also shows an EMPLOYEES table that contains an object column named employee. The employee column stores employee_type objects:

```
SQL> DESCRIBE employee_type
 Name                             Null?    Type
 -------------------------------- -------- ----
 EMPLOYEE_NAME                             VARCHAR2(40)
 EMPLOYEE_HIRE_DATE                        DATE
 EMPLOYEE_SALARY                           NUMBER(9,2)

SQL> DESCRIBE employees
 Name                             Null?    Type
 -------------------------------- -------- ----
 EMPLOYEE_ID                               NUMBER
 EMPLOYEE                                  EMPLOYEE_TYPE
```

When you select from this table using SQL*Plus, the employee object is treated as one database column, which in fact it is. The attributes of the employee object are displayed in parentheses, for example:

```
SQL> SELECT * FROM employees;
```

```
EMPLOYEE_ID
-----------
EMPLOYEE(EMPLOYEE_NAME, EMPLOYEE_HIRE_DATE, EMPLOYEE_SALARY)
--------------------------------------------------------------------------------
          1
EMPLOYEE_TYPE('Taras Shevchenko', '17-NOV-98', 57000)


          2
EMPLOYEE_TYPE('Ivan Mazepa', '17-NOV-98', 67000)


          3
EMPLOYEE_TYPE('Bohdan Khmelnytsky', '17-NOV-98', 77000)
```

This is some rather messy-looking output. You can tidy it up a bit by formatting the two columns so that both fit on one line. Note that as far as SQL\*Plus is concerned, there are only two columns: employee_id and employee. Here's an example that formats the columns a bit better.

```
SQL> COLUMN employee FORMAT A60 HEADING "Employee Data"
SQL> COLUMN employee_id HEADING "Employee ID"
SQL> SELECT * FROM employees;

Employee ID Employee Data
----------- ------------------------------------------------------------
          1 EMPLOYEE_TYPE('Taras Shevchenko', '17-NOV-98', 57000)
          2 EMPLOYEE_TYPE('Ivan Mazepa', '17-NOV-98', 67000)
          3 EMPLOYEE_TYPE('Bohdan Khmelnytsky', '17-NOV-98', 77000)
```

Now, this is a little better. However, there is still a bit more you can do. SQL\*Plus version 8 introduces a new command called ATTRIBUTE, which allows you to format the individual attributes of an object column. In this case, you can use ATTRIBUTE to format the employee salary so it prints as a dollar value. The following commands do this:

```
SQL> ATTRIBUTE employee_type.employee_salary ALIAS emp_sal
SQL> ATTRIBUTE emp_sal FORMAT $999,999.99
```

Notice that the ATTRIBUTE command referenced the object column's type and not the object column's name. In other words, employee_type was used, not employee. This is very important, and it's easy to overlook.

When you format an attribute for an object type, that format applies any time an object of that type is displayed. This is true even when the same object type is used in more than one column of a table or in more than one table. If you were to have two tables, each with an employee_type object column, the ATTRIBUTE commands just shown would affect the display format of data from *both* columns in *both* tables.

Having used the ATTRIBUTE command to format the employee salary attribute, you can reissue the SELECT to get the following results, which have the salary figures formatted as dollar amounts:

```
SQL> SELECT * FROM employees;

Employee ID Employee Data
----------- --------------------------------------------------------------
          1 EMPLOYEE_TYPE('Taras Shevchenko', '17-NOV-98', $57,000.00)
          2 EMPLOYEE_TYPE('Ivan Mazepa', '17-NOV-98', $67,000.00)
          3 EMPLOYEE_TYPE('Bohdan Khmelnytsky', '17-NOV-98', $77,000.00)
```

Look again at the ATTRIBUTE commands shown earlier. You will see that two commands were used instead of just one. The first command defined an alias for the attribute. An alias is simply another name you can use in subsequent ATTRIBUTE commands to save yourself the trouble of typing in the entire object type and attribute name again. The second ATTRIBUTE command referred to the alias. If you have deeply nested objects, the dot notation for an attribute can be quite long, so this aliasing ability can come in handy.

As with the COLUMN command, the effects of ATTRIBUTE commands are cumulative. That's why two commands were able to be used for the previous example in place of just one. Unlike COLUMN, there is no CLEAR ATTRIBUTES command. The CLEAR COLUMNS command will also erase any attribute settings you may have defined.

The syntax for the ATTRIBUTE command is similar to the COLUMN command, but because there aren't as many options to deal with, it's not quite as complex. It looks like this:

```
ATTRIBUTE [object_type.attribute|attribute_alias
          [ALI[AS] alias|
          CLE[AR]|
          FOR[MAT] format_spec|
          LIKE source_attribute|
          ON|
          OFF...]]
```

where:

*ATTRIBUTE*

Is the command. Issuing the ATTRIBUTE command with no parameters gets you a list of all current attribute settings.

*object_type*

Is the name of an Oracle8 object type.

*attribute*

Is the name of an attribute of the specified object type and the attribute you are formatting. If you stop here, and don't supply any other parameters, the current display settings for this attribute are shown.

*ALI[AS] alias*

May be abbreviated ALI. ALIAS allows you to specify an alternate name for this attribute that is meaningful to SQL\*Plus. This alias may be used in other ATTRIBUTE commands in place of having to spell out the full object type and attribute name again.

*CLE[AR]*

May be abbreviated to CLE. CLEAR erases any format settings for the attribute in question. This puts you back to the way things were before any ATTRIBUTE commands were issued for the attribute.

*FOR[MAT] format_spec*

May be abbreviated to FOR, and allows you to control how the data for the attribute is displayed. For text fields, you can control only the maximum length. For numeric fields, you can control the width, placement of commas, placement of the dollar sign, and so on. Appendix B describes the format specification elements that can be used with the ATTRIBUTE command.

*LIKE source_column*

Causes the attribute to be defined with the same format attributes as another attribute.

*ON*

Causes SQL\*Plus to print the attribute using the format you have specified. This is the default behavior. You don't need to use ON unless you have previously used OFF.

*OFF*

Disables the format settings for the attribute. SQL\*Plus acts as if you had never issued any ATTRIBUTE commands for the attribute in question.

The only format element that can be used with a text attribute is A. For example, you might specify A10 as the format for the employee object's employee name attribute. When used with the ATTRIBUTE command, a text format such as A10 serves to specify a maximum display length for the attribute. Any characters beyond that length are truncated and consequently not displayed. So, instead of a line like this:

```
1 EMPLOYEE_TYPE('Taras Shevchenko', '17-NOV-98', $57,000.00)
```

applying a format of A10 to the employee name field results in the name being truncated to 10 characters in length, as shown here:

```
1 EMPLOYEE_TYPE('Taras Shev', '17-NOV-98', $57,000.00)
```

Text attributes are never expanded to their maximum length. If you think about it, since they are delimited by quotes, that wouldn't make sense. You couldn't add the extra space inside the quotes, and there would be little point in putting it outside the quotes.

> Attributes of type DATE seem completely unaffected by any format settings you may specify, even though they, like text fields, are displayed within quotes.

## Summary Reports

Sometimes you are only interested in summarized information. Maybe you only need to know the total hours each employee has spent on each project, and you could care less about the detail of each day's charges. Whenever that's the case, you should write your SQL query to return summarized data from Oracle.

Here is the query used in the master/detail report shown earlier in this chapter:

```
SELECT P.PROJECT_ID,
       P.PROJECT_NAME,
       TO_CHAR(PH.TIME_LOG_DATE,'dd-Mon-yyyy') time_log_date,
       PH.HOURS_LOGGED,
       PH.DOLLARS_CHARGED,
       E.EMPLOYEE_ID,
       E.EMPLOYEE_NAME
  FROM EMPLOYEE E,
       PROJECT P,
       PROJECT_HOURS PH
 WHERE E.EMPLOYEE_ID = PH.EMPLOYEE_ID
   AND P.PROJECT_ID = PH.PROJECT_ID
 ORDER BY E.EMPLOYEE_ID, P.PROJECT_ID, PH.TIME_LOG_DATE;
```

This query brings down all the detail information from the PROJECT_HOURS table, and is fine if you need that level of detail. However, if all you were interested in were the totals, you could use the following query instead:

```
SELECT P.PROJECT_ID,
       P.PROJECT_NAME,
       max(PH.TIME_LOG_DATE) time_log_date
       sum(PH.HOURS_LOGGED) hours_logged,
       sum(PH.DOLLARS_CHARGED) dollars_charged,
       E.EMPLOYEE_ID,
       E.EMPLOYEE_NAME
  FROM EMPLOYEE E,
       PROJECT P,
       PROJECT_HOURS PH
 WHERE E.EMPLOYEE_ID = PH.EMPLOYEE_ID
   AND P.PROJECT_ID = PH.PROJECT_ID
```

```
GROUP BY E.EMPLOYEE_ID, E.EMPLOYEE_NAME, P.PROJECT_ID, P.PROJECT_NAME
ORDER BY E.EMPLOYEE_ID, P.PROJECT_ID;
```

You can practically plug this second query into your script in place of the first. There are only two other changes you would need to make. First, you would eliminate the project breaks and computations, changing the BREAK and COLUMN commands to:

```
BREAK ON REPORT -
     ON employee_id SKIP PAGE NODUPLICATES -
     ON employee_name NODUPLICATES
CLEAR COMPUTES
COMPUTE SUM LABEL 'Totals' OF hours_logged ON employee_id
COMPUTE SUM LABEL 'Totals' OF dollars_charged ON employee_id
COMPUTE SUM LABEL 'Grand Totals' OF hours_logged ON REPORT
COMPUTE SUM LABEL 'Grand Totals' OF dollars_charged ON REPORT
```

Then you might change the title of the date field, which now represents the most recent date an employee worked on a project, to something more descriptive:

```
COLUMN time_log_date HEADING 'Last Date|Worked' FORMAT A11
```

The resulting output would look like this:

```
                            The Fictional Company


I.S. Department                         Project Hours and Dollars Detail
========================================================================

Employee:   101 Jonathan Gennick


                            Last Date              Dollars
        Proj ID Project Name        Worked     Hours  Charged
    ------------ ------------------- ----------- ------ ------------
        1001 Corporate Web Site      01-Nov-1998    20   $3,380.00
        1002 Year 2000 Fixes         01-Dec-1998    24   $4,056.00
        1003 Accounting System       01-Nov-1998    24   $4,056.00
             Implementation

        1004 Data Warehouse Maintenance 01-Dec-1998 20   $3,380.00
        1005 TCP/IP Implementation   01-Nov-1998    28   $4,732.00
                                                 ------ ------------
                                                    116  $19,604.00
    ...

                                                 ------ ------------
    Grand Totals                                     786 $110,779.00
```

By letting the database handle the project-level summarization, you save both time and paper. You save time because SQL\*Plus doesn't need to pull all that data down from the database, and you save paper because you don't print all the unneeded detail.

# Taking Advantage of Unions

A *union* is a SQL construct that allows you to knit together the results of several SQL queries and treat those results as if they had been returned by just one query. I find them invaluable when writing queries, and one of the more creative uses I've discovered involves using unions to produce reports that need to show data grouped by categories, and that may need to show the same records in more than one of those categories.

## A typical example

A good example of this type or report would be one that fulfills the following request:

> Produce an employee turnover report that lists everyone employed at the beginning of the year, everyone hired during the year, everyone terminated during the year, and everyone still employed at the end of the year. The report should be divided into four sections, one for each of those categories.

This is not an unusual type of request, not for me at least. The interesting thing about this request, though, is that every employee will need to be listed in exactly two categories. That means you would need to write a query that returned each employee record twice, in the correct categories.

When you are faced with this type of query, it can be helpful to simplify the problem by thinking in terms of separate queries, one for each category. It's fairly easy to conceive of a query to bring back a list of employees that were on board at the beginning of the year. You just need to make sure the first of the year is between the hire and termination dates, and account for the fact that the termination date might be null. Here's the query to return a list of people employed as of January 1, 1998:

```
SELECT employee_id,
       employee_name,
       employee_hire_date,
       employee_termination_date
  FROM employee
 WHERE employee_hire_date < TO_DATE('1-Jan-1998','dd-mon-yyyy')
   AND (employee_termination_date IS NULL
        OR employee_termination_date >= TO_DATE('1-Jan-1998','dd-mon-yyyy'))
```

This gives you the first section of the report—those employed at the beginning of the year. Retrieving the data for the remaining sections is a matter of using a different WHERE clause for each section. Table 3-3 shows the selection criteria for each section of the report.

*Table 3-3. Union Query Selection Criteria*

| Report Section | WHERE Clause |
|---|---|
| Employed at beginning of year | ```
WHERE employee_hire_date < TO_DATE('1-Jan-1998','dd-mon-yyyy')
    AND (employee_termination_date IS NULL
        OR employee_termination_date
            >= TO_DATE('1-Jan-1998','dd-mon-yyyy'))
``` |
| Hired during the year | ```
WHERE employee_hire_date >= TO_DATE('1-Jan-1998','dd-mon-yyyy')
    AND (employee_hire_date < TO_DATE('1-Jan-1999',
        'dd-mon-yyyy'))
``` |
| Terminated during the year | ```
WHERE employee_termination_date >=
        TO_DATE('1-Jan-1998','dd-mon-yyyy')
    AND (employee_termination_date <
        TO_DATE('1-Jan-1999','dd-mon-yyyy'))
``` |
| Employed at end of year | ```
WHERE employee_hire_date < TO_DATE('1-Jan-1999','dd-mon-yyyy')
    AND (employee_termination_date IS NULL
        OR employee_termination_date
            >= TO_DATE('1-Jan-1999','dd-mon-yyyy'))
``` |

### The UNION query

After separately developing the four queries, one for each section of the report, you can use SQL's UNION operator to link those four queries together into one large query. There are four things to consider when doing this:

1. You need to return all the records retrieved by all four queries.

2. You need to be able to group the retrieved records by category.

3. You need to be able to control which category prints first.

4. You need to identify each category on the printed report so the end user knows what's what.

To be certain of getting all the records back from the query, use the UNION ALL operator to tie the queries together. Using UNION by itself causes SQL to filter out any duplicate rows in the result set. That's not really an issue with this example—there won't be any duplicate rows—but it's an important point to consider.

In order to properly group the records, you can add a numeric constant to each of the four queries. For example, the query to return the list of those employed at the beginning of the year could return an arbitrary value of 1:

```
SELECT 1 sort_column,
        employee_id,
        employee_name,
```

The other queries would return values of 2, 3, and 4 in the sort column. Sorting the query results on these arbitrary numeric values serves two purposes. First, the records for each section of the report will be grouped together because they will all have the same constant. Second, the value of the sort column controls the order in which the sections print. Use a value of 1 for the section to be printed first, a value of 2 for the second section, etc.

The final thing to worry about is identifying the results to the reader of the report. The values used in the sort column won't mean anything to the reader, so you also need to add a column with some descriptive text. Here's how the final query for people employed at the beginning of the year looks with that text added:

```
SELECT 1 sort_column,
       'Employed at Beginning of Year' employee_status_text,
       employee_id,
       employee_name,
       employee_hire_date,
       employee_termination_date
  FROM employee
 WHERE employee_hire_date < TO_DATE('1-Jan-1998','dd-mon-yyyy')
   AND (employee_termination_date IS NULL
        OR employee_termination_date >= TO_DATE('1-Jan-1998','dd-mon-yyyy'))
```

The first column returned by this query is used to sort these records to the top of the report, while the second column serves to identify those records for the reader. The full-blown UNION query to produce all four sections of the report looks like this:

```
SELECT 1 sort_column,
       'Employed at Beginning of Year' employee_status_text,
       employee_id,
       employee_name,
       employee_hire_date,
       employee_termination_date
  FROM employee
 WHERE employee_hire_date < TO_DATE('1-Jan-1998','dd-mon-yyyy')
   AND (employee_termination_date IS NULL
        OR employee_termination_date >= TO_DATE('1-Jan-1998','dd-mon-yyyy'))
UNION ALL
SELECT 2 as sort_column,
       'Hired During Year' as employee_status_text,
       employee_id,
       employee_name,
       employee_hire_date,
       employee_termination_date
  FROM employee
 WHERE employee_hire_date >= TO_DATE('1-Jan-1998','dd-mon-yyyy')
   AND (employee_hire_date < TO_DATE('1-Jan-1999','dd-mon-yyyy'))
UNION ALL
SELECT 3 as sort_column,
       'Terminated During Year' as employee_status_text,
       employee_id,
       employee_name,
       employee_hire_date,
       employee_termination_date
  FROM employee
 WHERE employee_termination_date >= TO_DATE('1-Jan-1998','dd-mon-yyyy')
   AND (employee_termination_date < TO_DATE('1-Jan-1999','dd-mon-yyyy'))
UNION ALL
SELECT 4 as sort_column,
```

```
            'Employed at End of Year' as employee_status_text,
            employee_id,
            employee_name,
            employee_hire_date,
            employee_termination_date
     FROM employee
    WHERE employee_hire_date < TO_DATE('1-Jan-1999','dd-mon-yyyy')
      AND (employee_termination_date IS NULL
            OR employee_termination_date >= TO_DATE('1-Jan-1999','dd-mon-yyyy'))
 ORDER BY sort_column, employee_id, employee_hire_date;
```

As you can see, the four queries have been unioned together in the same order in which the report is to be printed. That's done for readability, though. It's the ORDER BY clause at the bottom that ensures that the records are returned in the proper order.

### The final report

All that's left now that the query has been worked out is to follow the remaining steps in the report development methodology to format and print the report. To produce a fairly basic, columnar report, precede the query with the following commands:

```
--Setup pagesize parameters
SET NEWPAGE 0
SET PAGESIZE 55

--Set the linesize, which must match the number of equal signs used
--for the ruling lines in the headers and footers.
SET LINESIZE 75

TTITLE CENTER 'The Fictional Company' SKIP 2 -
       CENTER 'Employee Turnover Report' SKIP 1 -
       LEFT '===================================' -
            '===================================' -
       SKIP 3

--Format the columns
CLEAR COLUMNS
COLUMN sort_column NOPRINT
COLUMN employee_id NOPRINT
COLUMN employee_status_text HEADING 'Status' FORMAT A29
COLUMN employee_name HEADING 'Employee Name' FORMAT A20
COLUMN employee_hire_date HEADING 'Hire Date' FORMAT A11
COLUMN employee_termination_date HEADING 'Term Date' FORMAT A11

--Breaks and computations
BREAK ON employee_status_text SKIP 2 NODUPLICATES
CLEAR COMPUTES
COMPUTE NUMBER LABEL 'Total Count' OF employee_name ON employee_status_text

--Set the date format to use
ALTER SESSION SET NLS_DATE_FORMAT = 'dd-Mon-yyyy';
```

When you execute this report, the output will look like this:

```
                            The Fictional Company

                          Employee Turnover Report
==========================================================================


Status                            Employee Name        Hire Date   Term Date
-------------------------------   ------------------   ----------- -----------
Employed at Beginning of Year     Jonathan Gennick     15-Nov-1961
                                  Jenny Gennick        16-Sep-1964 05-May-1998
                                  Jeff Gennick         29-Dec-1987 01-Apr-1998
                                  Pavlo Chubynsky      01-Mar-1994 15-Nov-1998
                                  Taras Shevchenko     23-Aug-1976
                                  Hermon Goche         15-Nov-1961 04-Apr-1998
****************************       -------------------
Total Count                                        6


Hired During Year                 Horace Walker        15-Jun-1998
                                  Bohdan Khmelnytsky   02-Jan-1998
                                  Ivan Mazepa          04-Apr-1998 30-Sep-1998
                                  Jacob Marley         03-Mar-1998 31-Oct-1998
****************************       -------------------
Total Count                                        4


Terminated During Year            Jenny Gennick        16-Sep-1964 05-May-1998
                                  Jeff Gennick         29-Dec-1987 01-Apr-1998
                                  Pavlo Chubynsky      01-Mar-1994 15-Nov-1998
                                  Ivan Mazepa          04-Apr-1998 30-Sep-1998
                                  Hermon Goche         15-Nov-1961 04-Apr-1998
                                  Jacob Marley         03-Mar-1998 31-Oct-1998
****************************       -------------------
Total Count                                        6


Employed at End of Year           Jonathan Gennick     15-Nov-1961
                                  Horace Walker        15-Jun-1998
                                  Bohdan Khmelnytsky   02-Jan-1998
                                  Taras Shevchenko     23-Aug-1976
****************************       -------------------
Total Count                                        4
```

That's all there is to it. It wouldn't be a big leap to turn this report into a master/ detail report, with each section starting on a new page. Using this technique, you can develop similar reports with any number of sections you need.

# 4

# Writing SQL*Plus Scripts

In the previous chapter, you saw how to write a script to produce a report. This chapter delves more deeply into the subject of scripting, and shows you how to write interactive scripts. You will learn how to use substitution variables, which allow the user to dynamically supply values to a script at runtime. You will learn how to prompt the user for those values, and how to display other messages for the user to see. Finally, you will learn how to package your script for easy access when you need it.

## Why Write Scripts?

The most compelling reason to write scripts, in my mind, is to encapsulate knowledge. Say, for example, that you have developed a query that returns index definitions for a table. You certainly don't want to have to think through the entire process of developing that query each time you need to see an index. If you have a good script available, you just run it. Likewise, if someone asks you how to see index definitions for a table, just give them a copy of the script.

A second reason for developing scripts is that they save time. Look at the script to produce the first report in Chapter 3, *Generating Reports with SQL*Plus*. It contains 17 separate commands, some quite long. By placing those commands in a script, you save yourself the time and effort involved in retyping all of them each time you run the report.

Lastly, scripts can simplify tasks both for you and for others. When you know you have a good, reliable script, you can just run it, answer the questions, then sit back while it does all the work. You don't need to worry, thinking "did I enter the correct command?", "did I log on as the correct user?", or "did I get that query just right?"

Anytime you find yourself performing a task over and over, think about writing a script to do it for you. You'll save yourself time. You'll save yourself stress. You'll be able to share your knowledge more easily.

---

A good source of ready-to-run scripts for Unix users is *Oracle Scripts* by Brian Lomasky and David C. Kreines, O'Reilly & Associates, 1998.

---

# Using Substitution Variables

Substitution variables allow you to write generic SQL*Plus scripts. They allow you to mark places in a script where you want to substitute values at runtime.

## What Is a Substitution Variable?

A *substitution variable* is the same thing as a user variable. In the previous chapter, you saw how to get the contents of a database column into a user variable and how to place the contents of that user variable into the page header of a report. SQL*Plus also allows you to place user variables in your script to mark places where you want to supply a value at runtime. When you use them this way, they are called substitution variables.

A substitution variable is not like a true variable used in a programming language. Instead, a substitution variable marks places in the text where SQL*Plus does the equivalent of a search and replace at runtime, replacing the reference to a substitution variable with its value.

Substitution variables are set off in the text of a script by preceding them with either one or two ampersand characters. Say, for example, that you had this query to list all projects to which employee #107 had charged time:

```
SELECT DISTINCT p.project_id, p.project_name
  FROM project p,
       project_hours ph
 WHERE ph.employee_id = 107
   AND p.project_id = ph.project_id;
```

As you can see, this query is specific to employee number 107. To run the query for a different employee, you would need to edit your script file, change the ID number, save the file, then execute it. That's a pain. You don't want to do that.

Instead, you can generalize the script by rewriting the SELECT statement with a substitution variable in place of the employee ID number. It would look like this:

```
SELECT DISTINCT p.project_id, p.project_name
  FROM project p,
       project_hours ph
 WHERE ph.employee_id = &employee_id
   AND p.project_id = ph.project_id;
```

The ampersand in front of the word "employee_id" marks it as a variable. At runtime, when it reads the statement, SQL\*Plus will see the substitution variable and replace it with the current value of the specified user variable. If the employee_id user variable contained a value of 104, then "&employee_id" would be replaced by "104", and the resulting line would look like this:

```
WHERE ph.employee_id = 104
```

As stated earlier, and as you can see now, SQL\*Plus truly does a "search and replace" operation. The Oracle database does not know that a variable has been used. Nor does SQL\*Plus actually compare the contents of the employee_id column against the value of the variable. SQL\*Plus simply does the equivalent of a search and replace operation on each statement before that statement is executed. As far as the Oracle database is concerned, you might just as well have included constants in your script.

Substitution variables are the workhorse of SQL\*Plus scripts. They give you a place to store user input, and they give you a way to use that input in SQL queries, PL/SQL code blocks, and other SQL\*Plus commands.

## Using Single-Ampersand Variables

The easiest way to generalize a script is to take one you have working for a specific case and modify it by replacing specific values with substitution variables. In this section, we will revisit the Labor Hours and Dollars Detail report shown in Chapter 3. You will see how you can modify the script to print the report for only one employee, and you will see how you can use a substitution variable to generalize that script by making it prompt for the employee ID number at runtime.

When SQL\*Plus encounters a variable with a single leading ampersand, it always prompts you for a value. This is true even when you use the same variable multiple times in your script. If you use it twice, you will be prompted twice. Double-ampersand variables allow you to prompt a user only once for a given value, and are explained later in this chapter.

### The report for one specific employee

The report in the previous chapter produced detailed hours and dollars information for all employees. To reduce the scope to one employee, you can add this line to the WHERE clause:

```
        AND e.employee_id = 107
```

Since this report is now only for one employee, the grand totals don't make sense, so the COMPUTEs to create them can be removed. Finally, a SPOOL command has been added to capture the output in a file to be printed later. The complete script for the report looks like this:

```
--Setup pagesize parameters
SET NEWPAGE 0
SET PAGESIZE 55

--Set the linesize, which must match the number of equal signs used
--for the ruling lines in the headers and footers.
SET LINESIZE 71

--Get the date for inclusion in the page footer.
SET TERMOUT OFF
ALTER SESSION SET NLS_DATE_FORMAT = 'DD-Mon-YYYY';
COLUMN SYSDATE NEW_VALUE report_date
SELECT SYSDATE FROM DUAL;
SET TERMOUT ON

--Setup page headings and footings
TTITLE CENTER 'The Fictional Company' SKIP 3 -
       LEFT 'I.S. Department' -
       RIGHT 'Project Hours and Dollars Detail' SKIP 1 -
       LEFT '=================================================================' -
       SKIP 2 'Employee: ' FORMAT 9999 emp_id_var ' ' emp_name_var SKIP 3

BTITLE LEFT '=================================================================' -
       SKIP 1 -
       LEFT report_date -
       RIGHT 'Page ' FORMAT 999 SQL.PNO

--Format the columns
COLUMN employee_id NEW_VALUE emp_id_var NOPRINT
COLUMN employee_name NEW_VALUE emp_name_var NOPRINT
COLUMN project_id HEADING '    Proj ID' FORMAT 9999
COLUMN project_name HEADING 'Project Name' FORMAT A26 WORD_WRAPPED
COLUMN time_log_date HEADING 'Date' FORMAT A11
COLUMN hours_logged HEADING 'Hours' FORMAT 9,999
COLUMN dollars_charged HEADING 'Dollars|Charged' FORMAT $999,999.99

--Breaks and Computations
BREAK ON employee_id SKIP PAGE NODUPLICATES -
      ON employee_name NODUPLICATES -
      ON project_id SKIP 2 NODUPLICATES -
      ON project_name NODUPLICATES
CLEAR COMPUTES
COMPUTE SUM LABEL 'Project Totals' OF hours_logged ON project_name
COMPUTE SUM LABEL 'Project Totals' OF dollars_charged ON project_name
COMPUTE SUM LABEL 'Totals' OF hours_logged ON employee_id
COMPUTE SUM LABEL 'Totals' OF dollars_charged ON employee_id
```

```
--Execute the query to generate the report.
SPOOL C:\A\HOURS_DOLLARS
SELECT P.PROJECT_ID,
       P.PROJECT_NAME,
       TO_CHAR(PH.TIME_LOG_DATE,'dd-Mon-yyyy') time_log_date,
       PH.HOURS_LOGGED,
       PH.DOLLARS_CHARGED,
       E.EMPLOYEE_ID,
       E.EMPLOYEE_NAME
  FROM EMPLOYEE E,
       PROJECT P,
       PROJECT_HOURS PH
 WHERE E.EMPLOYEE_ID = PH.EMPLOYEE_ID
   AND P.PROJECT_ID = PH.PROJECT_ID
   AND E.EMPLOYEE_ID = 107
ORDER BY E.EMPLOYEE_ID, P.PROJECT_ID, PH.TIME_LOG_DATE;
SPOOL OFF

--Reset everything back to the defaults.
CLEAR BREAKS
CLEAR COMPUTES
TTITLE OFF
BTITLE OFF

SET NEWPAGE 1
SET PAGESIZE 24
SET LINESIZE 80
```

Running this script as shown will produce a report specifically for employee 107.

### Generalizing the report with substitution variables

You don't want to edit the script file and modify your script every time you need to produce a report for a different employee, and you don't have to. Instead, you can replace the reference to a specific employee number with a substitution variable and let SQL\*Plus prompt you for a value at runtime. Here's how the affected line of script looks with a substitution variable instead of a hardcoded value:

```
AND E.EMPLOYEE_ID = &employee_id
```

The variable name should be descriptive, and it needs to serve two purposes. It needs to inform the user and it needs to inform you. First and foremost, the variable name is used in the prompt, and must convey to the user the specific information needed. In this case, for example, using &id for the variable would leave the user wondering whether to enter an employee ID or a project ID. The second thing to keep in mind is that you will need to look at the script again someday, so make sure the name is something that will jog your memory as well.

### Running the report

When you run the report, SQL\*Plus will prompt you for the value of the &employee_id substitution variable. Assume that the script is in a file named *HOURS_DOLLARS.SQL*. Here's how the output will look:

```
SQL> @c:\hours_dollars_b
Enter value for employee_id: 111
```

As commands are executed, SQL*Plus constantly looks for the ampersand character, indicating a substitution variable. When an ampersand is encountered, the next token in the command is treated as a variable. SQL*Plus first looks to see if that variable has been previously defined. In this example it hasn't, so SQL*Plus automatically prompts for the value.

After prompting for a value and substituting it into the script in place of the corresponding variable, SQL*Plus will display both the old and the new versions of the particular line of script involved. During development, this aids you in verifying that your script is executing correctly. Here are the before and after versions of the line containing the &employee_id variable from the current example:

```
old  13:    AND E.EMPLOYEE_ID = &employee_id
new  13:    AND E.EMPLOYEE_ID = 111
```

Next, SQL*Plus goes on to read the remaining lines from the script, producing this hours and dollars report for Taras Shevchenko:

```
                     The Fictional Company


I.S. Department                      Project Hours and Dollars Detail
=====================================================================

Employee:   111 Taras Shevchenko


                                                           Dollars
          Proj ID Project Name         Date        Hours   Charged
          ------- -------------------- ----------- ------ -----------
             1001 Corporate Web Site   01-Jan-1998     1     $100.00
                                       01-Mar-1998     3     $300.00
                                       01-May-1998     5     $500.00
                                       01-Jul-1998     7     $700.00
                                       01-Sep-1998     1     $100.00
                                       01-Nov-1998     3     $300.00
                  *************************          ------ -----------
                  Project Totals                       20   $2,000.00
    ...
```

In addition to being displayed on the screen, the report is also spooled to the file specified in the script.

### When TERMOUT is off

In the example just shown, the report was both displayed on the screen and spooled to a file. In Chapter 3 you saw how the SET TERMOUT OFF command could be used to suppress output to the display while still allowing it to be spooled, thus making a report run much faster. Trying to do the same thing in this case presents a special problem. The problem is that the command to turn TER-MOUT off must precede the SELECT statement that generates the report, so terminal output is off by the time SQL*Plus reads the line containing the substitution variable. SQL*Plus does not handle this situation too well. You won't see a prompt for the substitution variable, because terminal output is off, but SQL*Plus will still be waiting for you to type in a value. Your session will appear to be hung. Here's what you will see:

```
SQL> @c:\hours_dollars_c
```

Strangely enough, even if you remember that SQL*Plus needs an employee number and you type one in, it won't be accepted. Try running the script like this:

```
SQL> @c:\hours_dollars_c
111
```

Even though you entered a value of 111, SQL*Plus will proceed as if you had entered an empty string. The end result will be the following error in the spool file:

```
Enter value for employee_id:
old  13:    AND E.EMPLOYEE_ID = &employee_id
new  13:    AND E.EMPLOYEE_ID =
ORDER BY E.EMPLOYEE_ID, P.PROJECT_ID, PH.TIME_LOG_DATE
      *
ERROR at line 14:
ORA-00936: missing expression
```

Looking at the before and after versions of the line with the &employee_id variable, which are written to the spool file, you can see that the input of 111 was totally ignored. The result was a syntactically incorrect SQL statement, so instead of a report all you got was an error.

There is a solution to this problem. The solution is to use the ACCEPT command to explicitly prompt the user for the employee ID prior to issuing the SET TER-MOUT OFF command. You will see how to do this later in this chapter in the section titled "Prompting for Values."

## *Using Double-Ampersand Variables*

Using a double ampersand in front of a substitution variable tells SQL*Plus to define that variable for the duration of the session. This is useful when you need to reference a variable several times in one script, because you don't usually want to prompt the user separately for each occurrence.

### An example that prompts twice for the same value

Take a look at the following script, which displays information about a table followed by a list of all indexes defined on the table:

```
SET HEADING OFF
SET RECSEP OFF
SET NEWPAGE 1

COLUMN index_name FORMAT A30 NEW_VALUE index_name_var NOPRINT
COLUMN uniqueness FORMAT A6 NEW_VALUE uniqueness_var NOPRINT
COLUMN tablespace_name FORMAT A30 NEW_VALUE tablespace_name_var NOPRINT
COLUMN column_name FORMAT A30
BREAK ON index_name SKIP PAGE on column_header NODUPLICATES

TTITLE uniqueness_var ' INDEX: ' index_name_var -
       SKIP 1 '  TABLESPACE: ' tablespace_name_var -
       SKIP 1

DESCRIBE &table_name
SELECT ui.index_name,
       ui.tablespace_name,
       DECODE(ui.uniqueness,'UNIQUE','UNIQUE','        ') uniqueness,
       '     COLUMNS:' column_header,
       uic.column_name
  FROM user_indexes ui,
       user_ind_columns uic
 WHERE ui.index_name = uic.index_name
   AND ui.table_name = UPPER('&table_name')
ORDER BY ui.index_name, uic.column_position;
TTITLE OFF
SET HEADING ON
SET RECSEP WRAPPED
CLEAR BREAKS
CLEAR COLUMNS
```

This script uses &table_name twice, once in the DESCRIBE command that lists the columns for the table, and once in the SELECT statement that returns information about the tables's indexes. When you run this script, SQL*Plus will issue separate prompts for each occurrence of &table_name. The first prompt will occur when SQL*Plus hits the DESCRIBE command:

```
SQL> @c:\list_indexes_d
Enter value for table_name: project_hours
 Name                             Null?    Type
 -------------------------------- -------- ----
 PROJECT_ID                       NOT NULL NUMBER
 EMPLOYEE_ID                      NOT NULL NUMBER
 TIME_LOG_DATE                    NOT NULL DATE
 HOURS_LOGGED                              NUMBER
 DOLLARS_CHARGED                           NUMBER
```

Since only a single ampersand was used, the value entered by the user was used for that one specific instance. It was not saved for future reference. The result is that next time SQL*Plus encounters &table_name, it must prompt again. This time it prompts for the table name to use in the SELECT statement:

```
Enter value for table_name: project_hours
old   9:     AND ui.table_name = UPPER('&table_name')
new   9:     AND ui.table_name = UPPER('project_hours')
```

Notice that SQL*Plus only displays before and after images of a line containing substitution variables when that line is part of a SQL query. When the DESCRIBE command was read, the user was prompted for a table name, and the substitution was made, but the old and new versions of the command were not shown.

The remaining output from the script, showing the indexes defined on the project_ hours table, looks like this:

```
        INDEX:  PROJECT_HOURS_BY_DATE
   TABLESPACE:  USER_DATA
      COLUMNS:  TIME_LOG_DATE

        INDEX:  PROJECT_HOURS_EMP_DATE
   TABLESPACE:  USER_DATA
      COLUMNS:  EMPLOYEE_ID
                TIME_LOG_DATE

 UNIQUE INDEX:  PROJECT_HOURS_PK
   TABLESPACE:  USER_DATA
      COLUMNS:  PROJECT_ID
                EMPLOYEE_ID
                TIME_LOG_DATE

6 rows selected.


Commit complete.
```

### A modified example that prompts once

Obviously there's room for improvement here. You don't want to type in the same value over and over just because it's used more than once in a script. Aside from being inconvenient, doing so introduces the very real possibility that you won't get it the same each time. One way to approach this problem is to use a double-ampersand the first time you reference the table_name variable in the script. Thus the DESCRIBE command becomes:

```
DESCRIBE &&table_name
```

The only difference between using a double ampersand rather than a single ampersand is that when a double ampersand is used, SQL*Plus will save the value. All subsequent references to the same variable use that same value. It doesn't even matter if subsequent references use a double ampersand or a single. Once the table_name variable has been defined this way, any other reference to &table_ name or &&table_name will be replaced with the defined value.

Now if you run the LIST_INDEXES script, you will only be prompted once for the table name, as the following output shows:

```
SQL> @c:\list_indexes_e
Enter value for table_name: project_hours
 Name                             Null?    Type
 -------------------------------- -------- ----
 PROJECT_ID                       NOT NULL NUMBER
 EMPLOYEE_ID                      NOT NULL NUMBER
 TIME_LOG_DATE                    NOT NULL DATE
 HOURS_LOGGED                              NUMBER
 DOLLARS_CHARGED                           NUMBER

old   9:    AND ui.table_name = UPPER('&table_name')
new   9:    AND ui.table_name = UPPER('project_hours')

        INDEX: PROJECT_HOURS_BY_DATE
   TABLESPACE: USER_DATA
      COLUMNS: TIME_LOG_DATE

        INDEX: PROJECT_HOURS_EMP_DATE
   TABLESPACE: USER_DATA
      COLUMNS: EMPLOYEE_ID
               TIME_LOG_DATE

 UNIQUE INDEX: PROJECT_HOURS_PK
   TABLESPACE: USER_DATA
      COLUMNS: PROJECT_ID
               EMPLOYEE_ID
               TIME_LOG_DATE

 6 rows selected.


Commit complete.
```

## A final caveat

If you run the LIST_INDEXES script again, you won't be prompted for a table name at all. Instead, the value entered earlier will be reused, and you will again see information about the project_hours table and its indexes. The reason for this is that once you define a variable, that definition sticks around until you either exit SQL*Plus or explicitly undefine the variable.

Because variable definitions persist after a script has ended, it's usually best to explicitly prompt a user for input rather than depending on SQL*Plus to do it for you. The ACCEPT command is used for this purpose and is described in the next section. At the very least, you should UNDEFINE variables at the end of a script so they won't inadvertently be reused later.

# Prompting for Values

The most reliable and robust method for getting input from the user is to explicitly prompt for values using the ACCEPT and PROMPT commands. The ACCEPT command takes input from the user and stores it in a user variable, and also allows you some level of control over what the user enters. The PROMPT command may be used to display messages to the user, perhaps supplying a short summary of what your script is going to accomplish.

There are several potential problems that arise when you simply place substitution variables in your scripts and rely on SQL\*Plus's default prompting mechanisms. All of these problems can be avoided through the use of the ACCEPT command. Table 4-1 provides a list of these problems together with a description of how the ACCEPT and PROMPT commands can be used to overcome them.

*Table 4-1. Potential Problems with SQL\*Plus's Default Prompting*

| Potential Problem | Solution |
| --- | --- |
| Using double ampersands to define a variable in a script results in your not being prompted for a value the second time you run the script. | Use the ACCEPT command to prompt for a value. This works regardless of whether the variable has previously been defined. |
| Setting terminal output off, such as when spooling a report to a file, prevents you from seeing the prompts for substitution variables used in the query. | Use the ACCEPT command to prompt for these values earlier in the script, before the SET TERMOUT OFF command is executed. |
| The default prompt provided by SQL\*Plus consists of little more than the variable name. | Use the ACCEPT command to specify your own prompt. For longer explanations, the PROMPT command may be used. |

This section shows how to enhance the LIST_INDEXES script with the PROMPT and ACCEPT commands. The PROMPT command will be used to better explain what the script is doing, while the ACCEPT command will be used to reliably prompt the user for the table name.

## The ACCEPT Command

The ACCEPT command is used to obtain input from the user. With it, you specify a user variable and text for a prompt. The ACCEPT command displays the prompt for the user, waits for the user to respond, and assigns the user's response to the variable.

### Syntax for the ACCEPT command

Here is the syntax for the ACCEPT command:

```
ACC[EPT] user_variable [NUM[BER]|CHAR|DATE]
        [FOR[MAT] format_specification]
        [DEF[AULT] default_value]
        [PROMPT prompt_text|NOPR[OMPT]]
        [HIDE]
```

where:

*ACC[EPT]*

> Tells SQL*Plus that you want to prompt the user for a value, and that you want the value stored in the specified user variable. The command may be abbreviated to ACC.

*user_variable*

> Is the variable you want to define. Do not include leading ampersands. If your script uses a "&table_name" for a substitution variable, you should used "table_name" here.

*NUMBER | CHAR | DATE*

> Is the type of data you are after. The default is CHAR, which allows the user to type in anything as a response. Use NUMBER to force the user to enter a number and DATE when you want a date.

*FOR[MAT] format_specification*

> This is an optional format specification, which may optionally be enclosed in quotes. If this is specified, ACCEPT will reject any input that does not conform to the specification. An error message will be displayed, and the prompt reissued. Specifying a format makes the most sense when dealing with numeric and date data, and SQL*Plus is actually somewhat loose in enforcing the format. Chapter 7, *Advanced Scripting*, delves into this aspect of the ACCEPT command in detail.

*DEFAULT default_value*

> Specifies a default value to assign to the variable. This is used if the user bypasses the prompt by pressing ENTER without actually entering a response. The default value should usually be enclosed within single quotes.

*PROMPT prompt_text*

> This is the prompt text displayed to the user before waiting for input.

*NOPROMPT*

> Indicates that you do not want the user to see a visible prompt.

*HIDE*

> Causes SQL*Plus not to echo the user's response back to the display. This is useful if you are prompting for a password.

The syntax for the ACCEPT command has evolved significantly with the past few releases of SQL\*Plus. The syntax shown here is valid for version 8.1. Not all of the clauses are available when using prior versions. Be sensitive to this, and check your documentation if you are writing scripts that need to work under earlier versions of SQL\*Plus.

### Using ACCEPT to get the table name

You can make the LIST_INDEXES script more reliable by using ACCEPT to get the table name from the user. This ensures that the user is prompted for a table name each time the script is run. The following ACCEPT command should do the trick:

```
ACCEPT table_name CHAR PROMPT 'Enter the table name >'
```

A good place to add the command would be just prior to the COLUMN commands, so the resulting script would look like this:

```
SET HEADING OFF
SET RECSEP OFF
SET NEWPAGE 1

--Get the table name from the user
ACCEPT table_name CHAR PROMPT 'Enter the table name >'

COLUMN index_name FORMAT A30 NEW_VALUE index_name_var NOPRINT
COLUMN uniqueness FORMAT A6 NEW_VALUE uniqueness_var NOPRINT
COLUMN tablespace_name FORMAT A30 NEW_VALUE tablespace_name_var NOPRINT
COLUMN column_name FORMAT A30
BREAK ON index_name SKIP PAGE on column_header NODUPLICATES

TTITLE uniqueness_var ' INDEX: ' index_name_var -
       SKIP 1 '  TABLESPACE: ' tablespace_name_var -
       SKIP 1

DESCRIBE &&table_name
SELECT ui.index_name,
       ui.tablespace_name,
       DECODE(ui.uniqueness,'UNIQUE','UNIQUE','        ') uniqueness,
       '    COLUMNS:' column_header,
       uic.column_name
  FROM user_indexes ui,
       user_ind_columns uic
 WHERE ui.index_name = uic.index_name
   AND ui.table_name = UPPER('&table_name')
ORDER BY ui.index_name, uic.column_position;
COMMIT;
TTITLE OFF
SET HEADING ON
SET RECSEP WRAPPED
CLEAR BREAKS
CLEAR COLUMNS
```

It doesn't really matter now whether the script uses &table_name or &&table_name for the substitution variable. Either will work just as well, and the script just shown uses both. When you run the script, here's how the prompt will look:

```
SQL> @c:\jonathan\sql_plus_book\xe_ch_5\list_indexes_f
Enter the table name >
```

Now you can run this script many times in succession, and you will be prompted for a different table name each time. In addition, this prompt is a bit more user-friendly than the default prompt generated by SQL*Plus.

## *The PROMPT Command*

The PROMPT command is used to print text on the display for the user to read. It allows you to provide informative descriptions of what a script is about to do. It can be used to provide very long and detailed prompts for information, and it can be used simply to add blank lines to the output in order to space things out a bit better.

### *Syntax for the PROMPT command*

PROMPT is a very simple command. The syntax looks like this:

```
PRO[MPT] text_to_be_displayed
```

where:

*PRO[MPT]*

Is the command, which may be abbreviated to PRO.

*text_to_be_displayed*

Is whatever text you want displayed for the user to see. This should not be a quoted string. If you include quotes, they will appear in the output.

If you are spooling output to a file when a PROMPT command is executed, the prompt text will also be written to the file. Any substitution variables in the prompt text will be replaced by their respective values before the text is displayed.

### *Using PROMPT to summarize the script*

It would be nice to add some messages to the LIST_INDEXES script to make it more self-explanatory to the user. You can do that by adding the following PROMPT commands to the beginning of the script:

```
PROMPT
PROMPT This script will first DESCRIBE a table, then
PROMPT it will list the definitions for all indexes
PROMPT on that table.
PROMPT
```

The first and last PROMPT commands simply space the output a bit better by adding a blank line above and below the description.

### Using PROMPT to explain the output

The PROMPT command can also be used to better explain the output of a script. In the LIST_INDEXES example, messages could be added prior to the DESCRIBE command, and prior to the SELECT statement, in order to explain the output. The resulting script would look like this:

```
...
PROMPT
PROMPT &table_name table definition:
PROMPT
DESCRIBE &&table_name

PROMPT
PROMPT Indexes defined on the &table_name table:
PROMPT
SELECT ui.index_name,
...
```

Here is the result of executing the script with all the PROMPT commands added. The messages not only make the output more clear, but space it out better as well.

```
SQL> @c:\jonathan\sql_plus_book\xe_ch_5\list_indexes_G

This script will first DESCRIBE a table, then
it will list the definitions for all indexes
on that table.

Enter the table name >project_hours

project_hours table definition:
```

| Name | Null? | Type |
|------|-------|------|
| PROJECT_ID | NOT NULL | NUMBER |
| EMPLOYEE_ID | NOT NULL | NUMBER |
| TIME_LOG_DATE | NOT NULL | DATE |
| HOURS_LOGGED | | NUMBER |
| DOLLARS_CHARGED | | NUMBER |

```
Indexes defined on the project_hours table:

old   9:     AND ui.table_name = UPPER('&table_name')
new   9:     AND ui.table_name = UPPER('project_hours')

        INDEX:  PROJECT_HOURS_BY_DATE
   TABLESPACE:  USER_DATA
      COLUMNS:  TIME_LOG_DATE
```

```
          INDEX: PROJECT_HOURS_EMP_DATE
     TABLESPACE: USER_DATA
        COLUMNS: EMPLOYEE_ID
                 TIME_LOG_DATE

   UNIQUE INDEX: PROJECT_HOURS_PK
     TABLESPACE: USER_DATA
        COLUMNS: PROJECT_ID
                 EMPLOYEE_ID
                 TIME_LOG_DATE

6 rows selected.


Commit complete.
```

# *Cleaning Up the Display*

As you've followed the development of the LIST_INDEXES script, you no doubt saw the following lines interspersed in the output:

```
old    9:    AND ui.table_name = UPPER('&table_name')
new    9:    AND ui.table_name = UPPER('project_hours')
...
6 rows selected.


Commit complete.
```

These lines add no value to the script and serve only to clutter up the output. It would be nice to get rid of them, and it is possible to do that by turning verification and feedback off. The commands to do that are described next.

## *Turning Verification Off*

*Verification* refers to what SQL*Plus does when it encounters a line of script containing substitution variables. By default, SQL*Plus verifies the substitution by displaying both the old and the new versions of the line involved. The output from verification looks like this:

```
old    9:    AND ui.table_name = UPPER('&table_name')
new    9:    AND ui.table_name = UPPER('project_hours')
```

Sometimes this verification is useful, especially when you are first developing a script, because it allows you to see for sure whether or not your substitutions are being made correctly. Once you've developed a script, though, it's nice to be able to turn this output off.

You can turn verification off by adding the following command to your script:

```
SET VERIFY OFF
```

Turning verification off makes your output a lot cleaner, and is especially helpful if the script is a report that may be run by an end user.

## *Turning Feedback Off*

*Feedback* refers to the short messages that SQL\*Plus displays after executing a SQL statement such as SELECT or COMMIT. Feedback looks like this:

```
6 rows selected.


Commit complete.
```

As with verification, feedback often clutters up the output from a script. The extra lines added by feedback are sometimes just enough to scroll output that you want to see off the top of the display, which can be a bit annoying.

You can turn feedback off by adding the following line to your scripts:

```
SET FEEDBACK OFF
```

You may want to turn it back on at the end of the script. Use SET FEEDBACK ON for this purpose, so that you get the normal feedback messages when executing interactive commands.

## *Turning Command Echoing Off*

The *echo* setting controls whether or not commands from script files are displayed to the screen as they are executed. Normally off by default, command echoing can be a useful debugging tool. To turn echo on, use the following command:

```
SET ECHO ON
```

Now when you execute a script, such as LIST_INDEXES, all the commands are echoed to the display as they are executed. Here's how that would look:

```
SQL> set echo on
SQL> @C:\jonathan\sql_plus_book\xe_ch_5\list_indexes_H
SQL> SET HEADING OFF
SQL> SET RECSEP OFF
SQL> SET NEWPAGE 1
SQL> SET FEEDBACK OFF
SQL> SET VERIFY OFF
SQL>
SQL> PROMPT

SQL> PROMPT This script will first DESCRIBE a table, then
This script will first DESCRIBE a table, then
SQL> PROMPT it will list the definitions for all indexes
it will list the definitions for all indexes
SQL> PROMPT on that table.
on that table.
```

```
SQL> PROMPT

SQL>
SQL> --Get the table name from the user
SQL> ACCEPT table_name CHAR PROMPT 'Enter the table name >'
Enter the table name >
...
```

As you can see, echoing is something you usually want turned off. As a safety measure, I often include SET ECHO OFF in my script files in order to avoid accidentally being deluged by output. The one case where I always turn echoing on is when I build a script file containing DDL commands. If I run a script to create tables, indexes, or some other object, I like to see exactly what is happening when I run it.

### *Turning Off All Terminal Output*

Sometimes it's helpful to turn off the display output completely. You've already seen this done in Chapter 3 when the script to produce the Project Hours and Dollars Report was modified to spool the output to a file. Usually you want to turn off the display when you are spooling a report to a file, or when you are extracting data to a file. You may not want to look at all the data scrolling by on the screen, and turning off the display can speed things up quite a bit. The command to turn off terminal output is SET TERMOUT OFF. To turn output back on again, use SET TERMOUT ON. When using these commands, you usually want to bracket the SQL query that produces the report, as shown here:

```
SET TERMOUT OFF
SELECT P.PROJECT_ID,
       P.PROJECT_NAME
       FROM PROJECT P;
SET TERMOUT ON
```

The more output a report produces, the more turning off the display will make it run faster. That's because updating and scrolling the display is one of the most time-consuming tasks SQL*Plus must perform.

## *Packaging Your Script*

For most scripts you write, you will be satisfied just invoking them from the SQL*Plus prompt. Sooner or later, however, you are going to write a script that you want to share with an end user who may not be familiar with SQL*Plus, or you may end up implementing a complex batch process as a SQL*Plus script. In either of these cases you may find it convenient to create a command or icon that can easily be used to execute the script in question. In the Microsoft Windows environment, for example, you could easily create an icon on which an end user could double-click in order to produce a report or extract data.

## Creating a Windows Shortcut

There are two decisions you need to make if you are going to create an icon or shortcut to execute a script. One is whether to embed the Oracle username and password into the shortcut or to prompt the user for this information. The second is to decide which version of SQL*Plus you want to use—the GUI version or the DOS version.

Both of these decisions affect the command used by the shortcut to invoke SQL*Plus and start the script. Your job is easiest if you can embed the Oracle username and password, or at least the username, into the shortcut. If you need to prompt for both username and password at runtime, then you will need to make some minor additions to your script.

For purposes of example, let's assume you are going to create a Windows shortcut to run the Project Hours and Dollars Report shown earlier in this chapter. This section will show you how to do that both for the case where you can hardcode the Oracle username in the shortcut, and for the case where you can't.

### Starting the SQL\*Plus executable

The Windows version of Oracle contains two SQL*Plus executables. One starts the command-line version while the other starts the GUI version. The exact executable names vary slightly from one release of Oracle to the next because the SQL*Plus version number is embedded in the last two characters of the filename. The locations of these executables vary as well, because the Oracle home directory is named differently under Windows 95 and NT.

---

> Beginning with version 8.1, Oracle has changed the naming convention used for the Windows and command-line implementations of SQL*Plus. *SQLPLUS.EXE* runs the command-line version, while *SQLPLUSW.EXE* starts the GUI version.

---

Before you can create the shortcut, you need to decide on the exact command you will use to start SQL*Plus. Table 4-2 shows three commands. Each starts the GUI version of SQL*Plus under Windows 95, and executes the SQL script to produce the report. The difference is in whether or not the user is to be prompted for an Oracle username, a username and password, or not prompted at all.

*Table 4-2. Commands to Start SQL\*Plus and Execute a Script*

| Command | Result |
|---|---|
| PLUS80W *username/password@connect* @hours_dollars_d | Username and password embedded in the command; user not prompted. |
| PLUS80W *username@connect* @hours_ dollars_d | Username embedded in the command; SQL\*Plus prompts for the password. |
| PLUS80W /NOLOG @hours_dollars_d | Your script must prompt for both user-name and password. |

> The @ sign is used both to mark the connect string and to start a script file. You must have at least one space between the login string and the command that starts the script; otherwise, SQL\*Plus will become confused and try to interpret the script file name as a connect string.

With the first command shown in Table 4-2, your script will simply run. SQL\*Plus will connect to Oracle with the username and password provided. The second command supplies only a username, so SQL\*Plus will prompt for the password, and then run your script. The third command deserves more explanation. If you leave off both the username and password entirely, yet specify a script file on the SQL\*Plus command line, SQL\*Plus gets confused. If you want to prompt the user for both his username and password, you have to do it from within your script. In order to allow for that, the /NOLOG option is used to tell SQL\*Plus to start up without first attempting to connect to a database.

> The implementation of SQL\*Plus that ships with Oracle8 Personal Edition doesn't seem to handle PLUS80 *username@connect* properly. Even though your connect string specifies a remote database, that implementation of SQL\*Plus will still attempt to connect you to the local database.

When you start up SQL\*Plus with the /NOLOG option, your script must log into a database before it executes any SQL statements. The CONNECT command is used to do this, and you can use substitution variables to allow the user to enter the required values at runtime. The following commands, for example, prompt for a username and password, then use that information to connect to Oracle.

```
ACCEPT username CHAR PROMPT 'Enter your Oracle username >'
ACCEPT password CHAR PROMPT 'Enter your password >'
CONNECT &username/&password
```

Once you have decided how to start SQL*Plus and which version to run, you are ready to create a Windows shortcut to run your script.

### Creating the shortcut

To create a Windows shortcut, right-click on the Windows 95 or NT desktop, and select New → Shortcut from the popup menu. Type the command to start SQL*Plus and execute your script in the "Command line:" field. For example, if your command is "PLUS80W /NOLOG @hours_dollars_d", the resulting screen should look like that shown in Figure 4-1.

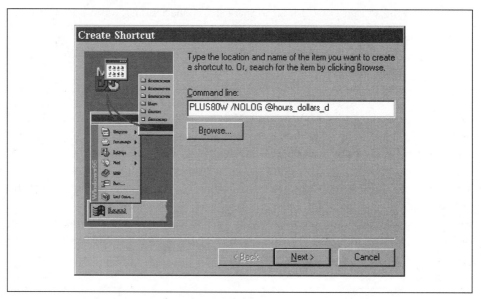

*Figure 4-1. The Windows shortcut wizard*

Press the Next button to advance to the next step, where you select a name for the shortcut. Be sure to pick a name that makes sense—one that will remind you later of what the script does. For this example, use the name Project Hours and Dollars Report. Figure 4-2 shows this screen after the name has been entered.

Finally, press the Finish button. The shortcut will be created, and will appear on your desktop. The icon will come from the SQL*Plus executable, and will be the familiar disk platter with a plus on top if you've chosen to use the GUI version. This is shown in Figure 4-3.

Now you can run the script. Double-click the icon and give it a try.

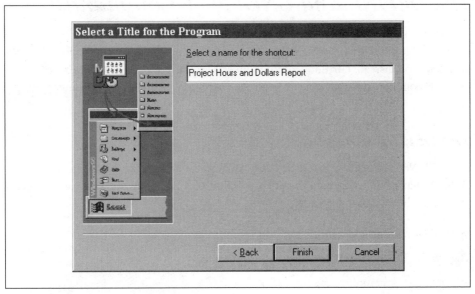

*Figure 4-2. Naming the shortcut*

*Figure 4-3. The shortcut icon*

## Creating a Unix Command

If you are running under Unix, you can write a simple shell script to invoke
SQL*Plus and run a SQL*Plus script. The command you need to place in your
script file is pretty much the same as the one used in the previous Windows 95
shortcut example. For example, if you are running the Korn shell, the following
command is all you need to run the Project Hours and Dollars Report:

```
sqlplus username @hours_dollars_d
```

Unlike with Windows, the Unix command to invoke SQL*Plus is almost always
*sqlplus*. Note that the above command does not include a password. It's always
best to avoid hardcoding passwords in script files. In this case, SQL*Plus will
prompt you for a password when you execute the script.

# The DEFINE and UNDEFINE Commands

The DEFINE and UNDEFINE commands allow you to explicitly create and delete user variables. DEFINE creates a variable and assigns it an initial value. DEFINE also lets you list all currently defined user variables with their values. The UNDEFINE command allows you to delete a user variable so it can no longer be referenced.

## The DEFINE Command

The DEFINE command is used to define a new user variable and assign it a value. DEFINE may also be used to display the value of a specific user variable or to display the values of all user variables.

### Syntax for the DEFINE command

The syntax for the DEFINE command is:

```
DEF[INE] [variable_name [= text]]
```

where:

*DEF[INE]*
  Is the command, which may be abbreviated to DEF.

*variable_name*
  Is the name of the variable you want to create.

*text*
  Is the text you want to assign to that variable. This may optionally be enclosed by single or double quotes, which you should use any time the value contains spaces or any other nonalphabetic character.

### Defining a variable

The first form of the DEFINE command is used to create a variable. Here are some examples:

```
SQL> DEFINE fiscal_year = 1998
SQL> DEFINE my_publisher = "O'Reilly"
SQL> DEFINE my_editor = Debby Russell
```

The last command is a good example of where quotes should have been used. The command will appear to execute correctly, but because of the space between the first and last name, my_editor will contain just "Debby". The remaining portion of the line is ignored.

## Examining a variable

The second form of the DEFINE command, where you specify only a variable name as an argument, shows you the contents of that variable. Here are some that examine the variables just created previously:

```
SQL> DEFINE fiscal_year
DEFINE FISCAL_YEAR     = "1998" (CHAR)
SQL> DEFINE my_publisher
DEFINE MY_PUBLISHER    = "O'Reilly" (CHAR)
SQL> DEFINE my_editor
DEFINE MY_EDITOR       = "Debby" (CHAR)
```

As you can see, because double quotes weren't used in the original DEFINE command, Debby's last name has been lost.

## Listing all variables

Issuing the DEFINE command with no arguments at all tells SQL*Plus to display all defined variables with their contents; for example:

```
SQL> DEFINE
DEFINE _SQLPLUS_RELEASE = "800040000" (CHAR)
DEFINE _EDITOR          = "Notepad" (CHAR)
DEFINE _O_VERSION       = "Oracle8 Enterprise Edition Release 8.1.3.0.0
With the Partitioning and Objects options
PL/SQL Release 8.1.3.0.0 - Beta" (CHAR)
DEFINE _O_RELEASE       = "801030000" (CHAR)
DEFINE FISCAL_YEAR      = "1998" (CHAR)
DEFINE MY_PUBLISHER     = "O'Reilly" (CHAR)
DEFINE MY_EDITOR        = "Debby" (CHAR)
SQL>
```

Not only are the variables just defined in the above list, but there are a number of others as well. That's because SQL*Plus automatically defines these at startup. You can define your own variables automatically as well, by taking advantage of the *LOGIN.SQL* file. See "The Site and User Profiles" in Chapter 11, *Customizing Your SQL*Plus Environment*, for more information on this.

## Usage notes

If you need to get a value from a user, DEFINE doesn't buy you much because you still have to use the ACCEPT command to get the user's input. However, using the DEFINE command to explicitly create all your variables at the beginning of a script can serve as a useful form of documentation. This is especially helpful in very long scripts, or when you have a chain of tightly coupled script files that call one another.

The DEFINE command can also be used to define certain magic constants, such as a company name, that may need to be used more than once in a script. Storing these types of constants in a user variable makes the script more maintainable because changes to the values can be made in one central place.

## The UNDEFINE Command

The UNDEFINE command deletes a variable definition. If you have created a variable containing sensitive information, such as a password, you can use UNDEFINE to delete it when it is no longer needed. It's also not a bad idea to UNDEFINE all your variables at the end of a script, so they don't linger and possibly affect the execution of other scripts that you run.

### Syntax for the UNDEFINE command

The syntax for UNDEFINE looks like this:

```
UNDEF[INE] variable_name [ variable_name...]
```

where:

*UNDEF[INE]*
> Is the command, and may be abbreviated to UNDEF.

*variable_name*
> Is the name of a user variable to delete. You can delete several variables with one command by listing them out, separated by spaces.

### Deleting a variable

The following example deletes the three variables created earlier when the DEFINE command was discussed:

```
SQL> UNDEFINE fiscal_year
SQL> UNDEFINE my_publisher my_editor
SQL> DEFINE my_publisher
symbol my_publisher is UNDEFINED
SQL> DEFINE my_editor
symbol my_editor is UNDEFINED
SQL> DEFINE fiscal_year
symbol fiscal_year is UNDEFINED
```

As you can see, after using UNDEFINE to delete the variables, they can no longer be referenced.

# Controlling Variable Substitution

As you use SQL\*Plus, two problems will eventually arise concerning the use of substitution variables. The first problem you are likely to encounter is that you will need to use an ampersand somewhere in your script, and you won't mean for it to be part of a substitution variable name. This is a very common problem, and happens most often when you're using an ampersand in a quoted string or as part of a comment.

The second problem, which you may never encounter at all, is that you may want to place a substitution variable smack in the middle of a word. This is a less common problem, and may not be an issue at all depending on the types of scripts you write.

SQL*Plus provides several ways to deal with these problems. A special *escape character* can be used whenever you need to place an ampersand in your script and have it stay there. A *concatenation character* is provided for those unusual cases where you want to place a substitution variable at the beginning or middle of a word. You can change the substitution character entirely if you don't like using the ampersand and want to use some other character instead. Finally, if you aren't really into writing scripts, you can turn the substitution feature completely off. Then you won't have to worry about it at all.

## *The Escape Character*

The escape character preceding an ampersand tells SQL*Plus to leave it alone—that it is not part of a substitution variable. Consider the following DEFINE command:

```
DEFINE company_name = "O'Reilly & Associates"
```

If you tried to execute that command, SQL*Plus would interpret "& Associates" as a substitution variable, and would prompt you to supply a value. The result would look like this:

```
SQL> DEFINE company_name = "O'Reilly & Associates"
Enter value for associates:
```

That's obviously not the behavior you want, yet the ampersand is legitimately part of the name, so what do you do? One solution is to precede the ampersand character with a backslash, which is the default SQL*Plus escape character, like this:

```
DEFINE company_name = "O'Reilly \& Associates"
```

The escape feature is not on by default. In order for this to work, you need to enable it first.

### *Turning on the escape feature*

By default, SQL*Plus does not check for escape characters when looking for substitution variables. This is a feature you must turn on before you use it. The command to do that is:

```
SET ESCAPE ON
```

Once turned on, this setting remains in effect until you turn it off again, or until you exit SQL*Plus.

### Escaping an ampersand

Now that the escape feature has been turned on, you can place a backslash in front of any ampersand characters that you need to embed in your script. The following is a modified version of the previous example that correctly assigns the text "O'Reilly & Associates" to the company_name variable:

```
SQL> DEFINE company_name = "O'Reilly \& Associates"
SQL> DEFINE company_name
DEFINE COMPANY_NAME    = "O'Reilly & Associates" (CHAR)
```

Because of the preceding backslash, SQL*Plus leaves the ampersand alone, and the company_name variable is created containing the desired text.

One thing to keep in mind when you have the escape feature turned on is that you must escape the escape character itself when you need to use it as part of your script. For example, to define a string containing one backslash, you must double the backslash character as shown in the following code:

```
SQL> DEFINE backslash = "\\"
SQL> DEFINE backslash
DEFINE BACKSLASH    = "\" (CHAR)
```

If you are using the backslash a lot, and this causes you problems or becomes cumbersome, you can change the escape character to something else.

### Changing the escape character

If you don't like using the backslash as the escape character, you can use the SET ESCAPE command to specify a different character more to your liking. The following command changes the escape character to be a forward slash:

```
SET ESCAPE /
```

Changing the escape character also turns the escape feature on. There is no need to subsequently issue a SET ESCAPE ON command.

> Any time you issue the SET ESCAPE ON command, the escape character is reset to the default backslash. This is true even if the escape feature was on to begin with. Keep this in mind whenever you issue SET ESCAPE ON, especially if you are using an escape character other than the default.

# The Concatenation Character

There may come a time when you want to use a substitution variable in a situation where the end of the variable name is not clear. Consider the following code example:

```
DEFINE sql_type = "PL/"
PROMPT &sql_typeSQL
```

The intent is to have SQL*Plus print the text "PL/SQL, but SQL*Plus won't substitute "PL/" in place of "&sql_type". Instead, it will interpret the entire string of "&sql_typeSQL" as a variable.

You can get around this problem by using the SQL*Plus concatenation character. The period is the default concatenation character, and it explicitly tells SQL*Plus where the variable name ends. The following code example shows the concatenation character being used to make the substitution work as intended:

```
SQL> DEFINE sql_type = "PL/"
SQL> PROMPT &sql_type.SQL
PL/SQL
```

### Turning off the concatenation feature

By default, the concatenation feature is always on. SQL*Plus looks for the period immediately following any substitution variables encountered in the script. If you need to, you can turn this feature off with the following command:

```
SET CONCAT OFF
```

It's usually not necessary to turn this feature off. You would only need to do it if you were using periods after your substitution variables and you didn't want those periods to disappear from your script. With concatenation on, any period immediately following a variable is used to mark the end of the variable name, and is removed from the script when the variable substitution is made.

### Changing the concatenation character

The default concatenation character can cause a problem if you intend to use a substitution variable at the end of a sentence. The problem is that the period at the end of the sentence will go away because SQL*Plus sees it as the concatenation character ending the variable name. Here's an example:

```
SQL> DEFINE last_word = 'period'
SQL> PROMPT This sentence has no &last_word.
This sentence has no period
```

Their are only two ways to deal with this problem. One is to turn the concatenation feature off. The other is to change it to something other than a period. The following command changes the concatenation character to an exclamation point:

```
SET CONCAT !
```

Now you can reexecute the example, and the period at the end of the sentence shows up as expected:

```
SQL> DEFINE last_word = 'period'
SQL> PROMPT This sentence has no &last_word.
This sentence has no period.
```

As with the SET ESCAPE command, using SET CONCAT to change the concatenation character also turns the feature on.

---

> Any time you issue the SET CONCAT ON command, the concatenation character is reset to the default period. This is true even if the concatenation feature was on to begin with. Keep this in mind whenever you issue SET CONCAT ON, especially if you are using a concatenation character other than the default.

---

## Enabling and Disabling Substitution

You can turn variable substitution completely off with this command:

```
SET DEFINE OFF
```

Sometimes it's easier just to turn substitution completely off rather than worry about how you use ampersand and escape characters in your scripts. If you have a large block of script that doesn't reference any variables, you can toggle substitution off just for that block, and turn it on again afterwards. For example:

```
...
SET DEFINE OFF     Toggle substitution off for the next few commands
...
Script that doesn't reference substitution
variables goes here.
...
SET DEFINE ON      Toggle substitution back on when needed again
...
```

To reenable substitution, simply issue:

```
SET DEFINE ON
```

## *Changing the Substitution Variable Prefix Character*

If you don't like prefixing your substitution variables with an ampersand, or if you need to use ampersands in your script, you can tell SQL*Plus to use a different character for substitution. You can pick any character you like, but it should be something that stands out.

### *Changing the substitution variable prefix character*

The following command changes the substitution variable prefix character to a caret:

```
SET DEFINE "^"
```

Changing the substitution character can be a handy thing to do if you need to use ampersands in a lot of text constants or if, like me, you tend to use them often in comments. The following code illustrates how to change from an ampersand to a caret and back again:

```
SQL> DEFINE message = "Brighten the corner where you are."
SQL> SET DEFINE ^
SQL> PROMPT &message
&message
SQL> PROMPT ^message
Brighten the corner where you are.
SQL> SET DEFINE &
SQL> PROMPT &message
Brighten the corner where you are.
SQL> PROMPT ^message
^message
```

Another way to reset the substitution character back to the default ampersand is to issue the SET DEFINE ON command. A side effect of issuing SET DEFINE ON is that the substitution character is always reset to the default. This is true regardless of whether substitution is currently on or off.

# *Commenting Your Scripts*

If you write extensive scripts, you should write extensive comments. In fact, any time you write a script, no matter how short, consider including a few comments to explain the purpose of the script.

Comments may be placed in a script using any of the following three methods:

1. By using the REMARK command
2. By using double-hyphen characters
3. By delimiting the comment by /* and */

Each method works just a bit differently from the others. You will probably find yourself gravitating towards the /*...*/ and -- delimiters. The REMARK command is cumbersome, and consequently isn't used very often.

## The REMARK Command

The REMARK command may be used to place comments in a SQL script. Any text on the same line following the REMARK command is considered a comment. The REMARK command may also be abbreviated to REM, as the following example shows:

```
REMARK This is a comment.
REM This is a comment too.
```

SQL*Plus does not look for substitution variables in the text following a REMARK command, so you are free to use ampersands, and any other characters you like, in your comments.

## The /* and */ Delimiters

The /* and */ delimiters are familiar to many programmers, and may also be used to delimit comments in SQL*Plus. Comments created using this method may span multiple lines, for example:

```
/*
This is the second line of a comment.
This is the third line.
*/
```

You can also use /* and */ to add comments to SQL queries, for example:

```
SELECT *
  FROM employee
 WHERE /* employees are current */
       SYSDATE BETWEEN employee_hire_date
               AND nvl(employee_termination_date,SYSDATE);
```

An interesting side effect of using /* and */ is that when you use them to mark off complete lines of comments in a script, those lines are echoed to the display. For example, if you place the following commands in a file:

```
/*
This script selects the current date from the
DUAL table, and displays it for you to see.
*/
SELECT SYSDATE FROM DUAL;
```

then execute that file, your output will look like this:

```
SQL> @c:\jonathan\sql_plus_book\xe_ch_5\comtest
SQL> /*
```

```
DOC>This script selects the current date from the
DOC>DUAL table, and displays it for you to see.
DOC>*/
SQL> SELECT SYSDATE FROM DUAL;

SYSDATE
---------
18-MAR-98
```

This echoing occurs regardless of whether the echo setting is currently on or off. It will only occur when the comment starts on a line by itself. Comments that you embed within a SQL query will not be displayed in this manner.

Note that comments may not be nested.

## Double Hyphens (--)

Double hyphens may be used to delimit comments in much the same manner as the REMARK command. Anything following the double hyphen is considered a comment. Here are some examples:

```
--Describe the employee table
DESCRIBE employee
--Select all currently employed people.
SELECT *
  FROM employee
 WHERE -- employees are current
       SYSDATE BETWEEN employee_hire_date
                   AND NVL(employee_termination_date,SYSDATE);
```

As with /*...*/, the double hyphen may be used to embed comments within SQL queries and PL/SQL blocks. The only difference is that double hyphen comments cannot span lines.

## Substitution Within Comments

SQL*Plus doesn't normally check comments for substitution variables, but the rules change when comments are embedded in a SQL query or a PL/SQL block. Thus, you can enter the following comment, and SQL*Plus won't treat &VAR as a substitution variable:

```
SQL> --In this comment, &VAR is not a substition variable.
```

However, if you enter a similar comment as part of a SQL query, SQL*Plus will see &VAR as a substitution variable, for example:

```
SQL> SELECT *
  2    FROM employee
  3        --Now, &VAR is treated as a substitution variable.
  4    WHERE employee_termination_date IS NULL;
Enter value for var:
```

The reason for this seemingly inconsistent behavior is that SQL*Plus does not parse your SQL statements; instead, they are sent to Oracle. As soon as SQL*Plus sees that you have begun to type in a SQL command, it stops parsing and accepts whatever text you enter into the buffer. Before the contents of the buffer are sent to Oracle, SQL*Plus must replace any substitution variables with their contents. In doing this, it simply scans the entire buffer, including any comments it contains.

Substitution is never an issue with the REMARK command, because REMARK is a SQL*Plus command and can never be used in a SQL query.

5

# Extracting and Loading Data

SQL*Plus can be used to extract data from Oracle for use in a spreadsheet or some other application. The need to do this is so common that it's a wonder Oracle doesn't supply an application specifically for that purpose. Unfortunately, they don't. Oracle does provide SQL*Loader, a utility that can load data into Oracle from almost any form of flat file, but there is no corresponding SQL*Unloader.

Oracle does, however, provide SQL*Plus. Even though it's not a generic data extraction utility, through the creative use of SQL and SQL*Plus's formatting options, you can extract numeric, date, and text data to a flat file. Depending on your needs, you can format the file as a comma-delimited file, a tab-delimited file, or you can format the data in fixed-width columns. Comma-delimited files are most useful if you are transferring data to a spreadsheet such as Lotus 1-2-3, or a desktop database such Microsoft Access. Fixed-width, columnar data files are often used to transfer data to legacy applications.

In addition to simply extracting data, you can get more creative and use SQL*Plus to generate a script file containing SQL statements. This is referred to as "using SQL to write SQL." You can do something as simple as generating a flat file of INSERT statements to be used in recreating the data at another site, or you can generate a file of Data Definition Language (DDL) statements to modify your own database. I've even seen people use SQL*Plus to generate operating-system shell scripts to use in modifying and maintaining their database.

In this chapter, I will walk you through the process of writing a script to extract data from the sample database into a flat file. You will see how SQL can be written to produce a comma-delimited text file, a fixed-width text file, or a file of INSERT statements. Once this is done, you will see how that same data can be loaded back into Oracle.

# Types of Output Files

Generally speaking, there are four types of output files you can produce when extracting data with SQL*Plus:

- Delimited columns
- Fixed-width columns
- DML (Data Manipulation Language)
- DDL (Data Definition Language)

There may be variations on these types—delimited files, for example, could be either tab-delimited or comma-delimited, and you may be able to dream up some novel format, but, generally speaking, these are the most useful.

## Delimited Files

Delimited files use a special text character to separate each data value in a record. Typically the delimiter is either a tab or a comma, but any character may be used. Here's an example of a comma-delimited file containing employee information (ID, rate, hire date, and name):

```
1,135,"15-Nov-1961","Jonathan Gennick"
2,95,"10-Jan-1991","Bohdan Khmelnytsky"
3,200,"17-Jul-1984","Ivan Mazepa"
```

This example illustrates a very commonly used format called the CSV (Comma Separated Values) format. CSV-formatted files use commas to delimit the values, and they enclose text fields within quotes. The CSV format is recognized by most spreadsheets and desktop databases, and is the format for the examples in this chapter.

## Fixed-Width Files

A fixed-width file contains data in columns, where each column is a certain width, and all values in that column are the same width. Here's an example of the same employee data shown earlier, but formatted into fixed-width columns:

```
00113515-Nov-1961Jonathan Gennick
00209510-Jan-1991Bohdan Khmelnytsky
00320017-Jul-1984Ivan Mazepa
```

In the above example, the columns abut each other with no space in between. If you aren't trying to match an existing file layout, you may prefer to allow at least one space between columns to aid readability.

## DML Files

A DML file contains Data Manipulation Language statements, such as INSERT, DELETE, UPDATE, and SELECT. This type of file can be used as a quick and dirty way of extracting data from one database for insertion into another. Here, for example, is a file of INSERT statements that recreate some employee data:

```
INSERT INTO employee
    (employee_ID,employee_billing_rate,employee_hire_date,employee_name)
    VALUES (1,135,TO_DATE('15-Nov-1961','DD-MON-YYYY'),'Jonathan Gennick');
INSERT INTO employee
    (employee_ID,employee_billing_rate,employee_hire_date,employee_name)
    VALUES (2,95,TO_DATE('10-Jan-1991','DD-MON-YYYY'),'Bohdan Khmelnytsky');
INSERT INTO employee
    (employee_ID,employee_billing_rate,employee_hire_date,employee_name)
    VALUES (3,200,TO_DATE('17-Jul-1984','DD-MON-YYYY'),'Ivan Mazepa');
```

You can generate these INSERT statements, based on existing data, using SQL\*Plus and SQL. Then you can easily apply those inserts to another database. This may not seem to be the most "efficient" way of moving data around, but if you have a low volume of data, such as a few dozen records that you want to send off to a client, it works very well.

## DDL Files

A DDL file contains Data Definition Language statements. It's not much different from a DML file, except that the goal is to modify your database rather than to extract data for another application. Say, for example, that you need to create public synonyms for all your tables. You could use a SQL query to generate the needed CREATE PUBLIC SYNONYM statements, spool those to a file, and then execute that file. You will find a brief example showing how to do this later in this chapter. Chapter 7, *Advanced Scripting*, explores this subject in greater depth.

# Limitations of SQL*Plus

When using SQL\*Plus to extract data, there are some limitations to keep in mind. Because SQL\*Plus was designed as a reporting tool and not a data extraction tool, the output must be text. If you need to write a file containing packed-decimal data or binary data, SQL\*Plus is not the tool to use.

A second SQL\*Plus limitation you may encounter when extracting data is the linesize. This maximum output line supported by SQL\*Plus varies from one platform to the next, but under Windows NT/95 it is 32,767 characters.

The final thing to keep in mind are the datatypes you can extract. SQL\*Plus was really designed to work with the traditional scalar datatypes, such as NUMBER,

VARCHAR2, etc. It can't be used to extract large object types, such as BLOBs and CLOBs, nor can it handle other large, complex data types, such as VARRAYs and Oracle8 objects. Here is a list of the datatypes you can easily extract using SQL*Plus:

VARCHAR2
NVARCHAR2
NUMBER
DATE
ROWID
CHAR
NCHAR

These types can be converted to character strings, and you can easily concatenate those strings together to produce whatever output format you want, whether that be comma-delimited, tab-delimited, or fixed-width. Text is the key to extracting data with SQL*Plus. Think text. If you have nonalphanumeric data to extract, you should use a different tool.

# Extracting the Data

To write a script to extract data from Oracle and place it in a flat file, follow these steps:

1. Formulate the query.

2. Format the data.

3. Spool the extract to a file.

4. Make the script user-friendly.

The last step, making the script user-friendly, isn't really necessary for a one-off effort. However, if it's an extraction you are going to perform often, it's worth taking a bit of time to make it easy and convenient to use.

## Formulate the Query

The very first step in extracting data is to figure out just what data you need to extract. You need to develop a SQL query that will return the data you need. For the example in this chapter, we will just extract the employee data, so the query will look like this:

```
SELECT employee_id,
       employee_name,
       employee_hire_date,
       employee_termination_date,
       employee_billing_rate
  FROM employee;
```

Keep in mind that you can write queries that are much more complicated than those shown here. If necessary, you can join several tables together, or you can UNION several queries together.

## Format the Data

The next step, once you have your query worked out, is to format the data to be extracted. The way to do this is to modify your query so it returns a single, long expression that combines the columns together in the format that you want in your output file. It's often necessary to include text literals in the SELECT statement as part of this calculation. For example, if you want to produce a comma-delimited file, you will need to include those commas in your SELECT statement.

Be sure to keep in mind the ultimate destination of the data. If your purpose is to pull data for someone to load into a spreadsheet, you will probably want to use a comma-delimited format. If you are passing data to another application, you may find it easier to format the data in fixed-width columns. Dates require some extra thought. With Oracle's built-in TO_CHAR function, you can format a date any way you want. Be sure, though, to use a format easily recognized by the application that needs to read that date.

### Comma-delimited

To produce a comma-delimited text file, you need to do two things. First, you need to add commas between each field. Second, you need to enclose text fields within quotes. The final query looks like this:

```
SELECT TO_CHAR(employee_id) || ','
       || '"' || employee_name || '",'
       || TO_CHAR(employee_hire_date,'MM/DD/YYYY') || ','
       || TO_CHAR(employee_termination_date,'MM/DD/YYYY') || ','
       || TO_CHAR(employee_billing_rate)
   FROM employee;
```

Oracle's TO_CHAR function has been used to explicitly convert numeric fields to text strings. TO_CHAR is also used to convert date fields to text, and a date format string is included to get the dates into MM/DD/YYYY format. SQL's concatenation operator, ||, is used to concatenate all the fields together into one long string, and you can see that commas are included between fields. The output from this query will look like this:

```
...
107,"Bohdan Khmelnytsky",01/02/1998,,45
108,"Pavlo Chubynsky",03/01/1994,11/15/1998,220
110,"Ivan Mazepa",04/04/1998,09/30/1998,84
111,"Taras Shevchenko",08/23/1976,,100
...
```

Notice that in addition to the commas, the employee_name field has been enclosed in quotes. This is done to accommodate the possibility that someone's name will contain a comma. Most commercial programs that load comma-delimited data will allow text strings to be optionally enclosed in quotes.

You can use the same technique to generate tab-delimited data. Instead of a comma, use CHR(9) to put a tab character between each field. CHR() is an Oracle SQL function that converts an ASCII code into a character. The ASCII code uses the value 9 to represent a tab character.

### Fixed-width

The easiest way to produce an output file with fixed-width columns is to use the SQL*Plus COLUMN command to format the output from a standard SQL query. The following example shows one way to dump the employee data in a fixed-width column format:

```
COLUMN employee_id FORMAT 09999 HEADING ''
COLUMN employee_name FORMAT A20 HEADING '' TRUNCATED
COLUMN employee_hire_date FORMAT A10 HEADING ''
COLUMN employee_termination_date FORMAT A10 HEADING ''
COLUMN employee_billing_rate FORMAT S099.99 HEADING ''
SELECT employee_id,
       employee_name,
       TO_CHAR(employee_hire_date,'MM/DD/YYYY') employee_hire_date,
       TO_CHAR(employee_termination_date,'MM/DD/YYYY')
            employee_termination_date,
       employee_billing_rate
  FROM employee;
```

Notice some things about the example:

- The heading for each column has explicitly been set to a null string. That's because, in the case of a numeric column, SQL*Plus will make the column wide enough to accommodate the heading. You don't want that behavior. You want the format specification to control the column width.

- Both numeric fields have been formatted to show leading zeros. Most programs that read fixed-width data, such as COBOL programs, will expect this.

- The employee_billing_rate column will always display a leading sign character, either a "+" or a "-". The employee_id field, on the other hand, displays a leading sign only for negative values. Positive employee_id values are output with a leading space. Neither field would ever be negative, and these two approaches were taken just for illustrative purposes.

- Finally, notice that the TRUNCATED option was used to format the employee_ name field. That's because the employee_name can be up to 40 characters long in the database. If TRUNCATED were not specified, any names that happened to be longer than 20 characters would wrap to a second line—definitely not what you want to happen in a flat file.

Here's how the output from the example will look:

```
. . .
00107 Bohdan Khmelnytsky   01/02/1998             +045.00
00108 Pavlo Chubynsky      03/01/1994 11/15/1998 +220.00
00110 Ivan Mazepa          04/04/1998 09/30/1998 +084.00
00111 Taras Shevchenko     08/23/1976             +100.00
. . .
```

Each column in the output is separated by one space, because that's the SQL*Plus default. If you like, you can use the SET COLSEP command to change the number of spaces or eliminate them entirely. To run the columns together, you could eliminate the space between columns by setting the column separator to a null string. For example:

```
SET COLSEP ""
```

Now the output will look like this:

```
. . .
00107Bohdan Khmelnytsky   01/02/1998                +045.00
00108Pavlo Chubynsky      03/01/199411/15/1998+220.00
00110Ivan Mazepa          04/04/199809/30/1998+084.00
00111Taras Shevchenko     08/23/1976                +100.00
. . .
```

You can use any column separation string that you like, and you aren't limited to just one character.

The command SET SPACE 0 has the same effect as SET COLSEP ""—it eliminates the space between columns. Oracle considers SET SPACE to be an obsolete command, but some people still use it.

Using SQL*Plus to format fixed-width output works best when you have some control over the format expected by the destination of that data. If you are also writing the program to load the data somewhere else, of course you can code it to match what you can easily produce with SQL*Plus. Sometimes though, you need to match an existing format required by the destination; one you cannot change. Depending on your exact requirements, it may be easier to code one large expression in your SQL statement, and use Oracle's built-in functions to gain more control over the output. The following example produces the same output as before, but without a leading sign character in the numeric fields:

```
SELECT LTRIM(TO_CHAR(employee_id,'09999'))
       || SUBSTR(RPAD(employee_name,20,' '),1,20)
```

```
                    || TO_CHAR(employee_hire_date,'MM/DD/YYYY')
                    || NVL(TO_CHAR(employee_termination_date,'MM/DD/YYYY'),'              ')
                    || LTRIM(TO_CHAR(employee_billing_rate,'099.99'))
              FROM employee;
```

The output from this example looks like this:

```
        00107Bohdan Khmelnytsky  01/02/1998            045.00
        00108Pavlo Chubynsky     03/01/199411/15/1998220.00
        00110Ivan Mazepa         04/04/199809/30/1998084.00
        00111Taras Shevchenko    08/23/1976            100.00
```

Look carefully, and you will see that neither the employee_id field nor the
employee_billing_rate field has a leading sign. Not only do they not have a leading sign, there isn't even space left for one. The LTRIM function was used to
remove it.

There is a wide variety of built-in Oracle functions available. Add to that the ability to write your own, and you should be able to generate output in any conceiv-
able format.

### DML

If you are extracting data from Oracle in order to move it to another database, and
if the volume of data isn't too high, you can use SQL*Plus to generate a file of
INSERT statements. Here is a query to generate INSERT statements for each
employee record:

```
        SELECT 'INSERT INTO employee' || chr(10)
            || '   (employee_id, employee_name, employee_hire_date' || chr(10)
            || '   ,employee_termination_date, employee_billing_rate)' || chr(10)
            || '   VALUES (' || TO_CHAR(employee_id) || ',' || chr(10)
            || '           ''' || employee_name || ''',' || chr(10)
            || '           TO_DATE('''
                        || TO_CHAR(employee_hire_date,'MM/DD/YYYY')
                        || ''',''MM/DD/YYYY''),' || chr(10)
            || '           TO_DATE('''
                        || TO_CHAR(employee_termination_date,'MM/DD/YYYY')
                        || ''',''MM/DD/YYYY''),' || chr(10)
            || '           ' || TO_CHAR(employee_billing_rate) || ');'
          FROM employee;
```

As you can see, this type of query can get a bit hairy. You have to deal with
nested, quoted strings; you have to concatenate everything together; and you have
to place line breaks so the output at least looks decent. The doubled-up quotes
you see in the above statement are there because single quotes are required in the
final output. So, for example, the string "''MM/DD/YYYY'')" will resolve to
"'MM/DD/YYYY')" when the SELECT statement is executed. The SELECT statement just shown will produce the following INSERT statement for each employee
record:

```
INSERT INTO employee
  (employee_id, employee_name, employee_hire_date
  ,employee_termination_date, employee_billing_rate)
  VALUES (111,
          'Taras Shevchenko',
          TO_DATE('08/23/1976','MM/DD/YYYY'),
          TO_DATE('','MM/DD/YYYY'),
          100);
```

This is not a technique I use very often, because it can be frustrating to get the SQL just right. I use it most often on code tables and other small tables with only two or three columns. I also use it sometimes when I'm sending data to a client. That way I just send one file, and my client doesn't have to mess with SQL*Loader or Oracle's Import utility.

### DDL

Another twist on using SQL to write SQL is to generate commands that help you maintain your database. Such commands are referred to as Data Definition Language, or DDL, commands. Using SQL*Plus to generate DDL scripts can help in automating many database administration tasks, and is often well worth the effort. The following command, for example, generates CREATE PUBLIC SYNONYM commands for each table you own:

```
SELECT 'CREATE PUBLIC SYNONYM ' || table_name
       || ' for ' || user || '.' || table_name || ';'
  FROM USER_TABLES;
```

It's not unusual to need public synonyms, and if you have a large number of tables, you can save yourself a lot of typing by letting SQL*Plus do the work for you. The output from the above command looks like this:

```
CREATE PUBLIC SYNONYM EMPLOYEE for JONATHAN.EMPLOYEE;
CREATE PUBLIC SYNONYM PROJECT for JONATHAN.PROJECT;
CREATE PUBLIC SYNONYM PROJECT_HOURS for JONATHAN.PROJECT_HOURS;
```

Once you have spooled the above commands to a file, you can then execute that file to create the synonyms. In addition to one-off tasks like creating synonyms, you can use SQL*Plus to generate DDL commands for use by ongoing maintenance tasks. Going beyond that, you can even use SQL*Plus to generate operating-system script files.

## Spool the Extract to a File

Once you have your query worked out and the data formatted the way you need it, it's time to spool your output to a file. In order to get a clean file, there are four things you must do.

1. Set the linesize large enough to accommodate the longest possible line. Pay close attention to this if you are generating comma-delimited data. You need to allow for the case where each field is at its maximum size. Use the SET LINESIZE command for this.

2. Turn off all pagination features. You can use SET PAGESIZE 0 for this purpose. It turns off all column headings, page headings, page footers, page breaks, etc.

3. Turn feedback off with the SET FEEDBACK OFF command.

4. Use the SET TRIMSPOOL ON command to eliminate trailing spaces in the output data file. Use this for comma-delimited output and when you generate a file of SQL statements. Do *not* use this command if you are generating a file with fixed-width columns.

The following script generates a clean, comma-delimited file containing employee information:

```
--
--This script extracts data from the employee
--table and writes it to a text file in
--a comma-delimited format.
--

--Set the linesize to accommodate the longest possible line.
SET LINESIZE 136

--Turn off all page headings, column headings, etc.
SET PAGESIZE 0

--Turn off feedback
SET FEEDBACK OFF

--Eliminate trailing blanks at the end of a line.
SET TRIMSPOOL ON

SET TERMOUT OFF
SPOOL C:\A\EMP_DATA.CSV
SELECT TO_CHAR(employee_id) || ','
       || '"' || employee_name || '",'
       || TO_CHAR(employee_hire_date,'MM/DD/YYYY') || ','
       || TO_CHAR(employee_termination_date,'MM/DD/YYYY') || ','
       || TO_CHAR(employee_billing_rate)
  FROM employee;
SPOOL OFF

--Restore the default settings.
SET LINESIZE 80
SET PAGESIZE 24
SET FEEDBACK ON
SET TERMOUT ON
```

The SPOOL command is used to send the output to *C:\A\EMP_DATA.CSV*, and SET TERMOUT OFF is used to disable the display while the data is being written to the file. Here's how you run this script:

```
SQL> @C\EMPLOYEE_EXTRACT
SQL>
```

The resulting output file looks like this:

```
101,"Jonathan Gennick",11/15/1961,,169
102,"Jenny Gennick",09/16/1964,05/05/1998,135
104,"Jeff Gennick",12/29/1987,04/01/1998,99
105,"Horace Walker",06/15/1998,,121
107,"Bohdan Khmelnytsky",01/02/1998,,45
108,"Pavlo Chubynsky",03/01/1994,11/15/1998,220
110,"Ivan Mazepa",04/04/1998,09/30/1998,84
111,"Taras Shevchenko",08/23/1976,,100
112,"Hermon Goche",11/15/1961,04/04/1998,70
113,"Jacob Marley",03/03/1998,10/31/1998,300
211,"Taras Shevchenko",08/23/1976,,100
```

You can see that the output contains no page or column headings of any kind. It's just plain, comma-delimited data, with one line for each record in the table.

## Make Your Extract Script User-Friendly

There are at least two things you can do to improve on the extract script just shown in the previous section. First, it might be nice to display a brief message to remind the user of what the script does. This will serve to give the user confidence that he or she has indeed started the correct script. The following PROMPT commands, added at the beginning of the script, should serve the purpose:

```
PROMPT
PROMPT This script creates a comma-delimited text file containing
PROMPT employee data. All records from the employee table will
PROMPT be output to this file.
PROMPT
```

It may not be much, but it always makes me feel better to have some indication that the script I am executing really does what I thought it did. For scripts that change data or do something difficult to reverse, I will often include a PAUSE command such as this:

```
PAUSE Press ENTER to continue, or ctrl-C to abort.
```

Another nice thing to do would be to prompt for the output filename. The following ACCEPT command will prompt the user for a filename, and put the user's response into the variable named output_file:

```
ACCEPT output_file CHAR PROMPT 'Enter the output filename >'
```

You can then replace the filename in the SPOOL command with the substitution variable &output_file. Here is the modified, more user-friendly version of the extract script:

```
--
--This script extracts data from the employee
--table and writes it to a text file in
--a comma-delimited format.
--

--Tell the user what he is about to do.
PROMPT
PROMPT This script creates a comma-delimited text file containing
PROMPT employee data. All records from the employee table will
PROMPT be output to this file.
PROMPT

--Give the user a chance to bail out.
PAUSE Press ENTER to continue, or ctrl-C to abort.

--Ask the user for a filename.
ACCEPT output_file CHAR PROMPT 'Enter the output filename >'

--Set the linesize to accommodate the longest possible line.
SET LINESIZE 136

--Turn off all page headings, column headings, etc.
SET PAGESIZE 0

--Turn off feedback
SET FEEDBACK OFF

--Eliminate trailing blanks at the end of a line.
SET TRIMSPOOL ON

SET TERMOUT OFF
SPOOL &output_file
SELECT TO_CHAR(employee_id) || ','
       || '"' || employee_name || '",'
       || TO_CHAR(employee_hire_date,'MM/DD/YYYY') || ','
       || TO_CHAR(employee_termination_date,'MM/DD/YYYY') || ','
       || TO_CHAR(employee_billing_rate)
  FROM employee;
SPOOL OFF

--Restore the default settings.
SET LINESIZE 80
SET PAGESIZE 24
SET FEEDBACK ON
SET TERMOUT ON
```

When you run this modified script, it's much more obvious what is going to happen. In addition, you have a chance to abort, and you can specify whatever filename you like for the output.

```
SQL> @C>EMPLOYEE_EXTRACT_FRIENDLY

This script creates a comma-delimited text file containing
employee data. All records from the employee table will
be output to this file.

Press ENTER to continue, or ctrl-C to abort.

Enter the output filename >C:\A\EMP_DATA.CSV
SQL>
```

Depending on your needs, you could even go further and allow the user to enter some selection criteria in order to specify which employee records to extract.

# Reloading the Data

Now that you know how to extract data from Oracle, you need to know how to load it back in again. This is easy if you have generated a file of SQL commands— you simply execute that file from within SQL*Plus. Loading data is a little tougher, however, if you have a file of comma-delimited or fixed-width data.

In order to load data into Oracle from a flat file, you need to use a tool called SQL*Loader. SQL*Loader is a generic utility provided by Oracle for the express purpose of loading data into the database from a file. An entire book could be written about SQL*Loader, so it's not possible to cover it exhaustively in the remainder of this chapter. What I can do is show you how to use SQL*Loader to reload the employee table from either a comma-delimited or fixed-width text file—the same files you learned how to create in this chapter. That should be enough to get you started.

## Executing DDL and DML

If you extract data by using SQL*Plus to create a file of INSERT commands, loading the data somewhere else is as simple as creating the necessary table and executing the file. If you created a file of DDL commands, such as the CREATE PUBLIC SYNONYM commands shown earlier, you only need to execute that file.

---

You may want to turn ECHO on, and spool the output of any files that you execute, so you can go back and check for errors later.

## *Running SQL\*Loader*

As I mentioned, SQL\*Loader is Oracle's data loading utility, a general-purpose utility that can be configured to read and load data from a wide variety of record formats. It's a very powerful and versatile utility, and, possibly because of that, it can be frustrating to learn. Certainly the manual can be a bit overwhelming the first time you look at it.

### *The control file*

In order to load data from a flat file into a database, you need to provide several types of information to SQL\*Loader. First of all, SQL\*Loader needs to know what database to connect to, how to connect to it, and what table to load. Then SQL\*Loader needs to know the format of the input file. It needs to know where the fields are, how long they are, and how they are represented. If, for example, your input file has date fields, SQL\*Loader needs to know whether they are in MM/DD/YYYY format, MM/DD/YY format, or some other format.

The database connection and login information are usually passed to SQL\*Loader as command-line arguments. The remaining information, describing the input file, needs to be placed in a text file called the *control file.* When you run SQL\*Loader, you tell it where the control file is. Then SQL\*Loader reads the control file and uses that information to interpret the data in the flat file you are trying to load. Figure 5-1 illustrates this, and shows the information flow into and out of SQL\*Loader.

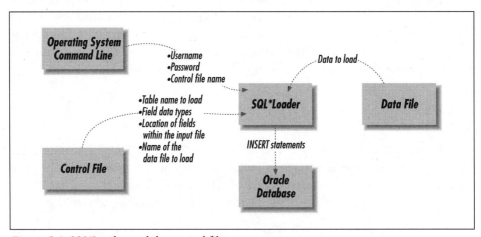

*Figure 5-1. SQL\*Loader and the control file*

In addition to describing the input file, the control file can be used to tell SQL\*Loader what to do with badly formatted data records, and it can be used to specify conditions limiting the data that is loaded. You can read more about SQL*Loader in the *Oracle8 Server Utilities* manual.

***Building a control file for comma-delimited data.*** The extract example shown earlier in this chapter produced comma-delimited output that looks like this:

```
107,"Bohdan Khmelnytsky",01/02/1998,,45
108,"Pavlo Chubynsky",03/01/1994,11/15/1998,220
110,"Ivan Mazepa",04/04/1998,09/30/1998,84
111,"Taras Shevchenko",08/23/1976,,100
```

In order to load this same data back into the employee table, or into another copy of the employee table, you need a control file that looks like this:

```
LOAD DATA
INFILE 'c:\a\emp_data.csv'
INTO TABLE employee
(
  employee_id              INTEGER EXTERNAL TERMINATED BY ',',
  employee_name            CHAR TERMINATED BY ',' OPTIONALLY ENCLOSED BY '"',
  employee_hire_date       DATE "MM/DD/YYYY" TERMINATED BY ',',
  employee_termination_date DATE "MM/DD/YYYY" TERMINATED BY ',',
  employee_billing_rate    DECIMAL EXTERNAL TERMINATED BY ','
)
```

You can think of the above as one long SQL*Loader command. The keywords LOAD DATA tell SQL*Loader to load data, and the rest of the command tells SQL*Loader where to get the data and how it is formatted. The remaining clauses are interpreted as described below:

*INFILE 'c:\a\emp_data.csv'*

> Tells SQL*Loader to read data from the file named *emp_data.csv* in the *c:\a* directory.

*INTO TABLE employee*

> Tells SQL*Loader to insert the data into the employee table owned by the current user. SQL*Loader will query Oracle's data dictionary tables for the columns and datatypes used in this table.

*(...column_specifications...)*

> A comma-delimited list of column specifications. Each column specification consists of the column name, followed by the representation (in the flat file) of the column, followed by the delimiter information.

The column names must correspond to the column names used in the database table you are loading, and they control the destination of each data element. For a delimited file, the order in which the column specifications appear in the control file must match the field order in the record.

The four elements of the column specifications used in this example are described in the following list. Table 5-1 describes the three datatypes that were used.

*column_name*
> Must be a column name in the destination table.

*datatype*
> A SQL*Loader datatype; See Table 5-1.

*TERMINATED BY ','*
> Tells SQL*Loader that a comma marks the end of the value for the data element.

*OPTIONALLY ENCLOSED BY '""'*
> Tells SQL*Loader that the data element may optionally be enclosed in quotes. If quotes are present, they are stripped off before the value is loaded.

SQL*Loader has its own set of datatypes, and they aren't the same as the ones used by the database. The most common datatypes used for loading data from text files are the numeric EXTERNAL types, CHAR, and DATE.

*Table 5-1. SQL*Loader Data Elements*

| Datatype | Description |
|---|---|
| INTEGER EXTERNAL | The data is numeric integer data stored as a character string. The character string must consist of the digits 0 through 9. Leading or trailing spaces are OK. Leading positive or negative signs (+ or -) are also OK. |
| DATE "format_string" | The data is a date, and the date is in the format specified by the format string. |
| DECIMAL EXTERNAL | Similar to INTEGER EXTERNAL, except that the number may contain a decimal point. This type was used for the employee_billing_rate field, because the billing rate is a dollar and cent value. |
| CHAR | Used for character data. |

***Building a control file for fixed-width data.*** The control file used to load fixed-width employee data is very similar to that used for delimited data. The only difference is that instead of specifying a delimiter for each field, you specify the starting and ending columns. Earlier in this chapter, you saw how to create a fixed-width file of employee data that looked like this:

```
00107 Bohdan Khmelnytsky   01/02/1998            +045.00
00108 Pavlo Chubynsky      03/01/1994 11/15/1998 +220.00
00110 Ivan Mazepa          04/04/1998 09/30/1998 +084.00
00111 Taras Shevchenko     08/23/1976            +100.00
```

Here is a control file that will load this fixed-width data back into the employee table:

```
LOAD DATA
INFILE 'c:\a\emp_data.dat'
INTO TABLE employee
(
  employee_id                POSITION (1:6) INTEGER EXTERNAL,
  employee_name              POSITION (8:28) CHAR,
  employee_hire_date         POSITION (29:38) DATE "MM/DD/YYYY",
  employee_termination_date  POSITION (40:49) DATE "MM/DD/YYYY"
                             NULLIF employee_termination_date=BLANKS,
  employee_billing_rate      POSITION (51:57) DECIMAL EXTERNAL
)
```

Each column in this control file contains a position specification that tells SQL*Loader where each field begins and ends. For some reason I have never been able to fathom, the position specification must precede the datatype, whereas a delimiter specification must follow the datatype. The position specification takes the form:

```
POSITION (starting_column : ending_column)
```

The starting and ending column numbers tell SQL*Loader where in the record to find the data, and the first character of a record is considered position 1. Unlike the case with delimited files, you do not have to list the column specifications for a fixed-width data file in any particular order.

---

The position specification for EMPLOYEE_ID, in this example, allows for six digits. The reason for this is to match the format of the fixed-width text file you saw generated in an earlier example in this chapter. Because the EMPLOYEE_ID field is numeric, it contains one space for a leading sign character. You will see this if you run the earlier example that generates a fixed-width file and look at the results in a text editor such as Notepad.

---

The employee_termination date column in this control file contains an extra element, a NULLIF clause. The NULLIF clause (the way it is written in the example) tells SQL*Loader to set the employee_termination_date column to null when the input data record contains spaces instead of a date. You didn't need this clause when loading the comma-delimited file because a null date was represented by a null string between two adjacent commas. In the case of this fixed-width data, a null date is represented as a string of spaces, or blanks. If SQL*Loader attempts to convert these blanks to a date, a validation error will occur, and the record will be rejected. The NULLIF clause avoids this problem because it is checked first. If the date field in the input file contains all blanks, the corresponding database column is set to null. No conversion is attempted, no validation error occurs, and the record will be loaded.

## Loading the data

Once you have the control file written, you can invoke SQL*Loader to load the data into the database. You can pass the following three items as command-line parameters:

- A login string
- The control file name
- A log file name

The last item, the log file name, is optional. If you include a log file name, SQL*Loader will generate a log of its activity and write it to that file. Among other things, any bad data records will result in log entries being made. At the end of the log file, SQL*Loader will print a summary showing how many records were loaded successfully and how many were rejected because of data errors. You won't get this information without a log file, so it's a good idea to generate one.

SQL*Loader is implemented as a command-line utility. To run it under Microsoft Windows, you must first open up a command prompt (or DOS) window. On most Unix systems, the command to run SQL*Loader will be *sqlldr*. In a Windows environment, the command has the Oracle version number appended to it. If you have Oracle8 installed, the command will look like this:

```
SQLLDR80 jonathan/secret CONTROL=emp_delimited.ctl
LOG=emp_delimited.log
```

The elements of this command are described next:

*SQLLDR80*

> This is the command to invoke SQL*Loader. The 80 in this example refers to the Oracle version number, and is only needed in a Windows environment. If you are running under Unix, the command will be *sqlldr*.

*jonathan/secret*

> This is the database username and password that SQL*Loader uses to connect to Oracle. This user must either own the table into which you are loading data, or must have INSERT access to that table.

*CONTROL=emp_delimited.ctl*

> This tells SQL*Loader where to find the control file. If your control file is not in the current working directory, you can include the path as part of the name.

*LOG=emp_delimited.log*

> This tells SQL*Loader what name to use for the log file. This name may include the path. It also tells SQL*Loader to create a log file. If you leave off this argument, you won't get a log file at all.

Here is how it looks to execute the command just shown and load the employee data from the comma-delimited file:

```
C>SQLLDR80 jonathan/secret CONTROL=emp_delimited.ctl LOG=emp_delimited.log

SQL*Loader: Release 8.0.3.0.0 - Production on Mon Mar 30 21:52:51 1998

(c) Copyright 1997 Oracle Corporation.  All rights reserved.

Commit point reached - logical record count 11

C>
```

You can see that you don't get much information at all about what happened. About all you can tell from SQL*Loader's output to the display is that there were 11 records in the input data file. The log file has more detail, however, and will look like this:

```
SQL*Loader: Release 8.0.3.0.0 - Production on Mon Mar 30 21:52:51 1998

(c) Copyright 1997 Oracle Corporation.  All rights reserved.

Control File:    emp_delimited.ctl
Data File:       c:\a\emp_data.csv
  Bad File:      emp_data.bad
  Discard File:  none specified

 (Allow all discards)

Number to load: ALL
Number to skip: 0
Errors allowed: 50
Bind array:     64 rows, maximum of 65536 bytes
Continuation:    none specified
Path used:       Conventional

Table EMPLOYEE, loaded from every logical record.
Insert option in effect for this table: INSERT

    Column Name                    Position   Len  Term Encl Datatype
    ------------------------------ ---------- ----- ---- ---- ------------------
EMPLOYEE_ID                        FIRST      *    ,         CHARACTER
EMPLOYEE_NAME                      NEXT       *    ,    O(") CHARACTER
EMPLOYEE_HIRE_DATE                 NEXT       *    ,         DATE MM/DD/YYYY
EMPLOYEE_TERMINATION_DATE          NEXT       *    ,         DATE MM/DD/YYYY
EMPLOYEE_BILLING_RATE              NEXT       *    ,         CHARACTER


Table EMPLOYEE:
  11 Rows successfully loaded.
  0 Rows not loaded due to data errors.
  0 Rows not loaded because all WHEN clauses were failed.
  0 Rows not loaded because all fields were null.
```

```
Space allocated for bind array:                    65040 bytes(60 rows)
Space allocated for memory besides bind array:         0 bytes

Total logical records skipped:          0
Total logical records read:            11
Total logical records rejected:         0
Total logical records discarded:        0

Run began on Mon Mar 30 21:52:51 1998
Run ended on Mon Mar 30 21:52:53 1998

Elapsed time was:      00:00:02.58
CPU time was:          00:00:00.00
```

The most important part of the log file to look at is the summary near the bottom, where SQL*Loader tells you how many rows were successfully loaded. In this case, all 11 records loaded cleanly. If any records were rejected because of bad data, there would be an entry for each in the log file telling you which record was rejected and why.

There is a lot more to SQL*Loader than what you have seen in this chapter. Here are some of the other things you can do with SQL*Loader:

- You can specify a *bad file*, which is where SQL*Loader places records that are rejected because of bad data. After a load, you can review the bad file, fix the records, and attempt to load them again.

- You can use a WHERE clause to place a restriction on the records to be loaded. Only those records that match the criteria in the WHERE clause will be loaded. Other records are ignored, or may optionally be placed in a *discard file*.

- You can build expressions, using any of Oracle's built-in SQL functions, to manipulate the data in the input file before it is loaded into Oracle.

The *Oracle8 Server Utilities* manual documents the SQL*Loader utility, and has a number of case studies that show you how to use these and other features.

# 6

# *Exploring Your Database*

You can create a variety of different objects in an Oracle database. You can create tables, indexes on those tables, objects, constraints, and so forth. It's important to be able to get information about the objects you have created. After a while you are going to find yourself asking questions like: "What tables do I have defined?" and "What do they look like?" You may have an application fail because of a constraint violation. In order to understand why the error occurred, you need to know what the definition is for that constraint. Unless you have an extremely good memory, you will need to go to the database itself for this information.

Using SQL*Plus, there are two ways you can display information about objects within your database. The easiest way is to use the DESCRIBE command. DESCRIBE will tell you about columns in a table or view. DESCRIBE will also show you the definition of an object type or of a PL/SQL package. The second method for getting information about objects in your database is to query the Oracle data dictionary. The data dictionary is a set of tables Oracle uses to keep track of object definitions. To facilitate your use of the data dictionary, Oracle provides a set of views known as *data dictionary views*. This chapter will show you how some of these views work and how you can write scripts to query them.

## *The DESCRIBE Command*

You may already be familiar with the SQL*Plus DESCRIBE command. DESCRIBE may be used to get a list of columns in a table or view, together with their datatypes. Beginning with Oracle8, DESCRIBE may also be used to see the definition of an Oracle8 object type, or to list definitions for all the functions and procedures in a stored PL/SQL package.

## Syntax for DESCRIBE

The syntax for the DESCRIBE command looks like this:

```
DESC[RIBE] [schema.]object_name[@database_link_name]
```

where:

*DESC[RIBE]*

Is the command, which may be abbreviated to DESC.

*schema*

Is the name of the object's owner. This defaults to your username.

*object_name*

Is the name of the object, often a table or a view, that you want to describe. You can describe any of the following: a table, a view, a stored procedure, a stored function, a stored package, or an Oracle8 object type.

*database_link_name*

Is the name of a database link pointing to the database where the object exists. You only need to use this if the object you want to describe exists in a database other than the one to which you are currently connected. Your DBA can help create a database link if you need one.

## Describing a Table

DESCRIBE is most often used to view the definition of a table or a view. Simply enter the command DESCRIBE, followed by the name of the table or view you are interested in, as the following example shows:

```
SQL> DESCRIBE employee
 Name                                      Null?    Type
 ---------------------------------------- -------- ----
 EMPLOYEE_ID                               NOT NULL NUMBER
 EMPLOYEE_NAME                                      VARCHAR2(40)
 EMPLOYEE_HIRE_DATE                                 DATE
 EMPLOYEE_TERMINATION_DATE                          DATE
 EMPLOYEE_BILLING_RATE                              NUMBER
```

If you aren't the owner of the table, you can qualify the table or view name using the standard *owner.table_name* notation. This next example describes the ALL_USERS view, which is owned by the user SYS.

```
SQL> DESCRIBE sys.all_users
 Name                                      Null?    Type
 ---------------------------------------- -------- ----
 USERNAME                                  NOT NULL VARCHAR2(30)
 USER_ID                                   NOT NULL NUMBER
 CREATED                                   NOT NULL DATE
```

As you can see, DESCRIBE just gives you a list of columns in the table or view, along with their resulting datatypes, lengths, and nullability. If you need to know more, such as whether or not a column has a default value, you will need to query the data dictionary directly. You will see how to do this later in the chapter.

> In early releases of Oracle8, in particular the 8.0.3 release, the DESCRIBE command does not function correctly when used with a public synonym. Thus, DESCRIBE ALL_TABLES will fail because ALL_TABLES is a public synonym. DESCRIBE SYS.ALL_TABLES will succeed because the view name is fully qualified. You can also create private synonyms that match public synonyms for objects you frequently look at. Create a private synonym named ALL_TABLES that refers to SYS.ALL_TABLES, and DESCRIBE will correctly interpret it.

## Describing Stored Functions and Procedures

DESCRIBE may also be used on stored procedures and functions. When used on a stored function, the DESCRIBE command tells you the data type of the return value, and also gives you a list of arguments that the function expects. For example:

```
SQL> DESCRIBE terminate_employee
FUNCTION terminate_employee RETURNS NUMBER(38)
 Argument Name                   Type                    In/Out Default?
 ------------------------------ ------------------------ ------ --------
 EMP_ID                          NUMBER                  IN
 EMP_HIRE_DATE                   DATE                    OUT
 EMP_TERM_DATE                   DATE                    IN
```

As you can see, DESCRIBE returns the following information for each argument:

- The datatype
- Whether it is an input, output, or both
- The default value, if there is one

The order in which the arguments are listed is also the order in which they should be passed into the function when you call it. The DESCRIBE command does not show you the source code for a function. To see that, you need to query the ALL_SOURCE data dictionary view. The following example shows how to get the source for the TERMINATE_EMPLOYEE function:

```
SQL> SELECT text
  2    FROM all_source
  3   WHERE owner = USER
```

```
  4      AND name = 'TERMINATE_EMPLOYEE'
  5   ORDER BY LINE;

TEXT
-----------------------------------------------------------------------
FUNCTION terminate_employee
    (emp_id IN employee.employee_id%TYPE,
     emp_hire_date OUT employee.employee_hire_date%TYPE,
     emp_term_date IN employee.employee_termination_date%TYPE)
RETURN INTEGER AS
BEGIN
  UPDATE employee
     SET employee_termination_date = emp_term_date
   WHERE employee_id = emp_id;

  SELECT employee_hire_date INTO emp_hire_date
    FROM employee
   WHERE employee_id = emp_id;

  RETURN 1;
EXCEPTION
WHEN OTHERS THEN
  RETURN 0;
END;

19 rows selected.
```

Describing a procedure works the same way as describing a function. The only difference is that procedures do not have a return type.

## Describing Packages and Object Types

With the release of Oracle8, the SQL*Plus DESCRIBE command was enhanced to return information about Oracle8 object types. The following example shows how this works:

```
SQL> DESCRIBE employee_type
 Name                              Null?    Type
 -------------------------------- -------- ----
 EMPLOYEE_NAME                              VARCHAR2(40)
 EMPLOYEE_HIRE_DATE                         DATE
 EMPLOYEE_SALARY                            NUMBER(9,2)

 METHOD
 ------
 MEMBER FUNCTION TERMINATE_EMPLOYEE RETURNS NUMBER
 Argument Name                    Type                    In/Out Default?
 -------------------------------- ----------------------- ------ --------
 EMP_ID                           NUMBER                  IN
 EMP_TERM_DATE                    DATE                    IN
```

Another Oracle8 enhancement provides the ability to describe a stored package and get back a list of all functions and procedures that make up the package. This is not surprising, because objects and packages are very similar in nature. For example, you can get a list of all the entry points in the DBMS_OUTPUT package by using DESCRIBE as shown here:

```
SQL> DESCRIBE sys.dbms_output
PROCEDURE DISABLE
PROCEDURE ENABLE
 Argument Name                    Type                     In/Out Default?
 ------------------------------   ----------------------   ------ --------
 BUFFER_SIZE                      NUMBER(38)               IN     DEFAULT
PROCEDURE GET_LINE
 Argument Name                    Type                     In/Out Default?
 ------------------------------   ----------------------   ------ --------
 LINE                             VARCHAR2                 OUT
 STATUS                           NUMBER(38)               OUT
PROCEDURE GET_LINES
 Argument Name                    Type                     In/Out Default?
 ------------------------------   ----------------------   ------ --------
 LINES                            TABLE OF VARCHAR2(255)   OUT
 NUMLINES                         NUMBER(38)               IN/OUT
PROCEDURE NEW_LINE
 ...
```

As with functions and procedures, you can get at the source for a package, or for an Oracle8 object type, by querying the ALL_SOURCE view. See the previous section for an example of how this is done.

> There have been some problems with the enhancements to DESCRIBE. Compatibility between different versions of SQL*Plus and different versions of the Oracle server has sometimes suffered. For example, if you use the 8.0.3 version of SQL*Plus, connect to a 7.x database and issue the DESCRIBE command on a table, it will fail. This particular problem was fixed in SQL*Plus 8.0.4.

## Why DESCRIBE Is Not Enough

Handy as DESCRIBE is, it just doesn't return enough information. While it shows you all the columns in a table, there are a lot of important details it leaves out. If you need to know the primary key for a table, DESCRIBE won't tell you. If you need to know the foreign key constraints defined on a table, DESCRIBE won't tell you that, either. DESCRIBE won't show you the indexes. DESCRIBE won't show you the default values. DESCRIBE won't show you the triggers, and DESCRIBE won't tell you anything about the table's security.

How then do you get at this other information? One way is to install Oracle's Enterprise Manager software. Enterprise Manager has a GUI-based schema browser that will show you everything there is to see about tables, indexes, views, triggers, and other objects. There are also several third-party software packages on the market that provide the same functionality. However, for many people, SQL*Plus is the only option available, or at least the only one conveniently available. If this is the case for you, you can still get the information you need by querying Oracle's data dictionary.

# Oracle's Data Dictionary Views

Oracle has to keep track of all the tables, views, constraints, indexes, triggers, and other objects you create. In order to do that, Oracle needs a place to store the information. This repository of information about your database is referred to as the *data dictionary*. Whenever you create a new object, such as a table, Oracle stores all the information about that object in the data dictionary. Modify the object, and Oracle modifies the data dictionary. It follows, then, that if you want to know anything about your database, the data dictionary is the place to go.

The data dictionary is a set of tables owned by the user SYS. The structure of these tables ends up being fairly complex, and much of the information is not stored in a very user-friendly form. You probably do not want to query these tables directly, and unless you have been given access to log in as user SYS, you won't be able to see them anyway. To help you out, Oracle provides a set of *data dictionary views*. These views have names that are easy to remember. The column names used in the views are also easy to remember and use a consistent naming convention. There are data dictionary views for each different type of schema object, and they present information in an easy-to-understand form. For example, if you are looking at a date column, the DBA_TAB_COLUMNS view will tell you it is of type 'DATE'. The underlying data dictionary table, which happens to be SYS.COL$, will simply tell you the type is 12.

Oracle has a large number of data dictionary views. This chapter concentrates only on the views that are used to return information about the structure of a table, its constraints, indexes, columns, triggers, and security. This is the most common type of information needed by application developers and other database users. I encourage you to dig deeper. If you want, or need, to know more, then the *Oracle Server Reference* manual would be a good place to start. The *Oracle Server Reference* manual contains a chapter titled *Static Data Dictionary Views*, which gives a comprehensive list of all the views available.

## The View Types: ALL, DBA, and USER

There are three different types of data dictionary views you need to be aware of. These control the scope of the information you can look at. The three view types are:

## USER

The USER views show you information only about objects that you own. There is a USER_TABLES view, for example, that will list only tables you own.

## ALL

The ALL views show you information about all objects you are able to access. Anything you own will be included in an ALL view, as well as anything owned by other users, but to which you have been granted access.

## DBA

The DBA views show you information about all objects—period. Usually only database administrators will have access to these views, and they could be considered a superset of the ALL views. DBA_TABLES, for example, will list every single table that exists. The typical way to gain access to the DBA views is to be granted the DBA role. However, the SELECT ANY TABLE privilege will also let you see them.

Generally speaking, for any given object type, one view of each type will exist. It's up to you to choose the one you want to look at. Table 6-1 shows how this works in terms of the views discussed in this chapter.

*Table 6-1. Correspondence Between USER, ALL, and DBA Views*

| USER View Name | ALL View Name | DBA View Name |
| --- | --- | --- |
| USER_TABLES | ALL_TABLES | DBA_TABLES |
| USER_TAB_COLUMNS | ALL_TAB_COLUMNS | DBA_TAB_COLUMNS |
| USER_CONSTRAINTS | ALL_CONSTRAINTS | DBA_CONSTRAINTS |
| USER_CONS_COLUMNS | ALL_CONS_COLUMNS | DBA_CONS_COLUMNS |
| USER_INDEXES | ALL_INDEXES | DBA_INDEXES |
| USER_IND_COLUMNS | ALL_IND_COLUMNS | DBA_IND_COLUMNS |
| USER_SYNONYMS | ALL_SYNONYMS | DBA_SYNONYMS |
| USER_TRIGGERS | ALL_TRIGGERS | DBA_TRIGGERS |
| USER_TAB_PRIVS | ALL_TAB_PRIVS | DBA_TAB_PRIVS |

As you delve more deeply into Oracle's data dictionary, you will occasionally find instances when corresponding views do not exist in all three categories. When a view is omitted it's either for security reasons, because it doesn't make sense in the context of a particular object, or because it would be redundant. The USER_JOBS and DBA_JOBS views provide a good example of this. A user can own a job, hence the USER_JOBS view. The database administrator needs to see everything, hence the DBA_JOBS view. There is no ALL_JOBS view, because there is no mechanism to grant another user access to your jobs. ALL_JOBS would be redundant with USER_JOBS, because the only jobs you can ever see are your own anyway.

When you write scripts, avoid the DBA views if at all possible. Using the DBA views limits your ability to share your scripts, because most users don't have access to them.

Which view should you use? The USER views limit you to seeing information only about objects that you own. If I'm working interactively, I'll frequently use the USER views to save myself some typing, because I don't need to enter a WHERE clause to restrict the results to my objects. When writing scripts, I try to use the ALL views in order to make the scripts more flexible. It's not unusual, for example, to need to see the definition for a table owned by another user. The ALL views allow this. I save the DBA views for database administration–related tasks.

The following sections show you how to get information about various types of schema objects. First I'll show how to list the tables you own and how to look at the column definitions for those tables. Next you will see how to look at the constraints, indexes, triggers, synonyms, and security for a table. Finally, you will see how to write one script that will give you a pretty complete dump of all this information just by issuing one command.

## *Dictionary Views Used in This Chapter*

A number of data dictionary views are referenced by the examples and scripts shown in this chapter. For your convenience, they are all shown together in this section. As you scan through these, it's not necessary to understand every single column of each view. Many of the view columns, particularly in ALL_TABLES and ALL_INDEXES, relate to the physical implementation of the objects, and aren't discussed in this chapter. The more experienced you become with Oracle, the more you will come to understand the information these columns contain.

### *The ALL_TABLES view*

The ALL_TABLES view contains one record for every table to which you have access. Table 6-2 lists the columns in this view and explains what information they contain. Many of the columns contain information about the physical implementation of the table, and if you are not the DBA, you may not be too interested in them. Some columns, beginning with NUM_ROWS and going through NUM_ FREELIST_BLOCKS, are set only when you use the ANALYZE TABLE command to compute statistics for the table.

*Table 6-2. Columns in the ALL_TABLES View*

| Column Name | Contents |
| --- | --- |
| OWNER | Username of the table's owner. |
| TABLE_NAME | Name of the table. |
| TABLESPACE_NAME | Name of the tablespace where the table is stored. This is a foreign key to the DBA_TABLESPACES view. |
| CLUSTER_NAME | A cluster name, if the table belongs to a cluster. This is a foreign key to the ALL_CLUSTERS view. |
| IOT_NAME | An index-organized table name. |
| PCT_FREE | Minimum percentage of free space in a block. When free space drops to this level, Oracle stops adding new rows to the block. |
| PCT_USED | Minimum percentage of used space in a block. When used space drops to this level, Oracle will again add new rows to the block. |
| INI_TRANS | Initial number of transactions that can concurrently touch this block. |
| MAX_TRANS | Maximum number of transactions that can concurrently touch this block. |
| INITIAL_EXTENT | The size, in bytes, of the initial extent for the table. This is how much space is allocated when the table is first created. |
| NEXT_EXTENT | The size, in bytes, of the next extent for the table. The next time the table needs to be expanded, this is how much space will be allocated. |
| MIN_EXTENTS | The minimum number of extents to be allocated for the table. This value affects the amount of space that is initially allocated for the table. See INITIAL_EXTENT and NEXT_EXTENT. |
| MAX_EXTENTS | The maximum number of extents allowed for the table. When these are used up, you won't be able to insert any more data into the table. |
| PCT_INCREASE | A percentage that controls growth of the NEXT_EXTENT value. Each time an extent is allocated, NEXT_EXTENT is recomputed to be NEXT_EXTENT + (NEXT_EXTENT * (PCT_INCREASE/100)). This value is then rounded up to the blocksize, or a multiple of the blocksize. |
| FREELISTS | The number of freelists allocated to the table. |
| FREELIST_GROUPS | The number of freelist groups allocated to the table. |
| LOGGING | The logging attribute for the table. |
| BACKED_UP | A Y/N flag that indicates whether or not the table has been backed up since the last change. |
| NUM_ROWS | The number of rows in the table.[a] |
| BLOCKS | The number of data blocks used by the table.[a] |

*Table 6-2. Columns in the ALL_TABLES View (continued)*

| Column Name | Contents |
| --- | --- |
| EMPTY_BLOCKS | The number of data blocks allocated to the table that have never been used.[a] |
| AVG_SPACE | The average amount of free space in all blocks allocated to this table. This value is in bytes. |
| CHAIN_CNT | The number of rows in the table that have had to be chained across more than one block, possibly because the row has been expanded. This also includes rows that have been moved entirely out of the block in which they were originally created. |
| AVG_ROW_LEN | The average length, in bytes, of the rows in the table. |
| AVG_SPACE_FREELIST_BLOCKS | The average freespace in all table blocks that are currently in the freelist. |
| NUM_FREELIST_BLOCKS | The number of blocks allocated to the table that still contain space for more rows. |
| DEGREE | The number of threads per instance for scanning the table. |
| INSTANCES | The number of instances allowed to scan the table at one time. |
| CACHE | A Y/N flag indicating whether or not the table should be cached in the buffer. |
| TABLE_LOCK | Either "ENABLED" or "DISABLED", indicating whether or not users are allowed to lock the entire table. |
| SAMPLE_SIZE | The sample size used when analyzing the table and computing statistics. |
| LAST_ANALYZED | The date on which the table was most recently analyzed. |
| PARTITIONED | Either "YES" or "NO", indicating whether or not the table is partitioned. |
| IOT_TYPE | Indicates whether or not the table is an index-only table. A null value indicates a normal table. A value of "IOT" or "IOT_OVERFLOW" is used for index-only tables. |
| TEMPORARY | Either "Y" or "N", indicating whether or not the table is a temporary table. |
| NESTED | Either "YES" or "NO", indicating whether or not the table is a nested table. |
| BUFFER_POOL | The name of the default buffer pool for the table. |

[a] Not maintained automatically by Oracle. This column is set when you use the ANALYZE TABLE command with the COMPUTE STATISTICS option.

### The ALL_TAB_COLUMNS view

The ALL_TAB_COLUMNS view contains one record for every column in a table. This is the view used by the DESCRIBE command to get column names, lengths, and datatypes. Table 6-3 lists the columns in this view and explains the information they contain.

*Table 6-3. Columns in the ALL_TAB_COLUMNS View*

| Column Name | Contents |
|---|---|
| OWNER | Username of the table's owner. |
| TABLE_NAME | Name of the table. |
| COLUMN_NAME | The column name. |
| DATA_TYPE | The column's datatype (e.g., VARCHAR2, NUMBER, etc). |
| DATA_TYPE_MOD | The datatype modifier for the column. |
| DATA_TYPE_OWNER | The datatype owner. This is used in Oracle8 and above when you create a column based on an object type owned by another user. |
| DATA_LENGTH | The length of the column in bytes. |
| DATA_PRECISION | The decimal precision, or the number of significant digits, the column will hold, if the column is type NUMBER. If the column is type FLOAT, then this is the binary precision, or the number of significant bits. For all other datatypes, this will be NULL. |
| DATA_SCALE | The number of digits allowed to the right of the decimal point in a NUMBER column. Remember, NUMBER columns are defined as NUMBER (*precision, scale*). |
| NULLABLE | Y = the column may contain null values. N = the column may not contain null values. This may be because of a NOT NULL constraint, or because the column is part of the table's primary key. |
| COLUMN_ID | The sequence number, indicating the column's position within each record. When you create a table, the first column in the list will have a COLUMN_ID of 1. The next column will have a COLUMN_ID of 2, and so on. |
| DEFAULT_LENGTH | The length of the default value for the column, if there is a default value. |
| DATA_DEFAULT | The default value for the column. |
| NUM_DISTINCT | The number of distinct values in the column.[a] |
| LOW_VALUE | The lowest value, up to the first 32 bytes of that value, in the column.[a] |
| HIGH_VALUE | The highest value, up to the first 32 bytes of that value, in the column.[a] |
| DENSITY | The density of the column.[a] |
| NUM_NULLS | The number of records with a null value for this column.[b] |
| NUM_BUCKETS | The number of buckets in the column's histogram.[b] |
| LAST_ANALYZED | The date on which the data in the column was last analyzed with an ANALYZE TABLE COMPUTE STATISTICS command.[b] |

*Table 6-3. Columns in the ALL_TAB_COLUMNS View (continued)*

| Column Name | Contents |
|---|---|
| SAMPLE_SIZE | The number of rows that were sampled when statistics were last computed for this column.[b] |
| CHARACTER_SET_NAME | For character columns, this indicates which character set is stored by the column. This value will be either NCHAR_CS or CHAR_CS. NCHAR_CS indicates that data in the column is stored using the national character set. CHAR_CS indicates that the database character set is used. |

[a] Not maintained automatically by Oracle; beginning with Oracle8, you should use the ALL_TAB_COL_STATISTICS view to retrieve this value. This column is set when you use the ANALYZE TABLE command with the COMPUTE STATISTICS option.
[b] Not maintained automatically by Oracle. This column is set when you use the ANALYZE TABLE command with the COMPUTE STATISTICS option.

### The ALL_CONSTRAINTS view

The ALL_CONSTRAINS view returns one row for each constraint you can see. Oracle will let you see all constraints on tables you own, as well as all constraints on tables to which you have been granted any type of access. Table 6-4 lists the columns in this view.

*Table 6-4. Columns in the ALL_CONSTRAINTS View*

| Column Name | Contents |
|---|---|
| OWNER | The owner of the constraint. This is usually the same as the owner of the table on which the constraint is defined. |
| CONSTRAINT_NAME | The name of the constraint. |
| CONSTRAINT_TYPE | Indicates the type of constraint,. Will be one of these values:<br>P = PRIMARY KEY<br>R = FOREIGN KEY<br>C = CHECK<br>U = UNIQUE KEY |
| TABLE_NAME | The table on which the constraint is defined. |
| SEARCH_CONDITION | If the constraint is a check constraint, this is the condition that must be satisfied for each row stored in the table. For other constraint types, this will be null. |
| R_OWNER | For foreign key constraints, this is the owner of the related primary key or unique constraint. |
| R_CONSTRAINT_NAME | For foreign key constraints, this is the related primary key or unique constraint. |
| DELETE_RULE | This has meaning only for foreign key constraints, and has these two values:<br>CASCADE: Deleting a record from the parent table will cause matching records in this table to be deleted automatically.<br>NO ACTION: Child records are not automatically deleted. You will not be able to delete a parent unless you first delete the children. |

*Table 6-4. Columns in the ALL_CONSTRAINTS View (continued)*

| Column Name | Contents |
|---|---|
| STATUS | Will be either ENABLED or DISABLED, depending on whether or not the constraint is currently being enforced. |
| DEFERRABLE | Will be either DEFERRABLE or NOT DEFERRABLE. |
| DEFERRED | Will be either DEFERRED or IMMEDIATE, depending on whether not the constraint is deferred by default. |
| VALIDATED | Will be either VALIDATED or NOT VALIDATED, depending on whether or not all rows in the table have been validated against the constraint. |
| GENERATED | Will be either GENERATED NAME or USER NAME depending on whether the constraint name was system-generated or specified by the user who created it. |
| BAD | Usually this is null. If this is "BAD", you have used a date constant that does not include the century, and you need to recreate the constraint prior to the year 2000. |
| LAST_CHANGE | The date when the constraint was most recently changed. Since the only change you can make is to enable or disable a constraint, this ends up being when that was most recently done. |

## The ALL_CONS_COLUMNS view

The ALL_CONS_COLUMNS view contains one row for each column specified in a primary key, foreign key, or unique constraint. Table 6-5 lists the columns in this view.

*Table 6-5. Columns in the ALL_CONS_COLUMNS View*

| Column Name | Contents |
|---|---|
| OWNER | The owner of the constraint, which is the same as the owner of the table on which the constraint is defined. |
| CONSTRAINT_NAME | The name of the constraint. |
| TABLE_NAME | The table on which the constraint is defined. |
| COLUMN_NAME | The name of a column that makes up the constraint. |
| POSITION | The position of the column in the constraint definition. |

## The ALL_INDEXES view

The ALL_INDEXES view returns one record for each index you can see. You should be able to see indexes for any table to which you have been granted access. The information in ALL_INDEXES pertains to the index as a whole. To get

the list of columns in an index, you need to look at the ALL_IND_COLUMNS view.
Table 6-6 describes the columns in ALL_INDEXES.

*Table 6-6. Columns in the ALL_INDEXES View*

| Column Name | Contents |
| --- | --- |
| OWNER | The username of the index's owner, which may not be the same as the owner of the underlying table. |
| INDEX_NAME | The index name. |
| INDEX_TYPE | The index type, one of the following values: NORMAL, BITMAP, CLUSTER, IOT-TOP, IOT-NESTED, SECONDARY, ANSI, or LOB. |
| TABLE_OWNER | The username of the table's owner. |
| TABLE_NAME | The name of the table on which the index was created. |
| TABLE_TYPE | The type of table which is indexed. |
| UNIQUENESS | Indicates whether or not the index is a unique index. Values are UNIQUE, NONUNIQUE, or UNDEFINED. |
| TABLESPACE_NAME | The name of the tablespace in which the index is stored. |
| INI_TRANS | The initial number of transactions. |
| MAX_TRANS | The maximum number of transactions. |
| INITIAL_EXTENT | The size, in bytes, of the first extent allocated for the index. |
| NEXT_EXTENT | The size, in bytes, of the next extent that will be allocated for the index. |
| MIN_EXTENTS | The minimum number of extents for the index. This number of extents is allocated when the index is first created. |
| MAX_EXTENTS | The maximum number of extents allowed for the index. When these fill up, any attempts to index new rows will result in an error. |
| PCT_INCREASE | Each time a new extent is allocated, the NEXT_EXTENT value is increased by this percentage. |
| PCT_THRESHOLD | The percentage of block space allowed for each index entry. |
| INCLUDE_COLUMN | Applies to indexes on index-organized table, and is the column ID number of the last column to be included in the top-level index blocks. |
| FREELISTS | The number of freelists allocated to this index. |
| FREELIST_GROUPS | The number of freelist groups allocated to this index. |
| PCT_FREE | Minimum percentage of free space in a block. When free space drops to this level, Oracle stops adding new rows to the block. |

*Table 6-6. Columns in the ALL_INDEXES View (continued)*

| Column Name | Contents |
| --- | --- |
| LOGGING | The logging attribute for the index. |
| BLEVEL | For B-Tree indexes, this is the number of different levels between the root (top) and the leaf (bottom) blocks.[a] |
| LEAF_BLOCKS | The number of leaf blocks contained in the index.[a] |
| DISTINCT_KEYS | The number of distinct index values. With a UNIQUE index, every value is a distinct value.[a] |
| AVG_LEAF_BLOCKS_PER_KEY | Each distinct indexed value appears in one or more leaf blocks. This is the average of the number of leaf blocks for each entry. For a UNIQUE index, this will always be 1.[a] |
| AVG_DATA_BLOCKS_PER_KEY | Each distinct index entry references one or more data blocks in the table. This is the average number of data blocks referenced by each entry.[a] |
| CLUSTERING_FACTOR | This indicates how well-ordered the table is in terms of the index. This value can range from the number of blocks in the table to the number of rows in the table. The more this value approaches the number of blocks in the table, the more closely the order of the rows in the table match the order in which they are indexed. As the rows are more randomized, this value will approach the row count for the table.[a] |
| STATUS | The status of the index; it has one of these values: DIRECT LOAD or VALID. A status of VALID indicates that the index is up to date and can be used. |
| NUM_ROWS | The number of rows indexed by this index.[a] |
| SAMPLE_SIZE | The sample size used when the index was last analyzed.[a] |
| LAST_ANALYZED | The date on which the index was last analyzed.[a] |
| DEGREE | The number of threads used by each instance scanning the index. This applies only to partitioned indexes, and will be null if the index is not partitioned. |
| INSTANCES | Similar to DEGREE, but refers to the number of instances that can simultaneously scan the index. If the index is not partitioned, this will be null. |
| PARTITIONED | A YES/NO flag indicating whether or not the index is a partitioned index. |
| TEMPORARY | A Y/N flag indicating whether or not the index is a temporary index. If the index is temporary, users will only see entries for rows they have inserted. |

*Table 6-6. Columns in the ALL_INDEXES View (continued)*

| Column Name | Contents |
|---|---|
| GENERATED | A Y/N flag indicating whether or not the index name was system-generated. A value of Y is used for system-generated names, which look like this: SYS_C001194. |
| BUFFER_POOL | The name of the default buffer pool to be used for the index. |

a Not maintained automatically by Oracle. This column is set when you use the ANALYZE TABLE command with the COMPUTE STATISTICS option.

### The ALL_IND_COLUMNS view

Indexes are made up of one or more columns. To find out what columns are included in an index, you need to use the ALL_IND_COLUMNS view. Table 6-7 describes this view.

*Table 6-7. Columns in the ALL_IND_COLUMNS View*

| Column Name | Contents |
|---|---|
| INDEX_OWNER | The owner of the index. |
| INDEX_NAME | The name of the index. |
| TABLE_OWNER | The owner of the table that is indexed. |
| TABLE_NAME | The name of the table that is indexed. |
| COLUMN_NAME | The name of a column in the index. |
| COLUMN_POSITION | The relative position of the column in the index. The first column will be number 1, the second column will be number 2, etc. |
| COLUMN_LENGTH | The number of bytes of the column that form part of the index entry. |

### The ALL_TRIGGERS view

The ALL_TRIGGERS view returns one row for each trigger on tables you own or to which you have access. Table 6-8 describes the columns in this view.

*Table 6-8. Columns in the ALL_TRIGGERS View*

| Column | Contents |
|---|---|
| OWNER | The owner of the trigger. |
| TRIGGER_NAME | The trigger name. |
| TRIGGER_TYPE | This indicates when the trigger fires and whether or not it fires for each row. The type will be one of these values: BEFORE EACH ROW, AFTER EACH ROW, BEFORE STATEMENT, or AFTER STATEMENT. |

*Table 6-8. Columns in the ALL_TRIGGERS View (continued)*

| Column | Contents |
| --- | --- |
| TRIGGERING_EVENT | The type of statement that fires the trigger, causing it to be executed. This will be one or more of the following: INSERT, UPDATE, DELETE: |
| TABLE_OWNER | The owner of the table on which the trigger is defined. Usually this is the same as the trigger owner, but it doesn't have to be. |
| TABLE_NAME | The name of the table on which the trigger is defined. |
| REFERENCING_NAMES | Tells you what correlation names are used in the trigger to reference columns in the table. If the defaults were taken when the trigger was created, the value for this column will be "REFERENCING NEW AS NEW OLD AS OLD". |
| WHEN_CLAUSE | The WHEN clause, if any, that was specified when the trigger was created. This will actually be the part of the WHEN clause between parentheses. Thus, if the CREATE TRIGGER statement specifies "WHEN (new.hire_date = sysdate)", this column will return only the "new.hire_date = sysdate" portion. A WHEN clause can only be specified for a row-level trigger, and the trigger only fires if this condition is true. |
| STATUS | This will be either ENABLED or DISABLED, and indicates whether or not the trigger will fire at all. |
| DESCRIPTION | This contains part of the original statement that was used to create the trigger. Everything following "CREATE TRIGGER" up until the keyword "REFERENCING" is stored here. This includes the trigger name, the table name, the trigger type, the triggering event, and the list of update columns. Using this field provides a more convenient way to get this information than selecting all the other columns separately. This is especially true if you are trying to recreate the original CREATE TRIGGER statement. |
| TRIGGER_BODY | This is a LONG column containing the PL/SQL code that makes up the body of the trigger. |

## The ALL_TRIGGER_COLS view

The ALL_TRIGGER_COLS view returns one row for each database column referenced or modified in triggers on tables you own or to which you have access. I rarely use this view, but if there is ever any doubt about whether or not a trigger uses a particular database column, this view can provide a quick answer. Table 6-9 describes the columns in this view.

*Table 6-9. Columns in the ALL_TRIGGER_COLS View*

| Column | Contents |
| --- | --- |
| TRIGGER_OWNER | The owner of the trigger. |
| TRIGGER_NAME | The trigger name. |

*Table 6-9. Columns in the ALL_TRIGGER_COLS View (continued)*

| Column | Contents |
|---|---|
| TABLE_OWNER | The owner of the table on which the trigger is defined. Usually this is the same as the trigger owner, but it doesn't have to be. |
| TABLE_NAME | The name of the table on which the trigger is defined. |
| COLUMN_NAME | The name of a column in the table that is used within the trigger, either within the trigger's specification, or within the PL/SQL block executed by the trigger. |
| COLUMN_LIST | Either YES or NO, depending on whether or not the firing of the trigger is dependent on this column being updated. This is only applicable to UPDATE triggers. A value of YES indicates that the column forms part of the column list following the keyword UPDATE in the CREATE TRIGGER statement. |
| COLUMN_USAGE | This tells you how the column is used within the trigger. It will contain some combination of the following strings, separated by one space:<br>    NEW: The new version of the column is referenced.<br>    OLD: The old version of the column is referenced.<br>    IN: The column is referenced, but not updated.<br>    OUT: The column's value is set, but never read.<br>    IN OUT: The column's value is both referenced and updated.<br>For example, a value of "NEW IN OUT" tells you that the trigger both sets the value of the column (OUT) and reads the value of the column (IN). It also tells you that it is the new version (NEW) of the column that is used. |

### The ALL_SYNONYMS view

The ALL_SYNONYMS view returns one row for each synonym you own and one for each public synonym. Table 6-10 describes the columns in this view.

*Table 6-10. Columns in the ALL_SYNONYMS View*

| Column | Contents |
|---|---|
| OWNER | The owner of the synonym. The owner name will be "PUBLIC" for public synonyms, which are accessible by all database users. |
| SYNONYM_NAME | The name of the synonym. |
| TABLE_OWNER | The name of the table's owner. |
| TABLE_NAME | The table name to which the synonym points. |
| DB_LINK | If the synonym points to a table in another database instance, this is the database link name that points to that instance. |

### The ALL_TAB_PRIVS view

The ALL_TAB_PRIVS view shows privileges granted to others on objects you own. It also shows privileges granted to you on objects owned by others. Table 6-11 describes this view.

*Table 6-11. Columns in the ALL_TAB_PRIVS View*

| Column | Contents |
| --- | --- |
| GRANTOR | The username of the person who granted the privilege. |
| GRANTEE | The username or rolename to which access was granted. |
| TABLE_SCHEMA | The owner of the object. |
| TABLE_NAME | The object's name. |
| PRIVILEGE | The privilege that was granted on the object (e.g., INSERT or DELETE). |
| GRANTABLE | This will be either YES or NO, depending on whether or not the privilege was granted with the administrative option. |

### The ALL_COL_PRIVS view

This view only comes into play when you have granted UPDATE privileges to a user, and when you have limited those update privileges to a specific set of columns. This view returns that list of updateable columns, and is described in Table 6-12.

*Table 6-12. Columns in the ALL_COL_PRIVS_MADE View*

| Column | Contents |
| --- | --- |
| GRANTOR | The username of the person who granted the privilege. |
| GRANTEE | The username or rolename to which access was granted. |
| TABLE_SCHEMA | The owner of the object. |
| TABLE_NAME | The object's name. |
| COLUMN_NAME | The column name on which the privilege was granted. |
| PRIVILEGE | The privilege that was granted on the object (e.g., INSERT or DELETE). |
| GRANTABLE | This will be either YES or NO, depending on whether or not the privilege was granted with the administrative option. |

# Tables

When it comes to looking at a table and its column definitions, there are two data dictionary views you need to be concerned with. These views are:

    ALL_TABLES
    ALL_TAB_COLUMNS

The ALL_TABLES view contains one row for each table. You can use this view to get a quick list of tables you own or to which you have been granted some type of access. ALL_TABLES has a one-to-many relationship to ALL_TAB_COLUMNS, which contains one record for each column in a table. ALL_TAB_COLUMNS is the source for information on column names, datatypes, default values, and so forth.

## *Listing Tables You Own*

To get a quick list of tables you own, it's easier to use the USER_TABLES view than ALL_TABLES. Remember, USER_TABLES shows you only the tables you own. To see a list of your tables, simply select the table_name column.

```
SQL> SELECT table_name FROM user_tables;

TABLE_NAME
------------------------------
DATA_TYPE_TEST
DT_TEST
EMPLOYEE
PROJECT
PROJECT_HOURS

5 rows selected.
```

To see tables owned by other users, you need to query the ALL_TABLES view. Just be sure to qualify your query by specifying the owner's username in the WHERE clause. Here's an example that lists all tables owned by the user SYSTEM:

```
SELECT table_name
  FROM all_tables
 WHERE owner = 'SYSTEM';
```

You can make things easy on yourself by writing a script to list tables. The following listing shows one approach you can take. It prompts you for a username, then lists all tables owned by that user. The table listing is in alphabetical order.

```
--DESCRIPTION
--List tables owned by the current user, or owned by a specified user.
--The user is prompted for an owner name. If an owner is not specified,
--i.e. the user just presses ENTER, then tables are listed for
--the current user.

SET ECHO OFF
SET FEEDBACK OFF
SET VERIFY OFF
SET DEFINE ON
SET HEADING OFF

--Ask the user for the owner.
ACCEPT username CHAR PROMPT 'List tables for user: '
PROMPT

--Set up the title to print the owner.
TTITLE LEFT 'TABLES OWNED BY: ' owner SKIP 1
COLUMN owner NOPRINT NEW_VALUE owner

--List the tables.
SELECT DECODE('&&username',NULL,USER,UPPER('&&username')) owner,
         '       ' indent,
```

```
          table_name
   FROM all_tables
  WHERE owner = DECODE('&&username',NULL,USER,UPPER('&&username'))
  ORDER BY table_name;

  --Clean up: undefine vars, clear columns, change settings back to defaults.
  UNDEFINE username
  UNDEFINE owner
  COLUMN owner CLEAR
  TTITLE OFF
  SET HEADING ON
  SET FEEDBACK ON
  SET VERIFY ON
```

When you run this script, it will prompt you for a username. Then it will list all the tables owned by that user. Here's an example:

```
SQL> @list_tables
List tables for user: jeff


TABLES OWNED BY: jeff
      EMPLOYEE
      MY_TABLE
      PROJECT
      PROJECT_HOURS
```

As you can see, the resulting list shows all the tables owned by the user named JEFF. The DECODE function in the SELECT statement translates any username you enter to uppercase. If you were to press ENTER at the username prompt, that same DECODE statement would translate your empty response to your username, so you would see your tables.

## Listing Column Definitions for a Table

To list the columns in a table, you will almost certainly want to write a script. The script shown next offers one possible approach to doing this. Some of the expressions, particularly the ones that call the DECODE function, get a bit complicated. I'll explain those after the listing.

### The LIST_COLUMNS.SQL script

```
--DESCRIPTION
--List all the columns for a table, together with
--their datatypes, default values, and nullability.
--
--INPUTS
--  Param 1   A table name, optionally qualified
--            optionally qualified by an owner name.
--            For example: "SYS.ALL_TAB_COLUMNS".
--
SET ECHO OFF
SET VERIFY OFF
```

```
SET FEEDBACK OFF
SET RECSEP OFF
SET HEADING ON
SET PAGESIZE 9999
SET LONG 1000
SET LINESIZE 80
CLEAR COLUMNS
CLEAR BREAKS
TTITLE OFF
BTITLE OFF

--Dissect the input argument, and get the owner name and
--table name into two seperate substitution variables.
--The owner name defaults to the current user.
DEFINE s_owner_name = ' '
DEFINE s_table_name = ' '
COLUMN owner_name NOPRINT NEW_VALUE s_owner_name
COLUMN table_name NOPRINT NEW_VALUE s_table_name
SELECT
  DECODE(INSTR('&&1','.'),
         0,USER,  /*Default to current user.*/
         UPPER(SUBSTR('&&1',1,INSTR('&&1','.')-1))) owner_name,
  DECODE(INSTR('&&1','.'),
         0,UPPER('&&1'),  /*Only the table name was passed in.*/
         UPPER(SUBSTR('&&1',INSTR('&&1','.')+1))) table_name
  FROM dual;

--Set up the page title, force just one page break by breaking on
--the table name column.
TTITLE LEFT -
       "COLUMN LISTING FOR " s_owner_name '.' s_table_name -
       SKIP 2
BREAK ON table_name SKIP PAGE

--Set up the formats and widths for the columns to be displayed.
COLUMN column_id NOPRINT
COLUMN table_name NOPRINT
COLUMN column_name FORMAT A30 HEADING 'Column Name'
COLUMN data_type FORMAT A17 HEADING 'Data Type'
COLUMN not_null FORMAT A9 HEADING 'Nullable?'

SELECT table_name,
       column_id,
       column_name,
       DECODE (data_type,
         'VARCHAR2','VARCHAR2 (' || TO_CHAR(data_length) || ')',
         'NVARCHAR2','NVARCHAR2 (' || TO_CHAR(data_length) || ')',
         'CHAR','CHAR (' || TO_CHAR(data_length) || ')',
         'NCHAR','NCHAR (' || TO_CHAR(data_length) || ')',
         'NUMBER',
            DECODE (data_precision,
              NULL, 'NUMBER',
               'NUMBER (' || TO_CHAR(data_precision)
                       || ',' || TO_CHAR(data_scale) || ')'),
```

```
              'FLOAT',
                DECODE (data_precision,
                  NULL, 'FLOAT',
                  'FLOAT (' || TO_CHAR(data_precision) || ')'),
              'DATE','DATE',
              'LONG','LONG',
              'LONG RAW','LONG RAW',
              'RAW','RAW (' || TO_CHAR(data_length) || ')',
              'MLSLABEL','MLSLABEL',
              'ROWID','ROWID',
              'CLOB','CLOB',
              'NCLOB','NCLOB',
              'BLOB','BLOB',
              'BFILE','BFILE',
              data_type || ' ???') data_type,
              DECODE (nullable, 'N','NOT NULL') not_null
    FROM all_tab_columns
   WHERE table_name = '&&s_table_name'
     AND owner = '&&s_owner_name'
  ORDER BY column_id;

--Now list any columns with default values defined.
--This is done as a separate select because SQL*Plus
--versions 8.0.3 and 8.0.4 do not handle null LONG
--columns properly.
TTITLE SKIP 2 LEFT -
        "DEFAULT VALUES FOR " s_owner_name '.' s_table_name -
        SKIP 2

COLUMN default_value HEADING 'Default Value' FORMAT A40 WORD_WRAPPED
SELECT table_name,
        column_name,
        data_default default_value
  FROM all_tab_columns
 WHERE table_name = '&&s_table_name'
   AND owner = '&&s_owner_name'
   AND data_default IS NOT NULL
ORDER BY column_id;

--Clean up by undefining variables, clearing break and
--column definitions, and changing all settings back to
--their defaults.
UNDEFINE s_owner_name
UNDEFINE s_table_name

CLEAR BREAKS
CLEAR COLUMNS
TTITLE OFF

SET ECHO OFF
SET VERIFY ON
SET FEEDBACK ON
SET RECSEP WRAPPED
SET HEADING ON
```

```
SET PAGESIZE 14
SET LONG 80
SET LINESIZE 80
```

### Notes about the LIST_COLUMNS script

The first part of the script simply initializes a few settings and clears any previously existing column and break settings. The next part of the script, which is a bit more complex, breaks the first argument up so the owner's name and the table name are in separate substitution variables. The script is intended to be invoked like this:

```
@LIST_COLUMNS [owner.]table_name
```

The first argument, referenced by &&1, will contain a table name that is possibly qualified with an owner name. The first task of the script is to interpret this first argument. The following DECODE statement will return the table owner, if one was specified:

```
DECODE(INSTR('&&1','.'),
       0,USER,  /*Default to current user.*/
       UPPER(SUBSTR('&&1',1,INSTR('&&1','.')-1))) owner_name,
```

If no period is contained in the argument, then no owner name was explicitly specified, and DECODE will call the USER function to return the name of the currently logged on user. If a table owner was specified, the position of the period will be non-zero, causing DECODE to return the value of the last expression, which uses SUBSTR to return all characters before the period as the owner. A similar approach is taken to get the table name:

```
DECODE(INSTR('&&1','.'),
       0,UPPER('&&1'),  /*Only the table name was passed in.*/
       UPPER(SUBSTR('&&1',INSTR('&&1','.')+1))) table_name
```

The issue here is that if a period was specified, the table name follows the period. Otherwise, the entire string is taken as the table name. The table name and owner name are selected from the DUAL table in order to get them into the substitution variables s_table_name and s_owner_name. The NEW_VALUE clause of the COLUMN command makes this happen.

The next part of the script is the SELECT statement, which returns information about each column in the table. The only complicated part of this query is the DECODE statement that starts out like this:

```
DECODE (data_type,
    'VARCHAR2','VARCHAR2 (' || TO_CHAR(data_length) || ')',
    'NVARCHAR2','NVARCHAR2 (' || TO_CHAR(data_length) || ')',
    'CHAR','CHAR (' || TO_CHAR(data_length) || ')',
    'NCHAR','NCHAR (' || TO_CHAR(data_length) || ')',
    'NUMBER',
        DECODE (data_precision,
```

```
                    NULL, 'NUMBER',
                    'NUMBER (' || TO_CHAR(data_precision)
                           || ',' || TO_CHAR(data_scale) || ')'),
      . . .
```

The long DECODE expression exists because some datatypes have a length associated with them, some have a precision and scale, and some have neither. This DECODE statement contains one expression for each possible datatype, and that expression returns the appropriate information for that datatype. Consider the VARCHAR2 datatype, for example. All VARCHAR2 columns have a length associated with them. In order to display that length, the following two expressions are included in the DECODE statement:

```
      'VARCHAR2','VARCHAR2 (' || TO_CHAR(data_length) || ')'
```

The two expressions are separated by commas. The first expression evaluates to the string VARCHAR2. When DECODE is evaluating a datatype that matches that string, it will return the value of the second expression in the pair. In the case of VARCHAR2, that second expression is:

```
      'VARCHAR2 (' || TO_CHAR(data_length) || ')'
```

As you can see, this second expression concatenates the string 'VARCHAR2 (' with the length, then follows that with a closing parentheses. The result will be a string resembling the one shown here:

```
      VARCHAR2 (40)
```

The NUMBER and FLOAT datatypes add a bit more complexity. A NUMBER, for example, can be defined as floating-point or fixed-point. Floating-point numbers have null values for data_precision and data_scale. If a NUMBER field is floating-point, the data_precision will be null, and the nested DECODE will return just "NUMBER" as the datatype. Otherwise, the nested DECODE will return "NUMBER (precision, scale)".

A second SELECT is done to return any default values defined for columns in the table. This is done in a separate query primarily because some versions of SQL*Plus delivered with early versions of Oracle8 (notably 8.0.3) generated errors whenever a LONG column contained a null value. The query in the preceding script avoids this problem by specifying "WHERE data_default IS NOT NULL" in the WHERE clause.

### Running LIST_COLUMNS

To run LIST_COLUMNS, execute the script from SQL*Plus and specify the table name as a command-line argument. You may optionally qualify the table name with an owner by using standard dot notation. The following example shows how to list columns for a table you own.

```
SQL> @list_columns employee

COLUMN LISTING FOR JEFF.EMPLOYEE

Column Name                      Data Type         Nullable?
------------------------------   ----------------  ---------
EMPLOYEE_ID                       NUMBER            NOT NULL
EMPLOYEE_NAME                     VARCHAR2 (40)
EMPLOYEE_HIRE_DATE                DATE
EMPLOYEE_TERMINATION_DATE         DATE
EMPLOYEE_BILLING_RATE             NUMBER

DEFAULT VALUES FOR JEFF.EMPLOYEE

Column Name                      Default Value
------------------------------   ----------------------------------------
EMPLOYEE_HIRE_DATE                sysdate
```

The following example shows how you can look at the column definitions for a table owned by another user, in this case the SYS user:

```
SQL> @list_columns sys.dual

COLUMN LISTING FOR SYS.DUAL

Column Name                      Data Type         Nullable?
------------------------------   ----------------  ---------
DUMMY                             VARCHAR2 (1)
```

# Table Constraints

Information about constraints can be obtained from two data dictionary views: ALL_CONSTRAINTS and ALL_CONS_COLUMNS. ALL_CONSTRAINTS returns one row for each constraint, and is the only view you need to look at for the definition of a check constraint. Foreign key, primary key, and unique constraints are defined on one or more columns, so for these there is a one-to-many relationship between ALL_CONSTRAINTS and ALL_CONS_COLUMNS. Foreign keys are the most complicated, because to get a complete picture of a foreign key constraint, you need to join the ALL_CONS_COLUMNS table to itself, then refer back to the ALL_CONSTRAINTS view again. The reason for this is that a foreign key may be attached to either a primary key constraint or a unique constraint. It's important to know which of the columns in the parent table matter.

## Different Constraint Types Need Different Queries

There are four different types of constraints that can be created on a table. The four types are:

    CHECK
    PRIMARY KEY

UNIQUE
FOREIGN KEY

These types are different enough that, with the exception of the PRIMARY KEY and UNIQUE constraints, you need a slightly different query for each in order to see the definition.

### CHECK constraints

A check constraint is simply an expression that must be true for each row in a table. This is the simplest of the constraint types when it comes to querying the data dictionary tables. The check expression is stored in the SEARCH_CONDITION column of the ALL_CONSTRAINTS table. The following query will get you the definition of all CHECK constraints on a particular table:

```
 SELECT constraint_name, search_condition
   FROM all_constraints
  WHERE owner = 'username'
    AND table_name = 'table_name'
    AND constraint_type ='C'
```

As you can see, the query is very simple. You don't even have to join any tables. With the other constraint types, the query gets more complex.

### PRIMARY KEY and UNIQUE constraints

Primary key and unique constraints are similar in that they both force each row in a table to have a unique value in one column or combination of columns. The only difference between the two is semantics. When looking at constraints of these two types, you need to include the ALL_CONS_COLUMNS view in your query in order to get a list of the columns involved. The following query shows how to do this:

```
SELECT ac.constraint_name, ac.constraint_type,
       ac.table_name, acc.column_name
  FROM all_constraints ac,
       all_cons_columns acc
 WHERE ac.owner = 'username'
   AND ac.table_name = 'table_name'
   AND ac.constraint_type in ('P','U')
   AND ac.constraint_name = acc.constraint_name
   AND ac.owner = acc.owner
ORDER BY ac.constraint_name, acc.position
```

Ordering the columns in the constraint definition by the POSITION column is done so the output matches the column order used when originally defining a constraint. Oracle enforces unique and primary key constraints by creating unique indexes. The column order used when creating the indexes will match that used in defining the constraints, and can affect the performance of queries issued against the table.

*FOREIGN KEY constraints*

Foreign key constraints are the most complex. A foreign key defines a list of columns in one table, called the child table, that correlates to either a primary key or a unique constraint on a parent table. When a row is inserted into the child table, Oracle checks to be sure a corresponding parent record exists. Foreign key constraints involve two lists of columns, one in the child table on which the constraint is defined, and another in the parent table.

The trick with foreign key constraints is to first find the name of the parent table, then find the names of the columns in the parent table that correspond to the columns in the child table. The key to doing this is to use the R_OWNER and R_CONSTRAINT_NAME columns in the ALL_CONSTRAINTS table. The constraint type code for foreign key constraints is "R". A foreign key always relates to either a primary key constraint or a unique constraint on the parent table. The name of this related constraint will be in the R_CONSTRAINT_NAME column. Usually, the R_OWNER column will match the OWNER column, but that doesn't have to be the case.

To see the definition of all the foreign key constraints for a given table, you can start with the query used for primary key constraints, and modify it to look only at constraint type 'R':

```
SELECT ac.constraint_name, ac.constraint_type,
       ac.owner, ac.table_name, acc.column_name
  FROM all_constraints ac,
       all_cons_columns acc
 WHERE ac.owner = 'username'
   AND ac.table_name = 'table_name'
   AND ac.constraint_type = 'R'
   AND ac.constraint_name = acc.constraint_name
   AND ac.owner = acc.owner
 ORDER BY ac.constraint_name, acc.position
```

This will give you the constraint name, the table name, and a list of column names. It won't tell you the name of the parent table or the names of the corresponding columns in that table. For that, you need to join ALL_CONSTRAINTS to itself via the R_CONSTRAINT_NAME and R_OWNER columns. This will give you access to the parent table's name.

```
SELECT ac.constraint_name, ac.constraint_type,
       ac.owner, ac.table_name, acc.column_name,
       r_ac.owner, r_ac.table_name
  FROM all_constraints ac,
       all_cons_columns acc,
       all_constraints r_ac
 WHERE ac.owner = 'username'
   AND ac.table_name = 'table_name'
   AND ac.constraint_type = 'R'
```

```
      AND ac.constraint_name = acc.constraint_name
      AND ac.owner = acc.owner
      AND ac.r_owner = r_ac.owner
      AND ac.r_constraint_name = r_ac.constraint_name
  ORDER BY ac.constraint_name, acc.position
```

Since most foreign key constraints relate to the parent table's primary key, you may want to just stop here. However, since it is possible to relate a foreign key to a unique key on the parent table, you may want see the corresponding list of parent table columns in order to fully understand the constraint. To do this, you must join with ALL_CONS_COLUMNS once again and pick up the columns that go with the related parent table constraint. For example:

```
SELECT ac.constraint_name, ac.constraint_type,
       ac.owner, ac.table_name, acc.column_name,
       r_ac.owner, r_ac.table_name,r_acc.column_name
  FROM all_constraints ac,
       all_cons_columns acc,
       all_constraints r_ac,
       all_cons_columns r_acc
 WHERE   ac.owner = 'username'
   AND ac.table_name = 'table_name'
   AND ac.constraint_type = 'R'
   AND ac.owner = acc.owner
   AND ac.constraint_name = acc.constraint_name
   AND ac.r_owner = r_ac.owner
   AND ac.r_constraint_name = r_ac.constraint_name
   AND r_ac.owner = r_acc.owner
   AND r_ac.constraint_name = r_acc.constraint_name
   AND acc.position = r_acc.position
 ORDER BY ac.constraint_name, acc.position
```

Notice that the ALL_CONS_COLUMN table's POSITION column forms part of the join criteria. This ensures that matching columns are output together, on the same line. You will see how this works in the next section, which presents a script that will list all constraints defined for a table.

## Listing the Constraints for a Table

With the three queries shown in the previous section, you have a good start on a script to show all constraints defined on a table. Start by putting the three queries in a script, then qualify each with a table name. Use a substitution variable for the table name so you can pass it to the script as a parameter. Next, format the results with some combination of the COLUMN, BREAK, and TTITLE commands. The LIST_CONSTRAINTS script, shown next, shows one possible approach you can take.

## The LIST_CONSTRAINTS.SQL script

```
--DESCRIPTION
--List all the constraints on a table.
--
--INPUTS
-- Param 1   A table name, optionally qualified
--              by an owner name.
--              For example: "SYS.ALL_TAB_COLUMNS".
--
SET ECHO OFF
SET NEWPAGE 1
SET VERIFY OFF
SET FEEDBACK OFF
SET HEADING OFF
SET PAGESIZE 9999
SET RECSEP OFF
SET CONCAT ON
CLEAR BREAKS
CLEAR COMPUTES
CLEAR COLUMNS
TTITLE OFF
BTITLE OFF

--Dissect the input argument, and get the owner name and
--table name into two seperate substitution variables.
--The owner name defaults to the current user.
DEFINE s_owner_name = ' '
DEFINE s_table_name = ' '
COLUMN owner_name NOPRINT NEW_VALUE s_owner_name
COLUMN table_name NOPRINT NEW_VALUE s_table_name
SELECT
   DECODE(INSTR('&&1','.'),
         0,USER,   /*Default to current user.*/
         UPPER(SUBSTR('&&1',1,INSTR('&&1','.')-1))) owner_name,
   DECODE(INSTR('&&1','.'),
         0,UPPER('&&1'),   /*Only the table name was passed in.*/
         UPPER(SUBSTR('&&1',INSTR('&&1','.')+1))) table_name
   FROM dual;

--Clear column definitions so that no future queries
--affect the substitution variables that were just set.
CLEAR COLUMNS

--Format the columns
COLUMN constraint_name NOPRINT NEW_VALUE constraint_name_var
COLUMN constraint_type_desc NOPRINT NEW_VALUE constraint_type_var
COLUMN r_owner NOPRINT NEW_VALUE r_owner_var
COLUMN r_table_name NOPRINT NEW_VALUE r_table_name_var
COLUMN status NOPRINT NEW_VALUE status_var
COLUMN delete_rule_desc NOPRINT NEW_VALUE delete_rule_var
COLUMN search_condition FORMAT A50 WORD_WRAPPED
COLUMN column_name FORMAT A30
COLUMN r_column_name FORMAT A30
```

```
--This script breaks on each constraint, and each constraint
--has its own page title. The page title shows information
--relating to the constraint as a whole.
BREAK ON constraint_name SKIP PAGE

--Tell the user he is going to see constraints.
PROMPT CONSTRAINTS ON TABLE &&s_owner_name..&&s_table_name

--First show the primary key and unique constraints.
--
--Set up the page title.
TTITLE LEFT '    ' constraint_name_var ' ' constraint_type_var -
       ' ' status_var SKIP 1

--Run the query to display primary key and unique constraints.
SELECT ac.constraint_name,
       DECODE(ac.constraint_type,
              'P','PRIMARY KEY','U','UNIQUE') constraint_type_desc,
       ' ' table_name,
       '        ' indent,
       acc.column_name,
       ac.status
  FROM all_constraints ac,
       all_cons_columns acc
 WHERE ac.owner='&&s_owner_name'
   AND ac.table_name = '&&s_table_name'
   AND ac.owner = acc.owner
   AND ac.constraint_name = acc.constraint_name
   AND ac.constraint_type IN ('P','U')
ORDER BY DECODE(ac.constraint_type,'P',1,'U',2),
         ac.constraint_name,
         acc.position;

--Then show the foreign key constraints
--
--Set up the page title for the foreign key constraints
TTITLE LEFT '    ' constraint_name_var ' ' status_var SKIP 1 -
       '    FOREIGN KEY TO ' r_owner_var '.' r_table_name_var SKIP 1

--Run the query to show foreign key constraints
SELECT ac.constraint_name,
       '        ' indent,
       acc.column_name,
       r_acc.owner r_owner,
       r_acc.table_name r_table_name,
       r_acc.column_name r_column_name
  FROM all_constraints ac,
       all_cons_columns acc,
       all_cons_columns r_acc
 WHERE ac.owner='&&s_owner_name'
   and ac.table_name = '&&s_table_name'
   AND ac.constraint_type = 'R'
   AND ac.owner = acc.owner
```

```
      AND ac.constraint_name = acc.constraint_name
      AND ac.r_owner = r_acc.owner
      AND ac.r_constraint_name = r_acc.constraint_name
      AND acc.position = r_acc.position
 ORDER BY ac.constraint_name, acc.position;

 --Then show the check constraints
 --
 --Set up the page title for the check constraints
 TTITLE LEFT '    ' constraint_name_var ' CHECK ' status_var SKIP 1

 SELECT ac.constraint_name,
        '        ' indent,
        search_condition
   FROM all_constraints ac
  WHERE ac.owner = '&&s_owner_name'
    AND ac.table_name = '&&s_table_name'
    AND ac.constraint_type = 'C';

 --Undefine variables and restore settings to their defaults.
 UNDEFINE s_owner_name
 UNDEFINE s_table_name

 SET NEWPAGE 1
 SET VERIFY ON
 SET FEEDBACK ON
 SET HEADING ON
 SET PAGESIZE 14
 SET RECSEP WRAPPED
 CLEAR BREAKS
 CLEAR COMPUTES
 CLEAR COLUMNS
 TTITLE OFF
```

### Running the LIST_CONSTRAINTS script

You can show all the constraints on a table by invoking the LIST_CONSTRAINTS script and providing the table name as the first argument. The following example shows the constraints defined on the PROJECT_HOURS table:

```
SQL> @list_constraints project_hours


CONSTRAINTS ON TABLE JEFF.PROJECT_HOURS

    PROJECT_HOURS_PK PRIMARY KEY ENABLED
          PROJECT_ID
          EMPLOYEE_ID
          TIME_LOG_DATE

    PROJECT_HOURS_UNIQUE UNIQUE ENABLED
          PROJECT_ID
          EMPLOYEE_ID
          TIME_LOG_DATE
          HOURS_LOGGED
          DOLLARS_CHARGED
```

```
PROJ_HOURS_FKTO_EMPLOYEE ENABLED
FOREIGN KEY TO JEFF.EMPLOYEE
     EMPLOYEE_ID                      EMPLOYEE_ID

PROJ_HOURS_FKTO_PROJECT ENABLED
FOREIGN KEY TO JEFF.PROJECT
     PROJECT_ID                       PROJECT_ID

HOURS_LOGGED_MUST_BE_INT CHECK ENABLED
     hours_logged = trunc(hours_logged)
```

# Indexes

Two views return information about indexes. Each index gets an entry in the ALL_INDEXES view, and the ALL_IND_COLUMNS view returns the columns included in each index.

## Listing Indexes for a Table

The problem of listing indexes for a table is much the same as that of listing constraints on a table. You have a master-detail relationship between the index and its columns, and you may have multiple indexes on one table. There are two approaches you can take. One approach is to write a script that describes one particular index, while the other is to write a script that lists all indexes on a table.

The tradeoff between these two approaches is that one lets you look at indexes by name, while the other lets you look at indexes by table. The problem is that you probably need both ways. Sometimes, as when a unique index is violated, you do need to look up an index by name. Other times, you just want to see what indexes have been defined on a particular table.

One thing to keep in mind when working with unique indexes is that Oracle will report a unique index violation as if it were a constraint violation. The error message you get is the same as the one used when you violate a unique constraint, and it looks like this:

```
ORA-00001: unique constraint (JEFF.UNIQUE_BILLING_RATE) violated
```

The reason for this is no doubt because Oracle enforces both unique and primary key constraints by creating indexes on the constrained fields. If you do get the error message just shown, there are two things you might want to check. First, list the constraints on the table you are updating. If you don't find one with a name that matches the one in the error message, check to see if there happens to be a unique index with that same name. The SHOW_INDEX script in the next section will help you do this.

Beginning with Oracle8i, it is possible to define a unique or primary key constraint without having a corresponding index created.

## Index Scripts

Since the previous section, "Table Constraints," showed you how to write one script to list all constraints, let's take the opposite approach this time and write a script that describes just one index. Following that, I'll show how you can expand on that first script by writing a second script that does list indexes by table. You *can* have it both ways.

### The SHOW_INDEX.SQL script

Shown below is a SQL*Plus script that describes just one index. The first part of the script resembles the other scripts shown in this chapter. It looks at the input argument to see whether or not it was qualified by an owner name, defaults it to the current user's userid if necessary, then stores the results in the substitution variables s_owner_name and s_index_name. Next, a SELECT is done on the ALL_ INDEXES table to retrieve information that is not column-specific about the index into a set of substitution variables. These substitution variables are then used to define the page title. So far, nothing has been displayed to the user. Finally, the index columns themselves are selected, causing the page title to print.

If the index does not exist, no columns will be selected and the page title will not be printed. The result will be that there is no output for the user to see. To avoid leaving the user in doubt about why there is no output, an extra SELECT is done to cover this case. This final SELECT statement only succeeds if the index does not exist, and it outputs a message informing the user that is the case.

The last thing the script does is reset anything it changed back to the default values. Here is the script:

```
--DESCRIPTION
--Displays information about an index. The index name
--is passed as a parameter to this script.
--
--INPUTS
--   param 1   Name of the index to be described.
--
SET ECHO OFF
SET RECSEP OFF
SET NEWPAGE NONE
```

```
SET VERIFY OFF
SET PAGESIZE 9999
SET HEADING OFF
SET LINESIZE 80
SET FEEDBACK OFF
CLEAR COMPUTES
CLEAR COLUMNS
CLEAR BREAKS

--Turn off terminal output to avoid spurious blank lines
--caused by the SELECTS that are done only to load the
--substitution variables.
SET TERMOUT OFF

--Dissect the input argument, and get the owner name and
--table name into two separate substitution variables.
--The owner name defaults to the current user.
DEFINE s_owner_name = ' '
DEFINE s_index_name = ' '
COLUMN owner_name NOPRINT NEW_VALUE s_owner_name
COLUMN index_name NOPRINT NEW_VALUE s_index_name
SELECT
  DECODE(INSTR('&&1','.'),
         0,USER,  /*Default to current user.*/
         UPPER(SUBSTR('&&1',1,INSTR('&&1','.')-1))) owner_name,
  DECODE(INSTR('&&1','.'),
         0,UPPER('&&1'),  /*Only the index name was passed in.*/
         UPPER(SUBSTR('&&1',INSTR('&&1','.')+1))) index_name
  FROM dual;

--Retrieve information about the index as a whole.
DEFINE s_table_owner
DEFINE s_table_name
DEFINE s_index_type
DEFINE s_uniqueness
DEFINE s_tablespace_name
COLUMN table_owner NOPRINT NEW_VALUE s_table_owner
COLUMN table_name NOPRINT NEW_VALUE s_table_name
COLUMN index_type NOPRINT NEW_VALUE s_index_type
COLUMN uniqueness NOPRINT NEW_VALUE s_uniqueness
COLUMN tablespace_name NOPRINT NEW_VALUE s_tablespace_name
SELECT table_owner, table_name, index_type, uniqueness, tablespace_name
  FROM all_indexes
 WHERE owner = '&&s_owner_name'
   AND index_name = '&&s_index_name';

--Information about the index as a whole is printed in
--the page title.
TTITLE SKIP 1 LEFT 'INDEX ' &&s_owner_name..&&s_index_name -
       ' ' &&s_index_type ' ' &&s_uniqueness SKIP 1 -
       'DEFINED ON TABLE ' &&s_table_owner..&s_table_name SKIP 1 -
       'STORED IN TABLESPACE ' &&s_tablespace_name SKIP 1 -
       'CONTAINING COLUMNS: '
```

```
--List the columns that make up the index.
--The indent column moves the column list over to the
--right so that it comes after the 'CONTAINING COLUMNS:'
--portion of the header.
SET TERMOUT ON
COLUMN indent FORMAT A19
COLUMN column_name FORMAT A30
SELECT ' ' indent,
       column_name
  FROM all_ind_columns
 WHERE index_owner = '&&s_owner_name'
   AND index_name = '&&s_index_name'
ORDER BY column_position;

--Spit out an error message if the index does not exist.
TTITLE SKIP 1
SELECT 'Index &&s_owner_name..&&s_table_name does not exist.'
  FROM DUAL
 WHERE NOT EXISTS (
                   SELECT *
                     FROM all_indexes
                    WHERE owner = '&&s_owner_name'
                      AND index_name = '&&s_index_name'
                  );

--Change all settings back to defaults
CLEAR COLUMNS
CLEAR BREAKS
UNDEFINE s_owner_name
UNDEFINE s_index_name
UNDEFINE s_index_type
UNDEFINE s_uniqueness
UNDEFINE s_tablespace_name
SET PAGESIZE 14
SET HEADING ON
SET NEWPAGE 1
SET FEEDBACK ON
```

### Running the SHOW_INDEX script

To describe an index, simply invoke SHOW_INDEX and pass the index name as a parameter. Here's an example:

```
SQL> @show_index project_hours_pk

INDEX JEFF.PROJECT_HOURS_PK NORMAL UNIQUE
DEFINED ON TABLE JEFF.PROJECT_HOURS
STORED IN TABLESPACE USERS
CONTAINING COLUMNS:
                    PROJECT_ID
                    EMPLOYEE_ID
                    TIME_LOG_DATE
```

If the specified index does not exist, you will get a message telling you that. For example:

```
SQL> @show_index this_does_not_exist

Index JEFF.THIS_DOES_NOT_EXIST does not exist.
```

Next you will see how you can write another script that uses SHOW_INDEX to describe all the indexes on a table.

### The LIST_INDEXES.SQL script

You now have a script that describes one specific index. If you wanted to describe all the indexes for a particular table, the obvious solution would be to run SHOW_ INDEX for each of those indexes. The only thing that makes this at all difficult is that SQL*Plus has no built-in looping construct.

You can't just write a simple loop to display each index for a table. However, you do have a view, the ALL_INDEXES view, from which you can select the names of all the indexes on a table. Instead of selecting just the index names, it's not too big a leap to select an expression such as this:

```
SELECT '@SHOW_INDEX ' || owner || '.' || index_name
```

Executing a SELECT such as the previous one against the ALL_INDEXES view results in output that looks like this:

```
@SHOW_INDEX JEFF.PROJECT_HOURS_PK
@SHOW_INDEX JEFF.PROJECT_HOURS_UNIQUE
```

Using the SPOOL command, you can send this output to a file, which will then contain commands to describe each index on a table. Then you execute that file. The following *LIST_INDEXES.SQL* script does this:

```
--DESCRIPTION
--Describe all the indexes that are defined on
--the specified table.
--
--INPUTS
--  param 1   The table name, optionally qualified by
--            an owner name using the standard dot notation.
--
SET ECHO OFF
SET TERMOUT OFF
SET FEEDBACK OFF
SET VERIFY OFF
CLEAR COLUMNS

--Dissect the input argument, and get the owner name and
--table name into two separate substitution variables.
--The owner name defaults to the current user.
DEFINE s_owner_name = ' '
```

```
DEFINE s_table_name = ' '
COLUMN owner_name NOPRINT NEW_VALUE s_owner_name
COLUMN table_name NOPRINT NEW_VALUE s_table_name
SELECT
  DECODE(INSTR('&&1','.'),
         0,USER,   /*Default to current user.*/
         UPPER(SUBSTR('&&1',1,INSTR('&&1','.')-1))) owner_name,
  DECODE(INSTR('&&1','.'),
         0,UPPER('&&1'),   /*Only the table name was passed in.*/
         UPPER(SUBSTR('&&1',INSTR('&&1','.')+1))) table_name
  FROM dual;

--
--Create a file of commands that will use the SHOW_INDEX script
--to describe each index defined on the table.
SET PAGESIZE 0
SET HEADING OFF
SPOOL list_indexes_1.sql

--Generate the show index commands.
SELECT '@SHOW_INDEX ' || owner || '.' || index_name
  FROM all_indexes
 WHERE table_owner = '&&s_owner_name'
   AND table_name = '&&s_table_name';

--Generate an error message if the table does not exist.
SELECT 'PROMPT Table &&s_owner_name..&&s_table_name does not exist.'
  FROM DUAL
 WHERE NOT EXISTS (
                   SELECT *
                     FROM all_tables
                    WHERE owner = '&&s_owner_name'
                      AND table_name = '&&s_table_name'
                  );

--Generate a message if no indexes at all exist for the table.
SELECT 'PROMPT Table &&s_owner_name..&&s_table_name has no indexes defined.'
  FROM all_tables
 WHERE owner = '&&s_owner_name'
   AND table_name = '&&s_table_name'
   AND NOT EXISTS (
                   SELECT *
                     FROM all_indexes
                    WHERE table_owner = '&&s_owner_name'
                      AND table_name = '&&s_table_name'
                  );

SPOOL OFF

--Reset everything back to its default.
SET PAGESIZE 14
SET TERMOUT ON
SET FEEDBACK ON
SET VERIFY ON
```

```
CLEAR COLUMNS

--Tell the user what she is going to see.
PROMPT
PROMPT INDEXES DEFINED ON TABLE &&s_owner_name..&&s_table_name

--Execute the script that was just created to
--display all the indexes on the table.
@list_indexes_1
```

This script builds a file named *LIST_INDEXES_1*, which runs the SHOW_INDEX script for each index on the specified table. There are two extra SELECTs to cover the cases where the table does not exist, or where there are no indexes defined on the table. This file is then executed in order to display information about each of the table's indexes.

### Running the LIST_INDEXES.SQL script

Here's what it looks like to run the LIST_INDEXES script on the PROJECT_HOURS table:

```
SQL> @list_indexes project_hours

INDEXES DEFINED ON TABLE JEFF.PROJECT_HOURS

INDEX JEFF.PROJECT_HOURS_UNIQUE NORMAL UNIQUE
DEFINED ON TABLE JEFF.PROJECT_HOURS
STORED IN TABLESPACE USERS
CONTAINING COLUMNS:
                PROJECT_ID
                EMPLOYEE_ID
                TIME_LOG_DATE
                HOURS_LOGGED
                DOLLARS_CHARGED

INDEX JEFF.PROJECT_HOURS_PK NORMAL UNIQUE
DEFINED ON TABLE JEFF.PROJECT_HOURS
STORED IN TABLESPACE USERS
CONTAINING COLUMNS:
                PROJECT_ID
                EMPLOYEE_ID
                TIME_LOG_DATE
```

As you can see, information about each index on the PROJECT_HOURS table is displayed. The next two examples show the results of running LIST_INDEXES with an invalid table name and for a table that does not have any indexes:

```
SQL> @list_indexes bad_table_name

INDEXES DEFINED ON TABLE JEFF.BAD_TABLE_NAME
Table JEFF.BAD_TABLE_NAME does not exist.
SQL>
SQL> @list_indexes x
```

```
INDEXES DEFINED ON TABLE JEFF.X
Table JEFF.X has no indexes defined.
```

# Triggers

Information about triggers can be retrieved from two views, the ALL_TRIGGERS view and the ALL_TRIGGER_COLS view. Most of the time you will be able to find all the information you need in ALL_TRIGGERS. The ALL_TRIGGER_COLS view contains a list of all database columns referenced in the trigger. This view is sometimes useful when you are troubleshooting because it can quickly show you which triggers reference or modify any given database column.

## Looking at Trigger Definitions

Retrieving the definition of a trigger from the database actually turns out to be quite easy compared to the effort you go through to see indexes and constraints. Mostly this is because you don't have a master/detail relationship to deal with—everything you need is in the ALL_TRIGGERS view. The DESCRIPTION field Oracle includes in the view helps a lot too. Everything you need to see is in just four columns.

There are just a couple of caveats you need to be aware of when looking at the ALL_TRIGGERS view. The first is that the format of the data in the DESCRIPTION and TRIGGER_BODY fields comes from the original CREATE TRIGGER statement. This can lead to some minor inconsistencies from one trigger to the next, depending on where the line breaks occur and whether the CREATE TRIGGER statement was entered in upper- or lowercase. There's also no guarantee that lines of code in the trigger body won't exceed your line length. For that reason, I usually set line length fairly high when I look at a trigger.

The second caveat is that the WHEN clause is returned as one long line in the WHEN_CLAUSE field, regardless of whether or not it was on one line in the original CREATE TRIGGER statement. Neither of these issues presents any great problem. It just helps to be aware of them.

## Trigger Scripts

The following sections describe scripts that will let you list trigger definitions.

### The SHOW_TRIGGER.SQL script

The following script shows the definition and code for a trigger on a table. Note the use of FOLD_BEFORE in the COLUMN commands. This results in the four columns printing vertically, one after the other, instead of the more usual horizontal format. The result makes for a very readable display of the trigger definition.

```
--DESCRIPTION
--This script lists the definition of the specified trigger.
--
--USAGE
--          @SHOW_TRIGGER [owner.]trigger_name
--

SET ECHO OFF
SET HEADING OFF
SET RECSEP OFF
SET NEWPAGE 1
SET VERIFY OFF
SET FEEDBACK OFF
SET PAGESIZE 0
SET LONG 10000
SET LINESIZE 80
--Dissect the input argument, and get the owner name and
--table name into two separate substitution variables.
--The owner name defaults to the current user.
DEFINE s_owner_name = ' '
DEFINE s_trigger_name = ' '
COLUMN owner_name NOPRINT NEW_VALUE s_owner_name
COLUMN trigger_name NOPRINT NEW_VALUE s_trigger_name
SELECT
  DECODE(INSTR('&&1','.'),
        0,USER,  /*Default to current user.*/
        UPPER(SUBSTR('&&1',1,INSTR('&&1','.')-1))) owner_name,
  DECODE(INSTR('&&1','.'),
        0,UPPER('&&1'),  /*Only the table name was passed in.*/
        UPPER(SUBSTR('&&1',INSTR('&&1','.')+1))) trigger_name
  FROM dual;

--Set up the formats
COLUMN description FORMAT A60 WORD_WRAPPED
COLUMN referencing_names FORMAT A60 WORD_WRAPPED FOLD_BEFORE
COLUMN when_clause FORMAT A60 WORD_WRAPPED FOLD_BEFORE
COLUMN trigger_body FORMAT A80 WRAPPED FOLD_BEFORE

SELECT 'TRIGGER ' || '&&s_owner_name..' ||
       RTRIM(description) description,
       RTRIM(referencing_names) referencing_names,
       'WHEN ' || when_clause when_clause,
       trigger_body
  FROM all_triggers
 WHERE owner = '&&s_owner_name'
   AND trigger_name = '&&s_trigger_name';

--Reset everything back to its default setting
TTITLE OFF
SET HEADING ON
SET RECSEP WRAPPED
```

```
SET VERIFY ON
SET FEEDBACK ON
SET PAGESIZE 24
SET LONG 80
CLEAR BREAKS
CLEAR COLUMNS
```

### Running the SHOW_TRIGGER.SQL script

Here are the results of executing the SHOW_TRIGGER script to see the definition of a trigger named TEST_1:

```
SQL> @show_trigger emp_hire_date_check

TRIGGER JEFF.emp_hire_date_check
BEFORE INSERT OR UPDATE ON employee
FOR EACH ROW
REFERENCING NEW AS NEW OLD AS OLD
WHEN
BEGIN
  IF :NEW.employee_hire_date < TRUNC(SYSDATE - 30) THEN
  RAISE_APPLICATION_ERROR (-20000,'An employee''s hire date may only be
  backdated 30 days, and not more.');
  END IF;
END;
```

### The LIST_TRIGGERS.SQL script

Instead of looking at one specific trigger, you may want to look at all the triggers that are defined on a specific table. It turns out that you can readily do this with only two slight modifications to the SHOW_TRIGGER script. One is to interpret the first argument as a table name, not a trigger name. The other is to use the table name in the WHERE clause of the SELECT statement. The following script will list all the triggers defined on a table:

```
--DESCRIPTION
--This script lists the definition of the specified trigger.
--
--USAGE
--        @LIST_TRIGGERS [owner.]table_name
--

SET ECHO OFF
SET HEADING OFF
SET RECSEP OFF
SET NEWPAGE 1
SET VERIFY OFF
SET FEEDBACK OFF
SET PAGESIZE 0
SET LONG 10000
SET LINESIZE 80
--Dissect the input argument, and get the owner name and
--table name into two separate substitution variables.
```

```
--The owner name defaults to the current user.
DEFINE s_owner_name = ' '
DEFINE s_table_name = ' '
COLUMN owner_name NOPRINT NEW_VALUE s_owner_name
COLUMN table_name NOPRINT NEW_VALUE s_table_name
SELECT
  DECODE(INSTR('&&1','.'),
         0,USER,  /*Default to current user.*/
         UPPER(SUBSTR('&&1',1,INSTR('&&1','.')-1))) owner_name,
  DECODE(INSTR('&&1','.'),
         0,UPPER('&&1'),  /*Only the table name was passed in.*/
         UPPER(SUBSTR('&&1',INSTR('&&1','.')+1))) table_name
  FROM dual;

--Set up the formats
COLUMN description FORMAT A60 WORD_WRAPPED
COLUMN referencing_names FORMAT A60 WORD_WRAPPED FOLD_BEFORE
COLUMN when_clause FORMAT A60 WORD_WRAPPED FOLD_BEFORE
COLUMN trigger_body FORMAT A80 WRAPPED FOLD_BEFORE

SELECT 'TRIGGER ' || '&&s_owner_name..' ||
       RTRIM(description) description,
       RTRIM(referencing_names) referencing_names,
       'WHEN ' || when_clause when_clause,
       trigger_body
  FROM all_triggers
 WHERE owner = '&&s_owner_name'
   AND table_name = '&&s_table_name';

--Reset everything back to its default setting
TTITLE OFF
SET HEADING ON
SET RECSEP WRAPPED
SET VERIFY ON
SET FEEDBACK ON
SET PAGESIZE 24
SET LONG 80
CLEAR BREAKS
CLEAR COLUMNS
```

### Running the LIST_TRIGGERS script

The following are the results of running the LIST_TRIGGERS script on a table that happens to have two triggers defined.

```
SQL> @list_triggers employee

TRIGGER JEFF.emp_delete_check
BEFORE DELETE ON employee
FOR EACH ROW
REFERENCING NEW AS NEW OLD AS OLD
WHEN
BEGIN
  IF (:OLD.employee_termination_date IS NULL)
```

```
        OR (:OLD.employee_termination_date >= TRUNC(SYSDATE)+1)
    THEN
            RAISE_APPLICATION_ERROR (-20001,'You must terminate an employee
            before deleting his record.');
    END IF;
END;

TRIGGER JEFF.emp_hire_date_check
BEFORE INSERT OR UPDATE ON employee
FOR EACH ROW
REFERENCING NEW AS NEW OLD AS OLD
WHEN
BEGIN
    IF :NEW.employee_hire_date < TRUNC(SYSDATE - 30) THEN
        RAISE_APPLICATION_ERROR (-20000,'An employee''s hire date may only be
        backdated 30 days, and not more.');
    END IF;
END;
```

# Synonyms

A *synonym* is an alternate name for a table. By coding your programs to use synonyms instead of table names, you insulate yourself from any changes in the name, ownership, or location of those tables. All of the scripts in this chapter have actually used synonyms instead of table names. ALL_TABLES, for example, is actually a public synonym for the SYS.ALL_TABLES table.

## Looking at Synonyms

To look at a synonym, you just select information from ALL_SYNONYMS for the synonym you are interested in. The following SELECT is an example:

```
SELECT *
  FROM all_synonyms
 WHERE synonym_owner = 'username'
   AND synonym_name = 'synonym_name'
```

So far, so good. However, there are two types of synonyms: public and private. Synonyms owned by a user are private synonyms and affect only that user. Public synonyms are owned by PUBLIC and affect all database users. If you are interested in a specific synonym, you probably also want to know if both public and private versions exist. Because of that, you might modify your query to look like this:

```
SELECT *
  FROM all_synonyms
 WHERE synonym_owner = 'username'
   AND synonym_name = 'synonym_name'
UNION
SELECT *
```

```
    FROM all_synonyms
  WHERE synonym_owner = 'PUBLIC'
    AND synonym_name = 'synonym_name'
```

Now you will see both synonym types, which is helpful in detecting cases where a private synonym conflicts with a public synonym. Private synonyms override public synonym definitions, so it's important to know when both types exist.

## Synonym Scripts

The following sections describe scripts that will let you list synonym definitions.

### The SHOW_SYN.SQL script

The following SQL*Plus script lists the definition of the synonym that you specify as an argument. If a matching public synonym exists, it will be listed as well. The results are sorted by owner and synonym name, and the owner column is decoded in such a way as to make PUBLIC sort first.

```
--DESCRIPTION
--This script displays the definition of a synonym.
--
--USAGE
--       @SHOW_SYN [owner.]synonym_name
--
SET ECHO OFF
SET VERIFY OFF
SET FEEDBACK OFF

--Dissect the input argument, and get the owner name and
--synonym name into two separate substitution variables.
--The owner name defaults to the current user.
SET TERMOUT OFF
DEFINE s_owner_name = ' '
DEFINE s_synonym_name = ' '
COLUMN owner_name NOPRINT NEW_VALUE s_owner_name
COLUMN synonym_name NOPRINT NEW_VALUE s_synonym_name
SELECT
  DECODE(INSTR('&&1','.'),
        0,USER,  /*Default to current user.*/
        UPPER(SUBSTR('&&1',1,INSTR('&&1','.')-1))) owner_name,
  DECODE(INSTR('&&1','.'),
        0,UPPER('&&1'),  /*Only the table name was passed in.*/
        UPPER(SUBSTR('&&1',INSTR('&&1','.')+1))) synonym_name
  FROM dual;
CLEAR COLUMNS
SET TERMOUT ON

--Display information about the synonym
--Information is displayed in three lines to accommodate the
--longest possible values for each data element.
--The matching public synonym, if one exists, is
```

```
--always shown as well.
SET HEADING OFF
SET NEWPAGE NONE
SET PAGESIZE 0
SET RECSEP OFF
SET LINESIZE 80
COLUMN owner NOPRINT
COLUMN synonym_name NOPRINT
COLUMN syn_def FORMAT A80 word_wrapped
PROMPT
SELECT DECODE(owner,'PUBLIC','1' || owner,'2' || owner) owner,
       synonym_name,
       owner || '.' || synonym_name
       || ' synonym for ' || table_owner || '.' || table_name
       || DECODE(db_link,NULL,NULL,CHR(10) || 'at ' || db_link) syn_def
  FROM all_synonyms
 WHERE owner = '&&s_owner_name'
   AND synonym_name = '&&s_synonym_name'
UNION
SELECT DECODE(owner,'PUBLIC','1' || owner,'2' || owner) owner,
       synonym_name,
       synonym_name
       || ' PUBLIC synonym for ' || table_owner || '.' || table_name
       || DECODE(db_link,NULL,NULL,CHR(10) || 'at ' || db_link) syn_def
  FROM all_synonyms
 WHERE owner = 'PUBLIC'
   AND synonym_name = '&&s_synonym_name'
ORDER BY owner,synonym_name;

--Reset everything back to its default.
CLEAR COLUMNS
UNDEFINE s_owner_name
UNDEFINE s_synonym_name
SET HEADING ON
SET NEWPAGE 1
SET PAGESIZE 14
SET VERIFY ON
SET RECSEP WRAPPED
SET FEEDBACK ON
```

### Running the SHOW_SYN.SQL script

Here are the results of executing the SHOW_SYN script to describe the ALL_TABLES synonym:

```
SQL> @show_syn all_tables

ALL_TABLES PUBLIC synonym for SYS.ALL_TABLES
JEFF.ALL_TABLES synonym for SYS.ALL_TABLES
```

As you can see, ALL_TABLES is a public synonym pointing to SYS.ALL_TABLES. In this case, the current user has a private synonym of the same name. This private synonym also points to SYS.ALL_TABLES.

### The LIST_SYN script

In addition to seeing the definition for one synonym, you may also want to see all synonyms owned by a particular user. The following script will let you do that:

```
--DESCRIPTION
--List synonyms owned by the current user, or owned by a specified user.
--The user is prompted for an owner name. If an owner is not specified,
--i.e., the user just presses ENTER, then synonyms are listed for
--the current user.

SET ECHO OFF
SET FEEDBACK OFF
SET VERIFY OFF
SET DEFINE ON
SET HEADING OFF

--Ask the user for the owner.
ACCEPT username CHAR PROMPT 'List synonyms for user: '
PROMPT

--Set up the title to print the owner.
TTITLE LEFT 'SYNONYMS OWNED BY: ' owner SKIP 1
COLUMN owner NOPRINT NEW_VALUE owner

   --List synonyms owned by the user specified
   --Information is displayed in three lines to accommodate the
   --longest possible values for each data element.
   COLUMN owner NOPRINT
   COLUMN synonym_name NOPRINT
   COLUMN db_link FORMAT A60 WRAPPED
   PROMPT
   SELECT owner,
          synonym_name,
          '       ' || owner || '.' || synonym_name
          || ' synonym for ' || table_owner || '.' || table_name
          || DECODE(db_link,NULL,NULL,CHR(10) || 'at ' || db_link) syn_def
      FROM all_synonyms
    WHERE owner = DECODE('&&username',NULL,USER,UPPER('&&username'))
    ORDER BY synonym_name;

--Clean up: undefine vars, clear columns, change settings back to defaults.
UNDEFINE username
UNDEFINE owner
COLUMN owner CLEAR
TTITLE OFF
SET HEADING ON
SET FEEDBACK ON
SET VERIFY ON
```

One thing you should be aware of when looking at synonyms is that unless you are the database administrator, you won't really be able to look at all synonyms owned by other users. The ALL_SYNONYMS view shows you three types of synonyms:

- Public synonyms (owned by PUBLIC)
- Synonyms you own
- Synonyms owned by other users that reference tables and other objects to which you have access

The only time the ALL_SYNONYMS view would show you all the synonyms in the database would be if you happened to have access to all the objects in the database.

### Running the LIST_SYN.SQL script

Here is a sample execution of the LIST_SYN script that shows all the public synonyms:

```
SQL> @list_syn
List tables for user: public

SYNONYMS OWNED BY: PUBLIC
        PUBLIC.ALL_ALL_TABLES synonym for SYS.ALL_ALL_TABLES
        PUBLIC.ALL_ARGUMENTS synonym for SYS.ALL_ARGUMENTS
        PUBLIC.ALL_CATALOG synonym for SYS.ALL_CATALOG
        PUBLIC.ALL_CLUSTERS synonym for SYS.ALL_CLUSTERS
        ...
```

The next example shows LIST_SYN being used to list all synonyms owned by the current user:

```
SQL> @list_syn
List synonyms for user:

SYNONYMS OWNED BY: JEFF
        JEFF.ALL_CONSTRAINTS synonym for SYS.ALL_CONSTRAINTS
        JEFF.ALL_INDEXES synonym for SYS.ALL_INDEXES
        JEFF.ALL_TABLES synonym for SYS.ALL_TABLES
```

You could also use LIST_SYN to see a list of synonyms owned by some other users that reference objects to which you have access. Just run the script, and enter the username of interest.

## Table Security

Information about who has been granted access to a particular table can be found in two views, the ALL_TAB_PRIVS view and the ALL_COL_PRIVS view. These views show you information about privileges granted on tables you own or privileges you have been granted on tables owned by other users. Unless you are the

DBA or otherwise have access to the DBA_TAB_PRIVS_MADE and DBA_COL_PRIVS_MADE views, you cannot fully see the security for tables you do not own.

## Looking at Table Security

As stated earlier, there are two views you need to look at when you want to find out who has access to a particular table. The ALL_TAB_PRIVS view gives you information about table-level grants. For example, if you issue the following statement, it will be reflected in ALL_TAB_PRIVS:

```
GRANT SELECT, DELETE ON employee TO user_a;
```

Some privileges, UPDATE and INSERT, for example, may be restricted only to certain columns of a table. For example, the following grant allows user_a to change just the employee's name:

```
GRANT UPDATE (employee_name) ON employee TO user_a;
```

Grants such as this, which are restricted to certain columns, are reflected in the ALL_COL_PRIVS view. To get a complete picture of the privileges you have granted on any particular table, you need to query both of these views. The query against ALL_TAB_PRIVS will look something like this:

```
SELECT grantee, privilege, grantable
  FROM all_tab_privs
 WHERE table_schema = 'owner_name'
   AND table_name = 'object_name';
```

This query will give you a list of all privileges that have been granted without any column restrictions. The GRANTABLE column will tell you whether or not the privilege was granted using the WITH GRANT OPTION keywords. Granting a privilege with GRANT OPTION allows the grantee to pass that privilege on to others.

You also need to know about any column-level privileges that have been granted. These will only be reflected in ALL_COL_PRIVS, so you must query that as well. This query looks similar to the previous query, except that it also returns the column names:

```
SELECT grantee, privilege, column_name, grantable
  FROM all_col_privs
 WHERE table_schema = 'owner_name'
   AND table_name = 'object_name';
```

## Security Scripts

The SHOW_SECURITY script you are about to see unions together the two queries we saw in the previous section.

*The SHOW_SECURITY.SQL script*

The following script shows you the grants that have been made on any table you own. You can also see grants made on tables owned by other users, so long as those grants apply to you. The two queries you saw previously have been unioned together, and the columns have been concatenated together to produce readable output. The table name and grantee are shown in the header, which changes each time the grantee changes.

```
--DESCRIPTION
--This script displays information about security on a table.
--
--USAGE
--        @SHOW_SECURITY [owner.]table_name
--
SET ECHO OFF
SET VERIFY OFF
SET FEEDBACK OFF
SET PAGESIZE 9999
SET HEADING OFF

--Dissect the input argument, and get the owner name and
--table name into two separate substitution variables.
--The owner name defaults to the current user.
SET TERMOUT OFF
DEFINE s_owner_name = ' '
DEFINE s_synonym_name = ' '
COLUMN owner_name NOPRINT NEW_VALUE s_owner_name
COLUMN table_name NOPRINT NEW_VALUE s_table_name
SELECT
  DECODE(INSTR('&&1','.'),
         0,USER,   /*Default to current user.*/
         UPPER(SUBSTR('&&1',1,INSTR('&&1','.')-1))) owner_name,
  DECODE(INSTR('&&1','.'),
         0,UPPER('&&1'),   /*Only the table name was passed in.*/
         UPPER(SUBSTR('&&1',INSTR('&&1','.')+1))) table_name
  FROM dual;
SET TERMOUT ON

COLUMN grantee NOPRINT NEW_VALUE s_grantee
BREAK ON grantee SKIP PAGE
TTITLE LEFT 'PRIVILEGES GRANTED TO ' s_grantee -
       ' ON ' s_owner_name '.' s_table_name

--Execute a query to show privileges granted at the table level.
SELECT grantee,
       '       ' || privilege ||
       DECODE(grantable, 'YES', ' with grant option', '') privilege
  FROM all_tab_privs
 WHERE table_schema = '&&s_owner_name'
   AND table_name = '&&s_table_name'
UNION
SELECT grantee,
```

```
            '      ' || privilege || ' of column ' || column_name
         || DECODE(grantable, 'YES', ' with grant option', '') privilege
   FROM all_col_privs
  WHERE table_schema = '&&s_owner_name'
    AND table_name = '&&s_table_name'
  ORDER BY grantee, privilege;

  --Reset everything back to its default.
  CLEAR COLUMNS
  CLEAR BREAK
  UNDEFINE s_owner_name
  UNDEFINE s_table_name
  SET VERIFY ON
  SET FEEDBACK ON
  SET HEADING ON
  SET PAGESIZE 24
```

### Running the SHOW_SECURITY script

The following example shows the results of running SHOW_SECURITY against the
EMPLOYEE table, after first granting some access to other users:

```
SQL> @show_security employee

PRIVILEGES GRANTED TO PUBLIC ON JEFF.EMPLOYEE
     SELECT
     UPDATE of column EMPLOYEE_TERMINATION_DATE

PRIVILEGES GRANTED TO USER_A ON JEFF.EMPLOYEE
     DELETE
     INSERT of column EMPLOYEE_BILLING_RATE with grant option
     INSERT of column EMPLOYEE_HIRE_DATE with grant option
     INSERT of column EMPLOYEE_ID with grant option
     INSERT of column EMPLOYEE_NAME with grant option
     SELECT

PRIVILEGES GRANTED TO USER_B ON JEFF.EMPLOYEE
     UPDATE of column EMPLOYEE_NAME
     UPDATE of column EMPLOYEE_TERMINATION_DATE

PRIVILEGES GRANTED TO USER_C ON JEFF.EMPLOYEE
     INSERT
     INSERT of column EMPLOYEE_ID
     SELECT
     UPDATE
```

# Finding More Information

It's well worth your time to learn more about Oracle's data dictionary views. Anything you want to know about the structure of your database and the objects
within it can be found by querying the appropriate view. The definitive reference
for these views is the *Oracle8 Server Reference* manual. However, if you don't

have that manual close by, you can get a quick list of useful views by executing the following query:

```
SELECT *
  FROM dictionary
  ORDER BY table_name;
```

Use the DESCRIBE command on any views of interest. The column names tend to be reasonably self-explanatory.

# Advanced Scripting

SQL*Plus was not designed to be a tool used for writing complex scripts. Its capabilities cannot compare to those of your typical Unix shell, such as the Korn shell or the Bourne shell. Nor does it have anywhere near the capabilities of an advanced scripting tool such as Perl. Most noticeably, SQL*Plus suffers from the following limitations:

- It lacks an IF statement.

- There are no looping constructs.

- It has very limited error handling.

- There is only marginal support for validating user input.

Because of these limitations, SQL*Plus is best suited to executing top-down scripts that don't require any branching, looping, or error handling. Most of the scripts you have seen so far in this book fall into this category. Many are reports that simply set up some column and page formatting, then execute a query. If something goes wrong, you either don't see any data in the report or may see some SQL or SQL*Plus error messages.

This limited scripting support is fine when it comes to producing a report. After all, if a report fails, you can simply fix the problem and rerun the report. But what if you are performing a more complex and critical task? What if you are summarizing some data, posting the summary results to a summary table, and then deleting the underlying detail? In that case, you certainly wouldn't want to delete the data if the summarization failed. You would need some sort of error-handling mechanism.

If you need to write scripts of any significant complexity, I strongly encourage you to investigate the use of PL/SQL in your script. PL/SQL is a powerful programming language in its own right, and includes support for error handling, branching, and looping—the very items that SQL*Plus lacks. Steven Feuerstein's and Bill Pribyl's book, *Oracle PL/SQL Programming*, 2nd edition (O'Reilly, 1997), is an excellent resource.

This chapter will show you some specific ways to work around these limitations of SQL*Plus. Believe it or not, it is possible, using just SQL*Plus, to implement branching and to validate user input. There are even ways to deal with repetitive tasks without resorting to a loop. You will learn about bind variables and see how they better enable you to mix PL/SQL code into your SQL*Plus scripts. You will also see how bind variables can make the job of developing queries for application programs a little bit easier.

## *Bind Variables*

Back in Chapter 4, *Writing SQL*Plus Scripts*, you learned about substitution variables. In addition to substitution variables, SQL*Plus supports another type of variable called a *bind variable*. Unlike substitution variables, bind variables are real variables, having both a datatype and a size.

Bind variables were created to support the use of PL/SQL in a SQL*Plus script. They provide a mechanism for returning data from a PL/SQL block back to SQL*Plus, where it can be used in subsequent queries or by other PL/SQL blocks. Here's a simple example showing how a bind variable can be used:

```
--Bind variables can be declared in your SQL*Plus script.
VARIABLE  s_table_name  varchar2(30)

--Preface a bind variable with a colon to reference it
--in a PL/SQL block.
BEGIN
   :s_table_name := 'EMPLOYEE';
END;
/

--Bind variables can even be referenced by SQL queries.
SELECT index_name
  FROM user_indexes
 WHERE table_name = :s_table_name;

--Bind variables persist until you exit SQL*Plus, so
--they can be referenced by more than one PL/SQL block.
SET SERVEROUTPUT ON
```

```
BEGIN
  DBMS_OUTPUT.PUT_LINE(:s_table_name);
END;
/
```

The scope of a bind variable is the SQL*Plus session in which it was defined. Variables defined within a PL/SQL block, on the other hand, cease to exist once that block has finished executing. Bind variables are defined one level higher (at the SQL*Plus level), so they can be referenced by many PL/SQL blocks and queries.

## *Declaring Bind Variables*

The SQL*Plus VARIABLE command is used to declare bind variables. The syntax looks like this:

```
VAR[IABLE] var_name data_type
```

where:

*VAR[IABLE]*

Is the command, which can be abbreviated to VAR.

*var_name*

Is whatever name you want to give the variable. A variable name must start with a letter, but after that, the name may contain any combination of letters, digits, underscores, pound signs, and dollar signs. 30 characters is the maximum length for a variable name.

*data_type*

Is the datatype of the variable. The following datatypes are allowed:

*NUMBER*

Results in a floating-point number, and is the same as a NUMBER variable in PL/SQL or a NUMBER column in a table. Unlike PL/SQL, SQL*Plus does not let you specify a length or a precision, so a declaration like NUMBER (9,2) would not be allowed.

*CHAR [(length)]*

Results in a fixed-length character string. Length is optional. If it's omitted, you get a one-character string.

*NCHAR [(length)]*

Results in a fixed-length character string in the national character set. Length is optional. If it's omitted, you get a one-character string.

*VARCHAR2 (length)*

Results in a variable-length character string.

*NVARCHAR2 (length)*

Results in a variable-length character string using the national language character set.

*CLOB*

Results in a character large object variable.

*NCLOB*

Results in a character large object variable using the national language character set.

*REFCURSOR*

Gives you a cursor variable that you can use to return the results of a SQL query from PL/SQL to SQL*Plus.

In addition to declaring variables, you can also use the VARIABLE command to list all the variables you have defined. To do that, simply issue the command VARIABLE, with no arguments, as shown in the following example:

```
SQL> VARIABLE
variable    jenny
datatype    NUMBER

variable    jeff
datatype    CHAR

variable    sharon
datatype    VARCHAR2(30)
```

If you are interested in one specific variable, you can specify that variable's name as an argument to the VARIABLE command, for example:

```
SQL> VARIABLE SHARON
variable    sharon
datatype    VARCHAR2(30)
```

There is no way to get rid of a variable once you've defined it.

## Using Bind Variables and Substitution Variables Together

Bind variables and substitution variables don't mesh together too well in SQL*Plus. Each was created for a different purpose, and the two types cannot be used interchangeably. For example, bind variables cannot be used with the ACCEPT command, while substitution variables can. Substitution variables can be used with the TTITLE and BTITLE commands that set up page headers and footers, while bind variables cannot. Bind variables are true variables, and can be passed as arguments to PL/SQL functions and procedures, while substitution variables cannot. Table 7-1 summarizes the best uses and capabilities of each type of variable.

*Table 7-1. Bind Variables versus Substitution Variables*

| Task | Bind Variable | Substitution Variable | Comments |
|------|---------------|----------------------|----------|
| Display information to the user—the PROMPT command. | | X | |
| Accept input from the user—the ACCEPT command. | | X | |
| Place information from a query into page headers and footers—the TTITLE and BTI-TLE commands. | | X | |
| Run a query with user-specified criteria in the WHERE clause. | X | X | User input must come through a substitution variable, but you can store the resulting value in a bind variable. |
| Pass values to a PL/SQL function or procedure. | X | X | Substitution variables may be used to pass input arguments as literals. |
| Return information back from a PL/SQL function or procedure. | X | | Bind variables must be used for OUT and IN OUT arguments. |

As you can see, each variable type pretty much exists in its own world, completely separate from the other. In fact, you cannot even directly assign values from a bind variable to a substitution variable, or vice versa. The following lines of script, though appearing perfectly reasonable on the surface, simply will not work:

```
DEFINE my_sub_var = ' '
VARIABLE my_bind_var VARCHAR2(30)
EXECUTE :my_bind_var := 'Donna Gennick'
my_sub_var = my_bind_var
```

This lack of interoperability between variable types can be a real frustration when writing scripts. As Table 7-1 shows, there are some tasks for which you can only use a bind variable, and others for which you can only use a substitution variable. Yet SQL*Plus does not let you easily move values back and forth between the two types. Fortunately, there are some relatively straightforward incantations that let you work around this problem.

### From substitution to bind

Putting the value of a substitution variable into a bind variable is actually the easier of the two tasks. Remember that as SQL*Plus executes your script, any substitution variables are simply replaced by their contents as each line of code is executed. You can easily take advantage of this in order to place a value into a bind variable. Take a look at the following short script:

```
DEFINE my_sub_var = 'Raymond'
VARIABLE my_bind_var VARCHAR2(30)
EXECUTE :my_bind_var := '&my_sub_var';
```

EXECUTE is a command that executes *one* line of PL/SQL code. When SQL*Plus encounters the EXECUTE command, it replaces the reference to the substitution variable with the value of that variable. The command after substitution, the one that is actually executed, looks like this:

```
EXECUTE :my_bind_var := 'Raymond';
```

Since the assignment involves a character string, the substitution variable must be contained in quotes; otherwise, you would not have a valid string. If you are working with numeric values, you shouldn't quote them. The following example declares a variable of type NUMBER and assigns a value to it:

```
DEFINE my_sub_num = 9
VARIABLE my_bind_num NUMBER
EXECUTE :my_bind_num := &&my_sub_num;
```

So quote your strings, don't quote your numbers, and remember that substitution is occurring.

### From bind to substitution

Taking a value from a bind variable and placing it into a substitution variable is a more difficult task. What you need to do is take advantage of SQL*Plus's ability to store the results of a SELECT statement into a substitution variable. Let's say you have the following in your script:

```
DEFINE my_sub_var = ' '
VARIABLE my_bind_var VARCHAR2(30)
EXECUTE :my_bind_var := 'This is a test.';
```

In order to get the value of the bind variable into the substitution variable, you need to go through the following steps:

1. Think up a column name.

2. Execute a COLUMN command for the column name you thought up. Use the NEW_VALUE clause and specify the substitution variable as the target.

3. Turn off terminal output by executing a SET TERMOUT OFF command. This is optional.

4. Issue a SELECT statement that selects the bind variable from Oracle's DUAL table. Use the column name you thought up in step 1 as the column alias.

5. Turn terminal output back on.

The SELECT statement will, of course, only return one value, but that value will be a new value for the column in question. The COLUMN command, with its NEW_ VALUE clause, causes this value to be stored in the specified substitution variable. It's a roundabout solution to the problem, but when it's all over the substitution variable will contain the value from the bind variable. The important thing is to be sure that the column alias matches the column name used in the COLUMN command. Here's a code sample that demonstrates this technique:

```
--Declare one bind variable and one substitution variable.
--Initialize the bind variable to a value.
DEFINE my_sub_var = ' '
VARIABLE my_bind_var VARCHAR2(30)
EXECUTE :my_bind_var := 'This is a test.';

--Store the new value of the my_alias column in my_sub_var.
COLUMN my_alias NEW_VALUE my_sub_var

--SELECT the value of the bind variable. SQL*Plus
--will store that value in my_sub_var because of the
--previous COLUMN command.
SET TERMOUT OFF
SELECT :my_bind_var my_alias
   FROM dual;
SET TERMOUT ON
```

Notice that a column alias is used in the SELECT statement to give the column a name. This same name must be used in the COLUMN command issued prior to the SELECT. If these two don't match, then the assignment won't be made, and my_sub_var will still be blank.

Strictly speaking, it's not necessary to turn the terminal output off for the SELECT statement. The variable assignment will still be made, even with the output on. However, if you are writing a script, you probably won't want the results of this SELECT to clutter up the display.

## Displaying the Contents of a Bind Variable

There are two ways to display the contents of a bind variable to a user. You can use the PRINT command, or you can list the variable in a SELECT statement.

### The PRINT command

The format for the PRINT command looks like this:

```
PRI[NT] [bind_variable_name]
```

where:

*PRI[NT]*
   Is the command, which can be abbreviated to PRI.

*bind_variable_name*

> Is the name of the bind variable you want to print. If you omit a name, the values of all bind variables are printed.

The results from the PRINT command look very much like the results you get from a SELECT. Here's an example:

```
SQL> PRINT my_string

MY_STRING
--------------------------------------------------
Brighten the corner where you are
```

The bind variable is treated like a database column, with the variable name being the default column heading. If you have page titles defined, they will print as well. You can even use the COLUMN commands to format the output. The following example shows how this works:

```
SQL> COLUMN my_string FORMAT A40 HEADING 'My Motto'
SQL> PRINT my_string

My Motto
----------------------------------------
Brighten the corner where you are

SQL>
SQL> TTITLE LEFT 'This is a Page Title' SKIP 2
SQL> COLUMN my_number FORMAT 99.99 HEADING 'My Age'
SQL> PRINT my_number

This is a Page Title

My Age
------
 36.00
```

All other formatting options, such as PAGESIZE and LINESIZE, apply when printing bind variables. You can even use the COLUMN command's NEW_VALUE clause to store the value of a bind variable in a substitution variable, as the following example demonstrates:

```
SQL> DEFINE s_my_string = ' '
SQL> COLUMN my_string NOPRINT NEW_VALUE s_my_string
SQL> PRINT my_string
SQL> PROMPT &&s_my_string
Brighten the corner where you are
```

Issuing the PRINT command by itself causes the contents of all bind variables to be displayed. Here's an example:

```
SQL> PRINT

My Motto
----------------------------------------
```

```
Brighten the corner where you are


My Age
------
 36.00
```

Some special considerations apply when printing bind variables of type CLOB and of type REFCURSOR. These are described in the following sections.

### Printing CLOB variables

The CLOB datatype is new with Oracle8. CLOB stands for character large object, and variables of this type can hold up to 2 gigabytes of text data. When printing variables of type CLOB or NCLOB, there are three SQL*Plus settings you can use to control what you see and how that works. See Table 7-2.

*Table 7-2. Settings That Affect the Printing of CLOBs*

| Setting | Default | Description |
|---------|---------|-------------|
| SET LONG | 80 | Controls the number of characters that are actually displayed from a CLOB variable. By default, only the first 80 characters will print. The rest are ignored. |
| SET LONGCHUNKSIZE | 80 | CLOB variables are retrieved from the database a piece at a time. This setting controls the size of that piece. |
| SET LOBOFFSET | 1 | An offset you can use to start printing with the nth character in the CLOB variable. By default, SQL*Plus will begin printing with the first character. A LOB-OFFSET of 80, for example, skips the first 79 characters of the string. |

By default, SQL*Plus will only display the first 80 characters of a CLOB value. This is rarely enough. After all, if you only needed 80 characters, you wouldn't have used a CLOB datatype in the first place. On the other hand, you may not want to risk printing 2 gigabytes of data either.

The following example shows the result of printing a CLOB value using the default settings for the values in Table 7-2:

```
SQL> SELECT clob_value FROM clob_example;

CLOB_VALUE
----------------------------------------------------------------------------
By default, SQL*Plus will only display the first 80 characters of a CLOB
value.

1 row selected.
```

As you can see, only 80 characters of the value were displayed. You can change the LONG setting to see more of the value, as the next example shows:

```
SQL> SET LONG 500
SQL> SELECT clob_value from clob_example;

CLOB_VALUE
----------------------------------------------------------------------------
By default, SQL*Plus will only display the first 80 characters of a CLOB
value. This is rarely enough. After all, if you only needed 80 characters,
you wouldn't have used a CLOB datatype in the first place.
On the other hand, you may not want to risk printing 2 gigabytes of data
either.

1 row selected.
```

By combining the LOBOFFSET and LONG settings, you can print any arbitrary substring of a CLOB variable. The following example prints the characters 81 through 102, which make up the second sentence in the example:

```
SQL> SET LONG 22
SQL> SET LOBOFFSET 81
SQL> SELECT clob_value FROM clob_example;

CLOB_VALUE
----------------------
This is rarely enough.

1 row selected.
```

Finally, the LONGCHUNKSIZE setting controls the amount of the CLOB that is fetched from the database at one time. If you have the memory available, you may want to set this to match the LONG setting. That way SQL*Plus will retrieve the value with one fetch from the database, possibly improving performance.

### Printing REFCURSOR variables

Beginning with Oracle8, SQL*Plus allows you to create bind variables of the type REFCURSOR. A REFCURSOR variable is a pointer to a cursor that returns a result set. Using PL/SQL, you can assign any SELECT query to a variable of this type, and then you can use the SQL*Plus PRINT command to format and display the results of that query. The following script makes use of this capability. It asks the user for a pattern match string and prints the list tables with names that match the pattern supplied by the user. A PL/SQL block is used to interpret the user's response, and to open a cursor that will return the desired results.

```
--Find out what tables the user wants to see.
--A null response results in seeing all the tables.
ACCEPT s_table_like PROMPT 'List tables LIKE > '

VARIABLE l_table_list REFCURSOR
```

```
--This PL/SQL block sets the l_table_list variable
--to the correct query, depending on whether or
--not the user specified all or part of a table_name.
BEGIN
  IF '&&s_table_like' IS NULL THEN
    OPEN :l_table_list FOR
      SELECT table_name
        FROM user_tables;
  ELSE
    OPEN :l_table_list FOR
      SELECT table_name
        FROM user_tables
        WHERE table_name LIKE UPPER('&&s_table_like');
  END IF;
END;
/

--Print the list of tables the user wants to see.
PRINT l_table_list
```

As you can see, this script defines a SQL*Plus REFCURSOR variable. The cursor is opened and a query assigned by code within a PL/SQL block. Then the SQL*Plus PRINT command is used to display the results of that query.

```
SQL> @ref_cursor
List tables LIKE >

TABLE_NAME
------------------------------
EMPLOYEE
PROJECT
PROJECT_HOURS
SQL>
SQL>
SQL> @ref_cursor
List tables LIKE > p%

TABLE_NAME
------------------------------
PROJECT
PROJECT_HOURS
```

The output you get when PRINTing a REFCURSOR variable is identical to the output you would get if you executed the same query directly from SQL*Plus.

### SELECTing a bind variable

The SQL*Plus manual, at least the one for versions 8.0.3 and before, will tell you that bind variables cannot be used in SQL statements. Don't believe it. Bind variables can be used in SELECT statements, both in the column list and in the WHERE clause. You will frequently see this done in scripts where there is a need to get the contents of a bind variable into a substitution variable. See the section titled "From bind to substitution" earlier in this chapter. Here's an example of a SELECT statement being used to display the contents of a bind variable:

```
SQL> VARIABLE l_user VARCHAR2(30)
SQL> EXECUTE :l_user := user;
SQL> SELECT :l_user FROM dual;

:L_USER
--------------------------------
NATHAN
```

Using SELECT like this offers no real advantage over the use of the PRINT command. If you just need to display one variable, you might as well PRINT it. Being able to use bind variables in a SELECT statement becomes more of an advantage when you need to display information from more than one column, when you want to use the bind variable in an expression for a computed column, or when you want to use it in the WHERE clause. Here's an example that combines all three of these:

```
SQL> SET HEADING OFF
SQL> SELECT 'User ' || :l_user || ' has '
  2           || TO_CHAR(COUNT(*)) || ' tables.'
  3      FROM all_tables
  4     WHERE owner = :l_user;
NATHAN
User SQLPLUS has 3 tables.
```

Two types of bind variables cannot be used in a SQL statement. These are the REFCURSOR and CLOB types. You must use the PRINT command with these.

## When and How to Use Bind Variables

There are three primary reasons to use bind variables in SQL*Plus:

- You need to call PL/SQL procedures or functions that return a value or that use IN OUT parameters.

- You need to conditionally execute one of several possible SELECT statements depending on user input or other circumstances.

- You want to test a query for use in an application, and that query uses colons to mark parameters.

The next few sections briefly describe each of these uses.

### Calling PL/SQL procedures and functions from SQL*Plus

Oracle provides a number of built-in PL/SQL packages that allow you to do such things as create and execute dynamic SQL queries (the DBMS_SQL package), submit and manage PL/SQL batch jobs (the DBMS_JOBS package), and many other very useful things. In many cases, the procedures and functions in these packages use OUT parameters to return information to the caller. To call these routines from within a SQL*Plus script and display the results to the person running the script, you need to use bind variables.

Consider the problem of writing a SQL*Plus script to submit a PL/SQL job for periodic execution by Oracle. To do this, you would use a procedure in Oracle's DBMS_JOBS package named SUBMIT. SUBMIT takes several arguments, one of which is an OUT argument. The declaration for SUBMIT looks like this:

```
DBMS_JOB.SUBMIT(  job         OUT   BINARY_INTEGER,
                  what        IN    VARCHAR2,
                  next_date   IN    DATE DEFAULT SYSDATE,
                  interval    IN    VARCHAR2 DEFAULT 'null',
                  no_parse    IN    BOOLEAN DEFAULT FALSE)
```

The job parameter is the job number, and is an output from the procedure. This job number uniquely identifies a job within Oracle, and is important to know because all the procedures to modify, delete, or otherwise manage database jobs require the job number as an input. Here is one approach you could use to write a script that submits a PL/SQL job for a user. In particular, note the use of a bind variable in the EXECUTE command. Also note the subsequent PRINT command that displays the job number to the user.

```
SET ECHO OFF
SET FEEDBACK OFF
SET VERIFY ON
SET HEADING ON
SET TERMOUT ON

--
--This script submits a job to the queue after first
--prompting the user for the required information.

--Get the neccessary information from the user.
PROMPT
prompt Submit a PL/SQL job.
PROMPT
ACCEPT what CHAR PROMPT 'Enter the PL/SQL statement to execute >'
PROMPT
ACCEPT when CHAR PROMPT 'When (e.g. 15-Nov-1961 18:30)?'
ACCEPT interval CHAR PROMPT 'Interval (e.g. sysdate+1)?'

--Submit the job
VARIABLE job_number NUMBER
EXECUTE DBMS_JOB.SUBMIT(:job_number, '&what', &when, '&interval');

--Tell the user the job's ID number.
PRINT job_number

SET FEEDBACK ON
SET VERIFY ON
```

Running the above script looks like this:

```
SQL> @submit_job

Submit a PL/SQL job.

Enter the PL/SQL statement to execute >NULL;

When (e.g. 15-Nov-1961 18:30)?sysdate
Interval (e.g. sysdate+1)?sysdate+1

JOB_NUMBER
----------
         4
```

NULL is a valid PL/SQL statement that does nothing, and is often used as a place-holder for code to be written later. In this example, Oracle will do nothing once each day.

### Using REFCURSOR variables

As mentioned earlier, the REFCURSOR datatype holds a pointer to a cursor, and is a new feature introduced with Oracle8. Using REFCURSOR variables, you can open a cursor for a SELECT statement in PL/SQL and print the results from SQL*Plus. One practical use for this is to write PL/SQL code that selects one query from many possibilities, based on user input or some other factor.

Earlier, in the section on printing, you saw a REFCURSOR example that printed a list of tables owned by the current user. Here is an enhanced version of that script that allows the user to optionally enter a pattern match string to narrow the list of table names to be displayed. The script executes one of two possible queries depending on whether or not a string was supplied.

```
--Find out what tables the user wants to see.
--A null response results in seeing all the tables.
ACCEPT s_table_like PROMPT 'List tables LIKE > '

VARIABLE l_table_list REFCURSOR

--This PL/SQL block sets the l_table_list variable
--to the correct query, depending on whether or
--not the user specified all or part of a table_name.
BEGIN
  IF '&&s_table_like' IS NULL THEN
    OPEN :l_table_list FOR
      SELECT table_name
        FROM user_tables;
  ELSE
    OPEN :l_table_list FOR
      SELECT table_name
        FROM user_tables
         WHERE table_name LIKE UPPER('&&s_table_like');
```

```
    END IF;
END;
/

--Print the list of tables the user wants to see.
PRINT l_table_list
```

This script first asks the user for a search string to be used with the LIKE operator. Entering this is optional. If a pattern match string is specified, then only table names that match that string are displayed; otherwise, all table names are listed. This conditional logic is implemented by the PL/SQL block, which checks the value of the substitution variable and then opens the REFCURSOR variable using the appropriate SELECT statement. Here's how it looks to run the script:

```
SQL> @ref_cursor
List tables LIKE >

TABLE_NAME
------------------------------
EMPLOYEE
PROJECT
PROJECT_HOURS
SQL>
SQL>
SQL> @ref_cursor
List tables LIKE > p%

TABLE_NAME
------------------------------
PROJECT
PROJECT_HOURS
```

You can see that when no search string was specified, all the tables were listed, whereas entering a search string of "p%" caused only tables starting with the letter "P" to be listed. The output is just like that from a standard SELECT statement, and all the column and page formatting options of SQL*Plus apply.

---

 You might be thinking now about using REFCURSOR variables with the DBMS_SQL package to return the results of dynamically generated SQL queries back to SQL*Plus. Unfortunately, that can't be done. DBMS_SQL returns integer values that reference cursors held internally, but there is no way to get a REFCURSOR value pointing to one of those cursors.

---

Using REFCURSOR variables is one way to add conditional logic to your SQL*Plus scripts. You'll see another example of this later in the section titled "Branching in SQL*Plus."

## *Testing application queries*

Bind variables can make it more convenient to take a query from an application development environment such as PowerBuilder and debug it using SQL*Plus. PowerBuilder queries often contain parameters to be supplied at runtime. Power-Builder parameters are preceded by colons, the same syntax SQL*Plus uses for bind variables. If you had a PowerBuilder datawindow that allowed you to edit just one employee record, here is how the query behind that datawindow might look:

```
SELECT employee.employee_id,
       employee.employee_name,
       employee.employee_hire_date,
       employee.employee_termination_date,
       employee.employee_billing_rate
  FROM employee
  WHERE employee.employee_id = :emp_id
```

Now if you want to test this query, and you just paste it into SQL*Plus as it is, you will get the following results:

```
SQL> SELECT employee.employee_id,
  2          employee.employee_name,
  3          employee.employee_hire_date,
  4          employee.employee_termination_date,
  5          employee.employee_billing_rate
  6    FROM employee
  7    WHERE employee.employee_id = :emp_id
  8  /
Bind variable "EMP_ID" not declared.
```

At this point, you have two choices. You can change the query and simply replace the parameter :emp_id with an employee number that you know exists. Then you can test the query, and when you are satisfied the query works, you can replace the hardcoded value with the parameter reference. Woe be unto you, however, if there are several parameters and you forget to change one back. A safer approach would be simply to declare bind variables to match the parameters in the query. In this case there's just one to declare:

```
SQL> VARIABLE emp_id NUMBER
```

Once the variable has been declared, it is a simple matter to initialize it to a known good value:

```
SQL> EXECUTE :emp_id := 101;

PL/SQL procedure successfully completed.
```

Having declared and initialized the variable, it's now a simple matter to copy the query directly from PowerBuilder, or wherever, and paste it unchanged into SQL*Plus:

```
SQL> SELECT employee.employee_id,
  2            employee.employee_name,
  3            employee.employee_hire_date,
  4            employee.employee_termination_date,
  5            employee.employee_billing_rate
  6    FROM employee
  7    WHERE employee.employee_id = :emp_id
  8    /
```

| EMPLOYEE_ID | EMPLOYEE_NAME | EMPLOYEE_ | EMPLOYEE_ | EMPLOYEE_BILLING_RATE |
|---|---|---|---|---|
| 101 | Jonathan Gennick | 15-NOV-61 | | 169 |

Once you are satisfied that everything is correct, you can paste the query directly back into your application without the risk that you might forget to manually change a hardcoded value back into a parameter.

# Branching in SQL*Plus

SQL*Plus has no IF statement. This is a very vexing thing. Script writing is similar to programming. It's natural to want to take different actions depending on user input or some other condition. Imagine how frustrated you would be if your favorite programming language suddenly lost its IF statement! Despite the lack of an IF statement in SQL*Plus, there are some approaches you can take to get equivalent results. Some are more straightforward than others. All involve some compromises.

## Approaches to Branching

There are at least six approaches you can take to the problem of conditional execution. These are:

- Simulate branching by adjusting the WHERE clause in a query.
- Use REFCUSOR variables.
- Use a multilevel file structure.
- Use SQL to write SQL.
- Use PL/SQL for conditional logic.
- Use an operating-system scripting language.

Some of these approaches are very specific to certain types of problems. Using REFCURSOR variables, for example, is a good solution when you simply need to choose which query to run based on user input or some other condition. Other approaches, such as the use of a multilevel file structure for your script, are more general in nature, and can be used for any type of branching.

## *Simulating Branching by Adjusting the WHERE Clause*

Suppose you are writing a script to delete all data from the project_hours table. Before you delete the data, you want to ask the user to confirm the operation. You really want to write something like this:

```
ACCEPT s_delete_confirm PROMPT 'Delete project hours data (Y/N)?'

IF s_delete_confirm = 'Y' THEN
   DELETE
      FROM project_hours;
  END IF
```

Of course, you can't do that! SQL*Plus has no IF statement, remember? However, you can add a WHERE clause to the DELETE statement that will have the same effect. Here's an example:

```
SET VERIFY OFF

ACCEPT s_delete_confirm PROMPT 'Delete project hours data (Y/N)?'

DELETE
  FROM project_hours
  WHERE UPPER('&&s_delete_confirm') = 'Y';
```

When you execute the script, the DELETE will always be executed. However, if the user answers with an N, the WHERE clause will always evaluate to FALSE, and no rows will be deleted. Verification is set off only to prevent SQL*Plus from echoing the line of the WHERE clause that references the substitution variable. The UPPER function is used in this case in order to allow the user's response to be case-insensitive. Here's how it looks when a user runs this script and doesn't confirm the delete:

```
SQL> @delete_hours
Delete project hours data (Y/N)?n

0 rows deleted.
```

If you wanted to, you could even write an additional query to give the user an error message if the response to the prompt was not a Y or an N. Adding these lines immediately after the ACCEPT statement would do that for you:

```
SET HEADING OFF
SET PAGESIZE 0
SET FEEDBACK OFF
SELECT 'You must answer with a Y or N.'
  FROM DUAL
 WHERE UPPER('&&s_delete_confirm') NOT IN ('Y','N')
    OR '&&s_delete_confirm' IS NULL;
```

```
SET FEEDBACK ON
SET PAGESIZE 1
SET HEADING ON
```

To make the results of this query look like an error message, both headings and pagination are turned off. Feedback is also turned off to avoid giving the "1 row selected" message to the user. After the SELECT executes, these settings are returned to their defaults. Now, here is what happens when you run the modified script and don't answer with a Y or N:

```
SQL> @delete_hours
Delete project hours data (Y/N)?X
You must answer with a Y or N.

0 rows deleted.
```

This technique has the advantage of keeping your entire script in one file, but it's pretty much limited to handling the case where you have several possible queries to execute and must choose the correct one based on input from the user.

## Using REFCURSOR Variables to Simulate Branching

If you want to present the user with a choice of reports to run, you can place the conditional logic within PL/SQL and use a REFCURSOR variable to return the selected query to SQL\*Plus, where the results can be formatted and printed.

 REFCURSOR variables are only available beginning with SQL\*Plus version 8 and above.

The following script gives the user a choice of three different reports. The conditional logic is implemented in a PL/SQL block, and the results are returned to SQL\*Plus via bind variables. A REFCURSOR bind variable is used to return a query that generates the report requested by the user.

```
--DESCRIPTION
--Print one of three user security reports

SET FEEDBACK OFF
SET PAGESIZE 20
SET LINESIZE 77
SET HEADING ON

--Ask the user what report to print
PROMPT
PROMPT 1 - List users
PROMPT 2 - List users and table privileges
PROMPT 3 - List users and system privileges
```

```
PROMPT
ACCEPT s_report_choice PROMPT 'Enter your choice (1,2,3) >'

--A PL/SQL block will set the b_report bind variable
--to a query based on the user's response. Text for the
--report title will be returned in b_report_type.
VARIABLE b_report REFCURSOR
VARIABLE b_report_type VARCHAR2(30)

--Interpret the user's choice.
BEGIN
  IF '&&s_report_choice' = '1' THEN
    --Return some text for the title to identify this report.
    :b_report_type := 'User Listing';

    --Return a query that will list all users.
    OPEN :b_report FOR
      SELECT username
        FROM dba_users
        ORDER BY username;
  ELSIF '&&s_report_choice' = '2' THEN
    --Return some text for the title to identify this report.
    :b_report_type := 'User Table Privileges';

    --Return a query that will list users and any
    --privileges they have on tables in the database.
    OPEN :b_report FOR
      SELECT username, privilege, owner, table_name
        FROM dba_users, dba_tab_privs
        WHERE username = grantee
        ORDER BY username, owner, table_name, privilege;
  ELSIF '&&s_report_choice' = '3' THEN
    --Return some text for the title to identify this report.
    :b_report_type := 'User System Privileges';

    --Return a query that lists users and any system
    --privileges they have been granted.
    OPEN :b_report FOR
      SELECT username, privilege
        FROM dba_users, dba_sys_privs
        WHERE username = grantee
        ORDER BY username, privilege;
  ELSE
    --Return some text for the title to identify this report.
    :b_report_type := 'Invalid Report Choice';

    --The user made an invalid choice, so
    --return a query that will display an error message.
    OPEN :b_report FOR
      SELECT 'You must choose either 1, 2, or 3' error_message
        FROM dual;
  END IF;
END;
/
```

```
--Specify formats for all possible report columns.
COLUMN username FORMAT A12 HEADING 'User'
COLUMN privilege FORMAT A20 HEADING 'Privilege'
COLUMN owner FORMAT A12 HEADING 'Table Owner'
COLUMN table_name FORMAT A30 HEADING 'Table Name'
COLUMN error_message FORMAT A40 HEADING 'Error Message'

--Set up the page title. First we have to get the contents of
--b_report_type into a substition variable.
set termout off
COLUMN b_report_type FORMAT A30 NOPRINT NEW_VALUE s_report_type
SELECT b_report_type FROM dual;
set termout on

TTITLE LEFT s_report_type RIGHT 'Page ' FORMAT 999 SQL.PNO SKIP 2

--Run the report requested by the user
PRINT b_report
```

Note that the script contains COLUMN commands for all possible columns from
the three different queries. These don't need to be conditionally executed, because
format definitions for columns not used in the final query are ignored by SQL*Plus.
Also note that the PL/SQL code does return a query even for the case where the
user's input is invalid; this query simply selects an error message from the DUAL
table. Here is the output from running this script, first showing the results of an
invalid input, then showing the output from one of the reports:

```
SQL> @user_security

1 - List users
2 - List users and table privileges
3 - List users and system privileges

Enter your choice (1,2,3) >4

User Listing                                                    Page    1

Error Message
-----------------------------------------
You must choose either 1, 2, or 3
SQL> @user_security

1 - List users
2 - List users and table privileges
3 - List users and system privileges

Enter your choice (1,2,3) >2

User Listing                                                    Page    1
```

| User | Privilege | Table Owner | Table Name |
| ------------ | -------------------- | ------------ | ---------------------------- |
| SYSTEM | EXECUTE | SYS | AQ$_AGENT |
| SYSTEM | EXECUTE | SYS | AQ$_DEQUEUE_HISTORY |
| SYSTEM | EXECUTE | SYS | AQ$_HISTORY |
| SYSTEM | EXECUTE | SYS | AQ$_RECIPIENTS |
| SYSTEM | EXECUTE | SYS | AQ$_SUBSCRIBERS |
| SYSTEM | EXECUTE | SYS | DBMS_AQADM |
| SYSTEM | EXECUTE | SYS | DBMS_AQ_IMPORT_INTERNAL |
| SYSTEM | EXECUTE | SYS | DBMS_DEFER_IMPORT_INTERNAL |
| SYSTEM | ALTER | SYS | INCEXP |
| SYSTEM | DELETE | SYS | INCEXP |
| SYSTEM | INDEX | SYS | INCEXP |

In this example, the query output is only displayed on the screen. If you wanted to print it, you would just need to add a SPOOL command to send the output to a file, which you could later send to a printer.

## *Branching Using a Multilevel File Structure*

The most generic and flexible approach to branching that you can implement using SQL*Plus is to write your script to execute one of several alternative files based on user input or other criteria. This is best explained by example, so here is a simplified version of the security reports menu shown previously in this chapter:

```
--Ask the user what report to print
PROMPT
PROMPT 1 - List users
PROMPT 2 - List users and table privileges
PROMPT 3 - List users and system privileges
PROMPT
ACCEPT s_report_choice PROMPT 'Enter your choice (1,2,3) >'

--Execute the appropriate report
@user_security_&&s_report_choice
```

The key to this approach is in the last line, where the user's response is used to form the name of another SQL file to execute. If the user chooses option 1, for example, the last line in the above script will be translated to:

```
@user_security_1
```

Of course, you have to make sure that a file named *USER_SECURITY_1.SQL* exists and that it will generate the correct report. When you use this approach to branching, you will end up with a set of script files that form an inverted tree structure. The tree diagram in Figure 7-1 shows the relationship between the menu script and the scripts that run the individual reports.

Because this branching technique executes another SQL*Plus script, you can continue to ask the user questions, and even branch again depending on the user's response. The one thing you have to watch out for is that SQL*Plus cannot nest

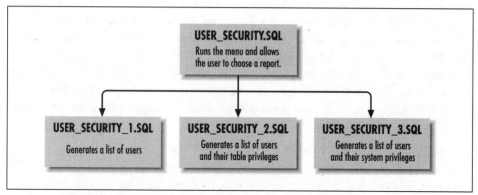

*Figure 7-1. Structure for the security reports menu, using a multilevel file structure*

scripts indefinitely. SQL\*Plus can currently nest scripts only 20 levels deep, and some older versions only allow 5 levels of nesting.

A useful variation on this technique is to code it using a SELECT statement to analyze the user's input and derive the name of the next script to call. You get two benefits from this: the script names are not directly linked to the user's input, and it's easier to designate one script to be called when the user makes an invalid choice. The only penalty is a small amount of added complexity in your script. The following script is an example of this technique:

```
--Ask the user what report to print
PROMPT
PROMPT A - List users
PROMPT B - List users and table privileges
PROMPT C - List users and system privileges
PROMPT
ACCEPT s_report_choice PROMPT 'Enter your choice (A,B,C) >'

--DECODE the user's input.
SET TERMOUT OFF
COLUMN user_choice NOPRINT NEW_VALUE s_next_script
SELECT DECODE (UPPER('&s_report_choice'),
              'A','USER_SECURITY_1.SQL',
              'B','USER_SECURITY_2.SQL',
              'C','USER_SECURITY_3.SQL',
              'USER_SECURITY_4.SQL') user_choice
  FROM DUAL;
SET TERMOUT ON

--Execute the appropriate report
@@&s_next_script
```

The key to this script is the call to DECODE in the SELECT statement. DECODE is a SQL function that allows you to arbitrarily specify an output value for any given input value. In this case, the input value is UPPER('&s_report_choice'). By using the UPPER function, we allow the user to respond in either uppercase or lower-case. Following the input are three value pairs, each specifying the output for a specific input value. An input of "A" causes this DECODE to return "USER_SECURITY_1.SQL", an input of "B" causes "USER_SECURITY_2.SQL" to be returned, and so forth. The final value, "USER_SECURITY_4.SQL", is returned if the user's choice did not match any of the others. In this case, the file *USER_SECURITY_4.SQL* would display some sort of error message, telling the user what he did wrong.

If you decide to develop a set of scripts like this, it's best to spend some time up front working out the structure before you begin scripting. Making changes after you've started writing a set of scripts like this can become cumbersome very quickly because so many files are involved. Try to keep things as modular as possible, too. In this example, any of the reports can be run as standalone scripts without going through the menu.

## *Using SQL to Write SQL*

Another way to branch that also involves a multilevel file structure is simply to spool some output to a new SQL file, then execute that file. To implement the security report menu using this technique, you could spool one of three SELECT statements to a file based on the user's report choice. Here's a version of the script that does that:

```
--DESCRIPTION
--Print one of three user security reports

SET FEEDBACK OFF
SET PAGESIZE 20
SET LINESIZE 77
SET HEADING ON

--Ask the user what report to print
PROMPT
PROMPT 1 - List users
PROMPT 2 - List users and table privileges
PROMPT 3 - List users and system privileges
PROMPT
ACCEPT s_report_choice PROMPT 'Enter your choice (1,2,3) >'

--Specify formats for all possible report columns.
COLUMN username FORMAT A12 HEADING 'User'
COLUMN privilege FORMAT A20 HEADING 'Privilege'
COLUMN owner FORMAT A12 HEADING 'Table Owner'
COLUMN table_name FORMAT A30 HEADING 'Table Name'
COLUMN error_message FORMAT A40 HEADING 'Error Message'

--Set up the page title. First we have to get the contents of
--b_report_type into a substitution variable.
```

```
set termout off
COLUMN b_report_type FORMAT A30 NOPRINT NEW_VALUE s_report_type
SELECT DECODE ('&&s_report_choice',
               '1','User List',
               '2','User Table Privileges',
               '3','User System Privileges',
               'Invalid Choice') b_report_type
  FROM dual;
set termout on

TTITLE LEFT s_report_type RIGHT 'Page ' FORMAT 999 SQL.PNO SKIP 2

--Generate the query for the report requested by the user.
--Spool that query to a file.
SET TERMOUT OFF
SET PAGESIZE 0
SET HEADING OFF
SET VERIFY OFF
SET FEEDBACK OFF
COLUMN next_query FORMAT A60
SPOOL user_security_choice.sql

--This query will be successful if the user chooses 1
SELECT 'SELECT username ' || CHR(10) ||
       '  FROM dba_users ' || CHR(10) ||
       'ORDER BY username;' || CHR(10) next_query
  FROM dual
 WHERE '&&s_report_choice' = '1';

--This query will be successful if the user chooses 2
SELECT 'SELECT username, privilege, owner, table_name' || CHR(10) ||
       '  FROM dba_users, dba_tab_privs' || CHR(10) ||
       ' WHERE username = grantee' || CHR(10) ||
       'ORDER BY username, owner, table_name, privilege;'
  FROM dual
 WHERE '&&s_report_choice' = '2';

SELECT 'SELECT username, privilege' || CHR(10) ||
       '  FROM dba_users, dba_sys_privs' || CHR(10) ||
       ' WHERE username = grantee' || CHR(10) ||
       'ORDER BY username, privilege;'
  FROM dual
 WHERE '&&s_report_choice' = '3';

SELECT 'PROMPT You must choose either 1, 2, or 3'
  FROM dual
 WHERE '&&s_report_choice' NOT IN ('1','2','3')
    OR '&&s_report_choice' IS NULL;

SPOOL OFF
SET TERMOUT ON
SET PAGESIZE 20
SET HEADING ON
SET VERIFY ON
```

```
--Now execute the query that we just spooled.
@user_security_choice

--Reset all the settings back to their defaults
SET FEEDBACK ON
CLEAR COLUMNS
TTITLE OFF
```

You have to be very careful when using this technique to turn off anything that could cause extraneous text to be written to the temporary command file. This includes page headings, column headings, and verification. That's why the script in the example included these commands:

```
SET TERMOUT OFF
SET PAGESIZE 0
SET HEADING OFF
SET VERIFY OFF
```

Terminal output was turned off to prevent the user from seeing the results of the SELECT on the display. One last thing you have to worry about is the filename itself. In the example shown above, the filename is hardwired into the script and does not include a path. Because no path is specified, the file will be written to the current directory. That's why a single ampersand or @ was used to run the intermediate file. Using @ causes SQL*Plus to look in the current directory for the script.

Having the filename hardwired into the script can cause problems if multiple users execute the script at the same time and from the same directory. If you are concerned about this, you could write some SQL or PL/SQL code to generate a unique filename based on the Oracle username or perhaps the session identifier (SID) from the V$SESSION view.

Be creative with this technique. You don't need to limit yourself to writing SQL*Plus scripts, either. You can use SQL*Plus to generate shell script files, SQL*Loader files, DOS batch files, or any other type of text file.

## Using PL/SQL

Always consider the possibility of using PL/SQL to implement any type of complex procedural logic. After all, that's the reason PL/SQL was invented in the first place. If you can manage to prompt the user up front for any needed information, and if you don't need to interact with the user during the operation, PL/SQL is the way to go.

The reports menu could not possibly be implemented in PL/SQL because the menu needs to run another SQL\*Plus script corresponding to the user's choice. PL/SQL runs inside the database, and cannot invoke a SQL\*Plus script.

An ideal candidate for the use of PL/SQL would be the example where we asked the user a simple yes/no question, and then deleted data from the PROJECT_ HOURS table if the user responded with a Y. Here's how that script looked:

```
SET VERIFY OFF

ACCEPT s_delete_confirm PROMPT 'Delete project hours data (Y/N)?'

DELETE
  FROM project_hours
 WHERE UPPER('&&s_delete_confirm') = 'Y';
```

This script works, and because the DELETE statement is so simple, it's not too hard to understand. Still, there are people who would look at it and become very confused. The more complicated the WHERE clause gets, the greater the likelihood of confusion. Wrapping a simple IF statement, which everyone understands, around the DELETE statement would add clarity to the script. The PL/SQL version of the above script looks like this:

```
SET VERIFY OFF

ACCEPT s_delete_confirm PROMPT 'Delete project hours data (Y/N)?'

SET SERVEROUTPUT ON

DECLARE
  users_yn_response CHAR := UPPER('&&s_delete_confirm');
BEGIN
  IF users_yn_response = 'Y' THEN
    DELETE
      FROM project_hours;
    COMMIT;

    DBMS_OUTPUT.PUT_LINE('All PROJECT_HOURS data has been deleted.');
  ELSIF users_yn_response = 'N' THEN
    DBMS_OUTPUT.PUT_LINE('No data was deleted.');
  ELSE
    DBMS_OUTPUT.PUT_LINE('You must answer with a Y or N.');
  END IF;
EXCEPTION
  WHEN OTHERS THEN
    DBMS_OUTPUT.PUT_LINE('The PROJECT_HOURS data could not be deleted. '
                          || SQLERRM);
    ROLLBACK;
END;
/
```

This script is a bit longer, but it's also more robust. The script will roll back the operation if the DELETE fails for any reason. It's also very clear now that the DELETE statement is going to delete *all* rows from the table.

### Using a Scripting Language Instead

Don't overlook the possibility that you can use your operating-system scripting language to good advantage. Any Unix shell will allow you to write more complex scripts than you could using SQL*Plus alone. Here's an implementation of the user security report menu using the Unix Korn shell:

```
while :
     do
     print " "
     print "1 - List users"
     print "2 - List users and table privileges"
     print "3 - List users and system privileges"
     print "4 - Quit"
     print
     print -n "Enter your choice (1,2,3,4) > "

     read

     case $REPLY in
          1 )
                    sqlplus -s jgennick/beaner @user_security_1
                    ;;
          2 )
                    sqlplus -s jgennick/beaner @user_security_2
                    ;;
          3 )
                    sqlplus -s jgennick/beaner @user_security_3
                    ;;
          4 )
                    exit
                    ;;
          * )
                    print "Please enter 1, 2, 3, or 4"
                    ;;
     esac
done
```

Perl is also something you should consider. The Perl scripting language is available for both Unix and Windows. It has the advantages of being widely used, and of not tying you to one specific operating system.

## Looping in SQL*Plus

There is no way to write a real loop using SQL*Plus. Your best option, if you need to do something iteratively, is to use PL/SQL. PL/SQL, however, doesn't allow you any interaction with the user, so it's not always suitable for the task at hand. Your second-best bet is to look into using your operating system's scripting language, if there is one. Having said this, I'll point out that there are a couple of things you can do in SQL*Plus that might get you the same result as writing a loop. These are:

- Recursive execution
- Generating a file of commands, and then executing it

The first option has some severe limitations, and I don't recommend it too strongly. The second option I use all the time, especially when performing database maintenance tasks.

## Recursive Execution

You can't loop, but you can execute the same script recursively. Say you have a script that displays some useful information, and you want to give the user the option of running it again. You can do that by recursively executing the script. Take a look at the following interaction, in which the user is looking at indexes for various tables. It looks like a loop. Each time through, the user is prompted for another table name, and the indexes on that table are displayed.

```
SQL> @list_indexes employee

INDEX_NAME                     COLUMN_NAME
------------------------------ ------------------------------
EMPLOYEE_PK                    EMPLOYEE_ID

Next table >project

INDEX_NAME                     COLUMN_NAME
------------------------------ ------------------------------
PROJECT_PK                     PROJECT_ID
PROJECT_BY_NAME                PROJECT_NAME

Next table >project_hours

INDEX_NAME                     COLUMN_NAME
------------------------------ ------------------------------
PROJECT_HOURS_PK               PROJECT_ID
                               EMPLOYEE_ID
                               TIME_LOG_DATE

Next table >

Thank you for using LIST_INDEXES. Goodbye!
```

It sure does look like a loop, but it's not. Here is the LIST_INDEXES script that is being run:

```
COLUMN index_name FORMAT A30
COLUMN column_name FORMAT A30
BREAK ON index_name NODUPLICATES
```

```
SELECT index_name, column_name
  FROM user_ind_columns
 WHERE table_name = UPPER('&1');

--Ask the user if he wants to do this again.
PROMPT
ACCEPT s_next_table PROMPT 'Next table >'

--Execute either list_indexes.sql or empty.sql,
--depending on the user's response.
COLUMN next_script NOPRINT NEW_VALUE s_next_script
SET TERMOUT OFF
SELECT DECODE ('&&s_next_table',
               '','empty.sql',
               'list_indexes ' || UPPER('&&s_next_table')) next_script
  FROM dual;
SET TERMOUT ON

@&&s_next_script
```

The key to the looping is in the last part of the script, following the ACCEPT statement. If the user enters another tablename, the SELECT statement will return another call to the LIST_INDEXES script. So when the user types "project" in response to the prompt, the s_next_script substitution variable ends up being:

```
list_indexes PROJECT
```

The only thing missing is the ampersand sign, and that is supplied by the command at the bottom of the script. In this case, the command:

```
@&&s_next_script
```

will be translated to:

```
@list_indexes PROJECT
```

If the user doesn't enter a table name at the prompt, the s_next_table variable will be null, and the DECODE statement will return "empty.sql". *EMPTY.SQL* is necessary because the @ command must be executed. *EMPTY.SQL* gives you a clean way out of the recursion. In this case *EMPTY.SQL* prints a message, and is implemented like this:

```
PROMPT
PROMPT Thank you for using LIST_INDEXES. Goodbye!
PROMPT
```

Recursive execution is a very limited technique. You can't nest scripts forever. SQL*Plus limits you to nesting only 20 scripts, and on some older versions the limit may be as low as 5. Exceed that limit, and you will get the following message:

```
SQL*Plus command procedures may only be nested to a depth of 20.
```

Still, recursion can be useful. What are the odds that you will want to type in 20 table names in one sitting? In this case, the convenience may outweigh any chance of exceeding that limit on nesting scripts. And if you do exceed the limit, so what? You can just rerun the script.

## Generating a File of Commands

If you need to loop a fixed number of times, say once for each table you own, you can use a SQL query to build a second file of SQL commands, then execute that file. This is known as *using SQL to write SQL*, and it's a very powerful scripting technique. You've already seen an example of this technique in a previous section, where it was used to implement the equivalent of an IF statement in a SQL\*Plus script. This technique can also be used to perform a repetitive operation, if the basis for that operation can be the results of a SQL query.

Suppose, for instance, that you want to write a script that will analyze and compute statistics for all your tables. You don't want to hardcode the table names in the script, because then you would need to remember to change the script each time you drop or create a table. Thinking in terms of pseudocode, you might envision a script like this:

```
FOR xxx = FIRST_TABLE TO LAST_TABLE
   ANALYZE xxx COMPUTE STATISTICS;
NEXT xxx
```

Of course, that script would never fly in SQL\*Plus. Instead, you need a way to execute the ANALYZE command for each table without really looping. One way to do that is to write a SQL query to create that command. Take a look at the following query:

```
SELECT 'ANALYZE ' || table_name || ' COMPUTE STATISTICS;'
   FROM user_tables;
```

Since SQL is a set-oriented language, it will return a result set consisting of one instance of the ANALYZE command for each table you own. Running this query against the sample database used for this book will give the following results:

```
ANALYZE EMPLOYEE COMPUTE STATISTICS;
ANALYZE PROJECT COMPUTE STATISTICS;
ANALYZE PROJECT_HOURS COMPUTE STATISTICS;
```

At this point, if this were just a once-off job, and if you were using a GUI version of SQL\*Plus, you could simply copy the output and paste it back in as input. The commands would execute and all your tables would be analyzed. To make a script you can run periodically, all you need to do is to spool the ANALYZE commands to a file and then execute that file. The following script does that.

```
SET ECHO OFF
--DESCRIPTION
--Analyze and compute statistics for all tables
--owned by the user.

--We only want the results of the query written to the
--file. Headings, titles, feedback, etc. aren't valid
--commands, so turn all that stuff off.
SET HEADING OFF
SET PAGESIZE 0
SET VERIFY OFF
SET FEEDBACK OFF
SET TERMOUT OFF

--Create a file of ANALYZE commands, one for
--each table. PROMPT commands are used to write
--SET ECHO ON and OFF commands to the spool file.
SPOOL analyze_each_table.sql
PROMPT SET ECHO ON
SELECT 'ANALYZE TABLE ' || table_name || ' COMPUTE STATISTICS;'
  FROM user_tables;
PROMPT SET ECHO OFF
SPOOL OFF

--Execute the ANALYZE commands.
SET TERMOUT ON
@analyze_each_table

--Reset settings back to defaults
SET HEADING ON
SET PAGESIZE 14
SET VERIFY ON
SET FEEDBACK ON
```

Most of the commands in the script are there to prevent any extraneous information, such as column headings or page titles, from being written to the spool file.
The real work is done by the SPOOL and SELECT commands, and also by the
command used to run the resulting script file. The ECHO setting is turned on prior
to running the ANALYZE commands so you can watch the ANALYZE commands
as they execute. A PROMPT command is used to write a SET ECHO ON command to the output file. Here are the results from running the script:

```
SQL> @analyze_tables
SQL> ANALYZE TABLE EMPLOYEE COMPUTE STATISTICS;
SQL> ANALYZE TABLE PROJECT COMPUTE STATISTICS;
SQL> ANALYZE TABLE PROJECT_HOURS COMPUTE STATISTICS;
SQL> SET ECHO OFF
```

All the tables in the schema were analyzed. Once this is set up, you never need to
worry about it again. Each time the script is run, ANALYZE commands are generated for all the tables currently in the schema.

My experience has been that the technique of using SQL to write SQL proves most useful when you are writing scripts to perform database maintenance tasks such as the one shown in the previous example. Information about all database objects is accessible via the data dictionary views, so it's usually a simple matter to issue queries against those views to generate whatever commands you need.

## Looping Within PL/SQL

You should always consider PL/SQL when you need to implement any type of complex procedural logic, and that includes looping. Because PL/SQL executes in the database, you can't use it for any type of loop that requires user interaction. The table index example shown earlier in this chapter, where the user was continually prompted for another table name, could never be implemented in PL/SQL. It's also impossible to call another SQL*Plus script from PL/SQL. However, if you can get around those two limitations, PL/SQL may be the best choice for the task.

### The ANALYZE TABLE script revisited

As an example of what you can do using PL/SQL, let's revisit the ANALYZE_ TABLE script shown earlier. It's very easy, using PL/SQL, to write a loop to iterate through all the tables you own. Here's one way to do that:

```
SQL> SET SERVEROUTPUT ON
SQL> BEGIN
  2    FOR my_table in (
  3      SELECT table_name
  4        FROM user_tables) LOOP
  5
  5      --Print the table name
  6      DBMS_OUTPUT.PUT_LINE(my_table.table_name);
  7    END LOOP;
  8  END;
  9  /
EMPLOYEE
PROJECT
PROJECT_HOURS

PL/SQL procedure successfully completed.
```

This example uses what is called a *cursor FOR loop*. A cursor FOR loop executes once for each row returned by the query you give it. In this example, that query returns a list of tables you own.

You might think you could just put an ANALYZE TABLE command inside the loop and pass it the table name as a parameter, but it's not quite that simple. The ANALYZE command is a DDL command, and prior to version 8.1 of Oracle, PL/SQL did not allow you to embed DDL commands within your code. The following is an example of what will happen if you try.

```
SQL> BEGIN
  2    ANALYZE TABLE employee COMPUTE STATISTICS;
  3  END;
  4  /
   ANALYZE TABLE EMPLOYEE COMPUTE STATISTICS;
              *
ERROR at line 2:
ORA-06550: line 2, column 11:
PLS-00103: Encountered the symbol "TABLE" when expecting one of the
following:
:= . ( @ % ;
```

With the earliest versions of PL/SQL, this was a hard-and-fast limitation, but now Oracle provides a PL/SQL package for executing dynamic SQL statements that you can also use to execute DDL. A *dynamic SQL* statement is one you build up programmatically, and often the exact statement isn't known until runtime. The package name is DBMS_SQL, and you can read about it in the *Oracle8 Server Application Developer's Guide.*[*]

There are five steps to using the DBMS_SQL package to execute a DDL statement:

1. Allocate a cursor for the statement.

2. Put the statement to be executed in a VARCHAR2 variable.

3. Parse the statement.

4. Execute the statement.

5. Deallocate the cursor.

Steps 2 through 4 are repeated for as many statements as you need to execute.

The first step is to allocate the cursor. Even though you aren't selecting data, all SQL statements are executed using a cursor. The code to do that looks like this:

```
ddl_cursor_id := DBMS_SQL.OPEN_CURSOR;
```

The variable ddl_cursor_id should be declared as an INTEGER. This integer is a cursor ID, used to refer to the actual cursor, which the DBMS_SQL package maintains internally. The call to DBMS_SQL.OPEN_CURSOR should go outside the loop. You can use the same cursor for multiple SQL statements, so you only need to allocate it once. The next step is to create the SQL statement you want executed. The following statement, placed inside the loop, will do that:

```
analyze_command := 'ANALYZE TABLE '
                   || my_table.table_name
                   || ' COMPUTE STATISTICS';
```

---

[*] Another good source of information on the DBMS_SQL package is *Oracle Built-in Packages*, by Steve Feuerstein, Charles Dye, and John Beresniewicz (O'Reilly & Associates, 1998). Not only does this book cover DBMS_SQL, it also covers all the other standard packages provided by Oracle.

Be sure not to include a semicolon to terminate the statement you
are creating. Semicolons are used to tell SQL\*Plus that a SQL statement has ended. They should never be passed to Oracle. If you ever
run a PL/SQL block and get an "invalid character" on the line containing your call to the DBMS_SQL.PARSE procedure, look for this
problem.

Once you have the SQL statement, pass it to the DBMS_SQL package with a call to
the PARSE procedure, like this:

```
DBMS_SQL.PARSE (ddl_cursor_id, analyze_command, DBMS_SQL.NATIVE);
```

The PARSE procedure takes three arguments: the cursor ID, the SQL statement to
be executed, and a flag telling it whether you want Oracle6 behavior, Oracle7
behavior, or *native* behavior. Specifying NATIVE results in the normal behavior for
whatever version of Oracle you are connected to. The statement is parsed and
stored in the cursor you previously allocated. Next, you execute it with a call like
the following to the EXECUTE function:

```
ignore_for_ddl := DBMS_SQL.EXECUTE (ddl_cursor_id);
```

The DBMS_SQL.EXECUTE function's return value indicates the number of rows
affected by an INSERT, UPDATE, or DELETE statement, and should be ignored
when executing anything else.

Currently, DDL statements are actually executed when they are
parsed, so the call to DBMS_SQL.EXECUTE is superfluous. Oracle
doesn't guarantee this behavior, however, so you shouldn't depend
on it.

Once you are done executing commands, you should dispose of the cursor with a
call like the following to the CLOSE_CURSOR procedure:

```
DBMS_SQL.CLOSE_CURSOR(ddl_cursor_id);
```

The final script to analyze all your tables, using PL/SQL and dynamic SQL, now
looks like this:

```
SET ECHO OFF
--DESCRIPTION
--Analyze and compute statistics for all tables
--owned by the user.

--Turn SERVEROUTPUT on so we see output from the
--PL/SQL block we are going to execute.
SET SERVEROUTPUT ON
```

```
--The following PL/SQL block will build up and execute
--an ANALYZE TABLE command for each table. The DBMS_SQL
--package is used for this purpose.
DECLARE
   ddl_cursor_id   INTEGER;
   analyze_command VARCHAR2(80);
   ignore_for_ddl  INTEGER;
BEGIN
   --Allocate a cursor to use when executing DDL commands.
   ddl_cursor_id := DBMS_SQL.OPEN_CURSOR;

   --Execute an ANALYZE command for each table.
   FOR my_table in (
     SELECT table_name
       FROM user_tables) LOOP

     --Create the command to analyze this table.
     analyze_command := 'ANALYZE TABLE '
                        || my_table.table_name
                        || ' COMPUTE STATISTICS';

     --Display the statement to be executed.
     DBMS_OUTPUT.PUT_LINE(analyze_command);

     --Parse & execute this ANALYZE command.
     DBMS_SQL.PARSE (ddl_cursor_id, analyze_command, DBMS_SQL.NATIVE);

     ignore_for_ddl := DBMS_SQL.EXECUTE (ddl_cursor_id);
   END LOOP;

   --Deallocate the cursor.
   DBMS_SQL.CLOSE_CURSOR(ddl_cursor_id);
END;
/
```

For a script like this, I think the technique of using SQL to write SQL is a better choice. It's certainly easier to write, and just as easy to understand, if not more so. Still, using PL/SQL gives you more control over the process if you need it.

# Validating and Parsing User Input

Whenever you ask a user for input, you run the risk that it won't make sense. Maybe you are asking for a number, and the user types in some letters. Maybe you are asking for a date, and the user enters a bad value for the month. The SQL*Plus ACCEPT command offers some support for dealing with these situations. You can do even more, if you need to, with some creative use of SQL.

## Validating Input with ACCEPT

Oracle has been steadily improving the ACCEPT command over the last few releases of SQL*Plus. These improvements all center around the issue of validation, and make it much easier to prevent a user from entering bad data in response to a prompt.

---

The ACCEPT command options illustrated in this section apply to SQL*Plus versions 8.0.3 and above. Not all options will be available under previous releases. The ACCEPT command is one that has changed a lot over the years. Check the documentation for the release you are using to see which options are available to you.

---

Throughout most of this book, the ACCEPT commands have all been written pretty much like this:

```
ACCEPT my_variable PROMPT 'Enter a value >'
```

This is a least-common-denominator version of the ACCEPT command that should work with any release of SQL*Plus. It will simply take whatever string the user types in and assign it to the variable. If you need to go beyond this, ACCEPT allows you to specify a datatype, and will not accept input that doesn't convert to the type you specify. ACCEPT also allows you to specify a format string that the input data must match. You can take good advantage of these options to make your scripts more bulletproof.

### ACCEPTing numeric values

If you are prompting the user for a number, the first and easiest thing to do is to use the NUMBER keyword with the ACCEPT command. Here's an example:

```
ACCEPT my_variable NUMBER PROMPT 'Enter a number >'
```

When NUMBER is specified, SQL*Plus won't accept any input that can't be converted to a number. Instead, it will keep repeating the prompt until the user gets it right; for example:

```
SQL> ACCEPT my_variable NUMBER PROMPT 'Enter a number >'
Enter a number >two
"two" is not a valid number
Enter a number >2.2.2
"2.2.2" is not a valid number
Enter a number >
```

SQL*Plus will accept a null input as a valid number, so if the user just presses ENTER, a "0" will be stored in the variable. Spaces, on the other hand, do not constitute numeric input. Using a FORMAT clause for a number will prevent null input from being accepted.

You can gain more control over numeric input by taking advantage of the ACCEPT command's FORMAT clause. With it, you can specify a numeric format string, and ACCEPT will only accept input that matches that format. Supposedly, any format string valid for use with the COLUMN command is also valid for use with the ACCEPT command. In practice, though, the "9", "0", and "." are the most useful as input formats.

Use "9"s when you want to limit the user to entering a certain number of digits.

```
SQL> ACCEPT my_variable NUMBER FORMAT 999 PROMPT 'Enter a number >'
Enter a number >1234
"1234" does not match input format "999"
Enter a number >123
SQL>
```

Note, though, that the user is not forced to enter the maximum number of digits allowed by the format string. The user may enter fewer digits, so long as the result is a valid number.

```
SQL> ACCEPT my_variable NUMBER FORMAT 999 PROMPT 'Enter a number >'
Enter a number >12
SQL>
```

One advantage of the FORMAT clause is that the user cannot get away without entering something. A valid number, even if it's zero, must be entered.

```
SQL> ACCEPT my_variable NUMBER FORMAT 999 PROMPT 'Enter a number >'
Enter a number >
"" does not match input format "999"
Enter a number >0
SQL>
```

If you want to allow a decimal value to be entered, then you must include a decimal point in the format string. The user will be limited to the number of decimal places you specify.

```
SQL> ACCEPT my_variable NUMBER FORMAT 999.99 PROMPT 'Enter a number >'
Enter a number >19.76
SQL> ACCEPT my_variable NUMBER FORMAT 999.99 PROMPT 'Enter a number >'
Enter a number >19.763
"19.763" does not match input format "999.99"
Enter a number >19.8
SQL>
```

You can use a leading zero in a format string to force the user to enter a specific number of digits.

```
SQL> ACCEPT my_variable NUMBER FORMAT 099 PROMPT 'Enter a number >'
Enter a number >1
"1" does not match input format "099"
Enter a number >12
"12" does not match input format "099"
Enter a number >123
SQL>
```

However, you cannot use the zero after the decimal point to force the user to enter a specific number of decimal digits. The user may always enter fewer digits after the decimal than you specify in the format string. For example, the following statement accepts an input with a single decimal digit, even though two are specified in the format string:

```
SQL> ACCEPT my_variable NUMBER FORMAT 099.90 PROMPT 'Enter a number >'
Enter a number >123.1
SQL>
```

Negative values are always allowed, regardless of whether the format string specifies a sign or not. The following example uses a format string of 999, but still accepts a negative value:

```
SQL> ACCEPT my_variable NUMBER FORMAT 999 PROMPT 'Enter a number >'
Enter a number >-123
SQL>
```

SQL*Plus will allow you to use other characters with the FORMAT clause (see the COLUMN command for a complete list), but they may not work as you would expect, and some don't work at all. The "S" character, for example, indicates a leading sign, but rather than being an optional sign, it is mandatory, so users must enter positive numbers with a leading "+". That behavior may make sense based on a strict interpretation of the manual, but it's unlikely to be what you want.

Things get even stranger if you use the dollar sign as part of a format string. Take a look at the following interaction with the ACCEPT command using a format of $999:

```
SQL> ACCEPT my_variable NUMBER FORMAT $999 PROMPT 'Enter a number >'
Enter a number >123
"123" does not match input format "$999"
Enter a number >$123
"$123" is not a valid number
```

SQL*Plus seems to be in a Catch-22 situation here. SQL*Plus correctly recognizes that "123" does not have a leading dollar sign, and thus does not match the input format. On the other hand, when you enter "$123", the value is not recognized as a number.

### ACCEPTing date values

You can deal with date values in much the same way as numeric values. The first thing to do is tell SQL*Plus you want a date. Do this by using the DATE keyword with the ACCEPT command, like this:

```
ACCEPT my_variable DATE PROMPT 'Give me a date >'
```

The date format accepted by SQL*Plus will depend on your NLS_DATE_FORMAT setting. Often this will be DD-MON-YY, but it could be something different depending on how Oracle is configured at your site. When the DATE option is specified, ACCEPT will reject any input that doesn't evaluate to a valid date; for example:

```
SQL> ACCEPT my_variable DATE PROMPT 'Give me a date >'
Give me a date >11/15/61
"11/15/61" does not match input format "DD-MON-YY"
Give me a date >November 15, 1961
"November 15, 1961" does not match input format "DD-MON-YY"
Give me a date >15-Nov-61
SQL>
```

You can see that if you enter an invalid date, ACCEPT will show you the format it's expecting. As with numbers, you can also specify a format string for dates. Any format string you can use with Oracle's TO_DATE function may also be used with the ACCEPT command. Here are a couple of typical examples:

```
SQL> ACCEPT my_variable DATE FORMAT 'MM/DD/YY' PROMPT 'Give me a date >'
Give me a date >15-Nov-1961
"15-Nov-1961" does not match input format "MM/DD/YY"
Give me a date >11/15/61
SQL> ACCEPT my_variable DATE FORMAT 'DD-MON-YYYY' PROMPT 'Give me a date >'
Give me a date >11/15/61
"11/15/61" does not match input format "DD-MON-YYYY"
Give me a date >15-Nov-1961
SQL>
```

---

 Remember that the result of an ACCEPT command is still a character string. The user may enter a date, but it is stored as a character string and will need to be converted again when your script next references that substitution variable.

---

ACCEPT is somewhat liberal when it comes to checking the date a user enters against the specified format. ACCEPT will allow either a two- or four-digit year, regardless of what you specify in the format string. ACCEPT is also not too picky about separators, and will allow hyphens even if your format string specifies slashes. The following examples illustrate this behavior:

```
SQL> ACCEPT my_variable DATE FORMAT 'DD-MON-YYYY' PROMPT 'Give me a date >'
Give me a date >15-Nov-61
SQL> ACCEPT my_variable DATE FORMAT 'MM/DD/YY' PROMPT 'Give me a date >'
Give me a date >11-15-1961
```

Time of day is not treated with too much respect by ACCEPT either. You may ask for it in your format string, but ACCEPT will take it or leave it. As long as the user enters a date, ACCEPT doesn't care about the rest; for example:

```
SQL> ACCEPT my_variable DATE FORMAT 'MM/DD/YYYY HH:MI:SS AM' PROMPT 'Give me
a date >'
Give me a date >11/15/1961
SQL>
```

Bear in mind that the user input in response to an ACCEPT command is always placed into a substitution variable, and that substitution variables are always text. This is true with numbers, and is just as true with dates. Look at the following example:

```
SQL> ACCEPT my_variable DATE FORMAT 'MM/DD/YY' PROMPT 'Give me a date >'
Give me a date >7/4/98
SQL> DEFINE my_variable
DEFINE MY_VARIABLE    = "7/4/98" (CHAR)
```

The date entered was July 4, 1998. It is stored as the character string "7/4/98", which matches the input format used with the ACCEPT command. To reference the date later in your script, you must use the TO_DATE function to convert it again, and you must use the same format string you used to ACCEPT the date. Failure to do this could result in the date being misinterpreted. The following SELECT, for example, interprets the same date using the European convention of having the day first, followed by the month and year:

```
SQL> select to_date('&&my_variable','dd/mm/yyyy') from dual;
old   1: select to_date('&&my_variable','dd/mm/yyyy') from dual
new   1: select to_date('7/4/98','dd/mm/yyyy') from dual

TO_DATE('
---------
07-APR-98

SQL>
```

Suddenly, July 4, 1998 has instead become April 7, 1998! I can't imagine ever wanting that type of behavior in a script. To avoid problems, use the same date format consistently every time you reference a substitution variable, whether it's in an ACCEPT command or somewhere else in your script.

## Validating Input with SQL

The validation you get with the ACCEPT command is rather limited. You can do more, if you need to, with the creative use of SQL (or PL/SQL) together with the branching techniques discussed earlier in this chapter. With a little thought and effort, you can:

• Code more specific validations than you get with ACCEPT

• Accept more complicated input from the user

You could, for example, write a script that asks the user for a date, and that requires all four digits of the year to be entered. You could also write a script that accepts several values in one string and then pulls apart that string to get at each value. An example of this would be allowing the user to specify a table using the standard *owner.tablename* syntax and defaulting the owner to the currently logged-on user.

If you are going to code a complex edit check using SQL*Plus, you need to be able to do two fundamental things:

1. Decide whether or not the user's input is valid

2. Take different actions depending on the result of that decision

The first thing you need to decide is which branching technique you are going to use, because that tends to drive how you structure the query you use for validation. Usually, if I'm in this deep, I will branch using a multilevel file structure. To facilitate this, I'll write the validation query to return all or part of the filename to run next. If the input is no good, the next script file will simply display an error message and quit. The second thing to do is write the SQL query to perform the validation. Implementing the validation requires these four steps:

1. ACCEPT input from the user.

2. Issue a COLUMN command to capture the value returned from the validation query.

3. Execute the validation query.

4. Execute the script file returned by the query, which you captured with the column command.

The following short script example illustrates how SQL can be used to validate input by to determining whether or not a date was entered with a four-digit year:

```
--Get a date from the user
ACCEPT start_date DATE FORMAT 'DD-MON-YYYY' PROMPT 'Start Date >'

--Get the next file to run, based on whether the date
--has a four-digit or a two-digit year.
COLUMN next_script_file NEW_VALUE next_script_file
SELECT DECODE (LENGTH(SUBSTR('&&start_date',
                INSTR(TRANSLATE('&&start_date','/','-'),'-',-1)+1,
                LENGTH('&&start_date')-
                INSTR(TRANSLATE('&&start_date','/','-'),'-',-1))),
```

```
         4,'four_digit_year.sql &&start_date',
         2,'two_digit_year.sql &&start_date',
         'bad_date.sql') next_script_file
  FROM dual;

--Execute the appropriate script
@&&next_script_file
```

Admittedly, the DECODE expression is a bit complex, but it serves to illustrate how much you can accomplish with Oracle's built-in functions.

## Parsing Input with SQL

In addition to simply validating input, you can also use SQL and PL/SQL to parse it. Imagine for a moment that you are writing a script to display information about the physical implementation of a table. The script has to know which table you want to look at, and one way to accomplish that is to pass the table name as an argument, like this:

```
@show_physical project_hours
```

That's fine if you always want to run the script on tables you own. But what if you are the DBA and want to examine tables owned by other users? As with the DESCRIBE command, you may want to allow for an optional owner name. Then you could also run the script like this:

```
@show_physical jeff.project_hours
```

The first problem you'll encounter in doing this is that the argument "jeff.project_hours" is one string, not two. The second problem is that you can't depend on the owner always to be specified, and when it's not specified, you want it to default to the currently logged-in user. The solution to these problems is to use SQL to parse the input. One way to do that is simply to extend the WHERE clauses of whatever queries are run by your script. Here's a query to return the amount of space used by a particular table:

```
SELECT SUM(bytes)
  FROM dba_extents
 WHERE segment_name = DECODE(INSTR('&&1','.'),
        0,UPPER('&&1'),
        UPPER(SUBSTR('&&1',INSTR('&&1','.')+1)))
   AND owner = DECODE(INSTR('&&1','.'),
        0,USER,
        UPPER(SUBSTR('&&1',1,INSTR('&&1','.')-1)));
```

This solution works, but it can be cumbersome and error-prone because the parsing logic has to be replicated in each query your script executes. A better solution is to write some SQL at the beginning of your script specifically to parse the input. That way you end up with two distinct substitution variables, one for the owner and one for the table name, to use in the rest of your script. There are two steps to doing this. First, set up some COLUMN commands with NEW_VALUE clauses. You need one of these COLUMN commands for each distinct value in your input string. In keeping with the owner.table example, the following two commands could be used:

```
COLUMN owner_name NOPRINT NEW_VALUE s_owner_name
COLUMN table_name NOPRINT NEW_VALUE s_table_name
```

Next, you need to execute a query that returns the results you want. In this case, the query needs to return the owner name and table name as separate columns. Be sure to use column aliases to name these columns, and be sure those aliases match the names used in the COLUMN commands. The following SELECT takes a string in the form owner.table, and returns two separate values. If the owner is not specified, the name of the current user is returned instead.

```
SELECT
  DECODE(INSTR('&&1','.'),
         0,USER,  /*Default to current user.*/
         UPPER(SUBSTR('&&1',1,INSTR('&&1','.')-1))) owner_name,
  DECODE(INSTR('&&1','.'),
         0,UPPER('&&1'),  /*Only the table name was passed in.*/
         UPPER(SUBSTR('&&1',INSTR('&&1','.')+1))) table_name
FROM dual;
```

Once the query has been executed, the substitution variables named in the COLUMN commands will hold the values returned by the SELECT. These substitution variables may now be used in the remainder of the script. The following is a rewrite of the previous SELECT using these variables:

```
SELECT SUM(bytes)
  FROM dba_extents
 WHERE segment_name '&&s_table_name'
   AND owner = '&&s_owner_name';
```

By using this technique, you have one point of change that controls how the input is parsed. If there's a bug in your logic, you only need to fix it in one place. The readability of your script is greatly increased, too. Your scripts will also be more clearly understood by others, and probably by yourself as well.

# *Error Handling*

SQL*Plus doesn't offer too much in the way of error handling. By default, SQL*Plus simply ignores errors and goes on to execute either the next command you type in, or the next command in the script you are running. For interactive use, this is good enough. If an error occurs, you will see the message and take appropriate action. However, the situation is different when you are running a script. Depending on what the script is doing, you may not want SQL*Plus to blindly proceed to the next command when an error occurs. Consider the following script, which creates a new table, copies data to it, then deletes the original table:

```
CREATE TABLE employees AS
    SELECT * FROM employee;
DROP TABLE employee;
```

If the CREATE TABLE command failed, you certainly wouldn't want the script to continue, because you would lose all your data! To help with this type of situation, SQL*Plus provides the WHENEVER command.

## *The WHENEVER Command*

With the WHENEVER command, you can give SQL*Plus instructions on what to do when an error occurs. Your choices are a bit limited: you can either continue when an error occurs, or you can exit SQL*Plus entirely, possibly returning an error code. Returning an error code is useful if you are calling SQL*Plus from a Unix shell script or a DOS batch file.

There are two types of errors you can handle with WHENEVER. Each has its own variation of the command. WHENEVER SQLERROR is used to handle SQL errors and errors raised from PL/SQL blocks. WHENEVER OSERROR is used to handle operating system errors, such as those you might get when you run out of disk space while spooling a large data extract.

There is one type of error you cannot detect: an error involving a SQL*Plus command. An example would be if you were to misspell a command, such as COLUMN. If your script contained a command like the following:

```
COLUM employee_name HEADEEN 'Employee Name' FLOORMAT A40
```

SQL*Plus would generate an error and continue on with the script as if nothing had happened. This isn't as much of a problem as you might first think. You should test your scripts to be sure your SQL*Plus commands are correct. This is easy to do, and the consequences of a failed SQL*Plus command are usually no worse than some messy formatting of the output. SQL commands, on the other hand, can fail for a variety of reasons that don't involve simple misspellings. A simple database change can easily cause a SQL command that worked one day to fail the next. Similarly, with operating-system errors, you don't know in advance when you will run out of disk space.

### *WHENEVER SQLERROR*

The WHENEVER SQLERROR command tells SQL*Plus what to do when a SQL statement or PL/SQL block fails to execute properly. The simplest way to use it is to issue the following command, which tells SQL*Plus to simply abort the script when an error occurs.

```
WHENEVER SQLERROR EXIT
```

Now, when a SQL error occurs, SQL*Plus will exit, as the following example shows:

```
SQL> WHENEVER SQLERROR EXIT
SQL> SELECT kristi FROM dual;
SELECT kristi FROM dual
       *
ERROR at line 1:
ORA-00904: invalid column name


Disconnected from Oracle7 Server Release 7.3.3.0.0 - Production Release
PL/SQL Release 2.3.3.0.0 - Production
$
```

When SQL*Plus exits like this, the default behavior is to commit any transaction that might be open. For a simple SELECT statement like that shown in the previous example, this is not a problem. When you are changing records, it might be. If your script executes several SQL statements that change data, you may not want to commit unless all the changes can be made. In this situation, use the ROLLBACK option to tell SQL*Plus to roll back when an error occurs, like this:

```
WHENEVER SQLERROR EXIT ROLLBACK
```

If you're calling SQL*Plus from a Unix shell script, DOS batch file, VMS command file, or the equivalent, you can have it pass back a return code so your shell script can tell whether your script executed successfully or not. The following command tells SQL*Plus to pass back a standard failure code when an error occurs:

```
WHENEVER SQLERROR EXIT FAILURE ROLLBACK
```

The precise code that gets passed back will vary from one operating system to the next. If a simple success/fail indication is not enough, you can have SQL*Plus pass back the specific Oracle error code or any other value you want. The following example shows how to pass back the Oracle error code when a SQL error occurs:

```
WHENEVER SQLERROR EXIT SQL.SQLCODE
```

You could also choose to return any arbitrary number, the value of a numeric bind variable, or the value of a substitution variable.

---

The default behavior of WHENEVER SQLERROR EXIT is to COMMIT any pending transaction. You may want to use the ROLLBACK option to change that behavior.

Using WHENEVER SQLERROR EXIT with the GUI version of SQL*Plus can be really annoying at times. Any error results in SQL*Plus terminating, causing the GUI window to close. Usually this happens before you even realize that an error occurred, making you miss any error message that may have been displayed.

Don't use THEN. It's WHENEVER SQLERROR EXIT, not WHENEVER SQLERROR THEN EXIT. I tend to get mixed up on this point often.

---

### PL/SQL errors and WHENEVER

The WHENEVER SQLERROR EXIT command will catch any errors in a PL/SQL block, but only if those errors are raised back to the SQL*Plus level. PL/SQL has its own error-handling mechanism, and using it can prevent SQL*Plus from knowing that an error ever occurred.

The following PL/SQL block does not contain an error handler, so any SQL errors will be implicitly raised to the calling routine, which in this case is SQL*Plus:

```
BEGIN
  UPDATE employee
     SET employee_billing_rate = employee_billing_rate * 1.10;
  COMMIT;
END;
/
```

However, you could rewrite the block so that it includes an error handler. In that case, the PL/SQL error handler would get the error, and SQL*Plus would not know about it. Here is the same block, but with an error handler:

```
DECLARE
  success_flag BOOLEAN;
BEGIN
  BEGIN
    UPDATE employee
       SET employee_billing_rate = employee_billing_rate * 1.10;
    success_flag := TRUE;
  EXCEPTION
    WHEN OTHERS THEN
      success_flag := false;
  END;

  IF success_flag THEN
    COMMIT;
  ELSE
    ROLLBACK;
    DBMS_OUTPUT.PUT_LINE('The UPDATE failed.');
  END IF;
END;
/
```

In this example, the UPDATE statement is contained in its own PL/SQL block, and any error related to that statement will be trapped by the exception handler for that block. Even if an error occurs, as far as SQL*Plus is concerned, this block will have executed successfully. If you want to handle an error within PL/SQL, but still abort the SQL*Plus script, you can use the RAISE_APPLICATION_ERROR procedure. This procedure is part of a PL/SQL package named DBMS_STANDARD, and should exist in all installations. You call it like this:

```
RAISE_APPLICATION_ERROR (error_code, error_message);
```

where:

*error_code*

Is a negative number. The range from −20000 to −20999 is reserved for user-defined errors.

*error_message*

Is a text message of up to 2048 characters.

When you call RAISE_APPLICATION_ERROR from a PL/SQL block, control immediately returns to the calling block. You must call the procedure from the outermost PL/SQL block in order to return the error to SQL*Plus. When that happens, SQL*Plus will print the error message and then take whatever action you specified in the most recent WHENEVER SQLERROR command. The next PL/SQL block is the same as the previous one, except for the addition of the RAISE_APPLICATION_ERROR command, which is used to notify SQL*Plus of an error:

```
DECLARE
   success_flag BOOLEAN;
BEGIN
  BEGIN
    UPDATE employee
       SET employee_billing_rate = employee_billing_rate * 1.10;
    success_flag := TRUE;
  EXCEPTION
    WHEN OTHERS THEN
       success_flag := false;
  END;

  IF success_flag THEN
    COMMIT;
  ELSE
    ROLLBACK;
    DBMS_OUTPUT.PUT_LINE('The UPDATE failed.');
    RAISE_APPLICATION_ERROR (-20000,
     'The UPDATE of employee billing rates failed.');
  END IF;
END;
/
```

Now if an error occurs, SQL*Plus will know about it and can abort the script.

## WHENEVER OSERROR

The WHENEVER OSERROR command tells SQL*Plus what to do when an operating system error occurs. Running out of disk space would be a likely operating-system error, one that you might encounter when spooling large amounts of output from a SQL query.

WHENEVER OSERROR works pretty much the same as the WHENEVER SQLER-ROR command. The simple version, which just causes SQL*Plus to exit when an error occurs, looks like this:

```
WHENEVER OSERROR EXIT
```

By default, any changes are committed when SQL*Plus exits. You can change that behavior using the ROLLBACK keyword as follows:

```
WHENEVER OSERROR EXIT ROLLBACK
```

As with WHENEVER SQLERROR, you can pass a return code back to a shell script in order to allow it to detect the error. For example:

```
WHENEVER OSERROR EXIT FAILURE
```

Unlike the SQLERROR version of the command, there is no equivalent to SQL.SQL-CODE for operating-system errors. The other options still apply, however, and you can return an arbitrary value, the value from a bind variable, or the value of a substitution variable.

> Be aware that the range of return codes you can pass back from SQL*Plus varies from one operating system to the next. Under Unix, return codes are limited to one byte, giving you a range of 0 to 255 to work with. VMS, on the other hand, allows much larger values to be returned. Keep this in mind if you are writing a script that needs to be portable across different operating systems.

The following example archives any project_hours data over one year old to a file, then deletes the data that was archived. In order to be sure no data is deleted without first being successfully archived, the WHENEVER commands are used to abort the script in the event of an error.

```
WHENEVER SQLERROR EXIT FAILURE
WHENEVER OSERROR EXIT FAILURE

--Turn off page headings, column titles, etc.
SET PAGESIZE 0
SET HEADING OFF
SET COLSEP ","

--Archive old records
SPOOL project_hours_archive.txt
SELECT *
  FROM project_hours
 WHERE TRUNC(time_log_date) <= ADD_MONTHS(TRUNC(SYSDATE),-12);
SPOOL OFF
```

```
--Delete the records just archived
DELETE
  FROM project_hours
 WHERE TRUNC(time_log_date) <= ADD_MONTHS(TRUNC(SYSDATE),-12);
```

# 8

# *Tuning and Timing*

Oracle offers two features that can be used from SQL\*Plus to monitor and improve the performance of your scripts and SQL statements. These two features are SQL\*Plus timers and the EXPLAIN PLAN command.

SQL\*Plus has a timing feature built into it that can be used to monitor the length of time it takes to execute a SQL command, a PL/SQL block, or any other part of a script. To measure the time it takes to execute a SQL statement, you start a timer prior to executing the statement, then display the value of the timer immediately after the statement is executed.

The EXPLAIN PLAN command, although it is a SQL command, not a SQL\*Plus command, is often used from SQL\*Plus. EXPLAIN PLAN can be used to find out exactly how Oracle intends to execute any given SQL query. It will tell you, for example, whether or not an index will be used, and what the name of that index will be. Once you know how Oracle intends to execute the query, you can use *hints* to influence or alter Oracle's default plan based on your knowledge of the data. A hint is a command to the optimizer that is embedded in a comment within a SQL query. The *optimizer* is the part of Oracle that determines how best to retrieve the data required by a SQL statement.

This chapter is not intended to be an exhaustive reference for tuning SQL statements. Several good books have been written on this subject. What this chapter does provide is a quick overview of the mechanics of tuning and a convenient summary of the hints available to you.

## *Using SQL\*Plus Timers*

SQL\*Plus has a crude timing facility built into it that allows you to measure the elapsed time of a script or any portion of a script. You can even have SQL\*Plus report the elapsed execution time of every SQL query and PL/SQL block automatically after each statement has executed. Timers can be nested so that you can time the overall execution of a script as well as the execution time of each individual statement.

Timer resolution varies with the hardware platform being used. Under Windows NT or 95, the elapsed time is reported in milliseconds. Under HP Unix, it is resolved only to the hundredth of a second, but the display format is much nicer. Here is how an elapsed time of 90.5 seconds will be shown under Windows:

```
real: 90500
```

90,500 milliseconds is equivalent to 90.5 seconds. With Unix versions of SQL*Plus, the display is much more user-friendly. Here's how the HP-UX version of SQL*Plus would report the same value:

```
Elapsed: 00:01:30.5
```

Unix uses an hour, minute, second, and hundredths format, so 90.5 seconds is reported as 1 minute, 30 seconds, and 50 hundredths. Remember, the timer is a SQL*Plus timer. The hardware that matters is the machine running the SQL*Plus executable, not the one running the Oracle server.

Timings can be useful in spotting trends. It may be helpful to know, for example, if a script is taking longer and longer to run. Timings can also be helpful in comparing the relative efficiency of two SQL statements. If you have two statements that return equivalent results, and one consistently runs faster than the other, that's the one you probably want to go with.

Take timing with a grain of salt, though. The timer measures elapsed time, not CPU time, and many factors can throw it off. The network throughput may vary between the execution of two queries. The load on the server could vary as well. For example, one query might run more slowly than another simply because many other users all happened to hit the database at the same time. Be skeptical of once-off results. Look for consistency over several timings.

## *The SET TIMING Command*

You can have SQL*Plus automatically report the elapsed time it takes to execute every query by using the SET TIMING ON command. For example:

```
SQL> SET TIMING ON
```

Now, whenever you execute a query, SQL*Plus will report the elapsed time. With the Windows versions of SQL*Plus, this time will be reported in milliseconds. The following example shows that it took 110 milliseconds, or about 1/10 of a second, for a query on DBA_VIEWS to complete:

```
SQL> SELECT view_name
  2    FROM dba_views
  3    WHERE view_name = 'DBA_TABLES';

VIEW_NAME
------------------------------
DBA_TABLES

 real: 110
```

Notice that the timing display is rather inelegant. Why a heading of "real" is used, instead of something more descriptive like "elapsed time," I don't know.

When timing is on, SQL\*Plus will also report the time it takes to execute a PL/SQL block. Here's an example:

```
SQL> BEGIN
  2    DBMS_OUTPUT.PUT_LINE('How long does this take?');
  3  END;
  4  /
How long does this take?

PL/SQL procedure successfully completed.

 real: 270
```

To turn timing off, simply issue the SET TIMING OFF command as follows:

```
SQL> SET TIMING OFF
```

When you have timing turned on, SQL\*Plus displays elapsed time only for commands executed by the database server. This includes SQL statements and PL/SQL blocks. Elapsed time for SQL\*Plus commands, such as ACCEPT and DEFINE, is not reported.

## The TIMING Command

The SQL\*Plus TIMING command gives you complete control over when timing starts and stops, and over what is measured. With it, you can turn on a timer at any point in your script. You can display the elapsed time at any point after a timer is turned on, and you can nest timers. Nesting timers gives you a way to time a set of operations, maybe an entire script, while still allowing you to time each individual operation separately.

The TIMING command is really useful only in scripts. You can use it interactively, but then the elapsed time will include your "think" time and the time it take you to type in commands.

The syntax for the TIMING command looks like this:

```
TIMI[NG] [START [timer_name ] | SHOW | STOP]
```

where:

*TIMI[NG]*

Is the command, which may be abbreviated to TIMI.

*START [timer_name]*

Starts a new timer, and optionally gives it the name you provide.

*SHOW*

Shows the current value of the most recently started timer.

*STOP*

Stops the most recently started timer, shows its current value, then deletes it.

Think of timers as being implemented on a stack. Each time you issue a TIMING START command, you push a new timer onto the stack. The TIMING SHOW and TIMING STOP commands each operate on whatever timer is currently at the top of the stack. To find out how many timers you have currently running, enter the TIMING command with no arguments.

### Starting and stopping a timer

Use the TIMING START command to start a timer. If you like, you can give the timer a name, but you don't have to. Timing starts the moment the command is executed. The following example starts a new timer, and gives it a name of for_testing:

```
SQL> TIMING START for_testing
```

You stop the timer and display its final value by issuing the TIMING STOP command as follows:

```
SQL> TIMING STOP
timing for: for_testing
 real: 56460
```

In this case, the timer ran for a total elapsed time of 56.460 seconds.

### Displaying the value of a timer

You can display the value of a timer without stopping it. This is useful if your script is executing several SQL queries and you want to see the cumulative elapsed time after each one. For example:

```
SQL> TIMING START for_show
SQL> TIMING SHOW
timing for: for_show
 real: 2250
```

```
SQL> TIMING SHOW
timing for: for_show
 real: 3790
SQL> TIMING SHOW
timing for: for_show
 real: 5380
SQL> TIMING SHOW
timing for: for_show
 real: 6920
```

You can see from this example that once I got going, it took me a tad more than 1 1/2 seconds to type each TIMING SHOW command.

### Nesting timers

Timers can be nested, allowing you to time a group of operations, while simultaneously timing each individual operation within the larger group. The following example shows a timer being started, and while that's running, two more timers are started and stopped. Finally, the first timer is also stopped.

```
SQL> TIMING START first
SQL> TIMING START second
SQL> TIMING STOP
timing for: second
 real: 2630
SQL> TIMING START third
SQL> TIMING STOP
timing for: third
 real: 2360
SQL> TIMING STOP
timing for: first
 real: 19160
```

The important thing to notice here is that the first timer kept running during this entire example. The total elapsed time was a bit over 19 seconds, while each of the intermediate operations took a bit over two seconds.

The following example shows how this nesting feature could be used. It runs a script to delete data and reports the elapsed time for each DELETE statement, as well as the total elapsed time for the script as a whole.

```
SET ECHO ON
TIMING START entire_script

--Delete project hours data and time the operation.
TIMING START delete_project_hours
DELETE FROM project_hours;
TIMING STOP

--Delete project data and time the operation.
TIMING START delete_projects
DELETE FROM project;
TIMING STOP
```

```
--Delete employee data and time the operation.
TIMING START
DELETE FROM employee;
TIMING STOP

COMMIT;

--Show the overall elapsed time for the entire script.
TIMING STOP
```

Here is the output from running the above script:

```
SQL> TIMING START entire_script
SQL>
SQL> --Delete project hours data and time the operation.
SQL> TIMING START delete_project_hours
SQL> DELETE FROM project_hours;
SQL> TIMING STOP
timing for: delete_project_hours
 real: 1100
SQL>
SQL> --Delete project data and time the operation.
SQL> TIMING START delete_projects
SQL> DELETE FROM project;
SQL> TIMING STOP
timing for: delete_projects
 real: 160
SQL>
SQL> --Delete employee data and time the operation.
SQL> TIMING START
SQL> DELETE FROM employee;
SQL> TIMING STOP
 real: 220
SQL>
SQL> COMMIT;
SQL>
SQL> --Show the overall elapsed time for the entire script.
SQL> TIMING STOP
timing for: entire_script
 real: 1750
```

You can see that the elapsed time was displayed for each statement and for the script as a whole.

### Finding out how many timers you have going

The TIMER command by itself will cause SQL*Plus to report the number of timers that are currently active. The following example shows how the count goes up each time you start a timer and back down each time you stop one:

```
SQL> TIMING START
SQL> TIMING
1 timing element in use
```

```
SQL> TIMING START
SQL> TIMING
2 timing elements in use
SQL> TIMING STOP
 real: 3510
SQL> TIMING
1 timing element in use
SQL> TIMING STOP
 real: 9170
SQL> TIMING
no timing elements in use
```

### Stopping all timers

You can stop and delete all timers at once with the CLEAR TIMING command. As each timer is stopped, its final value is displayed. Here's an example:

```
SQL> TIMING START first
SQL> TIMING START second
SQL> TIMING START third
SQL> CLEAR TIMING
timing for: third
 real: 2300
timing for: second
 real: 7250
timing for: first
 real: 10160
```

# *Using EXPLAIN PLAN*

EXPLAIN PLAN is a SQL statement that causes Oracle to report the execution plan it would choose for any SELECT, INSERT, UPDATE, or DELETE statement. An *execution plan* refers to the approach Oracle will take to retrieve the necessary data for a statement. One example of a plan would be to use an index to find the required rows. Another example of an execution plan would be to sequentially read all rows in the table. If you have a poorly-performing SQL statement, you can use EXPLAIN PLAN to find out how Oracle is processing it. With that information, you may be able to take some corrective action to improve performance.

When you use EXPLAIN PLAN, Oracle doesn't display its execution strategy on the screen; instead, it inserts rows into a table. This table is referred to as the *plan table*, and you must query it properly in order to see the results. Of course, the plan table must exist, so if you've never used EXPLAIN PLAN before, you may need to create the plan table first.

Oracle occasionally adds columns to the plan table. If you have a plan table created using a previous version of Oracle, you may want to drop and recreate it, just to be sure you have the most up-to-date version.

## Creating the Plan Table

Oracle provides a script to create the plan table. It is named *UTLXPLAN.SQL*, and it resides in the *RDBMS/ADMIN* directory for your database. Under Windows 95, for example, the script to create the plan table for Oracle8 will be *C:\ORAWIN95\ RDBMS80\ADMIN\UTLXPLAN.SQL*. You can run it from SQL*Plus like this:

```
SQL> @C:\ORAWIN95\RDBMS80\ADMIN\UTLXPLAN.SQL

Table created.
```

Here is what the Oracle8 plan table looks like:

```
SQL> DESCRIBE plan_table
 Name                              Null?     Type
 -------------------------------   --------  ----
 STATEMENT_ID                                VARCHAR2(30)
 TIMESTAMP                                   DATE
 REMARKS                                     VARCHAR2(80)
 OPERATION                                   VARCHAR2(30)
 OPTIONS                                     VARCHAR2(30)
 OBJECT_NODE                                 VARCHAR2(128)
 OBJECT_OWNER                                VARCHAR2(30)
 OBJECT_NAME                                 VARCHAR2(30)
 OBJECT_INSTANCE                             NUMBER(38)
 OBJECT_TYPE                                 VARCHAR2(30)
 OPTIMIZER                                   VARCHAR2(255)
 SEARCH_COLUMNS                              NUMBER
 ID                                          NUMBER(38)
 PARENT_ID                                   NUMBER(38)
 POSITION                                    NUMBER(38)
 COST                                        NUMBER(38)
 CARDINALITY                                 NUMBER(38)
 BYTES                                       NUMBER(38)
 OTHER_TAG                                   VARCHAR2(255)
 PARTITION_START                             VARCHAR2(255)
 PARTITION_STOP                              VARCHAR2(255)
 PARTITION_ID                                NUMBER(38)
 OTHER                                       LONG
```

The name of the table does not have to be plan_table, but that's the default, and it's usually easiest to leave it that way. If for some reason you don't have access to the *UTLXPLAN.SQL* script, you can create the table manually. Just be sure that the column names and datatypes match those shown here.

The columns in the plan table may vary a bit depending on the exact Oracle version you have. The table shown above is for Oracle 8.0.3, and includes at least three columns that are new with Oracle8. The PARTITION_START, PARTITION_STOP, and PARTITION_ID columns were added in support of Oracle8's new partitioning features.

## Explaining a Query

Once you have a plan table, getting Oracle to tell you the execution plan for any given query is a fairly easy task. You just need to prepend the EXPLAIN PLAN command to the front of your query. The syntax for EXPLAIN PLAN looks like this:

```
EXPLAIN PLAN
        [SET STATEMENT_ID = 'statement_id']
        [INTO table_name]
        FOR statement;
```

where:

*statement_id*

Can be anything you like, and is stored in the STATEMENT_ID field of all plan table records related to the query you are explaining. It defaults to null.

*table_name*

Is the name of the plan table, and defaults to "PLAN_TABLE". You only need to supply this value if you have created your plan table with some name other than the default.

*statement*

Is the DML statement to be "explained." This can be an INSERT, UPDATE, DELETE, or SELECT statement, but it must not reference any data dictionary views or dynamic performance tables.

Consider the following query, which returns the total number of hours worked by each employee on each project:

```
SELECT employee_name, project_name, sum(hours_logged)
  FROM employee, project, project_hours
 WHERE employee.employee_id = project_hours.employee_id
   AND project.project_id = project_hours.project_id
GROUP BY employee_name, project_name;
```

This query can be explained using the following two commands:

```
DELETE FROM plan_table WHERE statement_id = 'HOURS_BY_PROJECT';

EXPLAIN PLAN
SET STATEMENT_ID = 'HOURS_BY_PROJECT'
FOR
SELECT employee_name, project_name, sum(hours_logged)
  FROM employee, project, project_hours
```

```
WHERE employee.employee_id = project_hours.employee_id
  AND project.project_id = project_hours.project_id
GROUP BY employee_name, project_name;
```

When you execute this EXPLAIN PLAN command, you won't see any output. That's because Oracle stores the query plan in the plan table. Retrieving and interpreting the results is your next task.

You must include a DELETE statement prior to the EXPLAIN PLAN statement. When you explain a statement, Oracle does not clear the plan table of any previous rows with the same statement ID. If rows with the same statement ID exist from previous executions of EXPLAIN PLAN, you will get very strange results.

If you're the only person using the plan table, you can save yourself some typing by omitting the WHERE clause in the DELETE statement, thereby deleting all the records in the plan table.

## Interpreting the Results

Having done an EXPLAIN PLAN, you retrieve and view the results by querying the plan table. The statement ID is key to doing this. The plan table can contain execution plans for any number of queries. The rows for each query contain the statement ID you specified in your EXPLAIN PLAN statement, so you must use this same ID when querying the plan table in order to select the plan you are interested in seeing.

### The plan table query

The standard way to look at an execution plan is to display it using a hierarchical query. Oracle breaks query execution down into a series of nested steps, each of which feeds data up to a parent step. The ultimate parent is the query itself, the output of which is returned to the application. Here is a typical query used to display the plan output:

```
SELECT id, parent_id,
       LPAD(' ', 2*(level-1)) || operation || ' ' || options
       || ' ' || object_name || ' ' ||
       DECODE(id, 0, 'Cost = ' || position) "Query Plan"
  FROM plan_table
START WITH id = 0 AND statement_id = '&&s_statement_id'
CONNECT BY prior id = parent_id AND statement_id = '&&s_statement_id';
```

The result of this query will be a report showing the steps in the execution plan, with each child step being indented underneath its parent.

## The SHOW_PLAN script

You don't want to type a plan table query each time you need to see a plan, so you should consider placing it in a script file. The following script provides a user-friendly way to see the execution plan for a statement. It first lists the statements currently available in the plan table. Then you are prompted for the one you want to look at, and finally the plan for that statement is displayed. Here is the script:

```
SET ECHO OFF

--DESCRIPTION
--This script, SHOW_PLAN.SQL, displays a list of statement IDs from
--the plan table, and prompts the user to enter one. The plan for
--that statement is then displayed using a hierarchical query.
--
--MODIFICATION HISTORY
--19-Aug-1998 by Jonathan Gennick
--  1 Creation
--

SET VERIFY OFF
SET HEADING OFF
SET FEEDBACK OFF
SET PAGESIZE 0

--
--Display a list of statement ids for the user to choose from.
--
PROMPT
PROMPT The plan table contains execution plans
PROMPT for the following statements:
PROMPT

SELECT DISTINCT '     ', statement_id
  FROM plan_table
ORDER BY statement_id;

--
--Ask the user to enter the name of the statement for
--which the execution plan is to be shown.
--
PROMPT
ACCEPT s_statement_id CHAR PROMPT 'Enter Statement ID: '
PROMPT

--
--Show the execution plan for the statement the user selected.
--
COLUMN id FORMAT 999
COLUMN step_description FORMAT A80
SELECT id, LPAD(' ', 2*(level-1)) || operation || ' ' || options
       || ' ' || object_name || ' ' ||
       DECODE(id, 0, 'Cost = ' || position) step_description
```

```
     FROM plan_table
 START WITH id = 0 AND statement_id = '&&s_statement_id'
 CONNECT BY prior id = parent_id AND statement_id = '&&s_statement_id'
 ORDER BY id, position;

 SELECT 'PLAN_TABLE contains no execution plan for &&s_statement_id..'
   FROM dual
  WHERE '&&s_statement_id' NOT IN (
        SELECT DISTINCT statement_id
          FROM plan_table
        );

 --Restore settings to their defaults
 SET HEADING ON
 SET FEEDBACK ON
 SET PAGESIZE 14
```

### Executing the SHOW_PLAN script

You can execute the SHOW_PLAN script and display the plan for the HOURS_BY_
PROJECT query explained earlier as follows:

```
SQL> @show_plan

The plan table contains execution plans
for the following statements:

     HOURS_BY_PROJECT

Enter Statement ID: HOURS_BY_PROJECT

  0 SELECT STATEMENT    Cost = 21
  1    SORT GROUP BY
  2      HASH JOIN
  3        TABLE ACCESS FULL EMPLOYEE
  4        HASH JOIN
  5          TABLE ACCESS FULL PROJECT
  6          TABLE ACCESS FULL PROJECT_HOURS
SQL>
```

Each element of this execution plan contains three pieces of information: the operation, any options that apply, and the object of that operation. Usually these three
elements are enough to figure out what Oracle is doing with the query, but if you
need more information about a specific step, you can always query the plan table.

---

In order for Oracle to compute a reasonably accurate cost, you must
have up-to-date statistics on the tables involved in the query. Use
SQL's ANALYZE TABLE command to gather these statistics. If your
statistics are old, the optimizer may come up with an execution plan
that won't be efficient for the data you have now.

---

The SHOW_PLAN script also returns the overall cost of executing the query. In this example, the cost is 21. This number has no meaning in an absolute sense. It's simply a scoring mechanism used by the optimizer to facilitate choosing one plan from many possibilities. You should use it only when comparing two execution plans to see which is more efficient. A plan with a cost of 21, for example, would be approximately twice as efficient as a plan with a cost of 42.

 If you are using the rule-based optimizer, the cost will be null. Oracle will use the rule-based optimizer if you have not used the ANALYZE TABLE command to gather statistics for any of the tables involved in the query.

### Making sense of the results

The key to interpreting an execution plan is to understand that the display is hierarchical. A step may consist of one or more child steps, and these child steps are shown indented underneath their parent. Executing any given step involves executing all its children, so to understand the plan, you pretty much have to work your way out from the innermost step. In this example, there are three major steps to the plan. First, Oracle will join the PROJECT and PROJECT_HOURS tables, using a hash join method. Next, the results of this join will be joined with the EMPLOYEE table, also using a hash join method. Finally, the results are sorted on the GROUP BY columns. After the sort, the rows are returned as the result of the SELECT statement.

Table 8-1 gives a brief description of the various operations, together with their options, that you may see when querying the plan table. For more detailed information about any of these operations, refer to the *Oracle8 Server Tuning* manual.

*Table 8-1. EXPLAIN PLAN Operations*

| Operation | Options | Description |
|---|---|---|
| AND-EQUAL | | This step will have two or more child steps, each of which returns a set of ROWIDs. The AND-EQUAL operation selects only those ROWIDs that are returned by all the child operations. |
| BITMAP | CONVERSION TO ROWIDS | Converts a bitmap from a bitmap index to a set of ROWIDs that can be used to retrieve the actual data. |
| | CONVERSION FROM ROWIDS | Converts a set of ROWIDs into a bitmapped representation. |
| | CONVERSION COUNT | Counts the number of rows represented by a bitmap. |

*Table 8-1. EXPLAIN PLAN Operations (continued)*

| Operation | Options | Description |
|---|---|---|
| | INDEX SINGLE VALUE | Retrieves the bitmap for a single key value. For example, if the field was a YES/NO field, and your query wanted only rows with a value of "YES", then this operation would be used. |
| | INDEX RANGE SCAN | Similar to BITMAP INDEX SINGLE VALUE, but bitmaps are returned for a range of key values. |
| | INDEX FULL SCAN | The entire bitmap index will be scanned. |
| | MERGE | Merges two bitmaps together, and returns one bitmap as a result. This is an OR operation between two bitmaps. The resulting bitmap will select all rows from the first bitmap plus all rows from the second bitmap. |
| | MINUS | This is the opposite of a MERGE, and may have two or three child operations that return bitmaps. The bitmap returned by the first child operation is used as a starting point. All rows represented by the second bitmap are subtracted from the first. If the column is nullable, then all rows with null values are also subtracted. |
| | OR | Takes two bitmaps as input, ORs them together, and returns one bitmap as a result. The returned bitmap will select all rows from the first plus all rows from the second. |
| CONNECT BY | | Rows are being retrieved hierarchically because the query was written with a CONNECT BY clause. |
| CONCATENATION | | Multiple sets of rows are combined into one set, essentially a UNION ALL. |
| COUNT | | Counts the number of rows that have been selected from a table. |
| | STOPKEY | The number of rows to be counted is limited by the use of ROWNUM in the query's WHERE clause. |
| FILTER | | Takes a set of rows as input, and eliminates some of them based on a condition from the query's WHERE clause. |
| FIRST ROW | | Retrieves only the first row of a query's result set. |
| FOR UPDATE | | Locks rows that are retrieved. This would be the result of specifying FOR UPDATE in the original query. |
| HASH JOIN | | Joins two tables using a hash join method. |

*Table 8-1. EXPLAIN PLAN Operations (continued)*

| Operation | Options | Description |
|---|---|---|
| INDEX | UNIQUE | The lookup of a unique value from an index. You would see this only when the index is a unique index, such as those used to enforce a primary key or a unique key. |
| | RANGE SCAN | An index is being scanned for rows that fall into a range of values. The index is scanned in ascending order. |
| | RANGE SCAN DESCENDING | Same as RANGE SCAN, but the index is scanned in descending order. |
| INLIST ITERATOR | | One or more operations are to be performed once for each value in an IN predicate. |
| INTERSECTION | | Two rowsets are taken as input, and only rows that appear in both sets are returned. |
| MERGE JOIN | | Joins two rowsets based on some common value. Both rowsets will first have been sorted by this value. This is an inner join. |
| | OUTER | Similar to a MERGE JOIN, but an outer join is performed. |
| | ANTI | Indicates that an anti-join is being performed. |
| | SEMI | Indicates that a semi-join is being performed. |
| MINUS | | This is the result of the MINUS operator. Two rowsets are taken as inputs. The resulting rowset contains all rows from the first input that do not appear in the second input. |
| NESTED LOOPS | | This operation will have two children, each returning a rowset. For every row returned by the first child, the second child operation will be executed. |
| | OUTER | Represents a nested loop used to perform an outer join. |
| PARTITION | | Executes an operation for one or more partitions. The PARTITION_START and PARTITION_STOP columns give the range of partitions over which the operation is performed. |
| | SINGLE | The operation will be performed on a single partition. |
| | ITERATOR | The operation will be performed on several partitions. |
| | ALL | The operation will be performed on all partitions. |
| | INLIST | The operation will be performed on the partitions, and is being driven by an IN predicate. |

*Table 8-1. EXPLAIN PLAN Operations (continued)*

| Operation | Options | Description |
|---|---|---|
| PROJECTION | | Takes multiple queries as input, and returns a single set of records. This is used with INTERSECTION, MINUS, and UNION operations. |
| REMOTE | | Indicates that a rowset is being returned from a remote database. |
| SEQUENCE | | An Oracle sequence is being accessed. |
| SORT | AGGREGATE | Applies a group function, such as COUNT, to a rowset, and returns only one row as the result. |
| | UNIQUE | Sorts a rowset and eliminates duplicates. |
| | GROUP BY | Sorts a rowset into groups. This is the result of a GROUP BY clause. |
| | JOIN | Sorts a rowset in preparation for a join. See MERGE JOIN. |
| | ORDER BY | Sorts a rowset in accordance with the ORDER BY clause specified in the query. |
| TABLE ACCESS | FULL | Oracle will read all rows in the specified table. |
| | CLUSTER | Oracle will read all rows in a table that match a specified index cluster key. |
| | HASH | Oracle will read all rows in a table that match a specified hash cluster key. |
| | BY ROWID | Oracle will retrieve a row from a table based on its ROWID. |
| UNION | | Takes two rowsets, eliminates duplicates, and returns the result as one set. |
| VIEW | | Executes the query behind a view and returns the resulting rowset. |

# Using AUTOTRACE

Beginning with version 3.3 of SQL*Plus, Oracle provides a setting that automatically displays the execution plan for any query you execute. The name of this setting is AUTOTRACE, and you can turn it off and on with the SET command. There is one big catch. The query must actually be executed before you can see the results. If you are contemplating a query against a large table, it might take all day for a poorly-tuned query to execute. In that case, you might just want to see the execution plan before you run the query, not afterwards. You may also not want this behavior if you are writing a DELETE or an UPDATE statement, because you would need to actually delete or update some data in order to see the execution plan.

Before you can use AUTOTRACE to display execution plans, you must have created a plan table. AUTOTRACE uses this table, and expects the name to be PLAN_TABLE, which is the default name if you use the *UTLXPLAN.SQL* script to create it.

## Granting Access to the Performance Views

AUTOTRACE will do more than just display the execution plan for a query. It also displays statistics that show you how much disk I/O and network traffic occurred during a query's execution. Other information, such as the number of sorts performed on the data, is given as well.

In order to see the statistical data AUTOTRACE returns, you must have SELECT access to certain of Oracle's *dynamic performance views*. Dynamic performance views, whose names usually begin with V$ or V_$, are pseudoviews, maintained by Oracle, that contain real-time performance information. With Oracle8, version 8.0.3, you need SELECT access to the following three tables:

```
v_$sesstat
v_$statname
v_$session
```

Since the specific tables to which you need access may vary from one version of Oracle to the next, Oracle provides a script your DBA can run to simplify the process of granting the needed access to users of AUTOTRACE. The script name is *PLUSTRCE.SQL*, and it is stored in the *PLUS* directory under the Oracle home directory. The script must be executed while logged in as user SYS, and it creates a role named PLUSTRACE that has the needed privileges to use AUTOTRACE from SQL*Plus. Usually, only database administrators can log in as SYS. Here's how to run the script:

```
SQL> CONNECT sys/mgr
Connected.
SQL> @c:\orawin95\plus80\plustrce.sql
SQL>
SQL> drop role plustrace;

Role dropped.

SQL> create role plustrace;

Role created.

SQL>
SQL> grant select on v_$sesstat to plustrace;
```

```
Grant succeeded.

SQL> grant select on v_$statname to plustrace;

Grant succeeded.

SQL> grant select on v_$session to plustrace;

Grant succeeded.

SQL> grant plustrace to dba with admin option;

Grant succeeded.

SQL>
SQL> set echo off
```

Once the script has been run, the PLUSTRACE role will exist. PLUSTRACE should be granted to any user who needs to use AUTOTRACE; for example:

```
SQL> GRANT plustrace TO SARAH;

Grant succeeded.
```

Now the user SARAH will be able to execute the SET AUTOTRACE ON command from SQL*Plus.

## *Executing a Query with AUTOTRACE On*

There are several options you can use with SET AUTOTRACE. By default, when you turn AUTOTRACE on, SQL*Plus will show both the execution plan and some execution statistics for any query you execute. You can, if you like, limit AUTOTRACE to showing only the execution plan or only the execution statistics.

If you don't have the PLUSTRACE role, or don't otherwise have access to the required dynamic performance tables, you can issue the command SET AUTOTRACE ON EXPLAIN. This option is discussed later in this section; it limits the display to only the execution plan, and does not require access to the performance tables.

You also have the option of suppressing the output from the query you are executing. This is helpful if the query returns a large amount of data, because you aren't forced to watch all the results scroll by before the execution plan is displayed. You'll see how to do this later in this section.

*Showing statistics and the plan*

To enable AUTOTRACE and set it to show both the execution plan and the execution statistics, execute the following command from SQL*Plus:

```
SET AUTOTRACE ON
```

Now execute any query. You will see the query results, followed by the execution plan, followed by the execution statistics. Here is an example:

```
SQL> SET AUTOTRACE ON
SQL> SELECT employee_name, SUM(hours_logged)
  2    FROM employee, project_hours
  3   WHERE employee.employee_id = project_hours.employee_id
  4   GROUP BY employee_name;

EMPLOYEE_NAME                            SUM(HOURS_LOGGED)
---------------------------------------- -----------------
Bohdan Khmelnytsky                                     116
Hermon Goche                                            36
Horace Walker                                           68
Ivan Mazepa                                             57
Jacob Marley                                            80
Jeff Gennick                                            36
Jenny Gennick                                           49
Jonathan Gennick                                       116
Pavlo Chubynsky                                        112
Taras Shevchenko                                       116

10 rows selected.


Execution Plan
----------------------------------------------------------
   0      SELECT STATEMENT Optimizer=CHOOSE
   1    0   SORT (GROUP BY)
   2    1     NESTED LOOPS
   3    2       TABLE ACCESS (FULL) OF 'PROJECT_HOURS'
   4    2       TABLE ACCESS (BY INDEX ROWID) OF 'EMPLOYEE'
   5    4         INDEX (UNIQUE SCAN) OF 'EMPLOYEE_PK' (UNIQUE)

Statistics
----------------------------------------------------------
          0  recursive calls
          3  db block gets
        210  consistent gets
          0  physical reads
          0  redo size
        903  bytes sent via SQL*Net to client
        777  bytes received via SQL*Net from client
          4  SQL*Net roundtrips to/from client
          2  sorts (memory)
          0  sorts (disk)
         10  rows processed
```

One key statistic to look at would be the number of physical reads, particularly in relation to the number of rows processed. The fewer reads per row processed, the better. In the above example, all the data happened to be in memory as a result of previous queries, so no physical reads occurred.

The execution plan displayed by AUTOTRACE is formatted just a bit differently from previous plans shown in this chapter. The two leading numeric columns are the ID (of the step) and the PARENT_ID (ID of the parent step) columns.

### Showing just the plan

SQL*Plus allows you to turn AUTOTRACE on with an option to show only the execution plan. This is handy if you do not happen to have the needed privileges to access the execution statistics. Issue the following command from SQL*Plus:

```
SET AUTOTRACE ON EXPLAIN
```

Now, when you issue a SQL statement, only the execution plan is displayed, not the statistics. Here's an example:

```
SQL> SET AUTOTRACE ON EXPLAIN
SQL> SELECT employee_name, SUM(hours_logged)
  2    FROM employee, project_hours
  3   WHERE employee.employee_id = project_hours.employee_id
  4   GROUP BY employee_name;

EMPLOYEE_NAME                             SUM(HOURS_LOGGED)
----------------------------------------- -----------------
Bohdan Khmelnytsky                                      116
Hermon Goche                                            36
Horace Walker                                           68
Ivan Mazepa                                             57
Jacob Marley                                            80
Jeff Gennick                                            36
Jenny Gennick                                           49
Jonathan Gennick                                       116
Pavlo Chubynsky                                        112
Taras Shevchenko                                       116

10 rows selected.


Execution Plan
----------------------------------------------------------
   0      SELECT STATEMENT Optimizer=CHOOSE
   1    0   SORT (GROUP BY)
   2    1     NESTED LOOPS
   3    2       TABLE ACCESS (FULL) OF 'PROJECT_HOURS'
   4    2       TABLE ACCESS (BY INDEX ROWID) OF 'EMPLOYEE'
   5    4         INDEX (UNIQUE SCAN) OF 'EMPLOYEE_PK' (UNIQUE)
```

### Suppressing the query output

With AUTOTRACE, you also have the option of suppressing the output from any queries you run. This saves you from having to wait for the results to scroll by before you see the execution plan and statistics. To turn AUTOTRACE on and suppress any query output, issue the following command:

```
SET AUTOTRACE TRACEONLY
```

The EXPLAIN option is still valid, so if you only want to see the execution plan, issue the command like this:

```
SET AUTOTRACE TRACEONLY EXPLAIN
```

Now, execute a query, and you will see only the execution plan, not the data:

```
SQL> SET AUTOTRACE TRACEONLY EXPLAIN
SQL> SELECT employee_name, SUM(hours_logged)
  2    FROM employee, project_hours
  3   WHERE employee.employee_id = project_hours.employee_id
  4   GROUP BY employee_name;

Execution Plan
----------------------------------------------------------
   0      SELECT STATEMENT Optimizer=CHOOSE
   1    0   SORT (GROUP BY)
   2    1     NESTED LOOPS
   3    2       TABLE ACCESS (FULL) OF 'PROJECT_HOURS'
   4    2       TABLE ACCESS (BY INDEX ROWID) OF 'EMPLOYEE'
   5    4         INDEX (UNIQUE SCAN) OF 'EMPLOYEE_PK' (UNIQUE)
```

It's important to understand that even when the TRACEONLY option is used, the query is still executed. This is really important to remember if the query in question is a DELETE or UPDATE.

### Turning AUTOTRACE off

When you are done using AUTOTRACE, you can turn it off with the following command:

```
SET AUTOTRACE OFF
```

# Improving on EXPLAIN PLAN Results

If you don't like the results you get from EXPLAIN PLAN, there are some things you can do to change how Oracle executes your query. Generally speaking, these things fall into the following three categories:

- Restating the query
- Creating or modifying indexes
- Using hints

First, though, you have to be sure the default execution path is a bad one. This isn't as easy as you may think.

## Knowing Good Results from Bad

Knowing a good execution plan from a bad one requires some degree of experience and judgment. It also helps to understand your data. In many cases, it may not be enough to look at the plan. You may have to do some benchmarking as well.

Consider the issue of doing a full table scan—reading all the rows in the table—to find rows for a query. On the surface, reading the entire table to find the desired rows seems like a very inefficient approach. Many people avoid it out of hand, thinking that an indexed retrieval is always better. If you have a reasonably large table and are searching for only one or two rows, then a full table scan is not an efficient approach. However, if you are retrieving or summarizing a large percentage of the rows in the table, then a full table scan will likely outperform an indexed retrieval. The problem is that somewhere in between these two extremes lies a large grey area. That's where you have to do some benchmarking and use some judgment based on your expectations of what the query will be asked to do when it is in production.

Here are some questions to ask yourself as you look at an execution plan:

- Is a table scan being used to retrieve only a small percentage of rows from a large table? If so, you may want to create an index.

- Is an index scan being used when you are retrieving, or summarizing, a large percentage of a table's rows? If so, you may be better of forcing a full table scan.

- Is Oracle using the most selective index? An index on a YES/NO field would typically be much less selective than an index on last name, for example.

- Is Oracle joining the largest table last? It's generally better to eliminate as many rows as possible prior to any joins.

You should be able to make changes based on the above assumptions and be reasonably certain you will gain a performance improvement. It's always best, however, to test and validate that an improvement has occurred.

## Creating Indexes

Creating indexes is an easy way to affect a query. If, for example, you have a large employee table, much larger than the one used in this book, keyed on employee-id, and your query is searching for employees by name, then Oracle will be doing a full table scan for each name lookup. The response time won't be too good, and your users won't be too happy. Creating an index on the employee name field would improve your results a great deal.

Don't overlook the possibility of creating a multicolumn index, even if you don't use all the index columns in your query's WHERE clause. Suppose that you frequently execute the following query, which searches for an employee by name and displays that employee's current billing rate:

```
SELECT employee_name, employee_billing_rate
  FROM employee
 WHERE employee_name = :emp_name;
```

If you index the employee table by name, Oracle will look up the name in the index, get the ROWID, read the correct employee record into memory, and then return the billing rate. However, it takes an extra read from disk to fetch the employee record into memory. You can eliminate that extra I/O by creating an index such as this one:

```
CREATE INDEX employee_by_name ON employee
  (employee_name, employee_billing_rate);
```

Since the index now contains the billing rate column, Oracle does not need to read the actual employee record in order to retrieve it. Oracle is smart enough to recognize that all the columns needed to satisfy the query are in the index, and it will take advantage of that fact.

## *Rewriting the Query*

Sometimes you can restate a query, still get the results that you want, and have it run much more efficiently. Consider the following query, which lists all employees who have ever charged time to project 1001 or 1002:

```
SELECT DISTINCT employee.employee_id, employee.employee_name
  FROM employee, project_hours
 WHERE employee.employee_id = project_hours.employee_id
   AND project_hours.project_id in (1001,1002);
```

The execution plan for this query looks like this:

```
0 SELECT STATEMENT    Cost = 8
1    SORT UNIQUE
2       HASH JOIN
3          TABLE ACCESS FULL EMPLOYEE
4          TABLE ACCESS FULL PROJECT_HOURS
```

The query could be restated using an EXISTS predicate instead of joining the employee and project_hours tables together. Here's how that would look:

```
SELECT employee_id, employee_name
  FROM employee
```

```
      WHERE exists (SELECT *
                      FROM project_hours
                     WHERE project_hours.project_id = 1001
                       AND project_hours.employee_id = employee.employee_id)
         or exists (SELECT *
                      FROM project_hours
                     WHERE project_hours.project_id = 1002
                       AND project_hours.employee_id = employee.employee_id);
```

The execution plan for this version of the query looks like this:

```
   0 SELECT STATEMENT    Cost = 1
   1   FILTER
   2     TABLE ACCESS FULL EMPLOYEE
   3     INDEX RANGE SCAN PROJECT_HOURS_PK
   4     INDEX RANGE SCAN PROJECT_HOURS_PK
```

The second version of the query has a cost of 1, as opposed to a cost of 8 for the first. Thus, the second version of the query is the one to use. The higher cost of the first query probably comes from the SORT, which is necessary to eliminate duplicate rows, and from the full table scan on the PROJECT_HOURS table.

## *Using Hints*

Rather than allowing Oracle to have total control over how a query is executed, you can provide specific directions to the optimizer through the use of hints. A *hint*, in Oracle, is an optimizer directive embedded in a SQL statement in the form of a comment. Here is a query with an optimizer hint telling Oracle to do a full table scan:

```
   SELECT /*+ full(employee) */
          employee_id, employee_name, employee_billing_rate
     FROM employee
    WHERE employee_name = 'Jenny Gennick';
```

The hint in this case is "full(employee)", which tells Oracle to do a full table scan of the employee table. Oracle will honor this hint and perform a full table scan, even if there happens to be an index on the employee name field.

### *Syntax for a hint*

A hint applies to a single SQL statement, and hints may be specified only for SELECT, INSERT, UPDATE, and DELETE statements. The hint takes the form of a specially formatted comment, and must appear immediately following the key-word that begins the statement. The hint takes the form:

```
   keyword /*+ [hint|comment...] */
```

where:

*keyword*

Is the keyword that begins the statement. This will be one of the keywords SELECT, UPDATE, or DELETE. Hints do not apply to any other type of statement. The hint must immediately follow the keyword that begins the statement.

*hint*

The hint itself, sometimes with one or more arguments enclosed in parenthesis. Tables 8-2 through 8-7 provide a complete list of possible hints. Hints are not case-sensitive. A single comment may contain more than one hint, as long as the hints are separated by at least one space.

*comment*

A user-specified comment. Oracle allows you to intersperse comments with your hints.

Here are some examples of how hints may be specified:

```
SELECT /*+ full(employee) */ employee_id, employee_name
  FROM employee
 WHERE employee_billing_rate > 100;

SELECT /*+ full(e) do a full table scan on the employee table, because
                        most employees do have billing rates > 100. */
        employee_id, employee_name
  FROM employee e
 WHERE employee_billing_rate > 100;
```

Note the second example. The table name is "employee", but an alias of "e" has been specified. The hint for the table uses the same alias, and is specified as "full(e)". Whenever an alias is used, you must also use the alias name in any hints for the table.

If you want to supply multiple hints for a statement, they must all appear in the same comment, for example:

```
SELECT /*+ full(employee) first_rows */
        employee_id, employee_name
  FROM employee
 WHERE employee_billing_rate > 100;
```

When subqueries are used, they are allowed to have their own hints. The hint for a subquery follows immediately after the keyword that starts the query, for example:

```
SELECT /*+ first_rows */ employee_id, employee_name
  FROM employee
 WHERE exists (SELECT /*+ full(project_hours) */*
                  FROM project_hours
                 WHERE project_hours.project_id = 1001
                   AND project_hours.employee_id = employee.employee_id);
```

When using hints, be very careful to get the syntax exactly right. Because hints are embedded in the statements as comments, Oracle can't do any syntax checking. Oracle treats any incorrectly specified hint as a comment. In addition, you should always do an EXPLAIN PLAN after you code your hints, just to be sure that the optimizer is really doing what you think you told it to do.

Oracle hints can loosely be divided into the following categories:

- Optimizer goal hints
- Access method hints
- Join order hints
- Join operation hints
- Parallel execution hints
- Other hints

The next few sections describe the hints available in each category.

### Optimizer goal hints

Optimization goal hints allow you to influence the optimizer's overall goal when formulating an execution plan. You may, for example, specify that you want the plan optimized to return the first record as quickly as possible. Table 8-2 gives a list of these hints.

*Table 8-2. Optimization Goal Hints*

| Hint | Description |
| --- | --- |
| ALL_ROWS | Tells the optimizer to produce an execution plan that minimizes resource consumption. |
| FIRST_ROWS | Tells the optimizer to produce an execution plan with the goal of getting to the first row as quickly as possible. |
| CHOOSE | Allows the optimizer to choose between the rule-based mode and the cost-based mode. If statistics are present for any tables in the query, the cost-based approach will be taken. |
| RULE | Forces the optimizer to use a rule-based approach for the statement. |

You should avoid the RULE hint if at all possible. That hint causes the rule-based optimizer to be used. The rule-based optimizer uses a fixed set of rules when determining the execution plan for a statement, and does not attempt to factor in the ultimate cost of executing that plan. The cost-based optimizer, on the other hand, will base its decision on the estimated I/O and CPU overhead required by various alternative plans. While Oracle still supports the rule-based optimizer, it hasn't been enhanced in years, won't be enhanced in the future, and may be desupported at some point. Oracle is putting their development effort into the cost-based optimizer.

### Access method hints

Access method hints allow you to control the way data is accessed. For example, you can tell Oracle to do a full table scan, or to use an index when accessing a table. You can name the specific index to be used. Table 8-3 provides a list of these hints.

*Table 8-3. Access Method Hints*

| Hint | Description |
| --- | --- |
| FULL(*table_name*) | Requests a full table scan of the specified table, regardless of any indexes that may exist. |
| ROWID(*table_name*) | Tells Oracle to perform a scan of the specified table based on ROWIDs. |
| CLUSTER(*table_name*) | Tells Oracle to do a cluster scan of the specified table. This hint is ignored if the table is not clustered. |
| HASH(*table_name*) | Tells Oracle to do a hash scan of the specified table. This hint is ignored if the table is not clustered. |
| HASH_AJ(*table_name*) | Tells Oracle to do a hash anti-join of the specified table. |
| INDEX(*table_name [index_name...]*) | Tells Oracle to access the specified table via an index scan. Optionally, you may specify the index to use; otherwise, Oracle chooses the index. You may also specify a list of indexes to choose from, and Oracle will choose from that list. |
| INDEX_ASC(*table_name [index_name...]*) | Similar to the INDEX hint, but tells Oracle to scan the index in ascending order. |
| INDEX_COMBINE(*table_name [index_name...]*) | Tells Oracle to use some combination of two indexes. You may specify the indexes to choose from, or let Oracle make the choice. |
| INDEX_DESC(*table_name [index_name...]*) | Similar to INDEX_ASC, but forces Oracle to scan the index in descending order. |
| INDEX_FFS(*table_name [index_name...]*) | Tells Oracle to do a fast full index scan. |
| MERGE_AJ(*table_name*) | Turns a NOT IN subquery into a merge anti-join. |
| AND_EQUAL(*table_name index_name index name...*) | Tells Oracle to scan two or more indexes and merge the results. You must specify at least two index names. |
| USE_CONCAT | Turns a query with OR conditions into two or more queries unioned together with a UNION ALL. |

All access method hints take at least a table name as an argument. That's because you may want to specify different access methods for different tables in your query. The FULL hint, for example, takes one table name as an argument.

```
/*+ FULL(employee) */
```

Some of the access method hints are index-related, and allow you to specify one or more indexes to be used. In many cases, as with the INDEX hint, you have the choice of specifying an index name or not. The following hint, for example, tells Oracle you want to do an index scan on the employee table, but it's up to Oracle to pick the index:

```
/*+ INDEX(employee) */
```

This is useful if you think Oracle will make the correct choice, or if you don't want to hardcode an index name into the hint. You have the option, however, of specifying the exact index to use. Here's an example:

```
/*+ INDEX(empolyee employee_by_name) */
```

You may even specify a list of indexes, and Oracle will choose from the indexes in that list. If, for example, you had seven indexes on the employee table, but you believed that only two would be at all useful for the query in question, you could specify a hint like this:

```
/*+ INDEX(employee employee_by_name, employee_by_billing_rate) */
```

This tells Oracle that you want to use an index scan to access the employee table, and that you want to use either the name index or the billing rate index.

The AND_EQUAL hint is special in that it requires at least two indexes to be specified. That's because this hint causes Oracle to merge the results of two index scans together. You can't do that unless you have two indexes to scan.

If your choice conflicts with other hints, if it cannot be implemented, or if the indexes you specify do not exist, Oracle will simply ignore the hint altogether. Take a look at the following query:

```
SELECT /*+ USE_CONCAT */
       employee_id, employee_name
  FROM employee
 WHERE employee_name = 'Jeff Gennick';
```

The USE_CONCAT hint makes no sense here because the query does not contain an OR condition. You can't break this up into two queries and then UNION the results together, so Oracle will ignore the hint. A bad hint will be honored, however, whenever it is possible to implement. The following query contains a hint to do an index scan on the primary key index for the employee table:

```
SELECT /*+ INDEX(employee employee_pk) */
       employee_name
  FROM employee
 WHERE employee_name = 'Jeff Gennick';
```

The primary key for employee is the employee_id field. An index on employee name does exist. The query seeks one record based on the employee name. Even though it makes perfect sense to look up the name in the name index, Oracle will honor the request to use the primary key index. Here is the execution plan for this statement:

```
0 SELECT STATEMENT   Cost = 826
1    TABLE ACCESS BY INDEX ROWID EMPLOYEE
2       INDEX FULL SCAN EMPLOYEE_PK
```

Oracle is going to read every entry in the primary key index, retrieve the associated row from the employee table, and check the name to see if it has a match. This is worse than a full table scan! Oracle does this because the hint requested it, and because it physically can be done, so be careful what you ask for, and check the results. Change the index name used in the query to employee_by_name, and the execution plan looks like this:

```
0 SELECT STATEMENT   Cost = 1
1    INDEX RANGE SCAN EMPLOYEE_BY_NAME
```

You can see that the relative cost of using the name index is much, much less than that of using the primary key index. Be careful with these hints.

### Join order hints

Join order hints allow you to exercise some control over the order in which Oracle joins tables. There are only three of them, and they are listed in Table 8-4.

*Table 8-4. Join Order Hints*

| Hint | Description |
| --- | --- |
| ORDERED | Tells Oracle to join tables left to right, in the same order in which they are listed in the FROM clause. |
| STAR | Tells Oracle to use a star query execution plan, if at all possible. This can only work if there are at least three tables being joined, and the largest table has a concatenated index on columns that reference the two smaller tables. The two smaller tables are joined first, and then a nested-loop join is used to retrieve the required rows from the largest table. |
| STAR_TRANSFORMATION | Tells Oracle to transform the query into a star query, if possible, and then use the best plan for that query. |

### Join operation hints

Join operation hints allow you to control the manner in which two tables are joined. Oracle uses three basic methods whenever two tables are joined: the merge join, the nested loops join, and the hash join.

A *merge join* is done by sorting the rows from each table by the join columns. Once the two rowsets have been sorted, Oracle reads through both and joins any matching rows together. A merge join often uses fewer resources than the other options, but you have to wait for all the records to be sorted before you get the first one back. You also have to have enough memory and temporary disk space to handle the sort.

The method used for a *nested loops join* corresponds to the mental image most people have in mind when they think of joining tables. Oracle picks one table as the driving table, and reads through that table row by row. For each row read from the driving table, Oracle looks up the corresponding rows in the secondary table and joins them together. Because no sort is involved, a nested loops join will usually get you the first record back more quickly than a merge join. For the same reason, a nested loops join also does not require large amounts of disk space and memory. However a nested loops join may result in a considerably greater number of disk reads than a merge join.

A *hash join* is similar to a merge join, but a sort is not required. A hash table is built in memory to allow quick access to the rows from one of the tables to be joined. Then rows are read from the other table. As each row is read from the second table, the hash function is applied to the join columns, and the result is used to find the corresponding rows from the first table.

Aside from the hints used to specify the join method, there are a few other hints lumped into the join operation category. Table 8-5 lists all the join operation hints.

*Table 8-5. Join Operation Hints*

| Hint | Description |
| --- | --- |
| USE_NL(*table_name*) | Tells Oracle to use a nested loop when joining this table. The table specified by this hint will be the one accessed by the innermost loop. The other table will be the driving table. |
| USE_MERGE(*table_name*) | Tells Oracle to use the sort merge method when joining this table. |
| USE_HASH(*table_name*) | Tells Oracle to use a hash join for the specified table. |
| NO_MERGE | This is not the opposite of USE_MERGE. The NO_MERGE hint applies to queries that contain joins on one or more views. It prevents Oracle from merging the query from a view into the main query. |
| DRIVING_SITE(*table_name*) | This hint applies when you are executing a distributed join, one that joins tables from two or more databases. Without a hint, Oracle will choose which database actually collects the tables and does the join. By using the hint, you are telling Oracle that you want the join performed by the database containing the specified table. |

### Parallel execution hints

The hints shown in Table 8-6 allow you to influence the way Oracle executes a query in a parallel processing environment. In an environment with a single CPU, parallel processing is not possible, and these hints will be ignored.

*Table 8-6. Parallel Execution Hints*

| Hint | Description |
| --- | --- |
| PARALLEL(*table_name* [, *degree*[, *num_instances*]]) | Tells Oracle to access data from the indicated table in a parallel processing mode. You can optionally specify both the degree of parallelism to use and the number of instances that will be involved. The keyword DEFAULT may be used for both arguments, in which case Oracle decides the values based on parameters in the *INIT.ORA* file and the table definition. Using the PARALLEL hint in an INSERT statement automatically turns APPEND mode on. See the APPEND and NO_APPEND hints. |
| NO_PARALLEL(*table_name*) | Tells Oracle not to access the specified table in parallel. |
| APPEND | Applies only to INSERT statements. It tells Oracle not to attempt to reuse any freespace that may be available in any extents currently allocated to the table. |
| NOAPPEND | This is the opposite of APPEND, and tells Oracle to use any freespace in extents currently allocated to the table. This hint exists because APPEND becomes the default behavior whenever a PARALLEL hint is used in an INSERT statement. |
| PARALLEL_INDEX(*table_ name, index_name* [,*degree* [,*num_instances*]]) | Tells Oracle to access data from the indicated table by scanning the specified index in a parallel processing mode. The index must be a partitioned index. You can optionally specify both the degree of parallelism to use and the number of instances that will be involved. The keyword DEFAULT may be used for both arguments, in which case Oracle decides the values based on parameters in the *INIT.ORA* file and the table definition. |

### Other hints

There are a few hints that don't fit neatly into one of the other categories. These are listed in Table 8-7.

*Table 8-7. Other Hints*

| Hint | Description |
| --- | --- |
| CACHE(*table_name*) | Applies only when a full table scan is being performed on the specified table. It tells Oracle to place blocks for that table at the most recently used end of the buffer cache, so they will remain in memory as long as possible. This can be useful for small lookup tables that you expect to access repeatedly. |

*Table 8-7. Other Hints (continued)*

| Hint | Description |
|------|-------------|
| NOCACHE(*table_name*) | This is the opposite of CACHE, and tells Oracle to place blocks at the least recently used end of the buffer cache, where they will be cleared out as soon as possible. |
| PUSH_SUBQ | Tells Oracle to evaluate nonmerged subqueries as soon as possible during query execution. If you expect the subquery to eliminate a large number of rows, this can result in a performance improvement. |

# *Where to Find More Tuning Information*

Tuning Oracle SQL is a complex subject. The information in this chapter serves only to give you a brief overview of some of the features Oracle provides to help you during the tuning process. There is a lot of other information out there that you should avail yourself of.

To start with, read the manual. The *Oracle8 Server Tuning* manual contains a great deal of tuning information, though some of it is more oriented towards tuning the database server itself rather than tuning individual SQL statements. The *Server Tuning* manual contains information on Oracle hints, the use of EXPLAIN PLAN, and the TKPROF utility. TKPROF is a bit difficult to use, but can provide a great deal more information about the cost of a query than you will get with EXPLAIN PLAN.

There are two good books on Oracle tuning I can recommend. One is *Oracle Performance Tuning*, 2nd edition, by Mark Gurry and Peter Corrigan (O'Reilly & Associates, 1996). The other is *Oracle SQL High-Performance Tuning*, by Guy Harrison (Prentice-Hall, 1997). Guy Harrison's book is almost entirely focused on tuning SQL statements, as opposed to tuning the server, and it contains a great deal of helpful information for database programmers.

9

# The Product User Profile

In addition to the standard database security Oracle provides and enforces for all database objects—tables, views, and the like—Oracle also provides an application security scheme for SQL*Plus. This allows you to control the specific commands a SQL*Plus user is allowed to execute. At the core of the SQL*Plus application security scheme is the product user profile.

## What Is the Product User Profile?

The *product user profile* is an Oracle table, owned by the SYSTEM user, that contains a list of SQL*Plus command restrictions by user. The table may contain role restrictions as well. The name of this table used to be PRODUCT_USER_PROFILE. Now it is just PRODUCT_PROFILE, but a synonym named PRODUCT_USER_PROFILE exists to ensure backwards compatibility.

### Why Does the Product User Profile Exist?

Primarily, the product user profile enables you to give end users access to SQL*Plus for reporting and ad-hoc query purposes, yet restrict them from using SQL*Plus commands such as INSERT, DELETE, etc., that might damage production data.

Real-world applications typically implement a large number of business rules, edit checks, and even security at the application level rather than within the database. Modifying the data using an ad-hoc tool, such as SQL*Plus, bypasses the rules and puts data integrity at risk. Because of this, it's usually important to ensure that data is modified through the application, where the rules can be enforced.

If you give people an application that requires a database username and password, and those people also have access to SQL*Plus, it won't be too long before some curious and adventurous soul will figure out that the same userid and password that works for the application will also work for SQL*Plus. Next thing you know, you will have someone running ad-hoc queries that haven't been tuned, or, worse yet, you may have someone issuing ad-hoc INSERT, UPDATE, or DELETE commands. The product user profile allows you to defend against this risk.

## The PRODUCT_PROFILE Table

The PRODUCT_PROFILE table is owned by SYSTEM and has the following structure:

```
Name                             Null?     Type
-------------------------------- --------- ----
PRODUCT                          NOT NULL  VARCHAR2(30)
USERID                                     VARCHAR2(30)
ATTRIBUTE                                  VARCHAR2(240)
SCOPE                                      VARCHAR2(240)
NUMERIC_VALUE                              NUMBER(15,2)
CHAR_VALUE                                 VARCHAR2(240)
DATE_VALUE                                 DATE
LONG_VALUE                                 LONG
```

Most users will not have SELECT access on the table itself, so if you aren't logged in as SYSTEM, you may not be able to DESCRIBE the table. Instead, you should have access to a view on the table named PRODUCT_PRIVS. This view returns all the records from the PRODUCT_PROFILE table that apply to the currently logged-on user—you. Figure 9-1 shows the table, the view, the synonyms that normally exist, and the relationship between them.

Table 9-1 describes the purpose of each of the element shown in Figure 9-1.

## How the Product User Profile Works

When you log into an Oracle database using SQL*Plus, SQL*Plus will issue two SELECT statements against the product user profile. The first SELECT statement retrieves a list of command restrictions and looks like this:

```
SELECT attribute, scope,
       numeric_value, char_value, date_value
  FROM system.product_privs
 WHERE (UPPER('SQL*Plus') LIKE UPPER(product))
   AND (UPPER(user) LIKE UPPER(userid))
```

The two fields of interest to SQL*Plus are ATTRIBUTE and CHAR_VALUE. Together, these columns tell SQL*Plus which commands to disable for the cur-

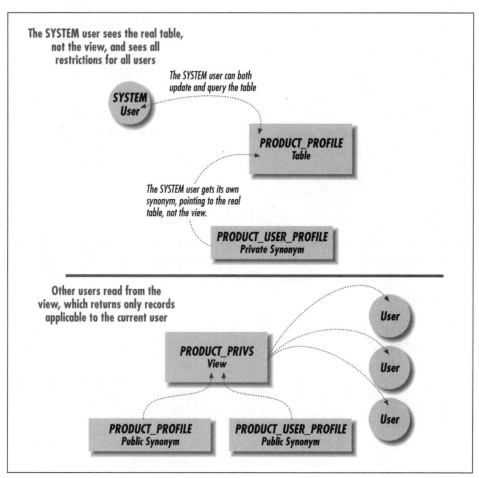

*Figure 9-1. The product user profile table, view, and synonyms*

*Table 9-1. Product User Profile Elements*

| Element | Who Sees It? | Purpose |
|---|---|---|
| PRODUCT_PROFILE table | SYSTEM | This is the product user profile table itself. |
| PRODUCT_USER_PROFILE private synonym | SYSTEM | Provides backwards compatibility, because the table name used to be PRODUCT_USER_PROFILE. |
| PRODUCT_PRIVS view | All users | A view that shows each user the restrictions that apply to him or her. |
| PRODUCT_USER_PROFILE public synonym | All users | A public synonym pointing to the view. |
| PRODUCT_PROFILE public synonym | All users | A public synonym pointing to the view. |

rently logged on user. For example, the following two rows will be returned for a user who has been denied access to the DELETE and HOST commands:

```
ATTRIBUTE   CHAR_VALUE
----------  --------------------
DELETE      DISABLED
HOST        DISABLED
```

A second SELECT statement is issued against the product user profile in order to retrieve any role restrictions for the user. Here's what that statement looks like:

```
SELECT char_value
  FROM system.product_privs
 WHERE (UPPER('SQL*Plus') LIKE UPPER(product))
   AND ( (UPPER(user) LIKE UPPER(userid))
         OR (UPPER(userid) = 'PUBLIC'))
   AND (UPPER(attribute) = 'ROLES')
```

In this case, the CHAR_VALUE column returns a list of roles that are to be disabled whenever the user connects using SQL*Plus. SQL*Plus then disables these roles with a SET ROLE command. By way of example, assume that the following data was returned:

```
CHAR_VALUE
--------------------
PAYROLL_ADMINISTRATOR
HR_ADMINISTRATOR
```

There are two roles to be disabled. SQL*Plus will turn them off by issuing the following command to Oracle:

```
SET ROLE ALL EXCEPT payroll_administrator, hr_administrator
```

This establishes the default condition for the user of having those roles turned off. The user may be able to issue another SET ROLE command to turn them back on again, but the starting condition is that the roles are off.

If SQL*Plus's attempt to query the product user profile results in an error, perhaps because the table does not exist, you will see the following message from SQL*Plus:

```
Error accessing PRODUCT_USER_PROFILE
Warning:  Product user profile information not loaded!
You may need to run PUPBLD.SQL as SYSTEM
Connected.
```

If you do happen to get the above error message, see the section titled "Creating the Profile Table" later in this chapter, or notify your DBA.

The SYSTEM user presents a special case. If you log into Oracle as SYSTEM, SQL*Plus detects this, and does not query the product user profile. Therefore, you can never restrict what the SYSTEM user is allowed to do.

## Product User Profile Limitations

The product user profile is used for application security. The application is SQL*Plus. No other applications respect the limitations set in the profile. In today's world, with ODBC (Open DataBase Connectivity) on every desktop, and every application under the sun capable of connecting to an Oracle database, securing SQL*Plus should be only a small part of your overall security plan. It is relatively easy for someone with Microsoft Access, for example, to connect to an Oracle database. Once that's done, that user will be able to freely edit, insert, and delete any data to which they have access. Guard against this by implementing as much of your security at the database level as possible.

There are also some potential security "holes" you should be aware of when using the product user profile to secure SQL*Plus. Oracle is a complex product, and often there is more than one way to accomplish any given task. You have to be particularly vigilant about the possible use of PL/SQL. The next two sections describe some known issues to be aware of when setting limits with the product user profile.

### Issues related to PL/SQL

Any SQL command you can issue from the SQL*Plus prompt can also be issued from a PL/SQL block. Remember this. It's important. Using the profile, you can restrict a user's access to a SQL command, but it may be possible to get around that restriction with PL/SQL. For this reason, you may want to restrict access to PL/SQL as well.

Take the UPDATE command, for example. Using the profile, you can restrict a SQL*Plus user from issuing the UPDATE command. Should the user try an update, an error will be returned, as the following example shows:

```
SQL> UPDATE sqlplus.employee
invalid command: update
```

This is all well and good, but the update can easily be coded in PL/SQL. Here's how:

```
SQL> BEGIN
  2  UPDATE sqlplus.employee
```

```
3      SET employee_billing_rate = 300
4    WHERE employee_id = 101;
5    END;
6    /
```

```
PL/SQL procedure successfully completed.
```

That was certainly easy enough, wasn't it? So much for your security. If you need to restrict a user from issuing any INSERT, UPDATE, DELETE, or SELECT commands, you should also restrict the user from using PL/SQL.

Data definition language (DDL) commands, such as GRANT or CREATE TABLE, are a bit more difficult to code from PL/SQL, but they can be done. As long as a user has EXECUTE access to the DBMS_SQL package, you should consider the possibility that the user may be able to code dynamic SQL statements.

 Beginning with Oracle8i, a new version of dynamic SQL is being implemented. This will allow users to code dynamic SQL by simply embedding the desired commands in the PL/SQL block. Thus, the lack of EXECUTE privileges on the DBMS_SQL package won't necessarily stop the user from being able to issue dynamic SQL.

There are two obvious ways to execute PL/SQL from SQL*Plus. One way is to type in a PL/SQL block at the command prompt and execute it. The other way is to use the SQL*Plus EXECUTE command. To restrict a user's access to PL/SQL, you must disable the following three SQL*Plus commands:

- DECLARE

- BEGIN

- EXECUTE

Leave any one of the above commands enabled, and you might as well leave them all enabled; the user will still have full access to PL/SQL. There are even less obvious ways to execute PL/SQL, and you may want to guard against these as well. The user could create a stored function and execute that from a SELECT statement, or the user could create a trigger on a table and then fire that trigger. The easiest way to guard against either of these possibilities is to ensure that the user does not have the system privileges required to do these things. An alternative would be to also restrict access to the CREATE command from SQL*Plus.

### Issues related to roles

When you disable a role, SQL*Plus turns that role off when the user first connects, but that doesn't prevent the user from turning the role on again. The user can simply issue a SET ROLE command of his own, as the following example shows, turning the desired role back on:

```
SQL> SELECT employee_name, employee_billing_rate
  2    FROM sqlplus.employee;
 FROM jeff.employee
               *
ERROR at line 2:
ORA-00942: table or view does not exist


SQL> SET ROLE ALL;

Role set.

SQL> SELECT employee_name, employee_billing_rate
  2    FROM jeff.employee;

EMPLOYEE_NAME                             EMPLOYEE_BILLING_RATE
---------------------------------------- ---------------------
Jonathan Gennick                                           300
Jenny Gennick                                              135
Jeff Gennick                                                99
...
```

In this example, the first SELECT failed because the PAYROLL_ADMINISTRATOR role had been disabled by SQL*Plus, and consequently the user could not see the EMPLOYEE table. Notice, though, that all the user had to do was issue a SET ROLE ALL command in order to enable the role, allowing him to see the data. It was not even necessary for the user to know the name of the specific role that needed to be enabled. For this reason, disabling the SET ROLE command should usually go hand in hand with disabling roles.

If you've disabled a role for a user, and also disabled the SET ROLE command, you should give some thought to disabling PL/SQL as well. At the very least, you might want to revoke EXECUTE privileges on the DBMS_SQL package. The reason for this is that by using dynamic SQL, the SET ROLE command can be executed from within a PL/SQL block. Admittedly, this would take a very knowledgeable and determined user, but it can be done. Here is an example:

```
SQL> SELECT employee_name, employee_billing_rate
  2    FROM sqlplus.employee;
 FROM sqlplus.employee
               *
ERROR at line 2:
ORA-00942: table or view does not exist


SQL> SET ROLE ALL;
invalid command: set role
SQL>
```

```
SQL> DECLARE
  2     set_role_cursor    INTEGER;
  3     rows_affected      INTEGER;
  4  BEGIN
  5     set_role_cursor := DBMS_SQL.OPEN_CURSOR;
  6     DBMS_SQL.PARSE (set_role_cursor,
  7                     'SET ROLE payroll_administrator',
  8                     DBMS_SQL.NATIVE);
  9     rows_affected := DBMS_SQL.EXECUTE(set_role_cursor);
 10     DBMS_SQL.CLOSE_CURSOR(set_role_cursor);
 11  END;
 12  /

PL/SQL procedure successfully completed.

SQL> SELECT employee_name, employee_billing_rate
  2     FROM sqlplus.employee;

EMPLOYEE_NAME                              EMPLOYEE_BILLING_RATE
---------------------------------------- ---------------------
Jonathan Gennick                                           300
Jenny Gennick                                              135
Jeff Gennick                                                99
...
```

SQL*Plus honors the restriction against using the SET ROLE command from the SQL*Plus prompt, but it has no way of knowing what is going on inside a PL/SQL block. Remember, PL/SQL is sent to the database for execution. SQL*Plus does not look inside a block.

# Using the Product User Profile

To use the product user profile, the first thing you need to do is create it. Oracle provides a script for this purpose. Once the product user profile table has been created, there are three things you need to know how to do:

- Restrict a user, or group of users, from using a specific command.

- Set a role so that it will be disabled for a given user or group of users when SQL*Plus first connects.

- Report the restrictions currently in the profile table.

The next few sections show you how to perform each of these tasks.

## Creating the Profile Table

Oracle supplies a script named *PUPBLD.SQL* that creates the table, views, and synonyms shown earlier in this chapter in Figure 9-1. On Windows-based systems, the script can be found in the *DBS* directory, underneath the Oracle home directory. On Windows NT, the full path and filename for the script is:

```
C:\ORANT\DBS\PUPBLD.SQL
```

On Unix systems, the script will be in the SQL*Plus product's *admin* directory. For example, under HP-UX, and running Oracle 7.3.3, the full path and filename for the script is:

```
$ORACLE_HOME/sqlplus/admin/pupbld.sql
```

In some instances, the SQL*Plus directory will be named *plusXX* instead of *sqlplus*. The *XX* in the name represents the Oracle version number, so with Oracle 7.1, the directory would be named *plus71*.

*PUPBLD.SQL* should be executed while logged in as user SYSTEM. Executing it while logged in as some other user will result in the profile table being created in the wrong schema, and may also result in a few privilege violations as it tries to create public synonyms. The following example shows the script being executed:

```
SQL> @c:\orant\dbs\pupbld
drop synonym product_user_profile
            *
ERROR at line 1:
ORA-01434: private synonym to be dropped does not exist


   date_value from product_user_profile
                   *
ERROR at line 3:
ORA-00942: table or view does not exist


drop table product_user_profile
          *
ERROR at line 1:
ORA-00942: table or view does not exist


alter table product_profile add (long_value long)
*
ERROR at line 1:
ORA-00942: table or view does not exist



Table created.
View created.
Grant succeeded.
Synonym created.
Synonym created.
Synonym created.
Table created.
```

```
Grant succeeded.
View created.
Grant succeeded.
Synonym created.
0 rows updated.
SQL>
```

Do not be alarmed by the error messages. They are nothing to worry about and are simply the result of the way Oracle wrote the script. If you now were to run the script again, you would see a different set of errors. Any errors returned because an object already exists, or because an object does not exist, may safely be ignored.

## Limiting Access to Commands

To limit access to a command, you simply need to insert a row into the PRODUCT_PROFILE table. This row tells SQL*Plus which command to disable and for what user. To reenable a command, simply delete the row with the restriction. The following sections show you how to do this.

### Commands that can be disabled

There is a specific list of commands that may be disabled using the product user profile. These are listed in Table 9-2.

*Table 9-2. Commands You Can Disable Using the Product User Profile*

| SQL*Plus | SQL | PL/SQL |
|---|---|---|
| CONNECT | ALTER | BEGIN |
| COPY | ANALYZE | DECLARE |
| EDIT | AUDIT | |
| EXECUTE | CREATE | |
| EXIT | DELETE | |
| GET | DROP | |
| HOST[a] | GRANT | |
| QUIT | INSERT | |
| PASSWORD | LOCK | |
| RUN | NOAUDIT | |
| SAVE | RENAME | |
| SET[b] | REVOKE | |
| SPOOL | SELECT | |
| START[c] | SET ROLE | |
| | SET TRANSACTION | |

*Table 9-2. Commands You Can Disable Using the Product User Profile (continued)*

| SQL*Plus | SQL | PL/SQL |
|----------|-----|--------|
| | TRUNCATE | |
| | UPDATE | |

a Disabling HOST also disables $, !, or any other operating-system-specific shortcut for executing a host command.
b Disabling the SET command takes SET ROLE and SET TRANSACTION with it. That's because SQL*Plus simply looks at the first word to see if it matches the entry in the profile table.
c Disabling the START command also disables @ and @@.

### Disabling a command

To disable a command for a user, insert a row into the PRODUCT_PROFILE table. You should normally log in as SYSTEM, and your INSERT statement should look like this:

```
INSERT INTO product_profile
    (product, userid, attribute, char_value)
    VALUES ('SQL*Plus','USERNAME','COMMAND_NAME','DISABLED');
```

where:

*'SQL*Plus'*

This is a constant. It identifies the product to which the restriction applies, in this case SQL*Plus. It should always be mixed-case, exactly as shown here.

*'USERNAME'*

The username of the user you are restricting. It should always be uppercase. You can wildcard this using the wildcard characters that are used with the LIKE predicate, the percent sign and the underscore. A value of '%' would make the restriction apply to all users.

*'COMMAND_NAME'*

This is the name of the command you wish to disable. It should always be uppercase.

*'DISABLED'*

The keyword 'DISABLED' must be stored in the CHAR_VALUE field.

Fields in the PRODUCT_PROFILE table other than the four listed above are not used by SQL*Plus. They should be left alone, and will default to NULL. The following example will disable the DELETE command for the user named SCOTT:

```
INSERT INTO product_profile
    (product, userid, attribute, char_value)
    VALUES ('SQL*Plus','SCOTT','DELETE','DISABLED');
```

You can wildcard the USERID field to disable a command for a number of users at once. You can even disable a command across the board for all users. The following statement inserts a row into the PRODUCT_PROFILE table that will disable the SQL*Plus HOST command for everyone:

```
INSERT INTO product_profile
    (product, userid, attribute, char_value)
    VALUES ('SQL*Plus','%','HOST','DISABLED');
```

Be careful when using wildcards other than %. You have to be sure you know which users you are affecting when you create the restriction, and you have to worry about the possibility that you might create a new username in the future that inadvertently matches some existing restriction. Wildcards also make it difficult to remove a restriction for just one of the users who meet the criteria. For example, you might use "J%" to disable DELETE for all usernames starting with "J". If you later decide that "JONES" needs DELETE access, but "JASON" and "JENNI-FER" don't, you have to rethink everything.

### Re-enabling a command

To remove a restriction you have created, simply delete that row from the PRODUCT_PROFILE table. For example, to once again allow all users to issue the HOST command, issue the following command:

```
DELETE
   FROM product_profile
  WHERE product='SQL*Plus'
    AND userid='%'
    AND char_value='HOST'
```

## Limiting Access to Roles

You disable roles for a user in much the same way that you disable commands. The primary reason to disable a role is that a user might have a role for purposes of running an application, but you do not want the user to have that role when issuing ad-hoc commands from SQL*Plus.

### Disabling a role

To disable a role for a user, log in as SYSTEM and insert a row into the PRODUCT_PROFILE table, as follows:

```
INSERT INTO product_profile
    (product, userid, attribute, char_value)
    VALUES ('SQL*Plus','USERNAME','ROLES','ROLE_NAME');
```

where:

*'SQL*Plus'*

Is a constant. It identifies the product to which the restriction applies, in this case SQL*Plus. It should always be mixed-case, exactly as shown here.

*'USERNAME'*

Is the username of the user you are restricting. It should always be upper-case. You can wildcard the username when restricting a role, but you must be very careful when doing so.

*'ROLES'*

Instead of a command, the keyword ROLES in this field tells SQL*Plus that you are restricting a role.

*'ROLE_NAME'*

Is the name of the role to disable.

Fields in the PRODUCT_PROFILE table that are not listed above should be left alone, and will default to NULL. The following example will disable the PAYROLL_ADMINISTRATOR role for the user named SCOTT:

```
INSERT INTO product_profile
    (product, userid, attribute, char_value)
    VALUES ('SQL*Plus','SCOTT','ROLES','PAYROLL_ADMINISTRATOR');
```

You can wildcard the username when disabling a role, but you must be very careful when doing this. SQL*Plus translates all the role restrictions for a user into a single SET ROLE command like this:

```
SET ROLE ALL EXCEPT role, role, role...
```

If any one of those roles is not valid for the user in question, the command will fail and none of the roles will disabled. If you wildcard the username when disabling a role, you must be absolutely certain either that each user has been granted the role in question, or that the role has been granted to PUBLIC.

### Re-enabling a role

The method for removing a role restriction is the same as that used to remove a command restriction—delete the row from the PRODUCT_PROFILE table. For example, to allow SCOTT to be a PAYROLL_ADMINISTRATOR when logged in using SQL*Plus, issue the following DELETE command:

```
DELETE
  FROM product_profile
 WHERE product='SQL*Plus'
   AND userid='SCOTT'
   AND command='ROLES'
   AND char_value='PAYROLL_ADMINISTRATOR'
```

You normally need to be logged in as SYSTEM to delete from the PRODUCT_PROFILE table.

## *Reporting on the Product User Profile*

The following sections show you two different ways to look at the product user
profile. The first section provides a script you can run to generate a report showing all the restrictions currently defined in the PRODUCT_PROFILE table. The second section provides a script that will show you the restrictions for a particular
user, which you can specify.

You should run these scripts while logged in as the SYSTEM user. If you run them
while logged in as anyone else, you will see only the restrictions that apply to
you.

### *Listing all restrictions*

The following script will generate a report showing all the command and role
restrictions defined in the PRODUCT_PROFILE table:

```
SET ECHO OFF
SET PAGESIZE 50
SET LINESIZE 60
SET NEWPAGE 0
SET FEEDBACK OFF
SET TRIMSPOOL ON

TTITLE LEFT 'Product User Profile Report' -
       RIGHT 'Page ' FORMAT 9999 SQL.PNO SKIP 6
BTITLE OFF

COLUMN userid FORMAT A12 HEADING 'User'
COLUMN sort_by NOPRINT
COLUMN command FORMAT A15 HEADING 'Disabled|Commands'
COLUMN role FORMAT A30 HEADING 'Disabled|Roles'

BREAK ON userid SKIP 1

PROMPT You are about to generate a product user profile report.
ACCEPT PUP_REPORT_FILE -
       PROMPT 'Enter the filename for the report output: ' -
       DEFAULT 'PUP_REPORT.LIS'

SPOOL &&PUP_REPORT_FILE
SET TERMOUT OFF

SELECT userid, 1 sort_by, attribute command, '' role
  FROM product_profile
 WHERE product = 'SQL*Plus'
   AND attribute <> 'ROLES'
   AND char_value = 'DISABLED'
UNION
SELECT userid, 2 sort_by, '' command, char_value role
  FROM product_profile
 WHERE product = 'SQL*Plus'
```

```
   AND attribute = 'ROLES'
ORDER BY userid, sort_by, command, role
;

SPOOL OFF
SET TERMOUT ON

--Restore these settings to their defaults
TTITLE OFF
CLEAR COLUMNS
SET PAGESIZE 14
SET LINESIZE 80
SET NEWPAGE 1
SET FEEDBACK ON
SET TRIMSPOOL OFF
```

When you run the script, you will be prompted for a filename, and the report output will be sent to that file. Here's an example showing how to run the script:

```
SQL> @report_product_profile
You are about to generate a product user profile report.
Enter the filename for the report output: c:\a\profile.lis
SQL>
```

When you look in the file, you will see that the report looks like this:

```
Product User Profile Report                     Page     1




              Disabled          Disabled
User          Commands          Roles
------------  ---------------   ------------------------------
GEORGE        BEGIN
              DECLARE
              EXECUTE

                                HR_ADMINISTRATOR
                                PAYROLL_ADMINISTRATOR


JONATHAN      BEGIN
              DECLARE
              DELETE
              EXECUTE
              HOST
              SET ROLE

JEFF          HOST
```

### Listing restrictions for a particular user

To find out what restrictions apply to any one user, you must keep in mind that the USERID field in the PRODUCT_PROFILE table may contain wildcards. The following script will prompt you for a username, then display a list of all the disabled commands and roles for that user. The queries involved use the LIKE operator to account for any possible wildcards.

```
SET ECHO OFF
SET FEEDBACK OFF
SET VERIFY OFF

BTITLE OFF
SET HEADING OFF
SET PAGESIZE 9999
SET NEWPAGE 1

ACCEPT user_to_show -
      PROMPT 'Show the product profile for which user? '

TTITLE LEFT restriction_heading SKIP 2
COLUMN restriction_type_heading NOPRINT NEW_VALUE restriction_heading
COLUMN sort_by NOPRINT
COLUMN restriction FORMAT A30
BREAK ON restriction_type_heading SKIP PAGE

SELECT 'User ' || UPPER('&&user_to_show')
      || ' is restricted from executing the following commands:'
      restriction_type_heading,
      1 sort_by, '    ', attribute restriction
  FROM product_profile
 WHERE product = 'SQL*Plus'
   AND attribute <> 'ROLES'
   AND char_value = 'DISABLED'
   AND UPPER('&&user_to_show') LIKE userid
UNION
SELECT 'User ' || UPPER('&&user_to_show')
      || ' has the following roles disabled:'
      restriction_type_heading,
      2 sort_by, '    ', char_value restriction
  FROM product_profile
 WHERE product = 'SQL*Plus'
   AND attribute = 'ROLES'
   AND ( UPPER('&&user_to_show') LIKE userid
        OR userid = 'PUBLIC')
UNION
SELECT 'User ' || UPPER('&&user_to_show')
      || ' does not exist.'
      restriction_type_heading,
      3 sort_by, '    ', ' ' restriction
  FROM dual
 WHERE NOT EXISTS (
          SELECT username
            FROM all_users
           WHERE username = UPPER('&&user_to_show'))
ORDER BY sort_by, restriction
;
```

```
--Restore these settings to their defaults.
SET HEADING ON
SET PAGESIZE 14
SET FEEDBACK ON
SET VERIFY ON
TTITLE OFF
CLEAR BREAKS
CLEAR COLUMNS
```

The following example shows how to run the script and what the output looks like:

```
SQL> @show_product_profile
Show the product profile for which user? george

User GEORGE is restricted from executing the following commands:

    BEGIN
    DECLARE
    EXECUTE

User GEORGE has the following roles disabled:

    HR_ADMINISTRATOR
    PAYROLL_ADMINISTRATOR
```

The script will even tell you whether or not the user really exists. It is possible to create entries in the PRODUCT_PROFILE table for users who do not exist. It is also possible to drop a user, leaving orphan entries in the profile. The following example demonstrates this:

```
SQL> @show_product_profile
Show the product profile for which user? Jonathan

User JONATHAN is restricted from executing the following commands:

    BEGIN
    DECLARE
    DELETE
    EXECUTE
    HOST
    SET ROLE

User JONATHAN does not exist.
```

# 10

*In this chapter:*
- *Connecting for Administrative Purposes*
- *Starting and Stopping a Database*
- *Looking at Your Database*
- *Database Backup and Recovery*

# Administration with SQL*Plus

Beginning with the release of Oracle8i, SQL*Plus has been enhanced to allow you to perform several administrative functions that previously required the use of Server Manager. Using SQL*Plus, you can now perform the following tasks:

- Start up or shut down an Oracle instance
- Turn archive log mode on and off
- View memory usage of the System Global Area (SGA)
- Look at the settings for various initialization parameters
- Initiate media recovery for a database

Server Manager is still around, at least in the initial release of Oracle8i, but Oracle's strategy is to make SQL*Plus the sole command-line interface to Oracle. Look for Server Manager to be desupported in some future release.

## Connecting for Administrative Purposes

In order to start up, shut down, change archive log settings, or recover an Oracle database, you must log into the database in a way that is different from your normal approach. Usually you connect as yourself, but to do many of the tasks described in this chapter, you need to log in either as an operator or as a database administrator. The section titled "Connecting in an Administrative Role," later in this chapter, shows you how to do this. In addition to logging in correctly, you must have the system privileges needed for the task you are performing. These are described next.

## Privileges You Will Need

To perform administrative tasks, you need to have been granted one of the following two roles:

SYSOPER
SYSDBA

Exactly what you can do depends on which of the two roles has been granted to you. The SYSOPER role was created for computer operators, who, in the absence of a database administrator, may need to perform such tasks as starting, stopping, and backing up the database. A user with the SYSOPER role is limited to the following commands:

STARTUP
SHUTDOWN
ALTER DATABASE OPEN
ALTER DATABASE MOUNT
ALTER DATBASE BACKUP
ARCHIVE LOG
RECOVER

The SYSDBA role, on the other hand, is intended for database administrators. There are no restrictions on what a user with SYSDBA can do.

These roles are granted at the database level, just like any other role, unless you are using operating-system authentication. In that case, the operating system roles OSOPER and OSDBA correspond to SYSOPER and SYSDBA, respectively.

## The Oracle Password File

When you connect to a database instance, Oracle needs a way to authenticate you as a valid user. Normally Oracle does this by looking at the DBA_USERS table to see if the password you have supplied matches the one stored in the database. This works fine when the database is up and running, but what if it's not? Most users do not connect to a database when it's closed. After all, what would be the point? Database administrators, however, need to be able to start and stop the database, as well as perform other administrative tasks. That means they need to be able to connect and be authenticated, even when the database is closed. The dilemma is that usernames and passwords are stored in the database and cannot be accessed when it's closed.

To resolve this dilemma of needing to authenticate database administrators when the database is closed, Oracle resorts to the method of storing their usernames and passwords in a file. This file is referred to as the *password file*, and is encrypted for obvious reasons. Any users who have been granted the SYSDBA or SYSOPER privileges have their passwords stored in this file as well as within the database.

 The INTERNAL password is also stored in the password file. See the section below titled "Connecting as INTERNAL."

Whenever you connect using one of the keywords SYSDBA, SYSOPER, or INTERNAL, Oracle validates your password using the password file, not the database. You can read more about this file, including how to create and manage it, in Chapter 1 of the *Oracle8 Administrator's Guide*.

## Connecting in an Administrative Role

To perform an administrative task, such as starting the database, you must connect to Oracle in your capacity as a database administrator. You do this by using the CONNECT command with the AS keyword to tell Oracle what role you intend to play. For example, if your username were RAYMOND, you would issue a command such as the following to connect in your role as an operator:

```
CONNECT raymond/my_secret AS SYSOPER;
```

This use of the AS keyword can be confusing to people, especially when they are first introduced to the subject. What exactly does it mean to connect "as" something? Many people take it to mean that you are really connecting as another user, but that's not quite the case. Take a look at the following command, and assume that you are the user named RAYMOND:

```
CONNECT raymond/good_man;
```

In this case, you are connecting to Oracle as yourself. This is easy enough to understand. You are attached to your own schema and see all of your own objects. If you are a database administrator, you may even have a number of system privileges that let you perform many administrative tasks without connecting as SYSOPER or SYSDBA.

When you connect AS a role, AS SYSOPER, for example, you are connected to Oracle and associated with the SYS schema. Why couldn't you just connect as user SYS in the first place? Because then every DBA would need to know the password for SYS. Sharing passwords is not a good security practice. Also, Oracle needs to be able to determine whether you should have SYSOPER privileges or SYSDBA privileges. Your username is key to making that determination.

The bottom line is this. When you connect to Oracle AS something, think of it as connecting to Oracle in your special capacity as a database administrator, or as an operator. You are connecting to perform some administrative task outside the scope of what you typically do.

### Connecting as SYSOPER or SYSDBA

In order to connect to Oracle in one of the administrative roles, you must run SQL*Plus and connect to the database using a special form of the CONNECT command, as shown in the following example:

```
C:\>SQLPLUS /NOLOG

SQL*Plus: Release 8.1.3.0.0 - Beta on Tue Oct 20 18:46:21 1998

(c) Copyright 1998 Oracle Corporation.  All rights reserved.

SQL> CONNECT raymond/good_man AS SYSDBA
Connected.
```

The /NOLOG option is used on the SQL*Plus command line so that SQL*Plus doesn't attempt to connect you as a normal user before you have a chance to connect as an operator or administrator. This is particularly necessary if the database is shut down and starting it is the reason you are connecting in the first place. As you can also see from the example, a special form of the CONNECT command is used. The syntax for it looks like this:

```
CONNECT [logon[@service]] AS role;
```

where:

*logon*
> If you are using operating-system authentication, this should simply be a forward slash (/) character. Otherwise, this should be your username and password, in the normal *username/password* notation.

*service*
> Is a SQL*Net or NET8 service name, and should match an entry in your *TNSNAMES* file.

*role*
> The role must be either SYSDBA or SYSOPER, depending on which you have.

When you connect like this, Oracle authenticates you using the Oracle password file. That way you can be authenticated as a privileged user even when the database is not open, which is important if you need to start the database.

If you are running on a Windows system, you may want to create a special short-cut to SQL*Plus that has /NOLOG as a command option. The Target field of the shortcut would look like this:

```
C:\ORAWIN95\BIN\SQLPLUSW.EXE /NOLOG
```

The exact path and executable name may vary depending on the specific versions of Windows and Oracle you are running. This will give you an icon to use when you need to start SQL*Plus without automatically connecting to the database. Once you've done that, you can use the CONNECT command as described earlier to connect as SYSDBA or SYSOPER.

### Connecting as INTERNAL

Another option for performing database administration tasks is to connect using the INTERNAL keyword. This option exists mainly for backwards compatibility with previous versions of Oracle, and normally shouldn't be used. However, it can be helpful, and sometimes necessary. It is possible to have a database where no user has SYSDBA or SYSOPER. It is always possible to connect as INTERNAL. Here is the command to use:

```
CONNECT INTERNAL[/password]
```

In some cases, you may not need to supply a password when connecting internally. Not all DBAs configure their systems to require an internal password. With an operating system such as Unix, the DBA, or the Oracle user, may have operating-system privileges that allow him to connect internally. If you do need to supply a password, it is authenticated against the one stored in your database's password file.

## Starting and Stopping a Database

Two SQL*Plus commands, STARTUP and SHUTDOWN, allow you to start and stop an Oracle instance. STARTUP, of course, is the command used to start an instance and open a database. In order to use it, you need to understand the various transitional states a database goes through on the way from being closed to open. These are described next, in "The States of a Database."

The SHUTDOWN command is used to close a database and stop an instance. There are four ways to stop an instance. First, there is the normal shutdown, which closes a database cleanly and has the least disturbing effect on any current users. Three other options allow you to terminate user connections and shut down an instance more quickly.

# The States of a Database

There are four states an Oracle database may be in on the continuum between being fully shut down and fully operational. Usually, you want the database to be at one extreme or the other, either fully closed or fully open. However, certain administrative tasks, renaming a datafile, for example, require that the database be in one of the intermediate states.

To understand the four states, you need to know the difference between an Oracle instance and an Oracle database. These terms are often used interchangeably, but each has a precise definition.

Oracle uses the term *instance* to refer to a set of background processes and their shared memory structures. These background processes are the ones that write data to the database, maintain the redo logs, archive the redo logs, and so on. These processes all share an area of memory referred to as the System Global Area, or SGA for short. The instance only exists when these processes are in memory, are running, and the System Global Area has been allocated. Think of a program like Microsoft Word. When you first open it, you see the default document. Close that default document, and you pretty much have a blank window. Word is still running. You still have a menu bar and a window, but no files are open and you can't do any word processing. Word in this state is analogous to an Oracle instance.

Oracle uses the term *database* to refer to the actual data being acted on by the instance. A database is stored in a collection of operating-system files on a host computer. To open a database, you first have to have an instance running. This makes sense if you think about it. Refer back to the Microsoft Word analogy. To open a document, you must start Word first.

Now, just as Windows lets you double-click a document's icon to both start Word and open the document in what looks like one step, so Oracle has a way to start an instance and open a database with one command, the STARTUP command.

When you issue the STARTUP command, Oracle will start an instance, associate it with a database, open the database, and allow users to connect. This process is illustrated in Figure 10-1.

As you can see from Figure 10-1, there are four possible states to be aware of. The first state is when the instance is stopped and the database is closed. None of the background processes are running, no memory is allocated for a System Global Area, and all the database files are closed. The database is fully shut down.

The next state may be referred to as the NOMOUNT state. When you issue the STARTUP command, Oracle first starts all the background processes and allocates memory for the SGA. It's possible to stop the process at this point. Why would

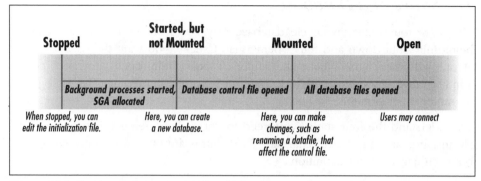

*Figure 10-1. Starting and opening an Oracle database*

you do this? One reason would be to create a new database. In the NOMOUNT state, the processes are all running, but no database files have been associated with the instance. This is like Word when all document files have been closed. It's the perfect time to create something new.

After the NOMOUNT state has been passed, the next point you reach is the MOUNT state. This is the point where you have told the instance what database you want to work with. The control files for the instance, and only the control files, will be open. The database datafiles remain closed. Renaming a datafile is an example of a task you could perform now. If you've moved one of the tablespace files or log files, you can use the ALTER DATABASE RENAME DATAFILE command to have Oracle write the file's new location to the database control files.

The final state to be reached is the OPEN state. All the datafiles associated with the database will now be open, and users will be allowed to connect. It's important to understand this process. Next you will see how to control it using the STARTUP command.

## Starting a Database

The STARTUP command is used to start an Oracle instance and open a database. Before issuing STARTUP, you must first decide whether you want the database to be fully open or not. If you don't want the database to be fully open, you must decide whether you want it to be mounted or not. Table 10-1 will help you decide, and shows you the basic command to reach each state.

*Table 10-1. STARTUP Commands for Each State*

| Command | Result | Why? |
|---------|--------|------|
| STARTUP | Instance started, database files open, users can connect | To make the database fully operational |

*Table 10-1. STARTUP Commands for Each State (continued)*

| Command | Result | Why? |
|---|---|---|
| STARTUP MOUNT | Instance started, database control files open, database data files closed, users cannot connect | To perform maintenance tasks such as renaming a data file |
| STARTUP NOMOUNT | Instance started, no database files open, users cannot connect | To create a new database |

Depending on your environment, there may be other options you need to use with this command in order for your database to start successfully. One commonly used parameter is PFILE, which points to the initialization file for the database being started. The following example shows the STARTUP command being used with PFILE to do a normal startup of a database:

```
SQL> CONNECT INTERNAL/plumtree@plum
Connected to an idle instance.
SQL> STARTUP PFILE=k:\instances\plum\initplum.ora
ORACLE instance started.
Total System Global Area     63475916 bytes
Fixed Size                      35760 bytes
Variable Size                37192988 bytes
Database Buffers             26214400 bytes
Redo Buffers                    32768 bytes
Database mounted.
Database opened.
```

This instance is started, the database is opened, and users may connect. In order to perform certain administrative tasks, you may need to only start the instance, or only mount the database. You do that with the NOMOUNT and MOUNT keywords, respectively. The following example starts an instance and mounts a database, but does not open it:

```
SQL> STARTUP MOUNT PFILE=k:\instances\plum\initplum.ora
ORACLE instance started.
Total System Global Area     63475916 bytes
Fixed Size                      35760 bytes
Variable Size                37192988 bytes
Database Buffers             26214400 bytes
Redo Buffers                    32768 bytes
Database mounted.
```

By using the NOMOUNT keyword instead of the MOUNT keyword, you could start the instance without associating a database. This is what you would need to do if you were planning to issue the CREATE DATABASE statement.

Sometimes you want to restrict access to a database after it is opened, so that only the DBA can connect. You can accomplish this with the RESTRICT keyword, as shown in the following example. In restricted mode, only users with the

RESTRICTED SESSION system privilege (usually just the database administrators) are allowed to connect.

```
SQL> STARTUP RESTRICT PFILE=k:\instances\plum\initplum.ora OPEN
ORACLE instance started.

Total System Global Area    5355764 bytes
Fixed Size                    63732 bytes
Variable Size               5013504 bytes
Database Buffers              204800 bytes
Redo Buffers                  73728 bytes
Database mounted.
Database opened.
```

 When opening a database in restricted mode, you need to use the OPEN keyword. Otherwise, the database is just mounted, but not opened.

There are other options that may be used with the STARTUP command. These are described fully in Appendix A, *SQL\*Plus Command Reference.*

## Stopping a Database

The SHUTDOWN command is used to stop an Oracle instance. If you are not running with the parallel server option, shutting down an instance also closes the database. If you are using multiple instances to access a database, the database files will be closed only after all instances have been shut down.

There are four ways to stop an instance. One way is to do a normal shutdown, which waits for all active users to disconnect before stopping the instance. Alternatively, you can use the TRANSACTIONAL, IMMEDIATE, or ABORT keywords to stop things more abruptly. Which keyword you should use depends on how quickly you need to stop the instance, and what effect you want that to have on the current users.

### SHUTDOWN NORMAL

A normal shutdown is generally considered the most prudent approach to stopping an instance and closing a database. It certainly is the least disruptive to any currently connected users. The command to issue is simply:

```
SHUTDOWN
```

When you issue this command, Oracle performs the following steps:

1. New user connections are disallowed.

2. Oracle waits for all users to disconnect.

3. The database files are closed.

4. The instance is stopped.

Step 2, waiting for the users to disconnect, may take a long time. In a normal shutdown, Oracle will not forcefully disconnect any active users, so the amount of time it takes to shut down the database depends largely on how quickly your users exit their applications.

---

 If all you want to do is quickly shut down and restart the database, the wait for active users to disconnect can be frustrating. On the one hand, you will have users who can't connect because the database is being shut down, yet on the other hand, you won't be able to finish the shutdown because there are active users still connected. In such a situation, you may have to take more drastic steps, such as doing a SHUTDOWN IMMEDIATE.

---

Here is an example showing a normal SHUTDOWN:

```
SQL> CONNECT INTERNAL/plumtree@plum
Connected.
SQL> SHUTDOWN
Database closed.
Database dismounted.
ORACLE instance shut down.
```

A normal shutdown results in the database activity being brought to an orderly halt. Recent changes contained in memory are flushed to files, the files are closed, memory structures are deallocated, and the instances's processes are stopped. At this point, the database files are all consistent with each other, and a cold backup could be taken. Other shutdown options, such as TRANSACTIONAL and IMMEDIATE, allow you perform a shutdown more quickly and still leave the database files in a consistent state.

### SHUTDOWN TRANSACTIONAL

A new feature of Oracle8i is the ability to perform a transactional shutdown. Unlike a normal shutdown, a *transactional shutdown* results in all users being forcibly disconnected. However, before being disconnected, users are allowed to complete their current transaction. Here is the syntax to use:

```
SHUTDOWN TRANSACTIONAL
```

When you issue the SHUTDOWN TRANSACTIONAL command, Oracle stops all new connections and begins waiting for each user to commit. As each user commits his current transaction, that user is disconnected. When no more users remain, the database is closed and the instance is stopped.

## SHUTDOWN IMMEDIATE

An immediate shutdown is very similar to a transactional shutdown, except that each user is disconnected when her current SQL statement completes, regardless of whether her transaction is complete or not. The command to use for an immediate shutdown is:

```
SHUTDOWN IMMEDIATE
```

In spite of its name, an immediate shutdown may not be very immediate. As users are kicked off, any open transactions must be rolled back. For short transactions, the rollback process is fairly quick, but in the case of a long transaction that affects a lot of a data, the rollback may take a noticeably long time. During this time, your session will appear "stuck," because SHUTDOWN IMMEDIATE does not provide any feedback until the rollback process is complete.

## SHUTDOWN ABORT

When you absolutely have to have the database down *now*, use the ABORT option. Aborting an instance is pretty much like kicking out the plug on your computer. All background processes are abruptly stopped. Files are not closed, at least not by Oracle, and open transactions are not rolled back. Instead, the rollback occurs when you restart the instance and Oracle performs crash recovery. The command to abort an instance is:

```
SHUTDOWN ABORT
```

Usually, you should only abort an instance when some critical event is imminent. Maybe an earthquake is occurring, and you expect to lose power any moment. Another reason to abort an instance is to remove any leftover background processes remaining after the instance has crashed. It's possible to get into a situation where STARTUP commands fail with errors saying that the instance is running, and where SHUTDOWN commands fail with errors saying that the instance is not running. In such a case, SHUTDOWN ABORT will usually set things right again.

Since processes are stopped immediately when you abort an instance, rollback of open transactions cannot occur in response to a SHUTDOWN ABORT. Instead, this work is deferred until the next time you start the instance. At that time, Oracle will detect the previous crash, and will initiate a process called *crash recovery*. During the crash recovery process, Oracle will roll forward through the redo logs to catch up on any updates that were lost, and will then roll back any transactions that weren't committed. The end result is the same as if you had done a SHUT-DOWN IMMEDIATE.

# Looking at Your Database

The SHOW command may be used to review information regarding the current state of your database. Use SHOW SGA to see the information about the size of your System Global Area, or SGA. With SHOW PARAMETER, you can look at the current settings for the database initialization parameters. SHOW LOGSOURCE and SHOW AUTORECOVERY give you information about archive logging and recovery.

Remember that the SHOW command options described in this chapter are new with release 8.1 of SQL*Plus, which was shipped with Oracle8i. In previous versions of Oracle, these SHOW commands were implemented only in Server Manager.

## Looking at the SGA

The SHOW SGA command may be used to display information regarding the size of the System Global Area. The SGA is shared by all Oracle processes and contains the database buffer cache, the redo log buffer, shared SQL statements, and a number of other items. Here is an example of SHOW SGA being used:

```
SQL> SHOW SGA
Total System Global Area      5508612 bytes
Fixed Size                      45584 bytes
Variable Size                 4529140 bytes
Database Buffers               409600 bytes
Redo Buffers                   524288 bytes
```

The values returned by SHOW SGA are as follows:

*Total System Global Area*
> The total maximum size of the SGA.

*Fixed Size*
> This is the minimum size of the SGA, and is the size used when the SGA is first allocated.

*Variable Size*
> This is the amount by which the SGA may expand.

*Database Buffers*

> The number of bytes allocated for buffering of data blocks from the data files. Oracle tries to keep the most recently used data in memory, in case it is needed again.

*Redo Buffers*

> The number of bytes allocated for buffering of redo log data. The log writer (LGWR) process reads these buffers and writes the information they contain to the redo log files.

For more information about the SGA, the structures within it, and the purpose of each of those structures, see Chapter 7 of the *Oracle8 Concepts* manual.

## *Looking at Initialization Parameters*

Each Oracle database has a number of initialization parameters that control its behavior. These parameters control a wide range of things, such as the number of job queue processes to run, the database block size, the shared pool size, and more. When an Oracle database starts, the initial settings for these parameters are read from an initialization file. Some of these parameters may be changed dynamically, while the database is up and running. Others may only be changed while the instance is shut down. Still others, such as the database block size, may never be changed at all.

The SHOW PARAMETERS command may be used to display the value of one or more selected parameters, or of all parameters. SHOW PARAMETERS with no arguments will get you a listing of everything, as shown in the following example:

```
SQL> SHOW PARAMETERS
NAME                                TYPE    VALUE
----------------------------------- ------- -----------------------------
O7_DICTIONARY_ACCESSIBILITY         boolean TRUE
allow_partial_sn_results            boolean FALSE
always_anti_join                    string  NESTED_LOOPS
aq_tm_processes                     integer 0
arch_io_slaves                      integer 0
audit_trail                         string  NONE
b_tree_bitmap_plans                 boolean FALSE
background_dump_dest                string  %RDBMS80%\trace
backup_disk_io_slaves               integer 0
backup_tape_io_slaves               boolean FALSE
bitmap_merge_area_size              integer 1048576
blank_trimming                      boolean FALSE
buffer_pool_keep                    string
buffer_pool_recycle                 string
cache_size_threshold                integer 20
cleanup_rollback_entries            integer 20
...
```

You can narrow down the results by using a specific parameter name as an argument, for example:

```
SQL> SHOW PARAMETERS log_checkpoint_interval
NAME                                 TYPE    VALUE
------------------------------------ ------- ------------------------------
log_checkpoint_interval              integer 10000
```

A useful variation on this theme is that you may specify any string you like as an argument to SHOW PARAMETERS, and SQL*Plus will display all the parameters whose names contain that string. The following example shows all the LOG-related parameters, plus a few others containing the string "LOG":

```
SVRMGR> SHOW PARAMETERS log
NAME                                 TYPE    VALUE
------------------------------------ ------- ------------------------------
dblink_encrypt_login                 boolean FALSE
delayed_logging_block_cleanouts      boolean TRUE
log_archive_buffer_size              integer 127
log_archive_buffers                  integer 4
log_archive_dest                     string  %RDBMS80%\
log_archive_duplex_dest              string
log_archive_format                   string  ARC%s.%t
log_archive_min_succeed_dest         integer 1
log_archive_start                    boolean FALSE
log_block_checksum                   boolean FALSE
log_buffer                           integer 8192
log_checkpoint_interval              integer 10000
log_checkpoint_timeout               integer 0
log_checkpoints_to_alert             boolean FALSE
log_file_name_convert                string
log_files                            integer 255
log_simultaneous_copies              integer 0
log_small_entry_max_size             integer 80
mts_rate_log_size                    string
remote_login_passwordfile            string  SHARED
```

## Looking at Archive and Recovery Information

SQL*Plus implements three commands that let you view information about archive logging and recovery. The SHOW LOGSOURCE command may be used to find out what directory your database's archive log files are being written to. Here's an example:

```
SQL> SHOW LOGSOURCE
Logsource                            G:\INSTANCES\PLUM\LOGS
```

If you want to see more information about the status of archive logging, use the ARCHIVE LOG LIST command as shown in this example:

```
SQL> ARCHIVE LOG LIST
Database log mode                    Archive Mode
```

```
Automatic archival              Enabled
Archive destination             G:\INSTANCES\PLUM\LOGS
Oldest online log sequence      35
Next log sequence to archive    36
Current log sequence            36
```

The output from ARCHIVE LOG LIST is as follows:

*Database log mode*

Tells you whether or not your database is running in archive mode. The value will be either "Archive Mode" or "NOArchive Mode".

*Automatic archival*

Tells you whether or not redo logs are automatically being archived. If automatic archival is enabled, that means you have an archiver process (ARCH) running, and your redo logs are automatically being copied to another device as each one is closed.

*Archive destination*

Tells you the archive destination. This is the same information you get from the SHOW LOGSOURCE command.

*Oldest online log sequence*

Tells you the sequence number of the oldest redo log group that hasn't been archived yet. Oracle increments this sequence each time a log switch occurs.

*Next log sequence to archive*

Tells you the sequence number of the next group of log files to be archived. If automatic archiving is disabled, this line won't be displayed. This value will always be less than the current log sequence.

*Current log sequence*

Tells you the sequence number of the redo log group currently in use.

You can get an idea of how well the archiving process, which is named ARCH, is keeping up by looking at the values for the next log sequence archive and the current log sequence. A large difference between these two values indicates that the ARCH process is falling behind. If the archiver falls too far behind, the log writer process won't be able to open another group, and database users will have to wait for one to be archived. If this happens frequently, you may be able to resolve the situation by creating more redo log groups, making your existing groups larger, or starting more archive processes.

# Database Backup and Recovery

Beginning with version 8.1, SQL*Plus implements commands to manage the archiving of redo log files and to perform point-in-time recovery of a database. In order to understand how these commands work, and to place them in their proper context, you need to understand something of how backup and recovery work in an Oracle environment.

This section explains the two fundamental approaches to backing up an Oracle database, and shows you how SQL*Plus may fit into your backup process. Archive logging will be explained, and you will see how SQL*Plus can be used to start, stop, and monitor that process. Finally, you will see how the SQL*Plus RECOVER command can be used to apply archive logs to a restored database in order to get up-to-the-minute recovery.

If you are responsible for backing up an Oracle database, please do not depend on just this one chapter to show you how to do that properly. There are several excellent books on the subject. One you should become very familiar with is the *Oracle8 Backup and Recovery Guide*—it's one of the manuals in the Oracle documentation set. Another book worth looking at is the *Oracle8 Backup and Recovery Handbook*, by Rama Velpuri and Anand Adkoli (Oracle Press, 1998). In addition, Oracle offers the three-day-long *Oracle8 Backup and Recovery Workshop*.

Of all the things that a database administrator is responsible for, protecting the data is probably first on the list.

The discussion of backup and recovery in this chapter is very high-level. The recovery scenario used as an example represents just one of many possibilities. It's a common scenario, and serves well to illustrate the use of the RECOVERY command, but there are a number of other possible scenarios you have to know how to handle in order to be confident that you can recover from a disaster.

## Backups

There are two fundamental approaches to backing up an Oracle database. The first and easiest approach is to shut down the database and copy the files to a backup medium such as a tape. This is referred to as making a *cold backup*, because the database is closed, or cold, when you make it. Cold backups carry with them one major disadvantage—you must shut down the database. In a 24×7 shop, this may not be an option.

With cold backups, you have to decide whether or not you need point-in-time recovery in the case of a failure. Enabling archive log mode gives you the ability to restore a cold backup and then reapply all committed transactions up to the point in time at which the failure occurred. Archiving is discussed in detail later in this chapter. Cold backups are the easiest to implement, and are often used for small databases.

Oracle provides a second approach to backing up a database that avoids the need for a shutdown. This involves copying the files while the database is open and being used, and is known as making a *hot backup*. You must have archive logging enabled in order to make a hot backup, so point-in-time recovery capabilities are automatically included.

### Cold backups

Making a cold backup of your database is a relatively painless process. You simply follow these three steps:

1. Shut down the database normally, so that you have a consistent set of database files. This must be done with the SHUTDOWN, SHUTDOWN IMMEDIATE, or SHUTDOWN TRANSACTIONAL command.

2. Copy all the database files to backup media, such as a tape. This copying can be done manually, or it can be done by whatever backup software you employ.

3. Restart the database using the STARTUP command.

To restore a database from a cold backup, you shut down the instance, copy the files from the backup media back to their original locations, then restart the instance. Your database will be restored to the way it was when you first took the backup.

---

 It is possible, when restoring a database from a cold backup, to place the datafiles somewhere other than their original locations. This may be necessary if you have lost a disk drive. If you do this, you will need to use the ALTER DATABASE RENAME DATAFILE command before opening your database.

---

If you aren't sure which files to back up, you can find out by querying the data dictionary. The V$DATAFILE view returns information about each datafile used by the database, while V$LOGFILE tells you about the redo log files. The following query will return a list of all data and log files:

```
SELECT name
   FROM v$datafile
UNION
SELECT member
   FROM v$logfile;
```

The only other files you need to worry about are the control files and the initialization file. You can get a list of control files by looking at the CONTROL_FILES entry in the initialization file, or by issuing the following command from SQL*Plus:

```
SHOW PARAMETERS control_files
```

The initialization file is the one used with the PFILE parameter on the STARTUP command. You should know where this is. Oracle won't keep track of it for you.

Cold backups are often done as part of a nightly backup process that makes a copy of all files on your system. At some point prior to making the backup, the database is shut down. The backup job then runs, copying all files on the system to tape. When the backup job is complete, the database is restarted.

 Generate a listing of all datafiles, log files, and control files associated with the database each night. You will need it when it comes time to restore.

If you are making cold backups as part of a nightly operating-system backup, you probably don't worry too much about which files are database files, since everything is being backed up anyway. You should worry. Knowing where your database files are is important when it comes time to restore, and for two reasons. First, if you need to restore your database, you will need to know which files to pull off the backup tape. You will also need to know where to place them. Second, you may be restoring the files to a different location, maybe to a different disk. If this is the case, you will need to issue ALTER DATABASE RENAME DATAFILE commands to tell Oracle the new location of the files. In order to do that, you will need to supply the old location as well.

### Hot backups

Hot backups allow you to back up the database while it is open and being used, avoiding the major disadvantage of the cold backup approach. Also, with a hot backup, you automatically get point-in-time recovery. In the event of a disk failure, this allows you to restore the database and recover all transactions up to the time of failure.

Because the files are open when you make a hot backup, they may not be consistent with one another. Consider, for example, a transaction that affects records stored in different datafiles. It isn't likely that the changes to both datafiles will be written to disk at exactly the same time. Thus, one datafile could be up-to-date, while changes to the second datafile could still be buffered in memory. If you take your hot backup at this moment, the two datafiles you copy won't be consistent in regard to a single point in time. Look at Figure 10-2 to see a simplistic representation of how this works. Assume that you have just added a new employee to your database and assigned him to a department. Figure 10-2 shows the database in a state where the employee record has been written to a datafile, but the department record has not.

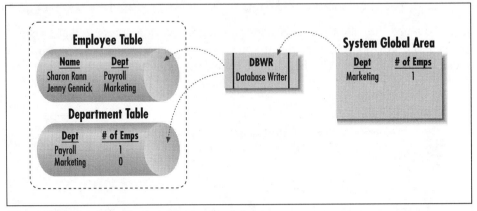

*Figure 10-2. Database files in an inconsistent state*

You can see from Figure 10-2 that the new employee record has been written to a database file. The updated department record, however, with its count of active employees, still remains buffered in memory. The dotted line in Figure 10-2 shows what you would get if you copied the files at this point in time. In order to restore a database from this type of backup, Oracle needs to know what changes to make to the department data file in order to bring it up to date with the rest of the database. Oracle can get this information from the redo logs, but in order to do that you must be saving these log files somewhere. You do that by running the database in archive log mode, which is described in the section titled "Archiving."

When taking a hot backup, you must use the ALTER TABLESPACE BEGIN BACKUP and ALTER TABLESPACE END BACKUP commands before and after copying each tablespace's datafiles. See the *Oracle8 Backup and Recovery Guide* for detailed information on performing a hot backup.

When restoring a database from a hot backup, you first shut down the database, then copy the data files back from tape. Finally, you go through a process called *recovery*. Recovery allows you to reapply transactions to the data files, bringing them up to date so they are consistent with one another and reflect the results of the last successful transaction prior to the failure. This is known as *point-in-time recovery,* because you can restore the database to the exact point of time that the failure occurred. See the section titled "Recovery," later in this chapter, for detailed information on the recovery process.

## Archiving

Archiving, in the Oracle world, is the process of saving redo log files for later use in a recovery process. Look at Figure 10-3. It's the same as Figure 10-2, except it also shows the redo log files. Whenever you change data in an Oracle database, the changes are written to a log file. This write occurs very quickly because it's a sequential write—the data is just appended to the end of the current log. This writing of the log file can lag somewhat behind your actual changes, but Oracle always catches up whenever you issue a COMMIT command. Transaction numbers are written with each log file record, so Oracle can keep track of which changes have been committed and which have not.

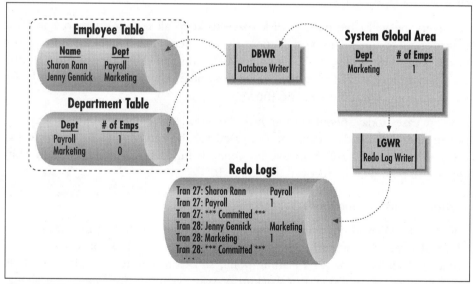

*Figure 10-3. Changes written to the redo log files*

These redo logs protect the database against a sudden interruption in the running of the software, such as you might get by kicking the computer's plug out of the wall. When you restart Oracle after a power failure, Oracle will immediately read through the redo log files to pick up any changes that weren't written to the database files before the crash. The database files are then updated with these changes, restoring things to the way they should have been had the crash not occurred. This process is known as *crash recovery,* and protects the database against any sudden interruptions that do not result in damage to the disks containing the database files.

To enable crash recovery, the logs only need to remain long enough for the same data to be written to the actual data files. Once that has happened, Oracle will reuse the log file for the next set of changes. In a running database, Oracle will continually cycle through a set of log files, moving from one to the next to the next as fast as each one is filled with data, saving only enough information to recover from an instance crash.

It stands to reason that if Oracle can use the log files to recover from an instance crash, it ought to be able to use the same log files to recover from a disk failure. Indeed it can; the only difference is in the number of log files you need to keep around. Saving all redo logs since the time of the most recent backup allows you to fully recover the database when files are lost or damaged. You recover the database by restoring the database files from the backup and reapplying subsequent changes from the log files.

Not everyone will have enough disk space to keep all redo log files online for a long period of time. This was particularly true years ago when the cost of the media was relatively high. This is where archiving comes in. Oracle provides the capability to archive redo log files to tape or some other media as they are being made. This gives you the scenario shown in Figure 10-4.

In many cases today, people just archive the redo logs to a separate disk, maybe a slower and cheaper disk than the one used for the redo log files. Whatever the case, running a database in archive log mode is fundamental to any backup strategy where point-in-time recovery is required.

### Turning on archive log mode

The ALTER DATABASE command can be used to put a database into archive log mode. It's important to remember that archive logs are useless for recovery without a full backup to use as a starting point, so before you turn archive log mode on, you should take a complete backup of your database. Generally, you should follow these steps:

1. Shut down the instance, closing the database.

2. Take a cold backup of the database.

3. Edit the initialization file. Check to make sure there is a LOG_ARCHIVE_DEST parameter, that it is uncommented, and that it is pointing to a valid directory.

4. Start the instance and mount, but don't open, the database. Use the STARTUP MOUNT command for this purpose.

5. Turn archive log mode on using the ALTER DATABASE command.

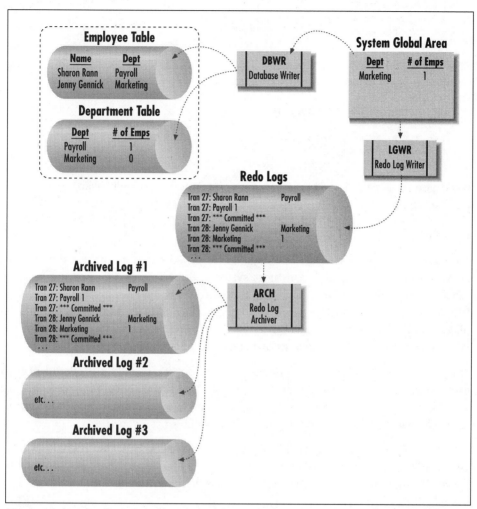

*Figure 10-4. A database in archive log mode*

6. Open the database for use.

7. Start the automatic archival process.

The ALTER DATABASE command has a number of options. The specific form used to put a database into archive log mode is:

```
ALTER DATABASE ARCHIVELOG;
```

In order to issue this command, you must be connected either as INTERNAL or SYSDBA. The following example shows how you would start a database using the MOUNT option, put it into archivelog mode, and then open the database:

```
SQL> CONNECT INTERNAL
Connected.
```

```
SQL> STARTUP MOUNT
ORACLE instance started.
Total System Global Area        5138580 bytes
Fixed Size                        47252 bytes
Variable Size                   4608000 bytes
Database Buffers                 409600 bytes
Redo Buffers                      73728 bytes
Database mounted.
SQL> ALTER DATABASE ARCHIVELOG;
Statement processed.
SQL> ALTER DATABASE OPEN;
Statement processed.
SQL>
```

Once you've put the database into archive log mode, you will want to start the archive log process.

### Starting the archive log process

The archive log process is an optional Oracle process that automates the task of archiving the redo log files. On most systems, the name of this process will be ARCH, or something close to that, and the Oracle documentation frequently refers to it by that name. ARCH runs in the background, and as each redo log file is filled, ARCH copies it to the archive log destination. ARCH also marks each file when it is copied so that Oracle knows it can be reused again.

Strictly speaking, ARCH is an optional process, but it's usually considered necessary when the database is in archive log mode. The alternative is for you to manually archive each redo log file as it fills, but that requires constant monitoring and attention—something most people don't have time for.

Use the ARCHIVE LOG command to start the archive log process. The ARCH process will be started, and redo logs will begin to be archived. You may optionally specify a destination for the archived files. Here is the syntax to use:

```
ARCHIVE LOG START [TO destination]
```

where:

*destination*
> Is an operating-system–specific path pointing to the directory or device where you want the archived log files written. This is an optional parameter. If you don't supply it, the archive log destination is taken from the LOG_ARCHIVE_DEST parameter in your database's initialization file.

You can start the archive process when the database is up and running, but you have to be connected in one of the administrative modes. The following example shows the archive log process being started:

```
SQL> CONNECT INTERNAL
Connected.
SQL> ARCHIVE LOG START
Statement processed.
SQL>
```

In this case, since no destination was supplied in the command itself, the location specified by the LOG_ARCHIVE_DEST initialization parameter will be used. After starting the archive log process, you should check the LOG_ARCHIVE_START parameter in your database's initialization file. Setting it to TRUE will ensure that the archive log process is automatically started. You should also be familiar with the value for the LOG_ARCHIVE_DEST parameter, which points to the destination directory, so you can find the log files in case you need to recover the database.

### Displaying the archive log status

Once archive log mode has been enabled, you can view the current status with the ARCHIVE LOG LIST command, as shown in the following example:

```
SQL> ARCHIVE LOG LIST
Database log mode              Archive Mode
Automatic archival             Enabled
Archive destination            C:\ORAWIN95\RDBMS80\
Oldest online log sequence     34
Next log sequence to archive   35
Current log sequence           35
SQL>
```

In fact, you can even view the archive log status when archiving is off. The output from ARCHIVE LOG LIST may be interpreted as follows:

### Database log mode

Tells you whether or not the database is in archive mode. When archive mode is on, redo log files must be archived before they can be reused. Whether that is happening automatically or not depends on the next piece of output.

### Automatic archival

Tells you whether automatic archival is enabled or disabled. If enabled, the ARCH process will be running. If disabled, you must manually archive log files as they are filled.

### Archive destination

Tells you where the archive log files are going. This will be a directory path or a device name. In this example, the log files are being archived to *C:\ORAWIN95\RDBMS80*.

### Oldest online log sequence

Redo log files are numbered sequentially. This tells you the number of the oldest file that has not yet been archived. The number itself has no meaning; it just increments forever.

### Next log sequence to archive

This is the sequence number of the next log file to be archived. When you first enable automatic archiving, this will be the same as the current log sequence. When Oracle switches to the next log file, this one will be archived.

### Current log sequence

This is the sequence number of the log file currently being used.

When the archive log process archives a redo log file by copying it to the archive destination, it gives the resulting file a new and unique name. The name usually includes the SID and the log sequence number, but the exact format is controlled by the LOG_ARCHIVE_FORMAT initialization parameter. See the *Oracle8 Server Reference* manual for detailed information on that and other initialization parameters.

### Manually archiving a log file

If you have automatic archiving turned off, you can use the ARCHIVE LOG command to manually archive a redo log file. The syntax to use is:

```
ARCHIVE LOG {[NEXT|ALL|integer]}
```

where:

*NEXT*

Archives the next redo log file in sequence.

*ALL*

Catches you up by archiving all filled redo log files that haven't yet been archived.

*integer*

Archives a specific redo log file. The number supplied must be a valid log file sequence number, and that log file must still be online.

The following example shows the NEXT option being used to manually archive the next log file in the sequence:

```
SQL> ARCHIVE LOG NEXT
1 log archived.
SQL>
```

### Stopping the archive log process

You can stop the archive process by issuing the ARCHIVE LOG STOP command. For example:

```
SQL> ARCHIVE LOG STOP
Statement processed.
```

Stopping the archive process does not take the database out of archive log mode. Oracle will continue to fill redo log files, and these files must be archived before they can be reused. Because you've stopped the archive log process, you will need to manually archive these files. Fail to keep up, and Oracle will come to a complete stop when the last redo log file is filled.

### Turning off archive log mode

To take the database out of archive log mode, you follow much the same process as you do when you put it into archive log mode. You should first shut down the database and take a cold backup. Even when turning archive log mode off, a backup is necessary because backups taken while archive log mode is on are not restorable without a complete set of archive logs. Once you've taken a cold backup, start the instance, mount the database, and issue the ALTER DATABASE NOARCHIVELOG command as shown in the following example:

```
SQL> CONNECT INTERNAL
Connected.
SQL> STARTUP MOUNT
ORACLE instance started.
Total System Global Area         5138580 bytes
Fixed Size                         47252 bytes
Variable Size                    4608000 bytes
Database Buffers                  409600 bytes
Redo Buffers                       73728 bytes
Database mounted.
SQL> ALTER DATABASE NOARCHIVELOG;
Statement processed.
SQL> ALTER DATABASE OPEN;
Statement processed.
SQL>
```

Once you've taken the database out of archive log mode, Oracle will cycle through and reuse the redo log files without waiting for them to be archived. You will no longer be able to perform point-in-time recovery of the database. The best you will be able to do if a disk failure occurs will be to restore the most recent full backup.

## Recovery

Recovery is the process of restoring a database from backups and replaying all the transactions from the archived redo log files in order to bring the database up to date. Running a database in archive log mode gives you a great deal of flexibility in what you recover and how you do it. In a worst-case scenario, you can restore and recover the entire database. If you have only lost part of the database, you can perform recovery on either a tablespace or datafile basis. When recovering specific tablespaces or datafiles, you may even be able to keep the rest of the database online and available.

The recovery process generally consists of the following six steps:

1. Restore the data files from the most recent backup.

2. Make sure the necessary archive logs are available in the archive log destination directory.

3. Start up the instance, mount the database exclusively, but do not open it.

4. Use the SQL\*Plus RECOVER command to reapply updates based on information in the archived log files.

5. Shut down the database.

6. Restart the instance, mount the database normally, and open it.

The SQL\*Plus RECOVER command is used in step 4 to reapply changes based on information in the redo log files.

The next few sections explain how to use the RECOVER command when restoring the entire database, and when restoring just one tablespace or datafile. The examples in this book assume that the required database files have been restored, and that the archive log files are in the archive log destination directory.

### Full database recovery

In order to restore and recover an entire database, you must first shut it down, then restore all the data files from the most recent backup. Do not restore the control file, and do not restore any redo log files. These should be multiplexed so you don't lose them in the event of a disk failure.

---

 It is possible to deal with extreme failures, such as losing all copies of your control file, but that information is well outside the scope of this book. The example here represents one of the simplest recovery scenarios, and is presented only to help explain the concepts behind the process.

---

The next step in the recovery process is to restart the instance and mount the database in exclusive mode. Do not open the database, just mount it. Here's how:

```
C:\Oracle\Ora81>SQLPLUS /NOLOG

SQL*Plus: Release 8.1.3.0.0 - Beta on Tue Oct 20 20:05:48 1998

(c) Copyright 1998 Oracle Corporation.  All rights reserved.
```

```
SQL> CONNECT INTERNAL
Connected to an idle instance.
SQL> STARTUP MOUNT
ORACLE instance started.

Total System Global Area      5355764 bytes
Fixed Size                      63732 bytes
Variable Size                 5013504 bytes
Database Buffers               204800 bytes
Redo Buffers                    73728 bytes
Database mounted.
```

Once the database has been mounted, it's time to issue the appropriate RECOVER command, which is RECOVER DATABASE in this case. Here is an example:

```
SQL> RECOVER DATABASE
ORA-00279: change 15447 generated at 11/29/98 15:31:37 needed for thread 1
ORA-00289: suggestion : C:\ORAWIN95\DATABASE\ARCHIVE\ARC26.1
ORA-00280: change 15447 for thread 1 is in sequence #26
  Specify log: {<RET>=suggested | filename | AUTO | CANCEL}
```

When you issue the RECOVER DATABASE command, Oracle will prompt you for the name of the first archive log file to apply. Part of this prompt will be a default path and filename, which is based on the current archive log settings in your database initialization file. Unless you have changed things or moved log files around, this default path and filename should be correct. If the log files are where Oracle expects them to be, all you have to do is press ENTER or RETURN. Otherwise, type in the correct path and filename, then press ENTER. Oracle will read changes from that log file and reapply those changes to the database.

As Oracle finishes reading each log file, you will be prompted for the path and filename of the next file in the sequence. If all the log files are online and in the correct directory, you have an easy task ahead of you. Just press ENTER in response to each prompt. To make things even easier, you can take advantage of the autorecovery feature. Autorecovery is described in the section titled "Autorecovery," later in this chapter.

When all the log files have been read and all the updates reapplied to the database, you will get a message telling you that recovery is complete. You are now ready to open the database for general use. You can do that with the ALTER DATABASE command shown in the following example:

```
SQL> ALTER DATABASE OPEN;

Database altered.
```

### Tablespace and datafile recovery

Running in archive log mode gives you the flexibility to recover a specific datafile or tablespace when it becomes damaged. This is faster than recovering the entire database, and, as long as the SYSTEM tablespace is not lost, you can even perform the recovery while the rest of the database is up and running.

As an example, let's say that you lose the disk containing one of the datafiles in the USER_DATA tablespace. The first thing you should do is take the tablespace offline. You can do that with the following command:

```
ALTER TABLESPACE USER_DATA OFFLINE;
```

Next, you need to restore the damaged datafile from the most recent backup. Since you will most likely need to put this file in a new location, you will need to issue the following command to update the database control file:

```
ALTER TABLESPACE USER_DATA
    RENAME DATAFILE 'G:\ORACLE\INSTANCES\ORCL\USER_DATA_1.DAT'
    TO 'H:\ORACLE\INSTANCES\ORCL\USER_DATA_1.DAT';
```

Now you are ready to begin the recovery process. Make certain you have the required archive log files online. You will need all the log files generated since the backup of the datafile. Issue the following command from SQL\*Plus:

```
RECOVER TABLESPACE
```

From this point forward, the recovery process works the same as when you are recovering the full database. You will be prompted for the name and location of each log file until the process is complete, at which time the tablespace will be back the way it was before you lost the disk. The last thing you need to do is bring the tablespace online again. The following command will do this:

```
ALTER TABLESPACE USER_DATA ONLINE;
```

Recovering a datafile can be done the same way as recovering a tablespace; the only difference is that you use the RECOVER DATAFILE command instead of RECOVER TABLESPACE.

### Autorecovery

When you are recovering a database, if there are a lot of redo logs to apply, being prompted for each file quickly becomes tiresome. The autorecovery feature can help with this. It's normally off, but you can turn it on with the following SQL\*Plus command:

```
SET AUTORECOVERY ON
```

With autorecovery on, you can issue the RECOVER command, and Oracle won't prompt you for the name of each log file. If you have already started recovering log files, you can kick the process into autorecovery mode by responding to one of the prompts with the keyword AUTO. The following example shows this:

```
SQL> RECOVER DATABASE
ORA-00279: change 340672 generated at 01/06/99 14:43:22 needed for thread 1
```

```
ORA-00289: suggestion : C:\ORACLE\ORADATA\ORCL\ARCHIVE\%ORCL%T001S00568.ARC
ORA-00280: change 340672 for thread 1 is in sequence #568

Specify log: {<RET>=suggested | filename | AUTO | CANCEL}
AUTO
ORA-00279: change 340721 generated at 01/06/99 16:52:34 needed for thread 1
ORA-00289: suggestion : C:\ORACLE\ORADATA\ORCL\ARCHIVE\%ORCL%T001S00569.ARC
ORA-00280: change 340721 for thread 1 is in sequence #569
ORA-00278: log file 'C:\ORACLE\ORADATA\ORCL\ARCHIVE\%ORCL%T001S00568.ARC' no
longer needed for this recovery

ORA-00279: change 340723 generated at 01/06/99 16:52:41 needed for thread 1
ORA-00289: suggestion : C:\ORACLE\ORADATA\ORCL\ARCHIVE\%ORCL%T001S00570.ARC
ORA-00280: change 340723 for thread 1 is in sequence #570
ORA-00278: log file 'C:\ORACLE\ORADATA\ORCL\ARCHIVE\%ORCL%T001S00569.ARC' no
longer needed for this recovery

ORA-00279: change 340725 generated at 01/06/99 16:52:50 needed for thread 1
ORA-00289: suggestion : C:\ORACLE\ORADATA\ORCL\ARCHIVE\%ORCL%T001S00571.ARC
ORA-00280: change 340725 for thread 1 is in sequence #571
ORA-00278: log file 'C:\ORACLE\ORADATA\ORCL\ARCHIVE\%ORCL%T001S00570.ARC' no
longer needed for this recovery

Log applied.
Media recovery complete.
```

After responding with AUTO, you won't be prompted for any more file names. Autorecovery works only if all the needed log files are where Oracle expects. This is the same location you see when you issue the ARCHIVE LOG LIST command. If Oracle looks for a file and can't find it, you will be prompted once again.

## Other Things You Need to Know

There are a lot of other permutations to backup and recovery than are covered in this chapter. The information in this chapter highlights the role SQL*Plus can play in a backup and recovery plan, but there are other tools you can use. Oracle's Recovery Manager, or RMAN, is one of them. RMAN can be used instead of operating-system commands to back up datafiles. RMAN can also be used instead of SQL*Plus to initiate the recovery process.

The examples in this chapter show you how to restore a full database or a tablespace. There are other things you could lose that would require a different recovery strategy. You could, for example, lose one of the disks containing your redo log files. Recovering from that requires a different procedure from that used by the examples in this chapter. When running in archive log mode, you don't necessarily need to back up your entire database at any one time. You can back up one tablespace today, another tomorrow, and so forth. There is even one situation where you can perform point-in-time recovery on a database that is not in archive log mode.

If you are responsible for backing up an Oracle database, make sure you know how to restore it! You should test yourself and your procedures by doing a trial restore of the database to another computer, or to another set of directories on the same computer. Many people have found holes in their backup methods only after a disaster forces them to attempt a restore—it's too late then. If you have never restored your database, then you do not have a good backup.

In order to be prepared for the day when you lose a disk, and consequently some critical database files, you should become familiar with the information in the *Oracle8 Backup and Recovery Guide*. You don't need to read it cover to cover, but you should be familiar with the concepts and procedures it describes. In addition, and I can't emphasize this enough, practice recovering your database. I am personally aware of cases where a database could not be recovered because the backups weren't being done correctly. I have even been burned myself. While writing this chapter, I discovered to my great chagrin that one of our disk drives was not being backed up each night. I was lucky. I only lost one table with old data that nobody cared about. Next time I may not be so lucky. Practice pays.

# 11

# *Customizing Your SQL\*Plus Environment*

This chapter will show you how you can modify the SQL\*Plus environment in order to make things more convenient for you or for the users you support. There are a number of settings that can be customized. Some, like the search path used for SQL scripts, are more useful than others. In addition, there are two SQL scripts that are automatically run whenever you start SQL\*Plus. These SQL scripts are useful, for example, if you have specific SET commands that you always want to execute at the beginning of a session.

## *SQL\*Plus Settings You Can Control*

The specific customizations you can make may vary a bit depending on the operating system and the specific version of SQL\*Plus you are using. Generally, though, there are two types of things you need to be aware of: the login scripts and the environment variable settings.

There are two SQL scripts that are executed whenever SQL\*Plus starts up. The first script is referred to as the *site profile,* and is named *glogin.sql.* It applies globally to all users on a particular computer. The second script is the *user profile* (not the same thing as the product user profile discussed in Chapter 9, *The Product User Profile),* and it is named *login.sql.* As you can guess from the name, each user may have his or her own user profile script. The most obvious use for these files is to execute SET commands to customize the environment settings to something other than their defaults.

There are several operating-system environment variables that affect how SQL\*Plus operates. These environment variables allow you to specify:

- The search path to use for SQL scripts (SQLPATH)

- The location of the site profile script (PLUS80)

- A default database connection (LOCAL)

- Whether the Windows or DOS version of SQL*Plus should be executed (PLUS_DFLT)

- The location of the *SQLUS.MSB* message file (PRO80)

- The language being used (NLS_LANG)

- The location of the message files for the language being used (RDBMS80)

Under Windows NT and Windows 95, these settings are made in the registry. On a Unix system, they are made using environment variables. For detailed information on each of these environment variables, including how to set them under different operating systems, see the section titled "Environment Variable Settings," later in this chapter.

# The Site and User Profiles

Two script files are executed every time SQL*Plus is started. These scripts define the site profile and the user profile, and are named, respectively, *glogin.sql* and *login.sql.*

## The Site Profile

The site profile is made up of the commands contained in *glogin.sql*, which is the *global login* file, and is automatically executed every time a user runs SQL*Plus on a given computer system. The location of *glogin.sql* varies from one operating system to the next, but it is always below the directory containing the SQL*Plus product. On a default Windows 95 installation of Oracle8, *glogin.sql* may be found in the following directory:

```
C:\ORAWIN95\PLUS80
```

On a typical Unix system, such as the HP-9000, the *glogin.sql* file will be found in this directory:

```
$ORACLE_HOME/sqlplus/admin
```

The specific version of SQL*Plus you are running makes a difference as well. If you have multiple versions of SQL*Plus installed, the default installation procedures will result in your having a separate *glogin.sql* file for each. For example, a Windows 95 PC running both SQL*Plus 8.0 and SQL*Plus 3.3 will have a *glogin.sql* file in each of the following two directories:

```
C:\ORAWIN95\PLUS80
C:\ORAWIN95\PLUS33
```

The specific file that is executed will depend on which version of SQL*Plus you are running.

> On Windows 95/NT, the PLUSXX registry setting, where XX refers to the specific SQL*Plus version, points to the location of *glogin.sql.* By pointing the PLUS80 and PLUS33 registry settings to the same directory, it is possible to end up with one global login file that is consistent across all versions of SQL*Plus.

The default *glogin.sql* file, supplied by Oracle for version 8.0 of SQL*Plus, looks like this:

```
--
--  $Header: /plus/v4/spam/precious/files/ACTIVE/glogin.sql,
--  v 1.1 1995/12/19 02:55:18 cjones Exp $
--  Copyright (c) Oracle Corporation 1988, 1994, 1995.  All Rights Reserved.
--
--  SQL*Plus Global Login startup file.
--
--  This is the global login file for SQL*Plus.
--  Add any sqlplus commands here that are to be
--  executed when a user invokes sqlplus

-- Used by Trusted Oracle
column ROWLABEL format A15

-- Used for the SHOW ERRORS command
column LINE/COL format A8
column ERROR     format A65  WORD_WRAPPED

-- For backward compatibility
set pagesize 14

-- Defaults for SET AUTOTRACE EXPLAIN report
column id_plus_exp format 990 heading i
column parent_id_plus_exp format 990 heading p
column plan_plus_exp format a60
column object_node_plus_exp format a8
column other_tag_plus_exp format a29
column other_plus_exp format a44
```

Most of the commands in the default *glogin.sql* file are COLUMN commands that format the output from the SQL*Plus autotrace facility and from the SHOW ERRORS command. It is interesting to note that the pagesize has been set to 14 for compatibility purposes. In Oracle 7.1 and earlier, the default pagesize was 14. In newer versions of Oracle, the pagesize is 24. In order to prevent problems with scripts that were written with the old default in mind, this *glogin.sql* file sets the pagesize to the old value.

## The User Profile

The user profile is similar to the site profile, except that it is intended to be user-specific. The command file name is *login.sql*, and it is executed immediately after the *glogin.sql* file. SQL\*Plus searches for the *login.sql* file in the current directory first; then it searches the directories listed in the SQLPATH environment variable. In a Unix installation, there will not be a default *login.sql* file, nor will there be a default SQLPATH variable. Under the various Windows environments, you will most likely have a default *login.sql* file in one of the following directories:

```
C:\ORAWIN95\DBS  --Windows 95
C:\ORANT\DBS     --Windows NT
C:\ORAWIN\DBS    --Windows 3.1, 3.11
```

You can add to the *login.sql* file, putting in whatever commands make your life easier. If you are running under Unix, you should make certain that your SQL-PATH environment variable points to the directory containing your *login.sql*; otherwise, SQL\*Plus won't be able to find it when you are working in another directory.

# Environment Variable Settings

There are a number of environment variables that can affect how SQL\*Plus operates. One of the most commonly used of these is the SQLPATH variable. SQL-PATH functions much like a command search path, except that it applies to SQL scripts. It contains a list of directories to search when looking for a script. The way you set SQLPATH and other variables depends on the specific operating system you are using. The next few sections demonstrate how SQLPATH is set under Windows 3.1, Windows 95, Windows 98, Windows NT, and Unix. Following these examples is a complete list of all the environment variables that apply to SQL\*Plus.

## Setting an Environment Variable

Under Unix, SQL\*Plus settings are stored in environment variables. You usually set these variables with the Unix *export* command. The situation is pretty much the same for Windows 3.1 and DOS, except that you use the DOS SET command. In later versions of Windows, such as Windows 95, these settings are stored in the registry.

### Unix

To set an environment variable from Unix, you generally use either the *export* or *setenv* command, depending on which shell you are using. The following example, using the Korn shell, shows how to set the SQLPATH variable to point to your home directory:

```
$ export SQLPATH=$HOME
```

Here is the same example using the C Shell's *setenv* command:

```
$ setenv SQLPATH $HOME
```

Note that with *export* you use an equals sign between the variable and the value, while with *setenv* you do not. You can use the *export* (or *setenv*) command by itself to get a listing of all the variables you have set, including SQLPATH.

```
$ export
...
SQLPATH=/home/oracle
...
```

All other environment variables are set using the same method.

### Windows 95/98/NT

Under Windows 95, 98, and NT, the SQL*Plus environment variable settings are stored in the registry. You can edit these registry settings using the REGEDIT program. Go to the Start menu, select Run, and type REGEDIT into the Run dialog box. Figure 11-1 shows how this will look.

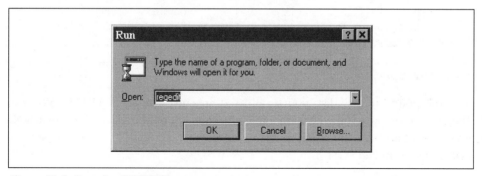

*Figure 11-1. Running REGEDIT*

Click the OK button to run REGEDIT. A window with two panes will open up (see Figure 11-2). The pane on the left contains a list of registry keys that you navigate through in a hierarchical manner very similar to that used in the Windows Explorer. You want to navigate to the following key:

```
My Computer\HKEY_LOCAL_MACHINE\SOFTWARE\ORACLE
```

Be sure to actually click on the key named ORACLE, so that you can see the entries associated with it. The resulting screen will look like that shown in Figure 11-2.

The right-hand side of the screen now shows a large number of registry entries used by the Oracle database server, SQL*Plus, and other Oracle products. Down

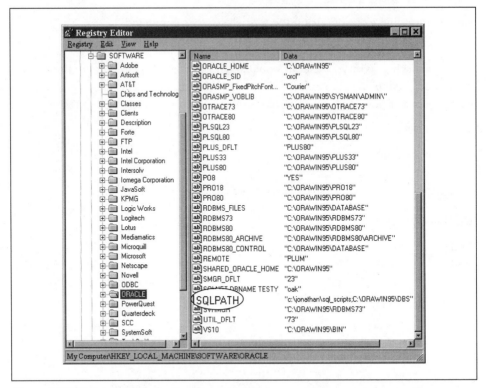

*Figure 11-2. Registry entries for Oracle*

near the bottom of this list, you should see an entry named SQLPATH. You can edit this entry by double-clicking on it. Be sure to double-click the word SQL-PATH itself, and not the string representing its current value. You should see the dialog shown in Figure 11-3.

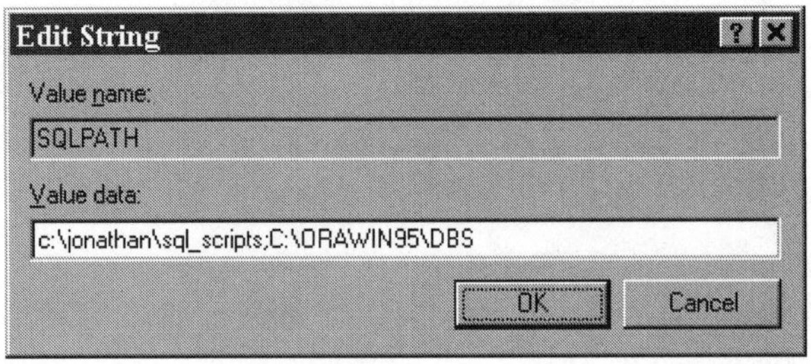

*Figure 11-3. Editing the SQLPATH registry entry*

When you have the entry edited the way you want it, click the OK button. The new value will be saved, and the Edit String dialog will close. In some cases, you may need to create an entirely new registry entry. Do this with the Edit → New → String Value menu item. Once you've created the new entry and given it the appropriate name, you can edit its value as described earlier. When you are done making changes, use the Registry → Exit menu option to exit REGEDIT.

Be extremely careful when using REGEDIT. Consider using REG-EDIT's File → Export Registry File menu item to make a backup first. Without a backup, there is no recourse if you make a mistake, and deleting the wrong key or entry could cause you some serious grief. If you've never used REGEDIT before, ask someone who has to help you.

If you open an MS-DOS window, you may use the SET command to change an environment variable. When you do this, that setting only takes effect when you start SQL*Plus from the same MS-DOS window. Thus, it is possible to have two or more MS-DOS windows open, each with a different SQLPATH setting.

### Windows 3.1

In a Windows 3.1 environment, the SQL*Plus environment variables are set using the DOS SET command. Often this is done from within the *autoexec.bat* file, so that all the settings are in place when the system starts. The following example shows how you would define the SQLPATH variable from a DOS prompt:

```
C:\>SET SQLPATH=C:\JONATHAN\SQL
```

You can use the SET command by itself to get a list of variables you have set; for example:

```
C:\>SET
...
SQLPATH=C:\JONATHAN\SQL
...
```

## Environment Variables That Affect SQL*Plus

This section describes the environment variables that affect SQL*Plus's operation. Not all settings are available in all environments, but most are. PLUS_DFLT is an example of a setting that's relevant only under Windows. The description for each setting will note whether or not it is operating-system-specific.

*LOCAL*

The LOCAL setting applies only to Windows environments, and specifies the default connect string to use when you start SQL\*Plus. For example, if you start SQL\*Plus under Windows, and enter only a username and password as shown in Figure 11-4, one of two things will happen. If you have Oracle8 Personal Edition installed, you will be connected to the local database on your PC. Otherwise, you will receive the following error:

```
ORA-03121: no interface driver connected - function not performed
```

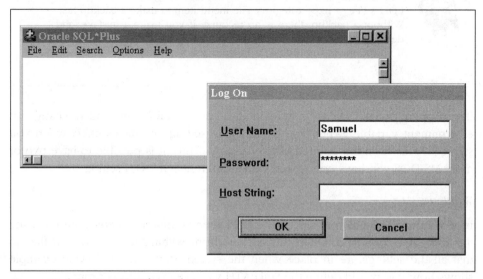

*Figure 11-4. Starting SQL\*Plus with no connect string*

The reason you get an error is that when you leave off the connect string, SQL\*Plus has no idea where to go. The only exception to this is that Oracle has added some extra code to the version of SQL\*Plus included with the Personal Edition, so it will default to the Personal Edition database if there is one.

By setting the LOCAL variable, you can make any Oracle database the default. Setting it to PRODUCTION, for example, makes SQL\*Plus interpret Figure 11-4 as if the user had really typed in PRODUCTION for the connect string. In other words, SQL\*Plus would reinterpret the inputs shown in Figure 11-4 as those shown in Figure 11-5.

By default, the Oracle installer will not create a LOCAL entry in the registry. You have to create it. Once you do, SQL\*Plus, even the version that ships with Oracle Personal Edition, will respect it.

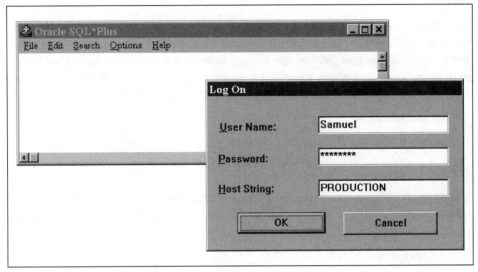

*Figure 11-5. Connecting to the PRODUCTION database*

### NLS_LANG

This parameter applies to all versions of SQL*Plus. It controls the language used for messages, the character set used, the sort order to be used, the manner in which dates are displayed, and other language-specific settings. The format for this setting is as follows:

```
LANGUAGE_TERRITORY.CHARACTER_SET
```

where:

### LANGUAGE

Specifies the language to be used. This controls the language used for messages and the names of days and months, among other things.

### TERRITORY

Specifies the territory. This controls the currency indicator, the decimal character, and the way dates are formatted.

### CHARACTER_SET

Specifies the character set to be used. This impacts sorting and the way characters are converted between upper- and lowercase.

The default value of the NLS_LANG setting for a Windows client installation is:

```
AMERICAN_AMERICA.WE8ISO8859P1
```

This setting is used by other Oracle products, and is not one to toy with lightly. If you aren't sure what you are doing, it's best to leave this alone. For detailed information on Oracle's language support, see the *Oracle8 Server Reference* manual.

### PRO80

The PRO80 variable specifies the location of the *SQLUS.MSB* message file. This message file is used by a number of different Oracle products, including some versions of SQL\*Plus. The "80" in the setting name refers to the specific Oracle version being used, so when Oracle 8.1 is shipped, the name of this setting will change to PRO81. The default value for this setting, under Windows 95, is:

    C:\ORAWIN95\PRO80

This setting applies to all operating systems.

### PLUS80

The PLUS80 variable points to the directory that contains the SQL\*Plus message files, the *glogin.sql* file, and the scripts to create the SQL\*Plus help. The default value for this setting, under Windows NT, is:

    C:\ORANT\PLUS80

The "80" corresponds to the SQL\*Plus version. SQL\*Plus 2.3, which shipped with Oracle 7.3, uses the PLUS23 variable. Under some operating systems, such as HP-UX, Oracle does not use this setting.

### RDBMS80

This variable points to the directory containing the message files that correspond to the particular language you're using. The default setting, under Windows NT, is:

    C:\ORANT\RDBMS80

The message files of interest to SQL\*Plus are: *LCDUS.MSB*, *ORAUS.MSB*, and *SOSDUS.MSB*. These are the names of the American English versions of the message files; if you are using a different language, the file names may be different.

As with PRO80 and PLUS80, the "80" in the setting name refers to the specific version of Oracle you are using.

### SQLPATH

Of all the variables, SQLPATH is probably the most useful. The SQLPATH variable contains a search path that is followed by SQL\*Plus when it's looking for a script file. It consists of one or more directory names, separated by semicolons. There is no default value under Unix, but under Windows, the default will be something like this:

    C:\ORAWIN95\DBS

The ...\*DBS* directory is where the default *login.sql* script file is installed under Windows. You can add your own directories to the search path; just be sure to separate each directory name from the next with a semicolon, as shown here:

```
c:\jonathan\sql_scripts;C:\ORAWIN95\DBS
```

When you invoke a SQL script without providing the full path, SQL*Plus will first look in the current directory; then it will search each directory listed in SQLPATH. The directories are searched in the order in which they are listed.

The SQLPATH setting applies to SQL*Plus on all operating systems.

### PLUS_DFLT

This is a Windows-specific setting that controls which version of SQL*Plus is executed when you invoke the *sqlplus.exe* executable. A Windows system will typically have at least two different SQL*Plus executables installed. One is a GUI version and the other is a DOS version. For SQL*Plus 8.0, the executables are named according to the following convention:

```
PLUS80       the DOS executable
PLUS80W      the GUI executable
```

In addition, it is possible to have two or more versions of SQL*Plus installed under Windows, and each version will still have two executables. Thus, a PC with SQL*Plus 3.3 and SQL*Plus 8.0 would have the following four executable files:

```
PLUS80       8.0 DOS
PLUS80W      8.0 GUI
PLUS33       7.3 DOS
PLUS33W      7.3 GUI
```

This makes for a bit of a problem if you are writing batch files that make use of SQL*Plus. You would need to hardcode the executable name in each batch file, then edit those files whenever you upgraded to a new version. To ease your pain, Oracle supplies a generic executable named *sqlplus.exe*. This generic executable reads the registry, gets the value of the PLUS_DFLT variable, and invokes the executable named by that value.

The default value of PLUS_DFLT will be that of the DOS executable, for example, *PLUS80*, in order to facilitate the writing of batch files. When you set this variable, do not include the *exe* extension as part of the filename. For example, *PLUS80* is correct, *PLUS80.EXE* is not.

# The SET Command

SQL*Plus contains a large number of internal variables that control various aspects of the way the product operates. The SET command is used to change these settings to suit your preferences. The number of settings is quite large, so for convenience I've divided them into the following categories:

- Report output and format settings

- Feedback settings

- Input settings

- Operational settings

- Substitution variable settings

- Large object settings

- Tuning and timing settings

- Database administration settings

- Miscellaneous settings

The following sections describe the settings available in each of these categories.

## Report Output and Format Settings

The largest group of SQL\*Plus settings exists to control the way data is formatted, displayed, and output for a report. These settings control such things as the number of lines on a page, the line length, whether or not tab characters are used to format the output, and so forth. The following list briefly describes each of these settings:

COLSEP
    Controls the text used to separate columns of data.

EMBEDDED
    Turns the embedded report feature on or off.

HEADSEP
    Controls the character used to mark a line break in a column heading.

HEADING
    Controls whether or not column headings are displayed when selecting data.

LINESIZE
    Specifies the maximum line width.

MAXDATA
    The maximum row length SQL\*Plus can handle.

NEWPAGE
    Controls what SQL\*Plus prints when advancing to a new page.

NULL
    Contains the text SQL\*Plus displays for any null values returned by a query.

*NUMFORMAT*

The default display format for numbers.

*NUMWIDTH*

The default column width used for numeric columns.

*PAGESIZE*

The number of printable lines on a page.

*RECSEP*

Controls whether or not a record separator is printed between rows of output.

*RECSEPCHAR*

The record separator character.

*SHIFTINOUT*

Controls the display of shift characters on IBM 3270 terminals.

*SPACE*

Specifies the number of spaces printed between columns.

*TAB*

Controls whether or not SQL*Plus uses tab characters to format whitespace.

*TRIMOUT*

Controls whether or not trailing spaces are displayed.

*TRIMSPOOL*

Controls whether or not trailing spaces are written to a spool file.

*TRUNCATE*

Controls whether or not SQL*Plus truncates long lines.

*UNDERLINE*

The character used to underline column headings.

*WRAP*

Controls whether or not SQL*Plus wraps or truncates long lines.

The following sections provide the syntax, and usage examples, for each of these settings.

## SET COLSEP

Use SET COLSEP to change the text that prints between columns of data.

```
SET COLSEP column_separator
```

where:

*SET COLSEP*

Is the command, which may not be abbreviated.

*column_separator*

    Is the text you want to print between columns. You should enclose this text in quotes if it contains any spaces or punctuation.

The default column separator is a single space. The following example shows how you can change it to a comma:

```
SQL> SET COLSEP ","
SQL> SELECT 'One' one,
  2            'Two' two
  3     FROM dual;

ONE,TWO
---,---
One,Two
```

Like a space, the comma in this example is a single character. You aren't limited to one character, though. You could just as easily change the column separator to a string of several characters.

### SET EMBEDDED

The SET EMBEDDED command controls the printing of embedded reports. The default setting is OFF, which causes the results of each new query to print on a new page, and also causes page numbering to start over each time a SELECT statement is executed.

```
SET EMB[EDDED] {ON|OFF}
```

*SET EMB[EDDED]*

    Is the command, which may be abbreviated to SET EMB.

*ON*

    Turns the embedded report feature on. Executing a SELECT statement will not force a page break, nor will it reset the page number.

*OFF*

    Turns the embedded report feature off. Executing a SELECT statement will force a page break, and the page number will be reset to 1.

An *embedded report* is one that prints as if it were the continuation of a previous report. The following example shows the results of executing two SELECT statements with the default setting. A page title has been created in order to show the effect on page numbering:

```
SQL> SET EMBEDDED OFF
SQL> SET PAGESIZE 24
SQL> SET NEWPAGE 1
SQL> TTITLE LEFT "Example of SET EMBEDDED, Page " SQL.PNO
SQL> SELECT * FROM dual;
```

```
Example of SET EMBEDDED, Page        1
D
-
X


SQL> SELECT * FROM dual;

Example of SET EMBEDDED, Page        1
D
-
X
```

Notice that the second SELECT statement generated a page break—you can see that the page title printed again. You can also see, by looking at the titles, that page numbering for each query began with page 1. Now take a look at the same example, but with SET EMBEDDED ON:

```
SQL> SET EMBEDDED OFF
SQL> SET PAGESIZE 24
SQL> SET NEWPAGE 1
SQL> TTITLE LEFT "Example of SET EMBEDDED, Page " SQL.PNO
SQL> SELECT * FROM dual;

Example of SET EMBEDDED, Page        1
D
-
X


SQL> SET EMBEDDED ON
SQL> SELECT * FROM dual;
D
-
X
```

This time, the second SELECT statement did not generate a page break. The second report began printing on the same page on which the first report ended.

Be sure to execute the first query of a report with SET EMBEDDED OFF. Otherwise, you may find that SQL*Plus continues the page numbering from a query executed earlier during the session.

If you have defined a page footer (BTITLE) for your report, then a page break will occur at the end of the report, regardless of the EMBEDDED setting. There are a couple of reasons for this behavior. One is that SQL*Plus processes commands one line at a time. SQL*Plus doesn't know about the second SELECT statement until after it is completely finished printing the results of the first one. If a page footer is defined, SQL*Plus must print it, because it has no way of knowing whether or not another SELECT statement is coming. In order for a page footer to print, SQL*Plus must advance printing to the bottom of the page. After the footer has printed, any new data must begin on a new page. The embedded setting, however, still controls whether or not the page number is reset.

### SET HEADSEP

Use the SET HEADSEP command when you want to change the character used when defining a two-line column heading:

```
SET HEADS[EP] heading_separator
```

where:

*SET HEADS[EP]*
> Is the command, which may be abbreviated to SET HEADS.

*heading_separator*
> Is the new heading separator character, which may be used in subsequent COLUMN commands to mark line breaks in multiline column headings.

Normally, this character is a vertical bar, and marks the place in a column's heading where you want a line break to occur. The following example shows a two-line heading being defined:

```
SQL> COLUMN dummy FORMAT A10 HEADING 'Line 1|Line 2'
SQL> SELECT * FROM dual;

Line 1
Line 2
----------
X
```

As you can see, the vertical bar in the column's heading text was replaced by a line break when the column heading was printed. If you need to use the vertical bar as part of a column heading, use SET HEADSEP to choose some other character to act as the line break marker.

> The line break in a heading is set when you first define that heading using the COLUMN command. Subsequently changing the heading separator character will not affect column headings you have already defined.

### SET HEADING

Use SET HEADING to control whether or not column headings print when you SELECT or PRINT data. The default value for this setting is ON, which allows column headings to print.

```
SET HEA[DING] [ON|OFF]
```

where:

*SET HEA[DING]*

Is the command, which may be abbreviated SET HEA.

*ON*

Causes column headings to print when you select data.

*OFF*

Suppresses column headings.

This setting is on by default, so you normally get a column heading whenever you select or print data using either the SELECT command or the PRINT command. For example:

```
SQL> SELECT * FROM dual;

D
-
X
```

Change the value to OFF, and your column headings go away. The following example shows this:

```
SQL> SET HEADING OFF
SQL> SELECT * FROM dual;

X
```

---

 Issuing a SET PAGESIZE 0 command will also turn headings off. If you are trying to enable headings, and SET HEADING ON does not appear to be working, then you should check the pagesize as well.

---

### SET LINESIZE

Use SET LINESIZE to control the number of characters SQL*Plus prints on one physical line. The default setting is 80. The maximum width is system-dependent. Under Windows 95, it is 32,767.

```
SET LIN[ESIZE] line_width
```

where:

*SET LIN[ESIZE]*

Is the command, which may be abbreviated to SET LIN.

*line_width*

Is the new line width, expressed as a number of characters.

The linesize setting is also referenced by SQL*Plus when you define any headers or footers (see TTITLE, BTITLE, REPHEADER, REPFOOTER) that are centered or right-justified.

### SET MAXDATA

MAXDATA is an obsolete setting that should no longer be used. SQL*Plus supports it in order to be backward-compatible. MAXDATA controls the maximum row length SQL*Plus can handle.

```
SET MAXD[ATA] max_row_width
```

where:

*SET MAXD[ATA]*

Is the command, which may be abbreviated to SET MAXD.

*max_row_width*

Is the new setting for the maximum row width you expect to process.

The default setting under Windows 95 is zero, but may vary from one operating system to the next. Under some operating systems, such as Windows 95, this setting seems to have no effect whatsoever on SQL*Plus's behavior.

### SET NEWPAGE

Controls the manner in which the transition from one page to the next is marked. You can have SQL*Plus print a formfeed character at the start of each new page, skip a specific number of lines between pages, or do nothing at all when advancing from one page to another:

```
SET NEWP[AGE] {lines_to_print|NONE}
```

where:

*SET NEWP[AGE]*

Is the command, which may be abbreviated to SET NEWP.

*lines_to_print*

Tells SQL*Plus to print a specific number of blank lines when a page break occurs. These lines will be printed following the footer (BTITLE) of the page just ending, and prior to the header (TTITLE) of the page just starting. If this value is zero, and only if it is zero, a formfeed character will be printed instead of any blank lines. The default value is 1.

*NONE*

Causes SQL*Plus to do nothing at all when a page break occurs—no blank lines, no formfeed.

Use SET NEWPAGE 0 if you want a formfeed printed at the start of each new page.

## SET NULL

SET NULL allows you to change the text SQL*Plus prints in a column when the value for that column is null:

```
SET NULL null_text
```

where:

*SET NULL*

Is the command, which may not be abbreviated.

*null_text*

Is the text you want to print in place of a null value.

The default null text setting is an empty string, which causes null values to print as blanks. The following example shows this, and also shows how the null text may be changed:

```
SQL> SELECT employee_termination_date
  2    FROM employee
  3    WHERE employee_id=101;


EMPLOYEE_
---------

SQL> SET NULL "*NULL*"
SQL> SELECT employee_termination_date
  2    FROM employee
  3    WHERE employee_id=101;


EMPLOYEE_
---------
*NULL*
```

If you use the COLUMN command to format a column, the NULL clause of that command will override this setting, but only for that one column.

## SET NUMFORMAT

SET NUMFORMAT allows you to specify the default formatting of numeric values returned from a SELECT statement. Any number format usable with the COLUMN command may also be used with SET NUMFORMAT.

```
SET NUMF[ORMAT] format_spec
```

where:

*SET NUMF[ORMAT]*

> Is the command, which may be abbreviated to SET NUMF.

*format_spec*

> Is a numeric format specification, which controls the default manner in which numeric values are displayed. See Appendix B, *SQL\*Plus Format Elements*, for a list of formats.

The following example shows the effect of changing the NUMFORMAT setting:

```
SQL> SELECT 123456.7 FROM dual;

 123456.7
----------
 123456.7

SQL> SET NUMFORMAT $999,999.99
SQL> SELECT 123456.7 FROM dual;

    123456.7
------------
$123,456.70
```

The NUMFORMAT setting controls the default display format for numeric values. You can use the COLUMN command to specify display formats on a column-by-column basis, and those take precedence over the NUMFORMAT setting.

### SET NUMWIDTH

SET NUMWIDTH controls the default width used when displaying numeric values:

```
SET NUM[WIDTH] width
```

where:

*SET NUM[WIDTH]*

> Is the command, which may be abbreviated to SET NUM.

*width*

> Is the default column width used when displaying a numeric value.

The default NUMWIDTH setting is 10. NUMWIDTH is used only when no other settings apply. The following example shows the effect of setting NUMWIDTH to 5:

```
SQL> SET NUMWIDTH 5
SQL> SELECT 123 FROM dual;

 123
----
 123
```

A numeric format specified by a COLUMN command or by a SET NUMFORMAT command will override NUMWIDTH. The following example shows this:

```
SQL> SET NUMWIDTH 5
SQL> SET NUMFORMAT 999,999.99
SQL> SELECT 123 FROM dual;

      123
-----------
     123.00

SQL> SHOW NUMWIDTH
numwidth 5
```

As you can see, NUMWIDTH is still 5, but that value is ignored because the NUM-FORMAT setting takes precedence. A long column title can also cause NUM-WIDTH to be ignored, as the following example demonstrates:

```
SQL> SET NUMWIDTH 5
SQL> SET NUMFORMAT ""
SQL> COLUMN a HEADING "This is a long column title"
SQL> SELECT 123 a FROM dual;

This is a long column title
---------------------------
                        123
```

As you can see, the column title takes precedence over NUMWIDTH when it comes to determining the width of the column.

## SET PAGESIZE

Use SET PAGESIZE to tell SQL*Plus the number of printed lines that will fit on one page of output. You can also use this setting to completely turn off all pagination functions.

```
SET PAGES[IZE] lines_on_page
```

where:

### SET PAGES[IZE]

Is the command, which may be abbreviated to SET PAGES.

### lines_on_page

Is the number of lines you want SQL*Plus to print on one page. This includes detail lines, header lines, and footer lines. The default value for PAGESIZE is 24. For SQL*Plus versions 2.1 and earlier, the default was 14.

The PAGESIZE must be set in conjunction with NEWPAGE. The sum of PAGESIZE and NEWPAGE should equal the number of lines that will physically fit on one page. SQL*Plus will print headers, detail, and footers until PAGESIZE lines have been printed. Then it will print NEWPAGE lines to advance to the next page, where the process starts over again. Your page titles will drift up or down with each new page if these settings don't match the page's physical size. The exception to this is when you use SET NEWPAGE 0.

If you use SET NEWPAGE 0 to cause a formfeed to print at the beginning of each page, you should set PAGESIZE to at least one less than the physical number of lines on a page. Failure to do so may result in alternating blank pages in your printed report.

You can completely turn off all pagination by issuing a SET PAGESIZE 0 command. This will eliminate page titles, page footers, column titles, and any blank lines or formfeeds from the NEWPAGE setting.

### SET RECSEP

SET RECSEP is used to tell SQL\*Plus whether or not to print a record separator between each record displayed as the result of a query. The default setting is not to print anything, except when a long record wraps to a second line. In that case, a blank line is printed as a record separator.

```
SET RECSEP {WR[APPED]|EA[CH]|OFF}
```

where:

### SET RECSEP

Is the command, which may not be abbreviated.

### WR[APPED]

Tells SQL\*Plus to print a record separator only when a line wraps. This is the default setting.

### EA[CH]

Tells SQL\*Plus to print a record separator after each record.

### OFF

Tells SQL\*Plus not to print any record separators at all.

The default setting is WRAPPED, which is probably a safe choice, because it causes a separator to print only in cases where a break between records may not be obvious—in other words, where each line does not necessarily start a new record. Here is an example of a record separator being printed:

```
SQL> COLUMN view_name FORMAT A15
SQL> SELECT view_name FROM all_views;
ALL_ALL_TABLES
ALL_ARGUMENTS
ALL_CATALOG
ALL_CLUSTERS
ALL_CLUSTER_HAS
```

```
H_EXPRESSIONS

ALL_COLL_TYPES
...
```

You can see that the record separator, by default a blank line, was printed after the ALL_CLUSTER_HASH_EXPRESSIONS view was listed. This blank line removes any ambiguity about whether H_EXPRESSIONS and ALL_CLUSTER_HAS are two separate views or if a long view name has wrapped to a second line. Setting REC-SEP to OFF yields the following results:

```
SQL> SET RECSEP OFF
SQL> SELECT VIEW_NAME from all_views;
ALL_ALL_TABLES
ALL_ARGUMENTS
ALL_CATALOG
ALL_CLUSTERS
ALL_CLUSTER_HAS
H_EXPRESSIONS
ALL_COLL_TYPES
```

Do you see six views listed or seven? How would you know?

In addition to controlling whether or not the record separator prints, you can control the character used as well. See the SET RECSEPCHAR command.

### SET RECSEPCHAR

Use SET RECSEPCHAR to change the record separator to something other than a line of space characters:

```
SET RECSEPCHAR separator_char
```

where:

### SET RECSEPCHAR

Is the command, which may not be abbreviated.

### separator_char

Is the character you want to use in the record separator line. The default value is a space.

The default record separator is a blank line. The following example shows how you can change it to be a line of asterisks instead:

```
SQL> SET RECSEPCHAR "*"
SQL> SET RECSEP EACH
SQL> SELECT view_name FROM all_views;
ALL_ALL_TABLES
*******************************************************************************
ALL_ARGUMENTS
*******************************************************************************
ALL_CATALOG
*******************************************************************************
```

This example uses SET RECSEP EACH to cause a separator to print after each
record, so that you will have something to look at. The separator character was set
to an asterisk, causing you to get a full line of asterisks between each record. The
length of the separator line will match the LINESIZE setting.

### SET SHIFTINOUT

The SHIFTINOUT setting controls whether or not shift characters are displayed as
part of the output. It is usable only with IBM 3270 terminals and their equivalent,
and only when SQL\*Plus is displaying data in a shift-sensitive character set.

```
SET SHIFT[INOUT] {VIS[IBLE]|INV[ISIBLE]}
```

where:

*SET SHIFT[INOUT]*

Is the command, which may be abbreviated to SHIFT.

*VIS[IBLE]*

Allows shift characters to be visible.

*INV[ISIBLE]*

Keeps shift characters from being displayed.

The default setting is INVISIBLE.

### SET SPACE

SET SPACE is an obsolete command similar to SET COLSEP. It allows you to specify the number of spaces SQL\*Plus prints between columns of output.

```
SET SPACE num_of_spaces
```

where:

*SET SPACE*

Is the command, which may not be abbreviated.

*num_of_spaces*

Is the new setting for the number of spaces you want to print between columns. The default setting is one space.

The following example shows how SET SPACE works by changing the spacing
between columns from one to five spaces:

```
SQL> SELECT 'A' a, 'B' b FROM dual;

A B
- -
A B

SQL> SET SPACE 5
```

```
SQL> SELECT 'A' a, 'B' b FROM dual;

A   B
-   -
A   B
```

Issuing SET SPACE 5 has the exact same effect as if you were to issue SET COLSEP " ". In fact, the two settings are kept in sync with one another. The SET SPACE command will change the COLSEP setting to match.

## SET TAB

The TAB setting controls whether or not SQL*Plus uses tab characters when generating whitespace in terminal output. This setting is a throwback to the days when terminal connections ran at very slow data rates, such as 1200 bits per second.

```
SET TAB {OFF|ON}
```

where:

### SET TAB

Is the command, which may not be abbreviated.

### ON

Is the default setting, and allows SQL*Plus to insert tabs into the output rather than displaying a large number of space characters.

### OFF

Forces SQL*Plus to use space characters for all whitespace.

The default setting is ON, which allows SQL*Plus to use tab characters in the output.

## SET TRIMOUT

The TRIMOUT setting controls whether or not SQL*Plus displays any trailing spaces that may occur at the end of a line. The default setting is ON, which causes SQL*Plus to display only up to the last non-blank character on a line.

```
SET TRIM[OUT] {ON|OFF}
```

where:

### SET TRIM[OUT]

Is the command, which may be abbreviated to SET TRIM.

### ON

Causes SQL*Plus to trim any trailing spaces from each line before it is displayed. This is the default setting.

### OFF

Causes SQL*Plus to display all characters on a line, even the trailing spaces.

The default setting of ON usually works well when displaying data on a terminal, so there's rarely a reason to turn this setting off. TRIMOUT has no effect on spooled output. If you are spooling output to a file, the TRIMSPOOL setting controls whether or not trailing spaces are spooled as well.

### SET TRIMSPOOL

The TRIMSPOOL setting controls whether or not SQL\*Plus writes trailing spaces when spooling data to a file. The default setting is OFF, which causes SQL\*Plus to write each line to the spool file in its entirety, trailing spaces and all.

```
SET TRIMS[POOL] {ON|OFF}
```

where:

*SET TRIMS[POOL]*

Is the command, which may be abbreviated to SET TRIMS.

*ON*

Causes SQL\*Plus to trim any trailing spaces from each line before it is written to the spool file.

*OFF*

Causes SQL\*Plus to write all characters of a line to the spool file, even the trailing spaces. This is the default setting.

If you are spooling data to a file in order to load it into another program, you will want to leave TRIMSPOOL ON. Otherwise, the program reading the spool file might return errors because the records are shorter than expected.

### SET TRUNCATE

SET TRUNCATE is an obsolete command that gives you the same choice as SET WRAP. You can choose whether or not to truncate lines that are longer than the LINESIZE setting.

```
SET TRU[NCATE] {OFF|ON}
```

where:

*SET TRU[NCATE]*

Is the command, which may be abbreviated to TRU.

*OFF*

Is the default setting, and allows long lines to be wrapped.

*ON*

Causes long lines of output to be truncated to match the current LINESIZE setting.

TRUNCATE and WRAP both affect the same internal setting. Turning one on results in the other being turned off, and vice versa. For example:

```
SQL> SHOW WRAP
wrap : lines will be wrapped
SQL> SET TRUNCATE ON
SQL> SHOW WRAP
wrap : lines will be truncated
```

 While you can issue the SHOW WRAP command to see the current value of the WRAP setting, you cannot issue SHOW TRUNCATE. The SHOW command does not recognize TRUNCATE as a valid SQL*Plus setting.

When you select data that is longer than the LINESIZE and the WRAP setting is off, some versions of SQL*Plus will print a warning message telling you that your rows may be truncated.

### SET UNDERLINE

With the SET UNDERLINE command, you can control the character used to underline column headings. You can also control whether or not column headings are underlined at all.

```
SET UND[ERLINE] {underline_char | {ON|OFF}}
```

where:

*SET UND[ERLINE]*

Is the command, which may be abbreviated to SET UND.

*underline_char*

Is the character you want to use when underlining column headings. By default, a dash character (-) is used.

*ON*

Causes column headings to be underlined, and resets the underline character back to the dash.

*OFF*

Keeps column headings from being underlined.

The following example shows the underline character being changed to an asterisk:

```
SQL> SET UNDERLINE *
SQL> SELECT USER FROM dual;
```

```
USER
******************************
JEFF
```

You can also use SET UNDERLINE to turn underlining off completely, for example:

```
SQL> SET UNDERLINE OFF
SQL> SELECT USER FROM dual;

USER
JEFF
```

One reason you might turn underlining off would be if you wanted some columns to print without any heading at all. First you would turn UNDERLINE off. Then you would define column headings for all columns with the COLUMN command. Those headings you did want to print would need to include the underlines as part of the heading definition. Other headings would be defined as empty strings.

### SET WRAP

The WRAP setting controls how SQL\*Plus prints lines that contain more characters than the current LINESIZE setting allows. With WRAP ON, long lines are wrapped around and continued on as many physical lines as necessary. With WRAP OFF, lines are truncated to match the LINESIZE setting.

```
SET WRA[P] {ON|OFF}
```

where:

*SET WRA[P]*
    Is the command, which may be abbreviated to SET WRA.

*ON*
    Causes long lines to be wrapped around to two or more physical lines, in order to print and still fit within the LINESIZE setting.

*OFF*
    Causes long records to be truncated to the current LINESIZE setting.

The following example shows the results of issuing the same SELECT statement, once with WRAP turned on, and once with it turned off:

```
SQL> SET WRAP ON
SQL> SELECT * FROM ALL_VIEWS WHERE VIEW_NAME = 'ALL_VIEWS';

OWNER                          VIEW_NAME                     TEXT_LENGTH
------------------------------ ----------------------------- -----------
TEXT
------------------------------------------------------------------------
TYPE_TEXT_LENGTH
```

```
----------------
TYPE_TEXT
--------------------------------------------------------------------------------
OID_TEXT_LENGTH
---------------
OID_TEXT
--------------------------------------------------------------------------------
VIEW_TYPE_OWNER                VIEW_TYPE
-----------------------------  -----------------------------
SYS                            ALL_VIEWS                          821
select u.name, o.name, v.textlength, v.text, t.typetextlength, t.typetext,


SQL> SET WRAP OFF
SQL> /
rows will be truncated

rows will be truncated

rows will be truncated

rows will be truncated

rows will be truncated

rows will be truncated


OWNER                          VIEW_NAME                    TEXT_LENGTH TEXT
-----------------------------  -----------------------------  ----------- ----
SYS                            ALL_VIEWS                            821 select
```

As you can see, SQL*Plus displays several warning messages telling you that the rows you are about to see displayed may have been truncated.

## Feedback Settings

The settings described in this section all control some aspect of the feedback SQL*Plus provides in response to the commands you issue. Feedback settings include the following:

*AUTOPRINT*
Controls whether or not SQL*Plus automatically prints bind variables after they are referenced.

*DOCUMENT*
Controls whether or not SQL*Plus prints documentation demarcated by the DOCUMENT command.

*ECHO*

Controls whether or not SQL\*Plus displays commands from a command file as they are executed.

*FEEDBACK*

Controls whether or not, and when, SQL\*Plus displays the number of rows affected by an SQL statement.

*PAUSE*

Controls whether or not SQL\*Plus pauses after each page of output.

*SERVEROUTPUT*

Controls whether or not SQL\*Plus prints output from PL/SQL routines.

*SHOWMODE*

Controls whether or not SQL\*Plus displays the before and after values when you change a setting.

*SQLPROMPT*

Contains the text string used as the SQL\*Plus command prompt.

*TERMOUT*

Controls whether or not SQL\*Plus displays output generated by SQL statements in a command file.

*TIME*

Controls whether or not SQL\*Plus displays the current time as part of the command prompt.

*VERIFY*

Controls whether or not SQL\*Plus displays before and after images of lines containing substitution variables.

The following sections describe each of these settings:

### SET AUTOPRINT

The AUTOPRINT setting controls whether or not SQL\*Plus automatically prints the contents of any bind variables referenced by a PL/SQL block after it executes.

```
SET AUTOP[RINT] {OFF|ON}
```

where:

*SET AUTOP[RINT]*

Is the command, which may be abbreviated to SET AUTOP.

*OFF*

Keeps bind variables from being automatically printed after being referenced by a PL/SQL block. This is the default setting.

*ON*

Causes bind variables to be printed automatically, following the execution of any PL/SQL block or SQL statement that references them.

## SET DOCUMENT

SET DOCUMENT controls whether or not SQL*Plus prints text created with the DOCUMENT command.

```
SET DOC[UMENT] {ON|OFF}
```

where:

*SET DOC[UMENT]*

Is the command, which may be abbreviated to SET DOC.

*ON*

Allows DOCUMENT text to be displayed. This is the default setting.

*OFF*

Keeps DOCUMENT text from being displayed.

This setting only affects the DOCUMENT command when it is issued from a command file. Say that you had a file with the following lines:

```
DOCUMENT
This is documentation.
#
```

The following example shows the results of executing this file with the DOCUMENT setting on, and then with it off.

```
SQL> SET DOCUMENT ON
SQL> @c:\a\doc
DOC>This is documentation.
DOC>#
SQL> SET DOCUMENT OFF
SQL> @c:\a\doc
```

## SET ECHO

Use SET ECHO to tell SQL*Plus whether or not you want the contents of command files to be echoed to the screen as they are executed.

```
SET ECHO {OFF|ON}
```

where:

*SET ECHO*

Is the command, which may not be abbreviated.

*OFF*

Keeps commands from being echoed to the screen while a command file is being executed. This is the default setting.

*ON*

Causes commands from a command file to be echoed to the screen as they are being executed.

SET ECHO is one of the few debugging tools SQL\*Plus has, if indeed you could call it a debugging tool. It's often very helpful to turn command echoing on while you are developing and testing a new script file. The following example shows the same script file being executed, once with ECHO on, and once with it off:

```
SQL> @c:\a\echo_test

D
-
X

SQL> SET ECHO ON
SQL> @c:\a\echo_test
SQL> SELECT * FROM dual;

D
-
X
```

For the second execution of the script, ECHO had been turned on, so the SELECT statement was displayed on the screen when SQL\*Plus executed it.

 If you are writing a script that spools data to a file, you will almost certainly want to leave ECHO off. Otherwise, the commands in your script would be spooled to the file along with the data.

### SET FEEDBACK

The FEEDBACK setting controls whether or not SQL\*Plus displays the number of records returned by a SELECT statement, deleted by a DELETE statement, updated by an UPDATE statement, or inserted by an INSERT statement. You can set a threshold below which you do not get any feedback regardless of whether the setting is on or not.

```
SET FEED[BACK] {OFF|ON|row_threshold}
```

where:

*SET FEED[BACK]*

Is the command, which may be abbreviated to SET FEED.

*OFF*

Turns feedback completely off. SQL\*Plus will not tell you how many rows are affected by any SQL statements you issue.

*ON*

> Turns feedback on, and is equivalent to SET FEEDBACK 1. For any SQL statement you issue, SQL*Plus will tell you how many rows were affected.

*row_threshold*

> Allows you to specify a row threshold, and also turns feedback on if it is not already on. A row threshold causes SQL*Plus to print the row count returned by a SELECT statement only when that row count exceeds the threshold. The default value for the threshold is 6 rows. The row threshold applies only to the SELECT command. As long as feedback is on, the INSERT, DELETE, and UPDATE statements will always return the number of rows affected, regardless of the row threshold.

The following example shows a feedback message from a SELECT statement:

```
SQL> SET FEEDBACK 1
SQL> SELECT * FROM dual;

D
-
X

1 row selected.
```

In this example, feedback was set to 1 prior to executing the SELECT statement. That caused a feedback message to be displayed, even though the statement returned only one row.

## SET PAUSE

You can use the SET PAUSE command to have SQL*Plus pause after each page of output when displaying rows returned by a query:

```
SET PAU[SE] {ON|OFF|pause_message}
```

where:

*SET PAU[SE]*

> Is the command, which may be abbreviated to SET PAU.

*ON*

> Causes SQL*Plus to pause after each page of output. The user must press ENTER to continue to the next page.

*OFF*

> Turns the pause feature off. This is the default setting.

*pause_message*

 Provides a message for SQL\*Plus to display after each page when prompting the user to continue. This does not turn pause on. You must issue a separate SET PAUSE ON command to do that.

The following example shows how the pause feature works:

```
SQL> SET PAGESIZE 10
SQL> SET PAUSE ON
SQL> SET PAUSE "Press ENTER to continue..."
SQL> SELECT view_name FROM all_views;
Press ENTER to continue...

VIEW_NAME
------------------------------
ALL_ALL_TABLES
ALL_ARGUMENTS
ALL_CATALOG
ALL_CLUSTERS
ALL_CLUSTER_HASH_EXPRESSIONS
ALL_COLL_TYPES
ALL_COL_COMMENTS
Press ENTER to continue...
```

The PAGESIZE setting controls the number of lines printed on a page. In this example, PAGESIZE was set to 10, so SQL\*Plus paused after every 10 lines of output.

## SET SERVEROUTPUT

The SERVEROUTPUT setting controls whether or not SQL\*Plus prints the output generated by the DBMS_OUTPUT package from PL/SQL procedures:

```
SET SERVEROUT[PUT] {OFF|ON}
                   [SIZE buffer_size]
                   [FOR[MAT] {WRA[PPED]|WOR[D_WRAPPED]|TRU[NCATED]}]
```

where:

*SET SERVEROUT[PUT]*

 Is the command, which may be abbreviated to SET SERVEROUT.

*OFF*

 Keeps PL/SQL output from being displayed. This is the default setting.

*ON*

 Causes SQL\*Plus to check for and display output generated by the DBMS_ OUTPUT package after each PL/SQL block, procedure, or function you execute.

*SIZE buffer_size*

> Sets the size of the buffer, in bytes, on the server that holds the output. This value can range from 2000 to 1,000,000, and controls the maximum amount of output any one PL/SQL routine can produce. The default buffer size is 2000 bytes.

*WRA[PPED]*

> Causes the output to be wrapped within the current linesize. Line breaks will occur in the middle of words, if necessary.

*WOR[D_WRAPPED]*

> Causes the output to be word-wrapped within the current linesize. Line breaks will only occur at word boundaries.

*TRU[NCATED]*

> Causes any output longer than the linesize to be truncated.

By default, SQL*Plus does not display output from PL/SQL. The following example shows this:

```
SQL> BEGIN
  2     DBMS_OUTPUT.PUT_LINE('Hello World');
  3  END;
  4  /

PL/SQL procedure successfully completed.
```

Now, the same block is executed again, after issuing a SET SERVEROUTPUT ON command:

```
SQL> SET SERVEROUTPUT ON
SQL> BEGIN
  2     DBMS_OUTPUT.PUT_LINE('Hello World');
  3  END;
  4  /
Hello World

PL/SQL procedure successfully completed.
```

Older versions of SQL*Plus do not support the SIZE and FORMAT clauses of this command.

## SET SHOWMODE

The SHOWMODE setting controls the feedback you get when you use the SET command to change a setting:

```
SET SHOW[MODE] {ON|OFF|BOTH}
```

where:

*SET SHOW[MODE]*

> Is the command, which may be abbreviated to SET SHOW.

*ON*

Turns SHOWMODE on, causing SQL\*Plus to list the before and after values of each setting you change using the SET command.

*OFF*

Turns SHOWMODE off, and is the default setting.

*BOTH*

Has the same effect as ON.

The following example shows the results of turning SHOWMODE on:

```
SQL> SET SHOWMODE ON
new:  showmode BOTH
SQL> SET LINESIZE 132
old:  linesize 80
new:  linesize 132
SQL> SET PAGESIZE 60
old:  pagesize 10
new:  pagesize 60
```

You can see that with SHOWMODE on, the old and new values of each setting are displayed when they are changed.

### SET SQLPROMPT

You can use the SET SQLPROMPT command to change the SQL\*Plus command prompt:

```
SET SQLP[ROMPT] prompt_text
```

where

*SET SQLP[ROMPT]*

Is the command, which may be abbreviated to SET SQLP.

*prompt_text*

Is the new prompt text. The default prompt text is "SQL>".

The following example shows the prompt being changed from "SQL>" to "SQL\*Plus>":

```
SQL> SET SQLPROMPT "SQL*Plus> "
SQL*Plus>
```

Some people like to set their prompt to the name of the database to which they are connected. One way to do this is to place the following commands in your *login.sql* file:

```
SET TERMOUT OFF
COLUMN dbname NEW_VALUE prompt_dbname
SELECT SUBSTR(global_name,1,INSTR(global_name,'.')-1) dbname
    FROM global_name;
```

```
SET SQLPROMPT "&&prompt_dbname> "
SET TERMOUT ON
```

These commands will set your prompt to the global database name. The global name comes from the global_name view, and may or may not be the same as the connect string you used to connect to the database. By placing these commands in your *login.sql* file, you ensure that the prompt will be set automatically, based on the database you are connecting to, whenever you start SQL*Plus.

*LOGIN.SQL* is executed only when SQL*Plus starts. Using the CONNECT command to connect to another database will not cause the prompt to be changed to reflect the new connection.

The *login.sql* file was discussed earlier in this chapter, in the section titled "The Site and User Profiles."

### SET TERMOUT

Controls whether or not SQL*Plus displays output generated by SQL statements, PL/SQL blocks, and SQL*Plus commands. This setting only applies when SQL*Plus is executing a script file. SQL*Plus always displays output from commands entered interactively.

```
SET TERM[OUT] {OFF|ON}
```

where:

*SET TERM[OUT]*

Is the command, which may be abbreviated to SET TERM.

*OFF*

Turns terminal output off.

*ON*

Turns terminal output on. This is the default setting.

Terminal output is often turned off while a command file is running to keep the user's screen from becoming cluttered with query output and feedback messages.

### SET TIME

The SET TIME command controls whether or not SQL*Plus displays the current time with each command prompt:

```
SET TI[ME] {OFF|ON}
```

where:

*SET TI[ME]*

Is the command, which may be abbreviated to SET TI.

*OFF*

Keeps the time from being displayed with the prompt. This is the default setting.

*ON*

Causes the time to be displayed as part of each prompt.

The following example shows the effect of issuing a SET TIME ON command:

```
SQL> SET TIME ON
22:44:41 SQL>
```

### SET VERIFY

The VERIFY setting controls whether or not SQL\*Plus displays before and after images of each line that contains a substitution variable:

```
SET VER[IFY] {OFF|ON}
```

where:

*SET VER[IFY]*

Is the command, which may be abbreviated to SET VER.

*OFF*

Turns verification off.

*ON*

Turns verification on. Lines containing substitution variables will be displayed before and after the substitution occurs. This is the default setting.

Verification is done only on lines that are part of a SQL statement or a PL/SQL block. When substitution occurs in a SQL\*Plus command, before and after images are never displayed. The following example shows what verification looks like:

```
SQL> DEFINE dummy_char = 'X'
SQL> SELECT * FROM dual
  2  WHERE dummy = '&&dummy_char';
old   2: where dummy = '&&dummy_char'
new   2: where dummy = 'X'

D
-
X
```

Notice that line 2, which contained the reference to the &&dummy_char substitution variable, was displayed both before and after the reference to the variable was replaced by its value. If you don't like this display, you can turn it off with SET VERIFY OFF.

## Input Settings

Input settings control some aspects of the way commands are entered. Many of these settings allow you to specify alternative characters for command separators, PL/SQL block terminators, continuation prompts, and so forth. Other settings let you force commands to be uppercased, and allow you to enter blank lines as part of an SQL statement. Here is complete list of input settings:

*BLOCKTERMINATOR*

Specifies the character used to terminate entry of a PL/SQL block.

*BUFFER*

Allows you edit using multiple buffers.

*CMDSEP*

Controls whether or not you may enter multiple SQL*Plus commands on one line, and also specifies the character used to separate those commands.

*SQLBLANKLINES*

Controls whether or not you may enter blank lines as part of a SQL statement.

*SQLCASE*

Controls automatic case conversion of SQL statements and PL/SQL blocks.

*SQLCONTINUE*

Contains the text of the prompt you get when you use the SQL*Plus continuation character to continue a long command to a new line.

*SQLNUMBER*

Controls whether or not SQL*Plus uses the line number as a prompt when you enter a multiline SQL statement.

*SQLPREFIX*

Specifies the SQL*Plus prefix character, which allows you to execute a SQL*Plus command while entering a SQL statement or PL/SQL block into the buffer.

*SQLTERMINATOR*

Controls whether or not you can use a semicolon to execute a SQL statement, and also lets you specify a different character to be used for that purpose.

*SUFFIX*

Contains the default extension used for command files.

The following sections describe each of these settings.

## BLOCKTERMINATOR

The BLOCKTERMINATOR setting controls the character used to terminate a PL/SQL block that is being entered into the buffer for editing:

```
SET BLO[CKTERMINATOR] block_term_char
```

where:

*SET BLO[CKTERMINATOR]*
> Is the command, which may be abbreviated to SET BLO.

*block_term_char*
> Is the new terminator character for use when entering PL/SQL blocks. The default value is a period.

When you enter a PL/SQL block into the buffer, you need a way to tell SQL\*Plus when the block has ended. By default, the period can be used for this purpose, but you can use the SET BLOCKTERMINATOR command to change that. The following example shows how this is done by changing the block terminator to a pound sign character:

```
SQL> SET BLOCKTERMINATOR #
SQL> BEGIN
  2    DBMS_OUTPUT.PUT_LINE('PL/SQL is powerful.');
  3  END;
  4  #
SQL>
```

Terminating the block this way leaves it in the buffer for you to edit. Do not confuse this with the use of the slash command, which both terminates and executes a block.

 Changing the terminator to a slash character, by using SET BLOCKTERMINATOR /, prevents you from subsequently using the / character to execute the contents of the buffer.

## BUFFER

The SET BUFFER command allows you to switch to another buffer for editing purposes:

```
SET BUF[FER] {buffer_name|SQL}
```

where:

*SET BUF[FER]*
> Is the command, which may be abbreviated to SET BUF.

*buffer_name*

Is the name of the buffer you want to edit. You can make up any name you like. If the named buffer does not yet exist, SQL*Plus will create it for you.

*SQL*

Switches you to the SQL buffer. This is the default setting. The SQL buffer is the one used when you type in a SQL statement at the command prompt, and is also the only buffer from which you can execute a SQL statement (or PL/SQL block).

Changing the buffer has limited use, because you can only execute a statement from the SQL buffer. The GET, SAVE, and EDIT commands work, as do all the editing commands. The following example shows a second buffer being used to edit a statement that exists in a text file without disturbing the statement currently in the SQL buffer:

```
SQL> SHOW BUFFER
buffer SQL
SQL> SELECT * FROM employee
  2
SQL> L
  1* SELECT * FROM employee
SQL> SET BUFFER project
SQL> L
No lines in PROJECT buffer.
SQL> GET c:\a\project.sql
  1* SELECT * FROM project
SQL> I
  2  WHERE project_budget > 1000000
  3
SQL> SAVE c:\a\project.sql REPLACE
Wrote file c:\a\project.sql
SQL> SET BUFFER SQL
SQL> L
  1* SELECT * FROM employee
SQL>
```

As you can see, using a second buffer made it possible to edit the SQL statement in the *project.sql* file without disturbing the statement currently in the SQL buffer. Of course, you could do the same thing more easily with the EDIT command, so SET BUFFER isn't used much anymore.

### CMDSEP

The SET CMDSEP command controls whether or not you can enter multiple commands on one line. The commands in question must both be SQL*Plus commands. SET CMDSEP is also used to change the character used to separate these commands:

```
SET CMDS[EP] {OFF|ON|separator_char
```

where:

*SET CMDS[EP]*
   Is the command, which may be abbreviated to SET CMDS.

*OFF*
   Turns the feature off, requiring you to enter each command on a separate line.
   This is the default setting.

*ON*
   Allows you to enter multiple SQL\*Plus commands on one line, and resets the
   separator character back to the default of a semicolon.

*separator_char*
   Causes SQL\*Plus to recognize the specified character as the command separator. You won't be allowed to make the command separator an alphabetic,
   numeric, or space character. This character may optionally be enclosed in
   either single or double quotes. In some cases, such as when you change it to
   a semicolon, you will need the quotes.

The following example turns this feature on, sets the separator character to an
exclamation point, and shows how two commands may be placed on one line:

```
SQL> SET CMDSEP ON
SQL> SET CMDSEP "!"
SQL> SHOW CMDSEP! SHOW BUFFER!
cmdsep "!" (hex 21)
buffer SQL
SQL>
```

### SQLBLANKLINES

The SQLBLANKLINES setting is a new feature in version 8.1 of SQL\*Plus, and
allows SQL statements to contain embedded blank lines:

```
SET SQLBLANKLINES {OFF|ON}
```

where:

*SET SQLBLANKLINES*
   Is the command.

*OFF*
   Turns this feature off. This is the default setting, and does not allow a SQL
   statement to have embedded blank lines.

*ON*
   Turns the feature on, and allows you to enter a SQL statement with an embedded blank line.

Pressing ENTER on a blank line while typing a SQL statement into SQL*Plus normally signals the end of the statement. The statement is then placed into the buffer, and you then have the option of making further edits or of executing the statement. Turning SQLBLANKLINES on allows you to put a blank line in the middle of your statement, as the following example demonstrates:

```
SQL> SET SQLBLANKLINES ON
SQL> SELECT
  2  *
  3
  4  FROM EMPLOYEE
  5
SQL>
```

This feature was added to SQL*Plus to allow it to execute existing Server Manager scripts, such as *CATPROC.SQL*, without having to go through and modify all the SQL statements in those scripts. Unlike SQL*Plus, the Server Manager utility allows blank lines in a SQL statement.

 Oracle plans to desupport Server Manager at some future date, leaving SQL*Plus as the only command-line interface into the Oracle database.

## SQLCASE

The SQLCASE setting controls whether or not SQL*Plus automatically uppercases or lowercases SQL statements and PL/SQL blocks as they are transmitted to the server for execution:

```
SET SQLC[ASE] {MIXED|UPPER|LOWER}
```

where:

*SET SQLC[ASE]*

Is the command, which may be abbreviate to SET SQLC.

*MIXED*

Leaves each statement just as you entered it. This is the default setting.

*UPPER*

Uppercases each statement, including any quoted text literals.

*LOWER*

Lowercases each statement, including any quoted text literals.

Be careful when changing this setting. Any case conversions SQL*Plus does will affect not only your SQL statement keywords, but also any quoted text literals as well. This is seldom desirable behavior. The following example demonstrates this.

```
SQL> SET SQLCASE UPPER
SQL> SELECT * FROM dual WHERE dummy='x';

D
-
X
```

You can see that the SELECT statement succeeded, even though the lowercase "x" in the WHERE clause does not match the uppercase "X" in the dummy column.

Case conversion occurs when the statement is transmitted to the database server. The contents of the buffer will always reflect what you actually typed.

### SQLCONTINUE

The SQLCONTINUE setting controls the prompt used when you continue a statement to a second line, using the SQL\*Plus continuation character:

```
SET SQLCO[NTINUE] continuation_prompt
```

where:

#### SET SQLCO[NTINUE]

Is the command, which may be abbreviated to SET SQLCO.

#### continuation_prompt

Is the new continuation prompt. The default value is ">"—the greater-than character. The prompt may optionally be enclosed in either single or double quotes.

The following example shows the effect of changing this setting:

```
SQL> SET SQLCONTINUE "Continue > "
SQL> DESCRIBE -
Continue >
```

Notice that the SQL\*Plus continuation character, a dash, was used following the DESCRIBE command. The continuation prompt is used only when you use the continuation character to continue a command to a new line. It is not used when you enter a multiline SQL statement.

### SQLNUMBER

The SQLNUMBER setting controls whether or not SQL\*Plus uses the line number as a prompt when you enter a multiline SQL statement:

```
SET SQLN[UMBER] {OFF|ON}
```

where:

#### SET SQLN[UMBER]

Is the command, which may be abbreviated to SET SQLN.

*OFF*

> Causes SQL*Plus to use the same prompt for all lines of a SQL statement or PL/SQL block.

*ON*

> Causes SQL*Plus to use the line number as the prompt for the second, and subsequent, lines of an SQL statement or PL/SQL block. This is the default setting.

The following example shows the difference between the ON and OFF settings:

```
SQL> SET SQLNUMBER ON
SQL> SELECT
  2  *
  3  FROM dual
  4
SQL> SET SQLNUMBER OFF
SQL> SELECT
SQL> *
SQL> FROM dual
SQL>
```

I can't imagine any reason to ever turn this setting off. Look at the first and second statements in the example. It's immediately obvious that the three lines of the first query all belong together as one statement. This is not so obvious with the second statement—you have to think about it a bit. The visual cue provided by the line numbers is missing, making you take more time to figure out what you are really looking at.

### SQLPREFIX

The SQLPREFIX setting controls the SQL*Plus prefix character. The prefix character allows you to execute a SQL*Plus command while in the middle of entering an SQL statement (or PL/SQL block).

```
SET SQLPRE[FIX] prefix_char
```

where:

*SET SQLPRE[FIX]*

> Is the command, which may be abbreviated to SET SQLPRE.

*prefix_char*

> Is the new prefix character. The default prefix character is a pound sign. This may optionally be enclosed in either single or double quotes.

The following example shows how the prefix character is used by using it to execute a DESCRIBE command while entering a SELECT statement:

```
SQL> SELECT
  2  #DESCRIBE EMPLOYEE
```

```
Name                                 Null?     Type
------------------------------------ --------  ----
EMPLOYEE_ID                          NOT NULL  NUMBER
EMPLOYEE_NAME                                  VARCHAR2(40
EMPLOYEE_HIRE_DATE                             DATE
EMPLOYEE_TERMINATION_DATE                      DATE
EMPLOYEE_BILLING_RATE                          NUMBER

  2  employee_id, employee_name
  3  FROM employee
  4
```

This ability to execute a SQL\*Plus command (and it must be a SQL\*Plus command) while entering a SQL statement can come in handy when you need to quickly refresh your memory regarding the column names in the table.

### SQLTERMINATOR

The SQLTERMINATOR setting controls whether or not SQL\*Plus allows you to use a semicolon to terminate and execute a SQL statement. This setting also controls the specific character used for this purpose.

```
SET SQLT[ERMINATOR] {OFF|ON|term_char}
```

where:

*SET SQLT[ERMINATOR]*

Is the command, which may be abbreviated to SET SQLT.

*OFF*

Turns off the feature that allows you to terminate and execute a SQL statement using a semicolon or other character.

*ON*

Turns this feature on, and resets the terminator character to the default value of a semicolon.

*term_char*

Is the character you want to use as a statement terminator. This may optionally be enclosed in single or double quotes.

The following example changes the terminator character to a percent sign and uses it to terminate and execute a SELECT statement:

```
SQL> SET SQLTERMINATOR "%"
SQL> SELECT employee_name FROM employee%

EMPLOYEE_NAME
----------------------------------------
Bohdan Khmelnytsky
Pavlo Chubynsky
Ivan Mazepa
Taras Shevchenko
...
```

If the feature had been turned off in the above example, the percent sign would have been placed in the buffer as part of the SELECT statement.

## SUFFIX

The SUFFIX setting controls the default extension used for command files:

```
SET SUF[FIX] extension
```

where:

*SET SUF[FIX]*

   Is the command, which may be abbreviated to SET SUF.

*extension*

   Is the default extension to use when referring to SQL files. The default value for this setting is SQL.

This setting is used by commands such as START, @, SAVE, and others that refer to SQL files. It does not apply to files created with the SPOOL command.

## Operational Settings

Operational settings control various aspects of how your commands are executed and how SQL*Plus interacts with the database. You can control the following items:

*APPINFO*

   Controls automatic registration of command files using the DBMS_ APPLICATION_INFO package.

*ARRAYSIZE*

   Is the number of rows SQL*Plus will return at once from the database.

*AUTOCOMMIT*

   Controls whether or not SQL*Plus automatically commits your changes.

*CLOSECURSOR*

   Controls whether or not SQL*Plus keeps the statement cursor open all the time.

*COMPATIBILITY*

   Controls whether SQL*Plus acts as if it is connected to a version 7 database or a version 8 database.

*COPYCOMMIT*

   Controls how often SQL*Plus commits during the execution of a COPY command.

*FLAGGER*

Controls whether or not SQL\*Plus checks your statements for compliance with ANSI/ISO syntax.

*FLUSH*

Controls whether or not output may be buffered.

The following sections describe the operational settings in detail.

### SET APPINFO

The APPINFO setting controls whether or not SQL\*Plus automatically registers command files using the DBMS_APPLICATION_INFO package:

```
SET APPI[NFO] {OFF|ON|app_text}
```

where:

*SET APPI[NFO]*

Is the command, which may be abbreviated to SET APP.

*OFF*

Disables the automatic registration of command file names. With this off, SQL\*Plus will make an entry using the current value of app_text whenever you execute a command file.

*ON*

Enables the automatic registration of command files. This is the default setting.

*app_text*

Provides a text string that is used instead of the command file name. The default setting for this is "SQL\*Plus".

The DBMS_APPLICATION_INFO package is defined in the *Oracle Tuning* manual. Among other things, this package controls the contents of the module field in both the V$SESSION and V$SQLAREA views.

Whenever you connect to a database, SQL\*Plus registers itself as the active application by making a call to the DBMS_APPLICATION_INFO.SET_MODULE procedure. This sets the module name for your session to "SQL\*Plus". This is reflected in the v$session view, as the following example demonstrates:

```
SQL> SELECT module FROM v$session WHERE username=USER;

MODULE
--------------------------------------------------
SQL*Plus
```

SQL\*Plus has the ability to update the module name whenever you execute a command file. The module name can be set to either the command file name or to some arbitrary text that you specify. The default setting for APPINFO causes

SQL*Plus to register the name of each command file you execute. So, if you execute a command file from one SQL*Plus session and query the v$session view from a second SQL*Plus session, you will get results like the following:

```
SQL> SELECT module FROM v$session WHERE username='JEFF';

MODULE
------------------------------------------------
01@ c:\a\project_hours_dollars.SQL
```

The module column now tells you the name of the command file being executed by the user named JEFF. SQL*Plus actually crams in a bit more information than just the filename. You can break down the format of the module field as follows:

NL@tFFFFFFFF

where:

NL    Is the nesting level. Command files executed from the SQL*Plus prompt will have a 01 in this position. If one command file executes another command file, then the nesting level will be 02, indicating that a second command file was invoked. The deeper the command files are nested, the larger this number becomes.

@     Is a constant.

t     Is a flag indicating whether or not SQL*Plus had to truncate the name of the command file in order for it to fit within the module field. The maximum length of a module is 48 bytes. If the filename was truncated, this value will be a less-than sign ("<").

*FFFFFFFF*
      Is the filename, or as much as will fit within 48 characters.

You may find that you don't care about command file names, but that you just want to know when users are using SQL*Plus. You can accomplish that by setting APPINFO to OFF. In that case, SQL*Plus will still register itself, but will not subsequently change the module name. It will always be "SQL*Plus". For this to apply to all users, you would need to place the setting in each user's global or site profile.

An additional option is to supply a fixed text string that SQL*Plus can use instead of a filename. This string is passed as the module name whenever a command file is executed. The result is that while you will know that a command file is being executed, you won't know which one.

## SET ARRAYSIZE

The ARRAYSIZE setting controls the number of rows SQL*Plus fetches from the database at one time.

```
SET ARRAY[SIZE] array_size
```

where:

*SET ARRAY[SIZE]*

   Is the command, which may be abbreviated to SET ARRAY.

*array_size*

   Is the number of rows fetched at one time. The default value is 15. The
   allowed range is from 1 to 5000.

Increasing the arraysize allows SQL\*Plus to return more rows in one fetch, thus
lessening the required number of network round trips between it and the database server. The tradeoff is that larger arraysize settings require more memory.
Using the default value of 15, SQL\*Plus would require 10 fetches to return 150
rows from a query. By increasing the arraysize to 50, you reduce the number of
fetches to three.

## SET AUTOCOMMIT

The autocommit setting controls whether or not SQL\*Plus automatically commits
changes you make to the database. It also controls how often those changes are
committed.

```
SET AUTO[COMMIT] {OFF|ON|IMMEDIATE|statement_count}
```

where:

*SET AUTO[COMMIT]*

   Is the command, which may be abbreviated to SET AUTO.

*OFF*

   Turns autocommit off, and requires you to commit (or rollback) changes manually. This is the default setting.

*ON*

   Causes SQL\*Plus to issue a COMMIT after each successful SQL statement or
   PL/SQL block you execute.

*IMMEDIATE*

   Has the same effect as ON.

*statement_count*

   Causes SQL\*Plus to issue a COMMIT after successfully executing the specified
   number of SQL queries or PL/SQL blocks. This value may range from 1 to
   2,000,000.

When you set autocommit to occur after a specified number of successful SQL
statements, be aware that manually executing a COMMIT, a ROLLBACK, or

another SET AUTOCOMMIT command will cause the counter to be reset back to zero. Take a look at the following example:

```
SET AUTOCOMMIT 5
DELETE FROM project_hours WHERE employee_id = 101 AND project_id = 1001;
DELETE FROM project_hours WHERE employee_id = 102 AND project_id = 1001;
COMMIT;
DELETE FROM project_hours WHERE employee_id = 103 AND project_id = 1001;
DELETE FROM project_hours WHERE employee_id = 104 AND project_id = 1001;
DELETE FROM project_hours WHERE employee_id = 105 AND project_id = 1001;
DELETE FROM project_hours WHERE employee_id = 106 AND project_id = 1001;
DELETE FROM project_hours WHERE employee_id = 107 AND project_id = 1001;
```

The COMMIT statement in the fourth line will cause the counter to be reset. Counting will start over again, and five more SQL statements must be executed successfully before an automatic commit occurs.

### SET CLOSECURSOR

The CLOSECURSOR setting controls whether or not SQL*Plus closes the cursor used to execute an SQL statement after the statement has executed:

```
SET CLOSECUR[SOR] {OFF|ON}
```

where:

*SET CLOSECUR[SOR]*
> Is the command, which may be abbreviated to SET CLOSECUR.

*OFF*
> Causes SQL*Plus to leave the cursor open for use by subsequent SQL statements. This is the default setting.

*ON*
> Causes SQL*Plus to close the cursor after a SQL statement has been executed.

While you normally think of a cursor only in the context of returning data from a SELECT statement, Oracle also uses cursors to execute other SQL statements, such as DELETE, INSERT, UPDATE, and so forth. The same cursor can be used to execute many SQL statements, so SQL*Plus leaves it open all the time by default.

### SET COMPATIBILITY

Use SET COMPATIBILITY to tell SQL*Plus the version of Oracle to which you are connected:

```
SET COM[PATIBILITY] {V7|V8|NATIVE}
```

where:

*SET COM[PATIBILITY]*
> Is the command, which may be abbreviated to SET COM.

*V7* Tells SQL*Plus you are connected to a version 7 server, or that you want SQL*Plus to act as if you were.

*V8* Tells SQL*Plus you are connected to a version 8 database.

*NATIVE*

Causes SQL*Plus to automatically determine the compatibility setting based on the version of the database to which you are connected. This is the default setting.

This setting controls the way SQL statements are transmitted to the server and the way the results are brought back. It's usually best just to leave this at the default setting, which causes SQL*Plus to automatically choose the correct method based on the database to which you are connected.

### SET COPYCOMMIT

The copycommit setting controls how often SQL*Plus commits during execution of a COPY command:

```
SET COPYC[OMMIT] batch_count
```

where:

*SET COPYC[OMMIT]*

Is the command, which may be abbreviated to SET COPYC.

*batch_count*

Is the maximum number of uncommitted batches you want to allow during a copy operation. After this many batches are sent to the server, SQL*Plus commits the changes and resets the counter before sending another. The default value is 0, which means that SQL*Plus commits changes only when the COPY command is finished. The maximum value for this setting is 5000.

Normally, when you execute a COPY command, SQL*Plus copies all the rows from the source table to the destination table, then commits those changes. This can make for a rather large transaction if you are copying a large number of records, and your rollback segments may not be big enough to accommodate it. You can use SET COPYCOMMIT to have SQL*Plus periodically commit the changes, thus reducing the transaction size.

The copycommit setting works in conjunction with the arraysize setting. The arraysize setting controls the number of rows in a batch. The copycommit setting controls how many batches are copied before committing. The number of rows copied before each commit is equal to ARRAYSIZE * COPYCOMMIT. Take a look at this example:

```
SET ARRAYSIZE 15
SET COPYCOMMIT 10
```

```
COPY TO jonathan/chatham@jonathan
CREATE employee_copy
USING SELECT * FROM employee;
```

Because the arraysize is 15 and the copycommit setting is 10, the COPY statement shown here will commit changes after every 150 rows (15 * 10).

## SET FLAGGER

Use SET FLAGGER to have your SQL statements checked for conformance to ANSI/ISO SQL92 syntax. There are three compliance levels to choose from: entry, intermediate, and full.

```
SET FLAGGER {OFF|ENTRY|INTERMED[IATE]|FULL}
```

where:

### SET FLAGGER

Is the command, which may not be abbreviated.

### OFF

Turns this feature off. This is the default setting.

### ENTRY

Allows SQL statements that use only the entry-level features of the standard.

### INTERMED[IATE]

Allows SQL statements that use the intermediate-level features of the standard.

### FULL

Allows any SQL statement that is defined in the standard.

Using the SET FLAGGER command has the same effect as executing the ALTER DATABASE SET FLAGGER command. However, SET FLAGGER is a SQL*Plus command, so you can execute it even before connecting to the database. Once you've turned this feature on, any attempt to execute a nonconforming command will result in an error message like the following:

```
ERROR:
ORA-00097: Use of Oracle SQL feature not in SQL92 Entry Level
```

This feature is useful if you are writing software for the federal government and are required to deliver an implementation that uses no non-standard, vendor-specific features.

## SET FLUSH

The flush setting indicates whether or not the host operating system is allowed to buffer output:

```
SET FLU[SH] {OFF|ON}
```

where:

*SET FLU[SH]*

Is the command, which may be abbreviated to SET FLU.

*OFF*

Allows output to be buffered.

*ON*

Causes output to be displayed immediately.

If you are running a command file, turning flush off might keep you from seeing any output until SQL\*Plus is finished executing that file.

## Substitution Variable Settings

Substitution variable settings allow you to change the way SQL\*Plus handles substitution variables. The following settings make up this category:

*CONCAT*

Specifies the concatenation character, which marks the end of a substitution variable.

*DEFINE*

Specifies the character used to mark a substitution variable.

*ESCAPE*

Specifies the escape character.

*SCAN*

Controls whether or not the substitution feature is enabled.

Most of these settings are described, with examples, in Chapter 4, *Writing SQL\*Plus Scripts.* They are described here as well, in the following sections.

### SET CONCAT

The SET CONCAT command allows you to change the character used to terminate a substitution variable reference. You can also use the command to turn the feature off so that SQL\*Plus doesn't recognize any character as the terminator.

```
SET CON[CAT] {OFF|ON|concat_char}
```

where:

*SET CON[CAT]*

Is the command, which may be abbreviated to SETCON.

*OFF*

Turns this feature off completely. SQL\*Plus won't recognize any character as the termination character for substitution variable names.

*ON*

Turns this feature back on, and resets the character back to the default value of a period.

*concat_char*

Is the new termination character. The default value is a period.

This setting is important only when you immediately follow a substitution variable name with characters that SQL*Plus might interpret as part of the name. Consider the following example:

```
DEFINE table="PROJECT"
SELECT &&table._name FROM &&table;
```

The period (or concatenation character) in the SELECT statement is used to terminate the reference to &&table. Without the period, SQL*Plus would recognize &&table_name as the substitution variable.

---

 The concatenation character is never left in the line. When SQL*Plus substitutes a value for the variable, the concatenation character goes away along with the variable name.

---

### SET DEFINE

The SET DEFINE command allows you to change the prefix character used to mark substitution variables. You can also use SET DEFINE to turn variable substitution off.

```
SET DEF[INE] {OFF|ON|prefix_char}
```

where:

*SET DEF[INE]*

Is the command, which may be abbreviated to SET DEF.

*OFF*

Disables variable substitution.

*ON*

Enables variable substitution, and resets the substitution prefix character back to the default ampersand (&) character. Variable substitution is on by default.

*prefix_char*

Is the new substitution prefix character.

When you start SQL*Plus, variable substitution will be on by default, and the default prefix character is an ampersand. If you are running a script that uses ampersands in text strings, you may want to change the prefix character to something else. If your script does not use substitution variables, you may find it easiest to just turn the feature off completely.

### SET ESCAPE

Use SET ESCAPE to specify the character used to escape the substitution variable prefix:

```
SET ESC[APE] {OFF|ON|escape_char}
```

where:

*SET ESC[APE]*

Is the command, which may be abbreviated to SET ESC.

*OFF*

Turns the escape feature off completely. SQL\*Plus will not recognize any character as an escape character. This is the default setting.

*ON*

Enables the escape feature, and resets the escape character back to the default value, a backslash (\).

*escape_char*

Is the new escape character. By default, this is a backslash.

You use the escape character when you want to place an ampersand in a command and you don't want that ampersand interpreted as a substitution variable prefix character. The following example shows a case where this can be a problem:

```
SQL> SELECT 'O''Reilly & Associates' FROM dual;
Enter value for associates:
```

The ampersand in front of the word "Associates" causes SQL\*Plus to interpret it as substitution variable name. To work around this behavior, you can turn the escape feature on and precede the ampersand with a backslash. Here is an example:

```
SQL> SET ESCAPE ON
SQL> SELECT 'O''Reilly \& Associates' FROM dual;

'O''REILLY&ASSOCIATES
--------------------
O'Reilly & Associates
```

You can also use the SET ESCAPE command to change the escape character to something other than a backslash.

### SET SCAN

SET SCAN is an obsolete command that allows you to choose whether or not SQL\*Plus scans for substitution variables:

```
SET SCAN {OFF|ON}
```

*SET SCAN*

Is the command, which may not be abbreviated.

*OFF*

Disables variable substitution, and has the same effect as SET DEFINE OFF.

*ON*

Enables variable substitution, and has the same effect as SET DEFINE ON.

The SET SCAN command duplicates functionality provided by the SET DEFINE command.

## Large Object Settings

Large object settings control the way SQL*Plus handles columns with a datatype of LONG. The most commonly adjusted setting is the LONG setting, which controls the maximum number of characters SQL*Plus will display from a LONG. The complete list of LONG settings is shown here:

*LOBOFFSET*

An index into the LONG column, specifying the first character to be displayed.

*LONG*

Specifies the maximum number of characters to display from a LONG column.

*LONGCHUNKSIZE*

Controls the number of characters retrieved from a LONG at one time.

Chapter 7, *Advanced Scripting*, contains examples showing how to use these three settings.

### SET LOBOFFSET

The LOBOFFSET setting represents an index into a LONG column. When SQL*Plus displays a LONG, it begins with the character pointed to by LOBOFFSET.

```
SET LOBOF[FSET] offset
```

where:

*SET LOBOF[FSET]*

Is the command, which may be abbreviated to SET LOBOF.

*offset*

Is the offset used when retrieving LONG values, and represents the first character you want to display.

Using the LOBOFFSET setting in conjunction with the LONG setting allows you to print any arbitrary substring from a LONG column.

### SET LONG

The LONG setting controls the number of characters displayed by SQL*Plus from any LONG columns returned by a query:

```
SET LONG long_length
```

where:

*SET LONG*

Is the command, which may not be abbreviated.

*long_length*

Represents the number of characters you want displayed from any LONG columns you select from the database. The default setting is to display 80 characters.

### SET LONGCHUNKSIZE

The LONGCHUNKSIZE is a performance-related setting. It controls the number of characters retrieved at one time from a LONG column.

```
SET LONGC[HUNKSIZE] size
```

where:

*SET LONGC[HUNKSIZE]*

Is the command, which may be abbreviated to SET LONGC.

*size*

Is the number of characters you want to retrieve from a LONG column in one fetch. The default value is 80.

With the default setting of 80 characters, SQL*Plus will need 10 round trips to the database to retrieve an 800-character LONG value. These network round trips take time, so you will tend to get better performance by increasing this setting. If you can afford the memory, make LONGCHUNKSIZE equal to the LONG setting. That way, the entire LONG value will be retrieved in one fetch.

## Tuning and Timing Settings

Two settings are useful when tuning SQL statements. They are:

*AUTOTRACE*

Enables the automatic display of the execution plan and execution statistics for a SQL statement.

*TIMING*

Controls whether or not SQL*Plus displays the elapsed execution time for each SQL statement or PL/SQL block.

Chapter 8, *Tuning and Timing*, describes the timing features of SQL*Plus in detail, and also explains how to interpret the execution plan for a SQL statement.

### SET AUTOTRACE

The AUTOTRACE setting is used to control whether or not SQL*Plus displays the execution plan and statistics for each SQL statement as it is executed:

```
SET AUTOT[RACE] {OFF|ON|TRACE[ONLY]} [EXP[LAIN]] [STAT[ISTICS]]
```

where:

*SET AUTOT[RACE]*

Is the command, which may be abbreviated to SETAUTOT.

*OFF*

Disables the autotrace feature. SQL*Plus will not display the execution plan or the statistics for each SQL statement.

*ON*

Turns the autotrace feature on. If no other parameters are supplied, SQL*Plus will default to displaying the statistics. SET AUTOTRACE ON is equivalent to SET AUTOTRACE ON STATISTICS.

*TRACE[ONLY]*

Inhibits the display of any data returned when the SQL statement in question is a SELECT statement.

*EXP[LAIN]*

Causes SQL*Plus to display the execution plan for each SQL statement you execute.

*STAT[ISTICS]*

Causes SQL*Plus to display execution statistics for each SQL statement you execute.

See Chapter 8 for comprehensive examples showing how to use the autotrace feature of SQL*Plus. Chapter 8 also shows you how to interpret the execution plan output and describes the operations that may be used in that plan.

### SET TIMING

The TIMING setting controls whether or not SQL*Plus displays the elapsed time for each SQL statement or PL/SQL block you execute:

```
SET TIMI[NG] {OFF|ON}
```

where:

*SET TIMI[NG]*

Is the command, which may be abbreviated to SET TIMI.

*OFF*

>   Turns the timing feature off. This is the default setting.

*ON*

>   Enables the display of elapsed execution time for SQL statements and PL/SQL blocks.

See Chapter 8, for examples of this command.

## Database Administration Settings

Database administration settings may be used only by database administrators, and control the way SQL\*Plus operates when performing administrative tasks such as database recovery. These settings are listed below:

*AUTORECOVERY*

>   Causes the RECOVER command to run without user intervention.

*LOGSOURCE*

>   Tells SQL\*Plus where to find archive log files for recovery.

### SET AUTORECOVERY

The AUTORECOVERY option causes the RECOVER command to run without user intervention, as long as the archived log files are in the destination pointed to by the LOG_ARCHIVE_DEST parameter and the names conform to the LOG_ARCHIVE_FORMAT parameter.

```
SET AUTORECOVERY {OFF|ON}
```

where:

*SET AUTORECOVERY*

>   Is the command, which may not be abbreviated.

*OFF*

>   Turns autorecovery off. This is the default setting.

*ON*

>   Turns autorecovery on, causing the RECOVER command to run without user intervention.

Chapter 10, *Administration with SQL\*Plus*, talks about recovery in more detail.

### SET LOGSOURCE

The LOGSOURCE setting specifies the location of the archive log files, and is referenced during recovery:

```
SET LOGSOURCE logpath
```

where:

*SET LOGSOURCE*
 Is the command, which may not be abbreviated.

*logpath*
 Is the path to the directory containing the archived redo log files.

## *Miscellaneous Settings*

This section describes the following three miscellaneous settings:

*COPYTYPECHECK*
 Controls whether or not type checking is done for the COPY command.

*EDITFILE*
 Specifies the name of the work file used when you invoke the EDIT command.

*INSTANCE*
 Specifies the default database instance to use with the CONNECT command.

### *SET COPYTYPECHECK*

The COPYTYPECHECK setting controls whether or not SQL*Plus checks the datatypes when you use the COPY command to move data between two databases:

```
SET COPYTYPECHECK {OFF|ON}
```

where:

*SET COPYTYPECHECK*
 Is the command, which may not be abbreviated.

*OFF*
 Turns type checking off.

*ON*
 Enables type checking. This is the default setting.

This option was created specifically for use when copying data to a DB2 database.

### *SET EDITFILE*

The SET EDITFILE command lets you change the name of the work file that is created when you use the EDIT command to edit the SQL statement in the buffer:

```
SET EDITF[ILE] edit_filename
```

where:

*SET EDITF[ILE]*

Is the command, which may be abbreviated to SET EDITF.

*edit_filename*

Is the filename you want SQL\*Plus to use when you issue an EDIT command. The default value is *afiedt.buf.* The filename you specify may optionally include a path.

If you do not include an extension as part of the filename, the current value of the SUFFIX setting will be used as the extension.

### SET INSTANCE

The SET INSTANCE command allows you to specify a default database to connect to when you use the CONNECT command without specifying a service name. You cannot issue this command while connected to a database; you must disconnect first.

```
SET INSTANCE [service_name|LOCAL]
```

where:

*SET INSTANCE*

Is the command, which may not be abbreviated. Issuing the command SET INSTANCE with no parameters has the same effect as SET INSTANCE LOCAL.

*service_name*

Is a Net8 (SQL\*Net) service name.

*LOCAL*

Sets the default instance to be your local database. This is the default setting. In a Windows environment, the local database is the one specified by the LOCAL registry setting.

# *The SHOW Command*

The SHOW command allows you to look at the current state of your SQL\*Plus environment. You can use it to display the current value of any setting controlled by the SET command. SHOW may also be used to look at current page titles, page footers, and so forth.

```
SHO[W] setting
       ALL
       BTI[TLE]
       ERR[ORS] [{FUNCTION|PROCEDURE|PACKAGE|PACKAGE BODY|
                  TRIGGER|TYPE|TYPE BODY|VIEW} [owner.]object_name]
       LNO
```

```
PARAMETERS [parameter_name]
PNO
REL[EASE]
REPF[OOTER]
REPH[EADER]
SGA
SPOO[L]
SQLCODE
TTI[TLE]
USER
```

where:

*SHO[W]*

Is the command, which may be abbreviated to SHO.

*setting*

Is any one of the settings you can set using the SET command.

*ALL*

Shows everything, except for errors and the SGA.

*BTI[TLE]*

Displays the current page footer.

*ERR[ORS]*

Displays an error listing for a stored object. The command SHOW ERRORS by itself causes the error listing for the most recently created object to be displayed. You can get the error listing for a specific object by specifying the object type (function, procedure, and so forth) and the object name.

*FUNCTION | PROCEDURE | PACKAGE | PACKAGE BODY | TRIGGER | TYPE | TYPE BODY | VIEW*

Used with SHOW ERRORS to specify the object type of interest. This is only necessary if you are specifying the name of the object.

*[owner.]object_name*

Used with SHOW ERRORS to name the object for which you want to display an error listing.

*LNO*

Displays the current line number.

*PARAMETER[S] [parameter_name]*

Displays the current value of one or more initialization parameters. Chapter 10 provides detailed examples of SHOW PARAMETERS in use.

*PNO*

Displays the current page number.

*REL[EASE]*

> Displays the release number (version) of the Oracle database to which you are connected.

*REPF[OOTER]*

> Displays the current report footer.

*REPH[EADER]*

> Displays the current report header.

*SGA*

> Displays information about the current state of the System Global Area. See Chapter 10 for more information about this option.

*SPOO[L]*

> Tells you whether or not output is currently being spooled to a file.

*SQLCODE*

> Displays the SQL code returned by the most recent SQL statement.

*TTI[TLE]*

> Displays the current page title.

*USER*

> Displays the current username.

The following few examples demonstrate how the SHOW command may be used to display the value of one item, such as a setting or a page title:

```
SQL> SHOW LINESIZE
linesize 80
SQL> SHOW USER
USER is "JEFF"
SQL> SHOW TTITLE
ttitle OFF and is the 1st few characters of the next SELECT statement
```

The ALL option may be used to display the value of all settings at once. Here is an example:

```
SQL> SHOW ALL
appinfo is ON and set to "SQL*Plus"
arraysize 15
autocommit OFF
autoprint OFF
autotrace OFF
shiftinout INVISIBLE
blockterminator "." (hex 2e)
...
```

As you can see, when you use SHOW ALL, the settings are displayed in alphabetical order.

The SHOW ERRORS command has more parameters than the other options, so it's a bit more complex. SHOW ERRORS is used to display error listings for stored procedures, stored functions, packages, triggers, and other such objects. Typically, you first issue a CREATE statement, and then, if errors are reported, you follow that with a SHOW ERRORS command. The following example uses SHOW ERRORS to display an error listing for the most recent creation attempt:

```
SQL> CREATE OR REPLACE TRIGGER employee_set_key
  2  BEFORE INSERT ON employee
  3  FOR EACH ROW
  4  BEGIN
  5    :new.employee_id := employee_seq.nextval;
  6  END;
  7  /

Warning: Trigger created with compilation errors.

SQL> SHOW ERRORS
Errors for TRIGGER EMPLOYEE_SET_KEY:

LINE/COL
-----------------------------------------------------------------
ERROR
-----------------------------------------------------------------
2/3
PL/SQL: Statement ignored

2/23
PLS-00201: identifier 'EMPLOYEE_SEQ.NEXTVAL' must be declared

SQL>
```

You can show errors for a specific object by telling SQL*Plus both the object type and the object name:

```
SQL> CREATE OR REPLACE PROCEDURE JEFF.DISABLE_TRIGGER AS
  2  BEGIN
  3    ALTER TABLE EMPLOYEE DISABLE TRIGGER EMPLOYEE_SET_KEY;
  4  END;
  5  /

Warning: Procedure created with compilation errors.

SQL> SHOW ERRORS PROCEDURE JEFF.DISABLE_TRIGGER
Errors for PROCEDURE JEFF.DISABLE_TRIGGER:

LINE/COL
--------------------------------------------------------------------------
ERROR
--------------------------------------------------------------------------
3/3
PLS-00103: Encountered the symbol "ALTER" when expecting one of the
following:
```

```
begin declare exit for goto if loop mod null pragma raise
return select update while <an identifier>
<a double-quoted delimited-identifier> <a bind variable> <<
close current delete fetch lock insert open rollback
savepoint set sql commit <a single-quoted SQL string>
```

The error listings stick around even after you end the session in which you tried to create the object. You can come back later, display the errors, and pick up where you left off. But when you do that, you must explicitly name the object you are working with.

# *SQL\*Plus Command Reference*

## *SQLPLUS*

The SQLPLUS command is used from the operating system prompt to start SQL*Plus, and is discussed in Chapter 2, *Interacting with SQL\*Plus*.

```
SQLPLUS [[-SILENT] [username[/password][@connect]|/|/NOLOG]
[@scriptfile [arg1 arg2 arg3...]]]|-|-?
```

where:

*SQLPLUS*

Is the command to use when invoking SQL*Plus. On a Unix system this will be lowercase *sqlplus*. From Windows or MS-DOS, you may need to use PLUS80 or PLUS80W. Beginning with release 8.1, the command under Windows, or from a DOS prompt, will always be *SQLPLUS*.

*-S[ILENT]*

Tells SQL*Plus to run in silent mode. No startup messages, such as the copyright message, will be displayed. No command prompt will be displayed, and no commands will be echoed to the screen. This is useful if you are invoking SQL*Plus from within some other program, and you want to do it transparently. Normally you would use this option in conjunction with invoking a script file.

*username*

Is your database username.

*password*

Is your database password.

*connect*

> Is the connect string, or host string, telling SQL*Plus the database to which you want to connect.

/    Use a forward slash instead of your username, password, and connect string when you want to connect to a local database using operating-system authentication.

*/NOLOG*

> Tells SQL*Plus not to connect you to any database at all. You will get a SQL> prompt, but you must issue a CONNECT command before you can do much else.

*scriptfile*

> Is the name of a SQL*Plus script file you want to run. SQL*Plus will start up, execute the file, then exit.

*arg1 agr2 arg3*

> Are optional command-line arguments to pass to your script. You can have as many as your script requires. Arguments are separated from each other by at least one space.

–    Causes SQL*Plus to display a short summary of the SQLPLUS syntax.

–?    Causes SQL*Plus to display version and copyright information.

# Comment Delimiters (/*...*/)

The /* and */ delimiters may be used to set off a comment in SQL*Plus. Comments entered this way may span multiple lines. If you use /*...*/ in a script file, the comments will be displayed on the screen when the script is executed. Chapter 4, *Writing SQL\*Plus Scripts*, talks about the different ways to enter comments in SQL*Plus.

```
/*
comment_text
comment_text
comment_text
*/
```

where:

/*    Marks the beginning of the comment.

*comment_text*

> Is the text making up the comment.

*/    Marks the end of the comment.

# Double Hyphen (--)

The double hyphen may be used to place a single-line comment in a SQL*Plus script, and is described in Chapter 4. The double hyphen works the same way as REMARK, except that it may also be used in SQL statements and PL/SQL blocks. When used in a SQL statement or PL/SQL block, the double-hyphen may also be used to add trailing comments to a line. The syntax looks like this:

```
--comment_text
```

where:

-- Is a double hyphen, and tells SQL*Plus that the line in question is a comment line.

*comment_text*
    Is your comment.

# At Sign (@)

The at sign is used to execute a SQL*Plus script file. A script file is simply a text file containing SQL*Plus commands. The commands appear in the file just as you would enter them from the keyboard. See Chapter 2 for a an introduction to this command. Also see the @@ and START commands.

```
@script_file [argument...]
```

where:

@   Is the command to execute a script file.

*script_file*
    Is the name of the file you want to execute, which may include the path and extension. The default extension is SQL. If you do not specify a path, SQL*Plus will look for the file first in the current working directory, then it will search each directory listed in the SQLPATH environment variable. See Chapter 10, *Administration with SQL*Plus*, for information about customizing the search path.

*argument*
    Is an argument you wish to pass to the script. You may pass as many arguments as you like. Arguments must be separated from each other by at least one space. Arguments may be enclosed in quotes, and should be if they contain spaces. Either single or double quotes may be used, at your discretion. Your script may reference the first argument as &1, the second as &2, and so forth.

# *Double At Sign (@@)*

The double at sign is used within a script file to execute another script file contained in the same directory as the first. This is very convenient if you have two scripts, one that calls the other. Use the @@ command in the first script file to call the second. Then put both files in the same directory. Now, regardless of whether or not that directory is in the search path, SQL\*Plus will find the second file whenever the first calls for it. If used interactively, @@ functions exactly the same as @.

A script file is simply a text file containing SQL\*Plus commands. The commands appear in the file just as you would enter them from the keyboard. See Chapter 2 for an introduction to this command. Also see the @ and START commands.

```
@@script_file [argument...]
```

where:

@@ Is the command to execute a script file.

*script_file*

Is the name of the file you want to execute, and may include the path and the extension. The default extension is SQL. The default path is the one pointing to the directory where the calling script is stored.

*argument*

Is an argument you wish to pass to the script. You may pass as many arguments as you like. Arguments must be separated from each other by at least one space. Arguments may be enclosed in quotes, and should be if they contain spaces. Either single or double quotes may be used, at your discretion. Your script may reference the first argument as &1, the second as &2, and so forth.

# *Forward Slash (/)*

A forward slash is used to execute the SQL statement or PL/SQL block that is currently in the buffer. See Chapter 2 for more information, and for examples.

```
/
```

where:

/ Causes SQL\*Plus to execute the statement in the buffer. The buffer is not changed by this command, and / can be used repeatedly to execute the same statement again and again.

# *ACCEPT*

The ACCEPT command is used to get input from a user. It causes SQL*Plus to display a prompt and wait for the user to type something in response. You can read about ACCEPT in Chapter 4 and in Chapter 7, *Advanced Scripting*.

```
ACC[EPT] user_variable [NUM[BER]|CHAR|DATE]
        [FOR[MAT] format_specification]
        [DEF[AULT] default_value]
        [PROMPT prompt_text|NOPR[OMPT]]
        [HIDE]
```

where:

*ACC[EPT]*

    Tells SQL*Plus you want to prompt the user for a value and that you want the value stored in the specified user variable. The command may be abbreviated to ACC.

*user_variable* ·

    Is the variable you want to define. Do not include leading ampersands. If your script uses "&table_name" for a substitution variable, you should use "table_name" here.

*NUM[BER] | CHAR | DATE*

    Is the type of data you are after. The default is CHAR, which allows the user to type in anything as a response. Use NUMBER to force the user to enter a number, and DATE when you want a date.

*FOR[MAT] format_specification*

    Is a format specification, which may optionally be enclosed in quotes. ACCEPT will reject any input that does not conform to the specification. An error message will be displayed and the prompt reissued. Specifying a format makes the most sense when dealing with numeric and date data, and SQL*Plus is actually somewhat loose in enforcing the format. Chapter 7 delves into this aspect of the ACCEPT command in detail. Format elements are described in Appendix B, *SQL*Plus Format Elements*.

*DEF[AULT] default_value*

    Specifies a default value to assign to the variable. This is used if the user bypasses the prompt by pressing ENTER without actually entering a response. The default value should usually be enclosed within single quotes.

*PROMPT prompt_text*

    This is the prompt text displayed to the user before waiting for input.

*NOPR[OMPT]*

    Indicates that you do not want the user to see a visible prompt.

*HIDE*

> Causes SQL\*Plus not to echo the user's response back to the display. This is useful if you are prompting for a password.

---

 The syntax for the ACCEPT command has evolved significantly with the past few releases of SQL\*Plus. The syntax shown here is valid for version 8.1. Not all of the clauses are available when using prior versions. Be sensitive to this and check your documentation if you are writing scripts that need to work under earlier versions of SQL\*Plus.

---

# APPEND

Append is an editing command that lets you add text onto the end of the current line in the SQL buffer:

```
A[PPEND] text
```

where:

*A[PPEND]*

> Is the command, which may be abbreviated to A.

*text*

> Is the text you want appended to the current line.

APPEND, and all other editing commands, are described in Chapter 2.

# ARCHIVE LOG

The ARCHIVE LOG command is used to control, or display information about, archive logging. It's discussed in Chapter 10 and may be used to start archiving, stop archiving, manually archive one or more log files, or display information about the current archive log state. You must be connected as SYSDBA, SYSOPER, or INTERNAL in order to use this command.

```
ARCHIVE LOG {LIST
            |STOP
            |START [TO destination]
            |NEXT [TO destination]
            |ALL [TO destination]
            |log_sequence_number [TO destination]}
```

where:

*ARCHIVE LOG*

> Is the command.

*LIST*

Causes SQL*Plus to display information about the current state of archiving. This includes the current destination, an indication of whether or not automatic archiving is enabled (the ARCH process), the oldest online log sequence number, the sequence number of the next log to be archived, and the current log sequence number.

*STOP*

Stops logs files from being automatically archived. You must manually archive redo log files as they fill; otherwise, you run the risk of the instance suspending operation because the log files have run out of space.

*START*

Turns on automatic archiving of redo log files.

*NEXT*

Manually archives the next log file group in the sequence, provided that it is filled. Use ARCHIVE LOG LIST to see the sequence number of this file.

*ALL*

Manually archives all log file groups that have been filled, but not previously archived.

*log_sequence_number*

Manually archives a specific log file group, provided that group is still online. Use ARCHIVE LOG LIST to find the sequence number of the oldest remaining log file group.

*destination*

Specifies a destination for archived log files. If used with ARCHIVE LOG START, this becomes the destination for all log files as they are archived. If used with NEXT, ALL, or a specific sequence number, this becomes the destination for files archived by that one command. If you do not specify a destination when using ARCHIVE LOG START, the value from the LOG_ARCHIVE_ DEST initialization parameter is used.

# *ATTRIBUTE*

The ATTRIBUTE command is used to format attributes of an Oracle8 object type. It functions like the COLUMN command, but with fewer parameters. Chapter 4 talks about this command.

```
ATTRIBUTE [object_type.attribute|attribute_alias
                [ALI[AS] alias|
                CLE[AR]|
                FOR[MAT] format_spec|
                LIKE source_attribute|
                ON|
                OFF...]]
```

where:

*ATTRIBUTE*

Is the command. Issuing the ATTRIBUTE command with no parameters gets you a list of all current attribute settings.

*object_type*

Is the name of an Oracle8 object type.

*attribute*

Is the name of an attribute of the specified object type, and is the attribute you are formatting. If you stop here and don't supply any other parameters, the current display settings for this attribute are shown.

*ALI[AS] alias*

May be abbreviated ALI. ALIAS allows you to specify an alternate name for this attribute that is meaningful to SQL\*Plus.

*alias*

Is an alternate name for the attribute that may be used in other ATTRIBUTE commands, in place of having to spell out the full object type and attribute name again.

*CLE[AR]*

May be abbreviated to CLE. CLEAR erases any format settings for the attribute in question. This puts things back the way they were before any ATTRIBUTE commands were issued for the attribute.

*FOR[MAT]*

May be abbreviated to FOR, and allows you to control how the data for the attribute is displayed. For text fields, the format controls the maximum display length. For numeric fields, you can control the width, placement of commas, placement of the dollar sign, and so on.

*format_spec*

Is a string that specifies the display format for the attribute. Appendix B describes the format specification elements that may be used with the ATTRIBUTE command.

*LIKE*

Causes the attribute to be defined with the same format attributes as another attribute.

*source_column*

Is the name of the source attribute used with the LIKE parameter. This may be either an alias or a complete attribute reference using the standard dot notation.

*ON*

> Causes SQL*Plus to print the attribute using the format you have specified. This is the default behavior. You don't need to use ON unless you have previously used OFF.

*OFF*

> Disables the format settings for the attribute. SQL*Plus acts as if you had never issued any ATTRIBUTE commands for the attribute in question.

When used with text attributes, formats such as A10 specify a maximum length to be displayed. Longer values are truncated to match the length specified, and shorter values are left alone.

# *BREAK*

The BREAK command is used to define page breaks and line breaks based on changing column values in a report. It controls whether or not duplicate values print in a column, and it controls the printing of computed values such as totals and subtotals. Chapter 3, *Generating Reports with SQL*Plus*, demonstrates the use of this command.

The BREAK command looks like this:

```
BRE[AK]  [ON {column_name|ROW|REPORT}
         [SKI[P] {lines_to_skip|PAGE}|
         NODUP[LICATES]|
         DUP[LICATES]...]...]
```

where:

*BRE[AK]*

> May be abbreviated BRE. Issuing the BREAK command with no parameters causes SQL*Plus to display the current break setting.

*column_name*

> Specifies a report column to watch. When the value in the column changes, SQL*Plus skips lines or pages as specified. SQL*Plus also inhibits repeating, or duplicate, values from printing more than once unless the DUPLICATES keyword is used.

*ROW*

> Causes SQL*Plus to break on each row. You could doublespace a report by using BREAK ON ROW SKIP 1.

*REPORT*

> Specifies a report-level break, and is used to cause SQL*Plus to print grand totals at the end of the report. SKIP PAGE will be ignored if it is specified as a

report break action, but, strangely enough, the other form of the SKIP parameter will work. You can skip lines on a report break.

### SKI[P] lines_to_skip

Tells SQL\*Plus to skip the specified number of lines when a break occurs. SKIP may be abbreviated to SKI.

### SKI[P] PAGE

Tells SQL\*Plus to advance to a new page when a break occurs.

### NODUP[LICATES]

Tells SQL\*Plus to print a column's value only when it changes. By default, whenever you put a break on a column, you get this behavior. May be abbreviated NODUP.

### DUP[LICATES]

Forces SQL\*Plus to print a column's value in every line on the report, regardless of whether or not the value is the same as that printed for the previous record. May be abbreviated as DUP.

# BTITLE

Use the BTITLE command to define page footers for a report. Chapter 3 discusses BTITLE and has several examples. Also see the TTITLE command. BTITLE and TTITLE work the same way.

```
BTI[TLE]  [[OFF|ON]|
          [COL x|
          S[KIP] x|
          TAB x|
          LE[FT]|
          CE[NTER]|
          R[IGHT]|
          BOLD|
          FOR[MAT] format_spec|
          text|
          variable...]
```

where:

### BTI[TLE]

May be abbreviated BTI. Issuing the BTITLE command with no parameters causes SQL\*Plus to display the current bottom title setting.

### OFF

Turns the page footer off, but does not erase its definition. You can turn it back on again with ON.

*ON*

> Turns on printing of page footers. The default footer, if you do not specify another, will be the first part of the SELECT statement.

*COL x*

> Causes any footer text following this parameter to print at the specified column position.

*S[KIP] x*

> May be abbreviated to S, and inserts the specified number of line breaks before printing any subsequent footer text.

*TAB x*

> TAB is similar to COL, but moves you the specified number of columns relative to the current position. Negative numbers move you backwards. TAB has nothing whatsoever to do with tab characters.

*LE[FT]*

> May be abbreviated LE, and causes subsequent footer text to be printed beginning at the leftmost column of the current footer line.

*CE[NTER]*

> May be abbreviated CE, and causes subsequent footer text to be centered within the current line. The LINESIZE setting controls the line width.

*R[IGHT]*

> May be abbreviated R, and causes subsequent footer text to be printed flush right. The LINESIZE setting controls where SQL*Plus thinks the right end of the line is.

*BOLD*

> Makes your footer "bold" by printing it three times. Only title text following the BOLD command is repeated on each line. There is not a NOBOLD parameter.

*FOR[MAT]*

> May be abbreviated to FOR, and allows you to control how subsequent numeric data in the footer is displayed.

*format_spec*

> Is a string that specifies the display format to use for subsequent numeric data in the footer. The format elements you can use here are the same as for the COLUMN command, and are described in Appendix B. It is possible to specify a character format, such as A20, but that has no effect on subsequent character strings.

*text*

> Is any text you want to have in the footer. To be safe, you should enclose this in quotes, but you don't have to as long as your title text doesn't include any

keywords like BOLD or TAB that have meaning to BTITLE. Either single or double quotes may be used. If you need to include a quote as part of your text, use two quote characters back to back.

*variable*

May be one of the variables shown in Table A-1.

*Table A-1. SQL\*Plus System Variables*

| System Variable | Value |
|---|---|
| SQL.PNO | The current page number |
| SQL.LNO | The current line number |
| SQL.RELEASE | The current Oracle release |
| SQL.SQLCODE | The error code returned by the most recent SQL query |
| SQL.USER | The Oracle username of the user running the report |

When using BTITLE, you should start off with one of the keywords such as LEFT, RIGHT, or CENTER. Otherwise, if the first parameter after the command is just text, SQL\*Plus will assume you have used a now-obsolete syntax for this command, and you won't get the results you want.

# *CHANGE*

CHANGE is an editing command that allows you to do a search and replace on the current line in the SQL buffer. The CHANGE command is also used to delete text.

```
C[HANGE] /old_text[/[new_text[/]]
```

where:

*C[HANGE]*

Is the command, which may be abbreviated to C.

*old_text*

Is the text you want to change or delete.

*new_text*

Is the replacement text.

/     The forward slash character is commonly used to delimit the old and new text strings, but any other character may be used as long as it is not a number or a letter, and as long as it is used consistently throughout the command.

CHANGE and all the other editing commands are described in Chapter 2.

# *CLEAR*

The CLEAR command allows you to easily delete all column definitions, break settings, compute definitions, and so forth:

```
CL[EAR] {BRE[AKS]|BUFF[ER]|COL[UMNS]|COMP[UTES]|SCR[EEN]|SQL|TIMI[NG]}
```

where:

*CL[EAR]*

Is the command, which may be abbreviated to CL.

*BRE[AKS]*

Deletes any break setting you may have defined using the BREAK command.

*BUFF[ER]*

Erases the contents of the buffer.

*COL[UMNS]*

Deletes any column definitions you may have made using the COLUMN command.

*COMP[UTES]*

Deletes any computations you may have defined using the COMPUTE command.

*SCR[EEN]*

Clears the screen.

*SQL*

Erases the contents of the SQL buffer.

*TIMI[NG]*

Deletes any timers you may have created using the TIMING command.

The different uses of the CLEAR command are described in various chapters throughout this book. Each option is described in the chapter relevant to that topic. CLEAR COMPUTES, for example, is described in Chapter 3, because that's where the COMPUTE command is explained.

# *COPY*

The COPY command allows you to use SQL*Plus as a conduit for transferring data between two Oracle databases:

```
COPY {FROM connection|TO connection}
    {APPEND|CREATE|INSERT|REPLACE}
    destination_table [(column_list)]
    USING select_statement
```

where:

*COPY*

Is the command.

*FROM/TO*

To use the COPY command, you must be connected to one of the databases involved. It doesn't matter which, but you must be connected either to the database containing the data or the database to which you want to copy the data. If you are connected to the source database, use the TO option to specify the destination database. If you are connected to the target database, use the FROM option to specify the source of the data.

*connection*

Is the login information to use when connecting to the other database. This must be in the typical username/password@connect_string format.

*APP[END]*

Causes SQL\*Plus to insert the copied rows into the destination table, creating it first if necessary.

*CRE[ATE]*

Causes SQL\*Plus to copy the data only if the destination table is a new table. If the destination table already exists, the COPY command will abort.

*INSERT*

Causes SQL\*Plus to insert the copied rows into the destination table only if it already exists. If the destination table is a new table, the COPY command will abort.

*REP[LACE]*

Causes SQL\*Plus to drop the destination table if it currently exists. A new table is then created, and the data is copied.

*destination_table*

Is the name of the table to which you want to copy the data.

*column_list*

Specifies column names to use when the COPY command creates a new destination table. This is a comma-delimited list, and the number of column names must match the number of columns in the SELECT statement.

*select_statement*

Is a SELECT statement that returns the data you want to COPY.

# COLUMN

The COLUMN command is used to format report output for columnar reports. Using this command, you can control column width, the column title, the way numbers are displayed, whether or not long values wrap to a new line, and a host of other things. Chapter 3 discusses this command.

```
COL[UMN] [column_name [ALI[AS] alias|
                       CLE[AR] |
                       FOLD_A[FTER] |
                       FOLD_B[EFORE] |
                       FOR[MAT] format_spec|
                       HEA[DING] heading_text|
                       JUS[TIFY] {LEFT|CENTER|CENTRE|RIGHT}|
                       LIKE source_column_name|
                       NEWL[INE] |
                       NEW_V[ALUE] user_variable|
                       NOPRI[NT] |
                       PRI[NT] |
                       NUL[L] null_text|
                       OLD_V[ALUE] user_variable|
                       ON|
                       OFF|
                       TRU[NCATED] |
                       WOR[D_WRAPPED] |
                       WRA[PPED]...]]
```

where:

*COL[UMN]*

May be abbreviated to COL. Issuing the COLUMN command with no parameters gets you a list of all current column formats.

*column_name*

Is the name of the column you are formatting. If it is a computed column, the expression is the name. If your SELECT statement aliases the column, you must use that alias name here. Issuing the command COLUMN *column_name* with no further parameters causes SQL*Plus to display the current format for that column.

*ALI[AS] alias*

May be abbreviated ALI. ALIAS allows you to specify an alternate name for this column that is meaningful to SQL*Plus. Do not confuse this with the column alias in a SELECT statement.

*alias*

Is an alternate name for the column that may be used in BREAK commands, COMPUTE commands, and other COLUMN commands.

*CLE[AR]*

> May be abbreviated to CLE. CLEAR erases any format settings for the column in question. This puts you back to the way things were before any COLUMN commands were issued for the column.

*FOLD_A[FTER]*

> May be abbreviated to FOLD_A, and causes SQL\*Plus to advance to a new line before displaying the next column. In other words, the output is wrapped after this column prints.

*FOLD_B[EFORE]*

> May be abbreviated to FOLD_B. This is the opposite of FOLD_AFTER, and causes SQL\*Plus to wrap to a new line *before* this column is printed.

*FOR[MAT]*

> May be abbreviated to FOR, and allows you to control how the data for the column is displayed. For text fields, you can control the width. For numeric fields, you can control the width, placement of commas, placement of the dollar sign, and so on.

*format_spec*

> Is a string that specifies the display format for the column. Appendix B describes the format specification elements that may be used with the COLUMN command.

*HEA[DING]*

> May be abbreviated HEA, and allows you to define a heading for the column. The heading text displays at the top of each column, and is redisplayed every time a page break occurs.

*heading_text*

> Is the text you want for the column heading. You should enclose this in quotes, but you don't have to if the heading is a single word. Either single or double quotes may be used. If you need to include a quote as part of your heading, use two quote characters back to back.

*JUS[TIFY]*

> May be abbreviated JUS, and controls where the heading text prints relative to the column width. By default, headings for numeric fields print flush right, and headings for text fields print flush left. This parameter allows you to change that behavior. You must follow this keyword with one of the following: LEFT, RIGHT, CENTER, or CENTRE. LEFT causes the heading to print flush left. RIGHT causes the heading to print flush right. CENTER and CENTRE cause the heading to print centered over the top of the column. Note that this parameter has no effect whatsoever on how the data for the column is displayed.

*LIKE*

Causes the column to be defined with the same format attributes as another column. LIKE must be followed by a column name, and that column becomes the source column.

*source_column_name*

Is the name of the source column used with the LIKE parameter.

*NEWL[INE]*

May be abbreviated NEWL. This is the same as FOLD_BEFORE. It causes SQL*Plus to wrap to a new line before the column is printed.

*NEW_V[ALUE]*

May be abbreviated NEW_V, and causes SQL*Plus to keep a user variable updated with the current value of the column. The user variable is updated whenever the column value changes.

*user_variable*

Is the name of a user variable for use with the NEW_VALUE and OLD_VALUE parameters.

*NOPRI[NT]*

May be abbreviated NOPRI, and tells SQL*Plus not to print the column. NOPRINT is sometimes used when you just want to get a column value into a user variable (see NEW_VALUE), but you don't want it displayed. This is often done when generating master/detail reports.

*PRI[NT]*

May be abbreviated to PRI, and is the opposite of NOPRINT. Use PRINT when you want to turn printing back on for a column.

*NUL[L]*

May be abbreviated NUL, and allows you to specify text to be displayed when the column value is null.

*null_text*

Is the text you want displayed when the column in question is null. As with the heading text, this may optionally be enclosed in quotes.

*OLD_V[ALUE]*

This may be abbreviated to OLD_V, and must be followed by a user variable name. OLD_VALUE works like NEW_VALUE, except that when the column changes, the previous value is stored in a user variable. This is useful when you need to print a value in the page footer of a master/detail report.

*ON*

Causes SQL*Plus to print the column using the format you have specified. This is the default behavior. You don't need to use ON unless you have previously used OFF.

*OFF*

> Disables the format settings for the column. SQL*Plus acts as if you had never issued any COLUMN commands for the column in question.

*TRU[NCATED]*

> May be abbreviated TRU, and causes the column text to be truncated to the width of the column. Longer values are not wrapped.

*WOR[D_WRAPPED]*

> May be abbreviated WOR. WORD_WRAPPED is similar to WRAPPED, but line breaks occur at word boundaries. Words that are longer than the column is wide will still be broken at the column boundary.

*WRA[PPED]*

> May be abbreviated WRA. WRAPPED affects the printing of values that are longer than the column is wide, and causes SQL*Plus to wrap those values to a new line as many times as necessary in order to print the entire value. Line breaks will occur exactly at the column boundary, even in the middle of a word.

# COMPUTE

The COMPUTE command defines summary calculations needed in a report. You can use COMPUTE in conjunction with BREAK to calculate and print column totals, averages, minimum and maximum values, and so on. These calculations are performed by SQL*Plus as the report runs. COMPUTE is a complex command, and must be used in conjunction with the BREAK command in order to get results. See the section "Totals and Subtotals" in Chapter 3 for help on this command.

### Syntax of the COMPUTE command

The syntax for the COMPUTE command looks like this:

```
COMP[UTE] [{AVG|COU[NT]|MAX[IMUM]|MIN[IMUM]|
          NUM[BER]|STD|SUM|VAR[IANCE]}... [LABEL label_text]
          OF column_name...
          ON {group_column_name|ROW|REPORT}...]
```

where:

*COMP[UTE]*

> May be abbreviated to COMP. Entering COMPUTE with no parameters causes SQL*Plus to list all currently defined computations.

*AVG*

> Computes the average of all non-null values for a column. AVG only applies to columns of type NUMBER.

*COU[NT]*

Computes the total number of non-null values for a column. COUNT may be used with columns of any datatype, and may be abbreviated to COU.

*MAX[IMUM]*

Computes the maximum value returned for a column. MAXIMUM may be abbreviated as MAX, and applies to columns of type NUMBER, CHAR, VARCHAR2, NCHAR, and NVARCHAR2.

*MIN[IMUM]*

Computes the minimum value returned for a column. MINIMUM may be abbreviated as MIN, and applies to columns of type NUMBER, CHAR, VARCHAR2, NCHAR, and NVARCHAR2.

*NUM[BER]*

Similar to COUNT, but computes the number of all values, including nulls. This applies to columns of any datatype, and may be abbreviated to NUM.

*STD*

Computes the standard deviation of all non-null values for a column. STD applies only to columns of type NUMBER.

*SUM*

Computes the sum of all non-null values for a column. SUM applies only to columns of type NUMBER.

*VAR[IANCE]*

Computes the variance of all non-null values for a column. VARIANCE applies only to columns of type NUMBER, and may be abbreviated to VAR.

*LABEL*

Allows you to specify a label for the computed value. If possible, this label will be printed to the left of the computed value.

*label_text*

Is the text you want to use as a label when the computed value is printed. This may be enclosed in quotes, either single or double. To embed a quote within the label when that label has been quoted, place two quote characters back to back.

*column_name*

Is the name of the column you are summarizing. If a computed column, the expression is the name. If your SELECT statement aliases the column, you must use that alias name here.

*group_column_name*

Causes SQL*Plus to restart the calculation every time this column changes. Typically, the report is sorted or grouped by this column, and the computed value is printed once for each distinct value of the group column.

*ROW*

Causes the computation to be performed once for each row returned by the query.

*REPORT*

Causes the computation to be performed at the end of the report and to include values from all rows. REPORT is used for grand totals.

# CONNECT

The CONNECT command is used to change your database connection, log in as a different user, or to connect to the database in an administrative mode. Chapter 2 describes CONNECT for normal users. Chapter 10 describes the administrative options.

```
CONN[ECT] [username[/password][@connect]|/|] [AS {SYSOPER|SYSDBA}]|[INTERNAL]
```

where:

*CONN[ECT]*

May be abbreviated CONN.

*username*

Is your database username.

*password*

Is your database password.

*connect*

Is the connect string, or host string, telling SQL\*Plus the database to which you want to connect.

/    Use a forward slash instead of your username, password, and connect string when you want to connect to a local database using operating-system authentication.

*AS*  Tells SQL\*Plus you are connecting in an administrative role.

*SYSOPER*

Tells SQL\*Plus you are connecting as an operator.

*SYSDBA*

Tells SQL\*Plus you are connecting as a database administrator.

*INTERNAL*

Tells SQL\*Plus you want to connect internally.

# *DEFINE*

The DEFINE command allows you to create a user variable (or substitution variable), and to assign it a value. DEFINE may also be used to list the value of a particular variable, or of all variables. DEFINE is discussed in Chapter 4.

```
DEF[INE] [variable_name [= text]]
```

where:

*DEF[INE]*

> Is the command, which may be abbreviated to DEF. Entering DEFINE by itself causes SQL*Plus to display list of all currently defined user variables.

*variable_name*

> Is the name of the variable you want to create. Issue the command with only a variable name, and SQL*Plus will display the current contents of that variable, if it exists.

*text*

> Is the text you want to assign to that variable. This may optionally be enclosed by single or double quotes, which you should use any time the value contains spaces or any other nonalphabetic character.

# *DEL*

The DEL command is an editing command used to delete the current line from the buffer:

```
DEL [{b|*|LAST}[ {e|*|LAST}]]
```

where:

*DEL*

> Is the command, which may not be abbreviated.

*b*  Is a line number representing the beginning of a range of lines to delete. If no ending line number is specified, then only this one line will be deleted.

*e*  Is a line number representing the end of a range of lines to delete.

*   The asterisk refers to the current line number. It may be used in place of a line number to mark either the beginning or the end (or both) of a range of lines to be deleted.

*LAST*

> LAST functions similarly to *, but refers to the last line in the buffer.

DEL, and all the other editing commands, are described in Chapter 2.

# DESCRIBE

The DESCRIBE command is used to display information about a table, a view, an Oracle8 object type, a stored package, a stored procedure, or a stored function. When used against a table or view, DESCRIBE returns a list of columns, including datatypes and lengths. When used against an Oracle8 object type or a stored package, DESCRIBE returns a list of procedures, functions, and variables that are accessible from outside the package or type. Parameters for each function, procedure, and method are listed as well. When used against a stored procedure or function, DESCRIBE returns a list of parameters. In the case of a function, DESCRIBE displays the return type as well. DESCRIBE is discussed in Chapter 6, *Exploring Your Database*.

```
DESC[RIBE]  [schema.]object_name[@database_link_name]
```

where:

*DESC[RIBE]*

Is the command, which may be abbreviated to DESC.

*schema*

Is the name of the object's owner. This defaults to your username.

*object_name*

Is the name of the object, often a table or a view, that you want to describe. You can describe any of the following: a table, a view, a stored procedure, a stored function, a stored package, or an Oracle8 object type.

*database_link_name*

Is the name of a database link pointing to the database where the object exists. You only need to use this if the object you want to describe exists in a database other than the one to which you are currently connected. Your DBA can help create a database link if you need one.

# DISCONNECT

The DISCONNECT command closes your database connection without terminating SQL\*Plus. DISCONNECT is discussed in Chapter 2.

```
DISC[ONNECT]
```

where:

*DISC[ONNECT]*

May be abbreviated to DISC.

# *EDIT*

The EDIT command allows you to invoke an external editor to edit the contents of the buffer, or to edit the contents of an operating system file:

```
ED[IT] [filename]
```

where:

*ED[IT]*

Is the command, which may be abbreviated to ED. The EDIT command with no parameters allows you to edit the current contents of the buffer.

*filename*

Specifies an external file to edit instead of the buffer. The filename may include a path and an extension.

EDIT, and all the other editing commands, are described in Chapter 2.

# *EXECUTE*

The EXECUTE command allows you to execute a single PL/SQL statement, and is discussed in Chapter 2.

```
EXEC[UTE] statement
```

where:

*EXEC[UTE]*

May be abbreviated to EXEC.

*statement*

Is the PL/SQL statement you want to execute.

# *EXIT*

The EXIT command is used to terminate a SQL*Plus session and return to the operating system:

```
EXIT [SUCCESS|FAILURE|WARNING|value|user_variable|:bind_variable]
    [COMMIT|ROLLBACK]
```

where:

*SUCCESS*

Returns a success status. The exact value of success is operating-system-dependent. This is the default setting, and applies if no other return value is specified.

*WARNING*

Returns a warning status. The exact value of a warning is operating-system-dependent.

*FAILURE*

Returns a failure status. The value of a failure is operating-system-dependent.

*value*

Returns an arbitrary value as the status.

*user_variable*

Returns the value of the specified user variable as the status. You can also specify SQL.SQLCODE here, to return the status of the most recently executed SQL statement.

*:bind_variable*

Returns the value of the specified bind variable as the status.

*COMMIT*

Causes SQL\*Plus to automatically commit before exiting.

*ROLLBACK*

Causes SQL\*Plus to automatically roll back any open transaction before exiting.

# GET

The GET command reads an SQL statement from a file and loads it into the buffer.

```
GET filename [LIS[T]|NOL[IST]]
```

where:

*GET*

Is the command.

*filename*

Is the name of the file containing the SQL statement you want to load. This can be any filename, including path and extension, that your operating system recognizes.

*LI[ST]*

Causes SQL\*Plus to display the buffer after loading the file. This is the default.

*NOL[IST]*

Causes SQL\*Plus to load the file without displaying it.

GET, and all the other editing commands, are described in Chapter 2.

# HELP

Use the HELP command to get help on SQL*Plus commands, SQL commands, PL/SQL statements, and other topics. HELP is described in Chapter 2.

```
HELP [topic]
```

where:

*HELP*

> May not be abbreviated.

*topic*

> Is the help topic you want to read about. Most SQL commands, SQL*Plus commands and PL/SQL statements are valid help topics. There are others as well. Entering HELP MENU will get you a complete list of valid topics.

# HOST

The HOST command allows you to execute an operating-system command or invoke the command interpreter so you can execute several such commands.

```
HO[ST] [os_command]
```

where:

*HO[ST]*

> Is the command, which may be abbreviated to HO. Issuing HOST without specifying a command will get you a command prompt from which you may enter several commands. Under Windows 95 and NT, for example, a DOS window will be opened.

*os_command*

> Is the operating-system command you wish to execute. SQL*Plus will execute this one command for you, and then you will be returned to the SQL*Plus prompt.

# INPUT

Inserts one or more lines of text into the buffer. The lines are inserted after the current line.

```
I[NPUT] [text]
```

where:

*I[NPUT]*

> Is the command, which may be abbreviated to I. When you issue the INSERT command with no text after it, SQL*Plus puts you in insert mode, allowing you

to type as many lines as you like. These are all inserted into the buffer following the current line. Press ENTER on a blank line to terminate insert mode.

*text*

Is the text you want to insert. Use this if you are only inserting one line.

INPUT, and all the other editing commands, are described in Chapter 2.

# *LIST*

The LIST command is an editing command used to list the current line from the buffer.

    L[IST] [{b|*|LAST}[ {e|*|LAST}]]

where:

*L[IST]*

Is the command, which may be abbreviated to L. LIST by itself will cause SQL\*Plus to display all lines in the buffer.

*b*    Is a line number representing the beginning of a range of lines to list. If no ending line number is specified, only this one line will be listed.

*e*    Is a line number representing the end of a range of lines to list.

*    The asterisk refers to the current line number. It may be used in place of a line number to mark either the beginning or the end (or both) of a range of lines to be list.

*LAST*

LAST functions similarly to *, but refers to the last line in the buffer.

LIST, and all the other editing commands, are described in Chapter 2.

# *PASSWORD*

The PASSWORD command allows you to change your Oracle password using SQL\*Plus, and is described in Chapter 2.

    PASSW[ORD] [username]

where:

*PASSW[ORD]*

May be abbreviated to PASSW.

*username*

Is the user whose password you want to change. Usually only database administrators (DBAs) can change passwords for other users. You do not need to supply a username if you are changing your own password.

# PAUSE

The PAUSE command is most commonly used from script files, and prompts the user to press the ENTER key before the script can continue:

> PAU[SE] [*pause_message*]

where:

*PAU[SE]*

> Is the command, which may be abbreviated to PAU.

*pause_message*

> Is an optional message you want displayed to the user. It's generally a good idea to include a message telling the user to press ENTER, lest they think the system has locked up on them.

# PRINT

The PRINT command is used to display the value of a bind variable. One of its most useful applications is to retrieve and print data from a REFCURSOR variable which has been opened within a PL/SQL block or returned from a PL/SQL procedure. PRINT is discussed in Chapter 7.

> PRI[NT] [*bind_variable_name*]

where:

*PRI[NT]*

> Is the command, which may be abbreviated to PRI.

*bind_variable_name*

> Is the name of the bind variable you want to print. If you omit a name, the values of all bind variables are printed.

# PROMPT

The PROMPT command is used to display a message for the user to see. See Chapter 4 for more information.

> PRO[MPT] *text_to_be_displayed*

where:

*PRO[MPT]*

> Is the command, which may be abbreviated to PRO.

*text_to_be_displayed*

Is whatever text you want displayed to the user. This should not be a quoted string. If you include quotes, they will appear in the output.

# QUIT

The QUIT command functions the same way as the EXIT command. It terminates a SQL\*Plus session and returns you to the operating system.

```
QUIT [SUCCESS|FAILURE|WARNING|value|user_variable|:bind_variable]
     [COMMIT|ROLLBACK]
```

where:

*SUCCESS*

Returns a success status. The exact value of success is operating-system-dependent. This is the default setting, and it applies if no other return value is specified.

*WARNING*

Returns a warning status. The exact value of a warning is operating-system-dependent.

*FAILURE*

Returns a failure status. The value of failure is operating-system-dependent.

*value*

Returns an arbitrary value as the status.

*user_variable*

Returns the value of the specified user variable as the status. You can also specify SQL.SQLCODE here, to return the status of the most recently executed SQL statement.

*:bind_variable*

Returns the value of the specified bind variable as the status.

*COMMIT*

Causes SQL\*Plus to automatically commit before exiting.

*ROLLBACK*

Causes SQL\*Plus to automatically roll back any open transaction before exiting.

# *RECOVER*

The RECOVER command initiates media recovery on a database, a tablespace, or a datafile. Chapter 10 provides an explanation of how recovery works. You must be connected as SYSDBA, SYSOPER, or INTERNAL in order to use this command.

```
RECOVER [DATABASE [[UNTIL {CANCEL|CHANGE system_change_number|TIME date_time}
                  [USING BACKUP CONTROLFILE]
                  [PARALLEL([DEGREE {num_of_procs|DEFAULT}
                  |INSTANCES {num_of_inst|DEFAULT}]...)
                  |NOPARALLEL]
                  |TABLESPACE tablespace_name [,tablespace_name...]
                  [PARALLEL([DEGREE {num_of_procs|DEFAULT}
                  |INSTANCES {num_of_inst|DEFAULT}]...)
                  |NOPARALLEL]
                  |DATAFILE datafile_name [,datafile_name...]
                  [PARALLEL([DEGREE {num_of_procs|DEFAULT}
                  |INSTANCES {num_of_inst|DEFAULT}]...)
                  |NOPARALLEL]
```

where:

*RECOVER DATABASE*

Initiates media recovery on the entire database. The database must be mounted, but not open.

*RECOVER TABLESPACE tablespace_name*

Initiates media recovery on the specified tablespace or list of tablespaces. A maximum of 16 tablespaces may be recovered with one command. The tablespace(s) must be offline, but the database must be mounted and open.

*RECOVER DATAFILE datafile_name*

Initiates media recovery on the specified datafile or list of datafiles. Unlike with tablespaces, there is no limit on the number of datafiles you can recover with one command. The datafiles to be recovered must be offline. As long as none of the datafiles are part of the SYSTEM tablespace, the database may remain open.

*UNTIL CANCEL*

Allows you to recover one log file at a time, with the opportunity to cancel after each log file has been processed.

*UNTIL CHANGE system_change_number*

Performs an incomplete recovery based on the system change number. Each transaction in an Oracle database has an assigned number. The UNTIL CHANGE option causes all transactions to be recovered up through the one *preceding* the system change number you specify. The transaction with the specified number is not recovered.

*UNTIL TIME date_time*

Similar to UNTIL CHANGE, but performs a time-based recovery. All transactions that were completed prior to the time specified are recovered.

*USING BACKUP CONTROLFILE*

Causes recovery to use a backup control file.

*PARALLEL*

Causes recovery to be done in parallel.

*NOPARALLEL*

Prevents recovery from being done in parallel.

*DEGREE {num_of_procs | DEFAULT}*

Controls the number of recovery processes running in parallel for each instance. You may specify a number or use the keyword DEFAULT. DEFAULT causes the number of processes to equal twice the number of datafiles being recovered.

*INSTANCES {num_of_procs | DEFAULT}*

Controls the number of instances that may be used in a parallel recovery. You may specify a number or use the keyword DEFAULT. The number of instances used when DEFAULT is specified is operating system–specific.

# REMARK

The REMARK command is used to place comments in a SQL\*Plus script. See Chapter 4. In addition to REMARK, comments may set off with /\*...\*/, or by preceding each comment line with a double hyphen (--).

```
REM[ARK] comment_text
```

where:

*REM[ARK]*

Is the command, which may be abbreviated to REM.

*comment_text*

Is your comment.

# REPFOOTER

The REPFOOTER command defines a report footer. Report footers print on the last page of a report, after the last detail line and before the bottom title. See Chapter 3 for more information.

```
REPF[OOTER]  [OFF|ON]|
             [COL x|
             S[KIP] x|
```

```
TAB x|
LE[FT]|
CE[NTER]|
R[IGHT]|
BOLD|
FOR[MAT] format_spec|
text|
variable...]
```

where:

*REPF[OOTER]*

> May be abbreviated REPF. Issuing the REPFOOTER command with no parameters causes SQL*Plus to display the current report footer setting.

*OFF*

> Turns the report footer off, but does not erase its definition. You can turn it back on again with ON.

*ON*

> Turns on printing of report footers.

*COL x*

> Causes any footer text following this parameter to print at the specified column position.

*S[KIP] x*

> May be abbreviated to S, and inserts the specified number of line breaks before printing any subsequent footer text.

*TAB x*

> TAB is similar to COL, but moves you the specified number of columns relative to the current position. Negative numbers move you backwards. TAB has nothing whatsoever to do with tab characters.

*LE[FT]*

> May be abbreviated LE, and causes subsequent footer text to be printed beginning at the leftmost column of the current footer line.

*CE[NTER]*

> May be abbreviated CE, and causes subsequent footer text to be centered within the current line. The LINESIZE setting controls the line width.

*R[IGHT]*

> May be abbreviated R, and causes subsequent footer text to be printed flush right. The LINESIZE setting controls where SQL*Plus thinks the right end of the line is.

*BOLD*

> Makes a footer "bold" by printing it three times. Only text following the BOLD command is repeated on each line. There is not a NOBOLD parameter.

*FOR[MAT]*

> May be abbreviated to FOR, and allows you to control how subsequent numeric data in the footer is displayed.

*format_spec*

> Is a string that specifies the display format to use for subsequent numeric data in the footer. The format elements you can use here are the same as for the COLUMN command, and are described in Appendix B. It is possible to specify a character format, such as A20, but that has no effect on subsequent character strings.

*text*

> Is any text you want to have in the footer. To be safe, you should enclose this in quotes, but you don't have to as long as your title text doesn't include any keywords like BOLD or TAB that have meaning to REPFOOTER. Either single or double quotes may be used. If you need to include a quote as part of your text, use two quote characters back to back.

*variable*

> May be one of the variables shown in Table A-1, which is shown under the BTITLE command.

# *REPHEADER*

The REPHEADER command defines a report header. Report headers print on the first page of a report, after the page title and before the first detail line. See Chapter 3 for more information.

```
REPH[EADER]  [OFF|ON]|
             [COL x|
             S[KIP] x|
             TAB x|
             LE[FT]|
             CE[NTER]|
             R[IGHT]|
             BOLD|
             FOR[MAT] format_spec|
             text|
             variable...]
```

where:

*REPH[EADER]*

> May be abbreviated REPH. Issuing the REPHEADER command with no parameters causes SQL\*Plus to display the current report header setting.

*OFF*

Turns the report header off, but does not erase its definition. You can turn it back on again with ON.

*ON*

Turns on printing of report headers.

*COL x*

Causes any header text following this parameter to print at the specified column position.

*S[KIP] x*

May be abbreviated to S, and inserts the specified number of line breaks before printing any subsequent footer text.

*TAB x*

TAB is similar to COL, but moves you the specified number of columns relative to the current position. Negative numbers move you backwards. TAB has nothing whatsoever to do with tab characters.

*LE[FT]*

May be abbreviated LE, and causes subsequent footer text to be printed beginning at the leftmost column of the current footer line.

*CE[NTER]*

May be abbreviated CE, and causes subsequent header text to be centered within the current line. The LINESIZE setting controls the line width.

*R[IGHT]*

May be abbreviated R, and causes subsequent header text to be printed flush right. The LINESIZE setting controls where SQL*Plus thinks the right end of the line is.

*BOLD*

Makes a footer "bold" by printing it three times. Only text following the BOLD command is repeated on each line. There is not a NOBOLD parameter.

*FOR[MAT]*

May be abbreviated to FOR, and allows you to control how subsequent numeric data in the header is displayed.

*format_spec*

Is a string that specifies the display format to use for subsequent numeric data in the header. The format elements you can use here are the same as for the COLUMN command, and are described in Appendix B. It is possible to specify a character format, such as A20, but that has no effect on subsequent character strings.

*text*

> Is any text you want to have in the header. To be safe, you should enclose this in quotes, but you don't have to as long as your title text doesn't include any keywords like BOLD or TAB that have meaning to REPHEADER. Either single or double quotes may be used. If you need to include a quote as part of your text, use two quote characters back to back.

*variable*

> May be one of the variables shown in Table A-1, which is shown under the BTITLE command.

# *RUN*

The RUN command displays and then executes the command currently in the SQL buffer.

    R[UN]

where:

*R[UN]*

> Is the command, which may be abbreviated to R. No parameters are necessary.

RUN, and all the other editing commands, are described in Chapter 2.

# *SAVE*

The SAVE command writes the contents of the SQL buffer to an operating-system file:

    SAV[E] filename [CRE[ATE]|REP[LACE]|APP[END]]

where:

*SAV[E]*

> Is the command, which may be abbreviated to SAV.

*filename*

> Is the filename, including the path and extension, to which you want to write the buffer contents.

*CRE[ATE]*

> Causes the operation to succeed only if the file does not already exist. This is the default setting.

*REP[LACE]*

> Overwrites any existing file of the same name.

*APP[END]*

   Appends the contents of the buffer to the file.

SAVE, and all the other editing commands, are described in Chapter 2.

# *SET*

The SET command is used to change the value of the many internal settings that
affect the operation of SQL*Plus:

```
SET APPI[NFO] {OFF|ON|app_text}
    ARRAY[SIZE] array_size
    AUTO[COMMIT] {OFF|ON|IMMEDIATE|statement_count}
    AUTOP[RINT] {OFF|ON}
    AUTORECOVERY {OFF|ON}
    AUTOT[RACE] {OFF|ON|TRACE[ONLY]} [EXP[LAIN]] [STAT[ISTICS]]
    BLO[CKTERMINATOR] block_term_char
    BUF[FER] {buffer_name|SQL}
    CLOSECUR[SOR] {OFF|ON}
    CMDS[EP] {OFF|ON|separator_char
    COLSEP column_separator
    COM[PATIBILITY] {V7|V8|NATIVE}
    CON[CAT] {OFF|ON|concat_char}
    COPYC[OMMIT] batch_count
    COPYTYPECHECK {OFF|ON}
    DEF[INE] {OFF|ON|prefix_char}
    DOC[UMENT] {ON|OFF}
    ECHO {OFF|ON}
    EDITF[ILE] edit_filename
    EMB[EDDED] {ON|OFF}
    ESC[APE] {OFF|ON|escape_char}
    FEED[BACK] {OFF|ON|row_threshold}
    FLAGGER {OFF|ENTRY|INTERMED[IATE]|FULL}
    FLU[SH] {OFF|ON}
    HEA[DING] [ON|OFF]
    HEADS[EP] heading_separator
    INSTANCE [service_name|LOCAL]
    LIN[ESIZE] line_width
    LOBOF[FSET] offset
    LOGSOURCE logpath
    LONG long_length
    LONGC[HUNKSIZE] size
    MAXD[ATA] max_row_width
    NEWP[AGE] {lines_to_print|NONE}
    NULL null_text
    NUMF[ORMAT] format_spec
    NUM[WIDTH] width
    PAGES[IZE] lines_on_page
    PAU[SE] {ON|OFF|pause_message}
    RECSEP {WR[APPED]|EA[CH]|OFF}
    RECSEPCHAR separator_char
    SCAN {OFF|ON}
```

```
SERVEROUT[PUT] {OFF|ON}
                [SIZE buffer_size]
                [FOR[MAT] {WRA[PPED]|WOR[D_WRAPPED]|TRU[NCATED]}]
SHIFT[INOUT] {VIS[IBLE]|INV[ISIBLE]}
SHOW[MODE] {ON|OFF|BOTH}
SPACE num_of_spaces
SQLBLANKLINES {OFF|ON}
SQLC[ASE] {MIXED|UPPER|LOWER}
SQLCO[NTINUE] continuation_prompt
SQLN[UMBER] {OFF|ON}
SQLPRE[FIX] prefix_char
SQLP[ROMPT] prompt_text
SQLT[ERMINATOR] {OFF|ON|term_char}
SUF[FIX] extension
TAB {OFF|ON}
TERM[OUT] {OFF|ON}
TI[ME] {OFF|ON}
TIMI[NG] {OFF|ON}
TRIM[OUT] {ON|OFF}
TRIMS[POOL] {ON|OFF}
TRU[NCATE] {OFF|ON}
UND[ERLINE] {underline_char | {ON|OFF}}
VER[IFY] {OFF|ON}
WRA[P] {ON|OFF}
```

Please see Chapter 11, *Customizing Your SQL\*Plus Environment,* for detailed information about each of these settings.

# SHOW

The SHOW command allows you to look at the current state of your SQL\*Plus environment. You can use it to display the current value of any setting controlled by the SET command. SHOW may also be used to look at current page titles, page footers, and so forth.

```
SHO[W] setting
       ALL
       BTI[TLE]
       ERR[ORS] [{FUNCTION|PROCEDURE|PACKAGE|PACKAGE BODY|
                 TRIGGER|TYPE|TYPE BODY|VIEW} [owner.]object_name]
       LNO
       PARAMETER[S] [parameter_name]
       PNO
       REL[EASE]
       REPF[OOTER]
       REPH[EADER]
       SGA
       SPOO[L]
       SQLCODE
       TTI[TLE]
       USER
```

where:

*SHO[W]*

Is the command, which may be abbreviated to SHO.

*setting*

Is any one of the settings you can set using the SET command.

*ALL*

Shows everything, except for errors and the SGA.

*BTI[TLE]*

Displays the current page footer.

*ERR[ORS]*

Displays an error listing for a stored object. The command SHOW ERRORS by itself causes the error listing for the most recently created object to be displayed. You can get the error listing for a specific object by specifying the object type (function, procedure, and so forth) and the object name.

*FUNCTION | PROCEDURE | PACKAGE | PACKAGE BODY | TRIGGER | TYPE | TYPE BODY | VIEW*

Used with SHOW ERRORS to specify the object type of interest. This is only necessary if you are specifying the name of the object.

*[owner.]object_name*

Used with SHOW ERRORS to name the object for which you want to display an error listing.

*LNO*

Displays the current line number.

*PARAMETER[S] [parameter_name]*

Displays the current value of one or more initialization parameters. Chapter 10 provides detailed examples of SHOW PARAMETERS in use.

*PNO*

Displays the current page number.

*REL[EASE]*

Displays the release number (the version) of the Oracle database to which you are connected.

*REPF[OOTER]*

Displays the current report footer.

*REPH[EADER]*

Displays the current report header.

*SGA*

Displays information about the current state of the System Global Area. See Chapter 10 for more information about this option.

*SPOO[L]*

Tells you whether or not output is currently being spooled to a file.

*SQLCODE*

Displays the SQL code returned by the most recent SQL statement.

*TTI[TLE]*

Displays the current page title.

*USER*

Displays the current username.

# SHUTDOWN

The SHUTDOWN command allows you to close a database and stop an Oracle instance. Chapter 10 discusses this command. In order to use SHUTDOWN, you must be connected as SYSDBA, SYSOPER, or INTERNAL.

```
SHUTDOWN [NORMAL|IMMEDIATE|TRANSACTIONAL|ABORT]
```

where:

*SHUTDOWN*

Is the command, which may not be abbreviated.

*NORMAL*

Causes a normal shutdown to take place. New users are blocked from con-necting. The database remains open until all currently connected users volun-tarily disconnect. When the last user disconnects, the database files are closed, the database is dismounted, and the instance is stopped.

*IMMEDIATE*

Causes users to be summarily disconnected when their current SQL statement completes execution. Users not in the middle of executing a statement are dis-connected immediately. As each remaining user's currently executing SQL statement completes, she is forcibly disconnected from the database. Any open transactions are rolled back, the database files are closed, the database is dis-mounted, and the instance is stopped.

*TRANSACTIONAL*

A compromise between NORMAL and IMMEDIATE. Users are allowed to fin-ish their current transactions. As each user completes his current transaction, he is forcibly disconnected. When the last user disconnects, the database is closed, then dismounted, and finally the instance is stopped.

*ABORT*

Is tantamount to pulling the plug on the server. All background processes are immediately aborted. Users are summarily disconnected. No rollback is done on open transactions, and dirty buffers are not written back to the disk. Crash recovery occurs the next time you start the database. This is the only shutdown option that does not leave the database files in a consistent state.

# SPOOL

The SPOOL command is used to write output to a text file. You must use this if you are going to print a report. The only way to print a report is to spool it to a file, then print that file. See Chapter 3 for an example of SPOOL being used to generate a report file. SPOOL may also be used to generate a new file of SQL commands to be executed. Chapter 7 shows you how to take advantage of that powerful technique.

```
SP[OOL] file_name|OFF|OUT
```

where:

*SP[OOL]*

May be abbreviated to SP.

*file_name*

Is the name of the file to which you want to write the report. The default extension depends on the operating system, and will be either LST or LIS. Under Windows 95 and NT, it is LST. A path may be specified as part of the filename.

*OFF*

Turns spooling off. You must have turned spooling on before you can turn it off.

*OUT*

Turns spooling off, and prints the file on the default printer. This option is not available in the Windows versions of SQL*Plus.

# START

The START command functions the same way as the @ command, and is used to execute a SQL*Plus script file:

```
STA[RT] script_file [argument...]
```

where:

*STA[RT]*

Is the command, which may be abbreviated to STA.

*script_file*

> Is the name of the file you want to execute, and may include the path and the extension. The default extension is SQL. If you do not specify a path, SQL\*Plus will look for the file first in the current working directory, then search each directory listed in the SQLPATH environment variable. See Chapter 11 for information about customizing the search path.

*argument*

> Is an argument you wish to pass to the script. You may pass as many arguments as you like. Arguments must be separated from each other by at least one space. Arguments may be enclosed in quotes, and should be if they contain spaces. Either single or double quotes may be used, at your discretion. Your script may reference the first argument as &1, the second as &2, and so forth.

# *STARTUP*

The STARTUP command allows you to start an Oracle instance and open a database. Chapter 10 discusses this command. In order to use STARTUP, you must be connected as SYSDBA, SYSOPER, or INTERNAL.

```
STARTUP [FORCE] [RESTRICT]
        [PFILE=parameter_filename]
        [MOUNT [OPEN [RECOVER]] [database_name]]
        [[EXCLUSIVE|PARALLEL|SHARED] [RETRY]] | [NOMOUNT]
```

where:

*STARTUP*

> Is the command, which may not be abbreviated.

*FORCE*

> Forces the instance to start. If the instance is currently running, then FORCE will cause the equivalent of a SHUTDOWN ABORT to be done first; then the instance will be restarted.

*RESTRICT*

> Opens the database in *restricted session* mode. Only users with the RESTRICTED SESSION system privilege will be allowed to connect.

*PFILE=parameter_filename*

> Tells SQL\*Plus to use the specified parameter file (initialization file) when starting the instance. You may specify a path with the filename.

SQL*Plus reads the parameter file, not the Oracle instance. The path to the parameter file must be relative to the machine running SQL*Plus. This matters, for example, if you are using SQL*Plus on a PC and connecting remotely to an instance on a server in order to start it.

*MOUNT*

Causes the database to be mounted, but not opened. The instance will be started. The control file will be opened, but none of the other database files will be opened. The MOUNT stage is the one between NOMOUNT and OPEN.

*OPEN*

Causes the database to be mounted, then opened for normal operation.

*RECOVER*

Tells Oracle to perform media recovery, if necessary. If no recovery is necessary, the database is opened as normal. If recovery is necessary, it proceeds automatically. You will be prompted for any needed log files that cannot be found. A failed recovery leaves the database mounted, but not opened.

*database_name*

Is a name you specify, which becomes the name of the database. This value overrides the DB_NAME parameter in the initialization file.

*EXCLUSIVE*

Causes the database to be opened, or mounted, exclusively by the current instance. No other instances may share it. This is the default setting, and is used if neither SHARE nor PARALLEL is specified.

*PARALLEL*

Causes the database to be opened, or mounted, in such a way as to allow multiple instances to access it simultaneously. This option cannot be used if the SINGLE_PROCESS parameter in the initialization file is set to TRUE.

*SHARED*

SHARED has the same effect as PARALLEL.

*RETRY*

Is provided for use when opening a database in parallel mode. RETRY affects the behavior of the instance when the database open fails because some other instance is performing recovery operations. When RETRY is specified, the instance will retry the open every five seconds until recovery is complete and the database is opened.

*NOMOUNT*

Causes an instance to be started, but no database is mounted or opened.

# STORE

STORE is a relatively new addition to the SQL*Plus command set. It generates a file of SET commands based on the current state of those settings. This file can be used after those settings have been changed to reset everything back to a known state.

```
STORE SET filename [CRE[ATE]|REP[LACE]|APP[END]]
```

where:

*STORE*

Is the command.

*SET*

Is an option indicating what you want to store. Currently, the only option available is SET.

*filename*

Is the name of the file, including the path and extension, to which you want to write the SET commands.

*CRE[ATE]*

Causes the command to fail if the file already exists.

*REP[LACE]*

Causes SQL*Plus to overwrite any existing file with the same name.

*APP[END]*

Causes the SET commands to be appended to an existing file.

# TIMING

The TIMING command lets you start, stop, or display the value of a timer. Timers let you measure elapsed time, and are described in Chapter 8, *Tuning and Timing*.

```
TIMI[NG] [START [timer_name ] | SHOW | STOP]
```

where:

*TIMI[NG]*

Is the command, and may be abbreviated to TIMI.

*START [timer_name]*

Starts a new timer, and optionally gives it the name you provide.

*SHOW*

Shows the current value of the most recently started timer.

*STOP*

Stops the most recently started timer, shows its current value, then deletes it.

# *TTITLE*

Use the TTITLE command to define page titles for a report. Chapter 3 discusses TTITLE, and has several examples. Also see the BTITLE command. TTITLE and BTITLE work the same way.

```
TTI[TLE] [OFF|ON]|
         [COL x|
         S[KIP] x|
         TAB x|
         LE[FT]|
         CE[NTER]|
         R[IGHT]|
         BOLD|
         FOR[MAT] format_spec|
         text|
         variable...]
```

where:

*TTI[TLE]*

May be abbreviated TTI. Issuing the TTITLE command with no parameters causes SQL*Plus to display the current top title setting.

*OFF*

Turns the page title off, but does not erase its definition. You can turn it back on again with ON.

*ON*

Turns on printing of page titles. The default title, if you do not specify another, will be the current date, the page number, and all or part of the SELECT statement.

*COL x*

Causes any title text following this parameter to print at the specified column position.

*S[KIP] x*

May be abbreviated to S, and inserts the specified number of line breaks before printing any subsequent title text.

*TAB x*

TAB is similar to COL, but moves you the specified number of columns relative to the current position. Negative numbers move you backwards. TAB has nothing whatsoever to do with tab characters.

*LE[FT]*

May be abbreviated LE, and causes subsequent title text to be printed beginning at the leftmost column of the current title line.

*CE[NTER]*

> May be abbreviated CE, and causes subsequent title text to be centered within the current line. The LINESIZE setting controls the line width.

*R[IGHT]*

> May be abbreviated R, and causes subsequent title text to be printed flush right. The LINESIZE setting controls where SQL\*Plus thinks the right end of the line is.

*BOLD*

> Makes your title "bold" by printing it three times. Only title text following the BOLD command is repeated on each line. There is no NOBOLD parameter.

*FOR[MAT]*

> May be abbreviated to FOR, and allows you to control how subsequent numeric data in the title is displayed.

*format_spec*

> Is a string that specifies the display format to use for subsequent numeric data in the title. The format elements you can use here are the same as for the COLUMN command, and are described in Appendix B. It is possible to specify a character format, such as A20, but that has no effect on subsequent character strings.

*text*

> Is any text you want to have in the title. To be safe, you should enclose this in quotes, but you don't have to as long as your title text doesn't include any keywords like BOLD or TAB that have meaning to TTITLE. Either single or double quotes may be used. If you need to include a quote as part of your text, use two quote characters back to back.

*variable*

> May be one of the system variables maintained by SQL\*Plus. See Table A-1, in the section on the BTITLE command, for a list of these variables.

When using TTITLE, you should start off with one of the keywords such as LEFT, RIGHT, or CENTER. Otherwise, if the first parameter after the command is just text, SQL\*Plus will assume you have used a now obsolete syntax for this command, and you won't get the results you want.

# UNDEFINE

UNDEFINE is the opposite of DEFINE, and erases a user variable definition. UNDEFINE is discussed in Chapter 4.

```
UNDEF[INE] variable_name [ variable_name...]
```

where:

*UNDEF[INE]*

Is the command, which may be abbreviated to UNDEF.

*variable_name*

Is the name of a user variable to delete. You can delete several variables with one command by listing them out separated by spaces.

# *VARIABLE*

The VARIABLE command is used to declare bind variables. Bind variables are discussed in Chapter 7. They are real variables that can be used within a PL/SQL block or SQL statement.

```
VAR[IABLE] var_name data_type
```

where:

*VAR[IABLE]*

Is the command, which may be abbreviated to VAR.

*var_name*

Is whatever name you want to give the variable. A variable name must start with a letter, but after that, the name may contain any combination of letters, digits, underscores, pound signs, and dollar signs. 30 characters is the maximum length for a variable name.

*data_type*

Is the datatype of the variable. The following datatypes are allowed:

*NUMBER*

This results in a floating-point number, and is the same as a NUMBER variable in PL/SQL or a NUMBER column in a table. Unlike PL/SQL, SQL*Plus does not let you specify a length or a precision, so a declaration like NUMBER (9,2) would not be allowed.

*CHAR [(length)]*

Results in a fixed-length character string. Length is optional. If it's omitted, you get a one-character string.

*NCHAR [(length)]*

Results in a fixed-length character string in the national character set. Length is optional. If it's omitted, you get a one-character string.

*VARCHAR2 (length)*

Results in a variable-length character string.

*NVARCHAR2 (length)*

> Results in a variable-length character string using the national language character set.

*CLOB*

> Results in a character large object variable.

*NCLOB*

> Results in a character large object variable using the national language character set.

*REFCURSOR*

> Gives you a cursor variable you can use to return the results of a SQL query from PL/SQL to SQL\*Plus.

# WHENEVER

The WHENEVER command controls the behavior of SQL\*Plus when an operating-system or SQL error occurs, and is discussed in Chapter 7. You can choose between having SQL\*Plus exit immediately or continue on whenever an error occurs. You can also choose whether to automatically COMMIT or ROLLBACK in the event of an error. Finally, if you decide to abort in the event of an error, you can pass a value back to the operating system. If you are calling SQL\*Plus from an operating-system script, you can use this return value to determine that script's next course of action.

```
WHENEVER {OSERROR|SQLERROR}
         {EXIT [SUCCESS|FAILURE|value|:bind_variable|]
               [COMMIT|ROLLBACK]
         |CONTINUE [COMMIT|ROLLBACK|NONE]}
```

where:

*WHENEVER OSERROR*

> Use this form of the command to tell SQL\*Plus what to do in the event of an operating-system error.

*WHENEVER SQLERROR*

> Use this form of the command to tell SQL\*Plus what to do in the event that an error is returned from a SQL statement or PL/SQL block.

*EXIT SUCCESS*

> Exit with a success status. The exact value of success is operating-system-dependent. This is the default setting, and it applies if the EXIT keyword is used without specifying any return value.

*EXIT FAILURE*

> Exit with a failure status. The value of failure is operating-system-dependent.

*EXIT value*

Exit, and return the value specified as the status.

*EXIT :bind_variable*

Exit, and return the value of the specified bind variable as the status.

*CONTINUE*

Do not exit if an error occurs. This is the default behavior when you first start SQL*Plus.

*COMMIT*

This keyword may be used in conjunction with both EXIT and CONTINUE. It causes SQL*Plus to automatically COMMIT the current transaction when an error occurs. This is the default behavior when you use the EXIT keyword.

*ROLLBACK*

May also be used in conjunction with EXIT and CONTINUE, and causes SQL*Plus to roll back the current transaction when an error occurs.

*NONE*

May only be used in conjunction with CONTINUE, and causes SQL*Plus to neither COMMIT nor ROLLBACK when an error occurs. This is the default behavior when you use the CONTINUE keyword.

# B

## SQL*Plus Format Elements

Several SQL*Plus commands allow you to control data formats using what is called a format specification. A *format specification* is a string of characters that tells SQL*Plus exactly how to format a number, date, or text string when it is displayed. The most notable of these commands is the COLUMN command, which is used to format columns of output from a SELECT query. There are other commands as well. The complete list of SQL*Plus commands that accept format specification strings is shown here:

*ACCEPT*
Prompts the user to enter a value from the keyboard.

*COLUMN*
Controls various aspects of the way a column of data is displayed.

*SET NUMBER*
Defines the default display format for numbers.

*TTITTE, BTITLE, REPHEADER, REPFOOTER*
These commands all allow number format specifications to control the way numbers are formatted in page headers, page footers, report headers, and report footers.

There are three different, broad types of values SQL*Plus can format: numbers, character strings, and dates. Not all commands can handle each type. With most commands, you can only specify number and date formats. The COLUMN command is a good example. The ACCEPT command is the only one that allows you to specify a date format string.

Format specification strings are made up of special characters that have meaning to SQL*Plus in the context of formatting a value for display. Numeric format strings, for example, tend to have lots of 0s, 9s, decimal points, and dollar signs.

Date format strings tend to include things like MM, DD, YYYY, and so forth. Character string formats are the simplest of all, because you basically have only one thing you can influence: length.

# *Formatting Numbers*

SQL*Plus offers the most options when it comes to formatting numbers. Numeric format strings may contain any of the elements shown in Table B-1.

*Table B-1. Numeric Format Elements*

| Format Element | Function |
| --- | --- |
| 9 | 9s are used to control the number of significant digits to be displayed. |
| 0 | A 0 is used to mark the spot in the result where you want to begin displaying leading zeros. It replaces one of the 9s. The most common location for a 0 is at the extreme left of the format string, but you can place it elsewhere. |
| $ | Causes a number to be displayed with a leading dollar sign. |
| , | Places a comma in the output. |
| . | Marks the location of the decimal point. |
| B | Forces zero values to be displayed as blanks. |
| MI | Used at the end of a format string to cause a trailing negative sign to be displayed for negative values. |
| S | May be used at either the beginning or end of a format string, and causes a sign to be displayed. The + sign is used to mark positive numbers, and the – sign marks negative numbers. When you use S, a sign will always be displayed. |
| PR | Causes negative values to be displayed within angle brackets. For example, –123.99 will be displayed as "<123.99>". Positive values will be displayed with one leading and one trailing space in place of the angle brackets. |
| D | Marks the location of the decimal point. |
| G | Places a group separator (usually a comma) in the output. |
| C | Marks the place where you want the ISO currency indicator to appear. For US dollars, this will be USD. |
| L | Marks the place where you want the local currency indicator to appear. For US dollars, this will be the dollar sign character. You cannot use L and C in the same format specification. |
| V | Used to display scaled values. The number of digits to the right of the V indicates how many places to the right the decimal point is shifted before the number is displayed. |
| EEEE | Causes SQL*Plus to use scientific notation to display a value. You must use exactly four Es, and they must appear at the right end of the format string. |

*Table B-1. Numeric Format Elements (continued)*

| Format Element | Function |
|---|---|
| RN | Allows you to display a number using Roman numerals. This is the only format element where case makes a difference. An uppercase "RN" yields uppercase Roman numerals, while a lowercase "rn" yields Roman numerals in lowercase. Numbers displayed as Roman numerals must be integers, and must be between 1 and 3,999, inclusive. |
| DATE | Causes SQL\*Plus to assume that the number represents a Julian date, and to display it in MM/DD/YY format. |

To format a numeric column or other number, simply string together the format elements that yield the result you want. Except for the RN element, none of the numeric format elements are case-sensitive. Table B-2 contains a number of examples showing you how these format elements really work.

The ACCEPT command is unique in that it uses a format string to constrain the user's input. However, in doing so, it takes a rather loose interpretation of the format elements shown in Table B-1. You can read more about this in Chapter 7, *Advanced Scripting*. For the most part, though, only the 9, 0, and period are very useful with ACCEPT.

SQL\*Plus always allows for a sign somewhere when you display a number. The default is for the sign to be positioned to the left of the number, and the sign is only displayed when the number is negative. Positive numbers will have a blank space in the leftmost position. Because space is always made for a sign character, number columns will typically be one space wider than your format specification seems to account for. That's the default behavior. Things change when you use S, MI, or PR. With S, you always get a sign. With MI, you get a trailing sign, or a trailing blank for positive numbers. PR gives you angle brackets, or spaces in place of them.

*Table B-2. Numeric Format Examples*

| Value | Format | Result | Comments |
|---|---|---|---|
| 123 | 9999 | 123 | A basic number |
| 1234.01 | 9,999.99 | 1,234.01 | Comma and decimal point |
| 23456 | $999,999.99 | $23,456.00 | A dollar value |
| 1 | 0999 | 0001 | Leading zeros |
| 1 | 99099 | 001 | Leading zeros only within the rightmost three digits |
| 23456 | 9,999.99 | ######### | An overflow condition |
| 0 | 099B | | Display zeros as blanks |
| 1 | 099B | 001 | Leading zeros displayed, even with B, when the value is nonzero |

*Table B-2. Numeric Format Examples (continued)*

| Value | Format | Result | Comments |
|---|---|---|---|
| -1000.01 | 9,999.99mi | 1,000.01- | Trailing minus sign |
| 1000.01 | 9,999.99mi | 1,000.01 | Trailing space |
| -1001 | S9,999 | -1,001 | Leading sign |
| -1001 | 9,999PR | <1,001> | Negative values in angle brackets |
| 1001 | 9,999PR | 1,001 | Spaces instead of angle brackets |
| 1001 | 9.999EEEE | -1.001E+03 | Scientific notation |
| 1995 | RN | MCMXCV | Roman numerals, uppercase |
| 1988 | rn | mcmlxxxviii | Roman numerals, lowercase |
| 1 | date | 01/01/12 | Julian date, day one |

# Formatting Character Strings

SQL*Plus offers only one format element when it comes to character strings. That element is "A". "A" is always followed by a number specifying the column width in characters. Character strings shorter than the column width are displayed left-justified within the column. Character strings that exceed the column width are either wrapped or truncated based on the option specified in the COLUMN command. The following example shows a text column that has been formatted wide enough to display the entire character string:

```
SQL> COLUMN a FORMAT A40
SQL> SELECT 'An apple a day keeps the doctor away.' A
  2     FROM dual;

A
----------------------------------------
An apple a day keeps the doctor away.
```

You can format the column so that it is 18 characters wide, which results in the text being wrapped within that space:

```
SQL> COLUMN a FORMAT A18
SQL> SELECT 'An apple a day keeps the doctor away.' A
  2     FROM dual;

A
------------------
An apple a day kee
ps the doctor away
```

By default, SQL*Plus wraps the text right in the middle of a word, if necessary. You can use the WORD_WRAPPED option of the COLUMN command to wrap text only at word boundaries.

```
SQL> COLUMN a FORMAT A18 WORD_WRAPPED
SQL> SELECT 'An apple a day keeps the doctor away.' A
  2    FROM dual;

A
------------------
An apple a day
keeps the doctor
away.
```

You also have the ability to truncate text at the column boundary.

```
SQL> COLUMN a FORMAT A18 TRUNCATE
SQL> SELECT 'An apple a day keeps the doctor away.' A
  2    FROM dual;

A
------------------
An apple a day kee
```

When used with the ACCEPT command, a character format defines the maximum number of characters SQL*Plus will accept from the user. This is shown in the following example:

```
SQL> ACCEPT some_text CHAR FORMAT A10
thisthatthen
"thisthatthen" does not match input format "A10"

SQL>
```

While the character format used with ACCEPT specifies a maximum length, it does not specify a minimum length. You can always enter fewer characters than the format calls for, even to the point of entering nothing at all.

## *Formatting Dates*

SQL*Plus doesn't really format dates at all. If you are selecting a date column from the database, you must use Oracle's built-in TO_CHAR function to convert the date to a character string, formatting it the way you want it. As far as SQL*Plus is concerned, that makes it just another character column. Table B-3 shows the date format elements that can be used with the TO_CHAR function.

The one SQL*Plus command that does recognize these date format elements is the ACCEPT command. When you ask the user to enter a date, you can also provide a date format specification. SQL*Plus will reject any date the user enters that does not match that format.

When displaying a date, you must use the TO_CHAR function to specify the format. The following example displays the current value of SYSDATE, including the time:

*Table B-3. Date Format Elements*

| Format Element | Function |
|---|---|
| -/,.;: | Punctuation may be included anywhere in the date format string, and will be included in the output. |
| 'text' | Quoted text may also be included in the date format string, and will be reproduced in the output. |
| AD or A.D.<br>BC or B.C. | Includes an AD or BC indicator with the date. |
| AM or A.M.<br>PM or P.M. | Prints AM or PM, whichever applies, given the time in question. |
| CC | The century number. This will be 20 for years 1900 through 1999. |
| SCC | Same as CC, but BC dates will be negative. |
| D | The number of the day of the week. This will be 1 through 7. |
| DAY | The name of the day. This will be Saturday, Sunday, Monday, and so forth. |
| DD | The day of the month. |
| DDD | The day of the year. |
| DY | The abbreviated name of the day. This will be Sat, Sun, Mon, and so forth. |
| HH | The hour of the day. This will be 1 through 12. |
| HH12 | The hour of the day. This will be 1 through 12, the same as HH. |
| HH24 | The hour of the day on a 24-hour clock. This will be 0–23. |
| IW | The week of the year. This will be 1–53. |
| IYYY | The four-digit year. |
| IYY | The last three digits of the year number. |
| IY | The last two digits of the year number. |
| I | The last digit of the year number. |
| J | The Julian day. Day 1 is equivalent to Jan 1, 4712 BC. |
| MI | The minute. |
| MM | The month number. |
| MON | The three-letter month abbreviation. |
| MONTH | The month name, fully spelled out. |
| Q | The quarter of the year. Quarter 1 is Jan–Mar, quarter 2 is Apr–Jun, and so forth. |
| RM | Is the month number in Roman numerals. |
| RR | When used with TO_CHAR, returns the last two digits of the year. |
| RRRR | When used with TO_CHAR, returns the four-digit year. |
| SS | The second. |
| SSSSS | The number of seconds since midnight. |
| WW | The week of the year. |

*Table B-3. Date Format Elements (continued)*

| Format Element | Function |
|---|---|
| W | The week of the month. Week one starts on the first of the month.. Week two starts on the 8th of the month, and so forth. |
| Y,YYY | The four-digit year with a comma after the first digit. |
| YEAR | The year spelled out in words. |
| SYEAR | The year spelled out in words, with a leading negative sign when the year is BC. |
| YYYY | The four-digit year. |
| SYYYY | The four-digit year, with a leading negative sign when the year is BC. |
| YYY | The last three digits of the year number. |
| YY | The last two digits of the year number. |
| Y | The last digit of the year number. |

```
SQL> SELECT TO_CHAR(SYSDATE,'dd-Mon-yyyy hh:mi:ss PM')
  2    FROM dual;

TO_CHAR(SYSDATE,'DD-MON
-----------------------
13-Dec-1998 09:13:59 PM
```

When you use a date format element that displays a text value, such as the name of a month, you need to pay attention to the case. The case of the element displayed will follow the case used when you specified the element. Suppose you want to display the three-letter abbreviation for a month. You could place either "Mon", "mon", or "MON" in your format string, and you would get back "Dec", "dec", or "DEC" respectively. You will see examples of this in Table B-4, which shows the results of several sample date format specifications.

To find out how to use a date format with the ACCEPT command, consult Chapter 7. ACCEPT uses the date format to validate what the user enters, and there are some limits on how closely the user is forced to follow that format.

*Table B-4. Date Format Examples*

| Value | Format | Result |
|---|---|---|
| 13-Dec-1998 09:13:59 PM | dd-mon-yyyy | 13-dec-1998 |
| 13-Dec-1998 09:13:59 PM | dd-Mon-yyyy | 13-Dec-1998 |
| 13-Dec-1998 09:13:59 PM | DD-MON-YYYY | 13-DEC-1998 |
| 13-Dec-1998 09:13:59 PM | Month dd, yyyy | December 13, 1998 |
| 13-Dec-1998 09:13:59 PM | Month dd, yyyy "at" hh:mi am | December 13, 1998 at 09:13 pm |
| 13-Dec-1998 09:13:59 PM | mm/dd/yy | 12/13/98 |
| 13-Dec-1998 09:13:59 PM | mm/dd/rr | 12/13/98 |

*Table B-4. Date Format Examples (continued)*

| Value | Format | Result |
|---|---|---|
| 13-Dec-1998 09:13:59 PM | mm/dd/yyyy | 12/13/1998 |
| 13-Dec-1998 09:13:59 PM | Day | Sunday |
| 13-Dec-1998 09:13:59 PM | ddd | 347 |
| 13-Dec-1998 09:13:59 PM | ww | 50 |
| 13-Dec-1998 09:13:59 PM | q | 4 |
| 13-Dec-1998 09:13:59 PM | year | nineteen ninety-eight |
| 13-Dec-1998 09:13:59 PM | Year | Nineteen Ninety-Eight |
| 13-Dec-1998 09:13:59 PM | YEAR | NINETEEN NINETY-EIGHT |

# *Index*

## *Symbols*

& (ampersand)
&& with substitution variables, 128–132
changing for variable substitution, 151
escaping, 147–148
marking variables, 124
prompting for variable values, 124
* (asterisk)
identifying errors in SQL statements, 52
line editing keyword, 43, 48, 443, 448
@ command, 62, 425
@@ command, 426
\ (escape character), 147–148
- command-line option, 25
-- (hyphens) for comments, 153, 425
-? command-line option, 25
. (period)
concatenation character, 149–150
terminating PL/SQL blocks, 39
; (semicolon) to end SQL statements, 34, 402
text editors, 59
/ (slash)
executing SQL buffer, 51, 53, 426
terminating PL/SQL blocks, 39
terminating SQL statements, 34
/* and */ comment delimiters, 152, 424

## *A*

A (APPEND) command, 42, 45, 428
ABORT parameter (SHUTDOWN), 336, 461

aborting database instance, 336, 461
ACC[EPT] command, 132–135, 427
in extract scripts, 165
format specifications with, 470, 472, 474–477
validating user input, 263–267
access method hints, 303–305
administration, 326–356
automating routine tasks, 8
backup and recovery, 340–356
RMAN for, 355
logging in as administrator, 31, 329, 442
looking at database, 337–340
settings for, 416
starting/stopping databases, 330–337, 460, 462
advancing to new page (reports), 82
AFIEDT.BUF file, 58
ALI[AS] clause
ATTRIBUTE command, 114, 430
COLUMN command, 69, 437
ALL parameter
ARCHIVE LOG command, 350, 429
SHOW command, 419, 459
ALL views, 181–182
ALL_COL_PRIVS view, 193, 222
ALL_CONS_COLUMNS view, 187, 200, 203
ALL_CONSTRAINS view, 186, 200
ALL_IND_COLUMNS view, 190, 207
ALL_INDEXES view, 187–190, 207, 211
ALL_SOURCE view, 177

# About the Author

Jonathan Gennick is a manager in KPMG's Public Services Systems Integration practice. Jonathan has over seven years of experience working with relational database technology, and is currently the lead database administrator for the utilities group working out of KPMG's Detroit office. In his day-to-day work as a DBA, Jonathan has come to depend heavily on SQL*Plus, and uses it extensively.

When he is not managing databases, Jonathan can often be found writing or editing books about them. His writing career began in 1997, when he coauthored *Teach Yourself PL/SQL in 21 Days* (Sams). Since then, he has been involved with four other book projects. He was the technical editor for *Oracle8 Server Unleashed* (Sams), the development editor for *Teach Yourself Access 2000 in 24 Hours* (Sams), a technical reviewer for *Oracle Database Administration: The Essential Reference* (O'Reilly & Associates), and the author of the book you are holding now.

Jonathan is a member of MENSA, and he holds a bachelor of arts degree in Information and Computer Science from Andrews University in Berrien Springs, Michigan. Jonathan currently resides in Lansing, Michigan, with his wife Donna and their two children: ten-year-old Jenny, who often wishes her father wouldn't spend quite so much time writing, and three-year-old Jeff, who has never seen it any other way. Jonathan may be contacted by email at *jonathan@gennick.com*.

# Colophon

The animal on the cover of *Oracle SQL*Plus: The Definitive Guide* is a moving leaf (*Phyllium giganteum*), a large (about 10 cm in length) Malaysian leaf insect related to stick insects; together these constitute the order *Phasmatida*, derived from the Greek word for "ghost." These stunning insects imitate local foliage with intricate detail, down to the leaf-like veins on their legs and tattered brown edges to mimic dead leaves. Moving leaf insects feed on bramble and other plant material. Kept by many entymologists as exotic pets, they require high temperature and humidity.

Ellie Fountain Maden was the production editor and project manager for *Oracle SQL*Plus: The Definitive Guide*, and also copyedited the book. Quality assurance was provided by Madeleine Newell, Sarah Jane Shangraw, and Sheryl Avruch, who was also the production manager. Ellie Cutler proofread the book, and Seth Maislin wrote the index.

Edie Freedman designed the cover of this book, using a 19th-century engraving from the Dover Pictorial Archive. The cover layout was produced by Kathleen Wilson with Quark XPress 3.32 using the ITC Garamond font.

The inside layout was designed by Nancy Priest and implemented in FrameMaker 5.5 by Mike Sierra. The text and heading fonts are ITC Garamond Light and Garamond Book. The illustrations that appear in the book were created in Macromedia FreeHand 8 and Adobe Photoshop 5 by Robert Romano. This colophon was written by Nancy Kotary.

Whenever possible, our books use RepKover™, a durable and flexible lay-flat binding. If the page count exceeds RepKover's limit, perfect binding is used.

# How to stay in touch with O'Reilly

## 1. Visit Our Award-Winning Web Site

### http://www.oreilly.com/

★ "Top 100 Sites on the Web" —*PC Magazine*
★ "Top 5% Web sites" —*Point Communications*
★ "3-Star site" —*The McKinley Group*

Our web site contains a library of comprehensive product information (including book excerpts and tables of contents), downloadable software, background articles, interviews with technology leaders, links to relevant sites, book cover art, and more. File us in your Bookmarks or Hotlist!

## 2. Join Our Email Mailing Lists

### New Product Releases
To receive automatic email with brief descriptions of all new O'Reilly products as they are released, send email to:
**listproc@online.oreilly.com**
Put the following information in the first line of your message (*not* in the Subject field):
**subscribe oreilly-news**

### O'Reilly Events
If you'd also like us to send information about trade show events, special promotions, and other O'Reilly events, send email to:
**listproc@online.oreilly.com**
Put the following information in the first line of your message (*not* in the Subject field):
**subscribe oreilly-events**

## 3. Get Examples from Our Books via FTP

There are two ways to access an archive of example files from our books:

### Regular FTP
- ftp to:
  **ftp.oreilly.com**
  (login: anonymous
  password: your email address)
- Point your web browser to:
  **ftp://ftp.oreilly.com/**

### FTPMAIL
- Send an email message to:
  **ftpmail@online.oreilly.com**
  (Write "help" in the message body)

## 4. Contact Us via Email

**order@oreilly.com**
To place a book or software order online. Good for North American and international customers.

**subscriptions@oreilly.com**
To place an order for any of our newsletters or periodicals.

**books@oreilly.com**
General questions about any of our books.

**software@oreilly.com**
For general questions and product information about our software. Check out O'Reilly Software Online at **http://software.oreilly.com/** for software and technical support information. Registered O'Reilly software users send your questions to: **website-support@oreilly.com**

**cs@oreilly.com**
For answers to problems regarding your order or our products.

**booktech@oreilly.com**
For book content technical questions or corrections.

**proposals@oreilly.com**
To submit new book or software proposals to our editors and product managers.

**international@oreilly.com**
For information about our international distributors or translation queries. For a list of our distributors outside of North America check out:
**http://www.oreilly.com/www/order/country.html**

O'Reilly & Associates, Inc.
101 Morris Street, Sebastopol, CA 95472 USA
TEL    707-829-0515 or 800-998-9938
       (6am to 5pm PST)
FAX    707-829-0104

# International Distributors

## UK, EUROPE, MIDDLE EAST AND AFRICA (EXCEPT FRANCE, GERMANY, AUSTRIA, SWITZERLAND, LUXEMBOURG, LIECHTENSTEIN, AND EASTERN EUROPE)

**INQUIRIES**
O'Reilly UK Limited
4 Castle Street
Farnham
Surrey, GU9 7HS
United Kingdom
Telephone: 44-1252-711776
Fax: 44-1252-734211
Email: josette@oreilly.com

**ORDERS**
Wiley Distribution Services Ltd.
1 Oldlands Way
Bognor Regis
West Sussex PO22 9SA
United Kingdom
Telephone: 44-1243-779777
Fax: 44-1243-820250
Email: cs-books@wiley.co.uk

## FRANCE

**ORDERS**
GEODIF
61, Bd Saint-Germain
75240 Paris Cedex 05, France
Tel: 33-1-44-41-46-16 (French books)
Tel: 33-1-44-41-11-87 (English books)
Fax: 33-1-44-41-11-44
Email: distribution@eyrolles.com

**INQUIRIES**
Éditions O'Reilly
18 rue Séguier
75006 Paris, France
Tel: 33-1-40-51-52-30
Fax: 33-1-40-51-52-31
Email: france@editions-oreilly.fr

## GERMANY, SWITZERLAND, AUSTRIA, EASTERN EUROPE, LUXEMBOURG, AND LIECHTENSTEIN

**INQUIRIES & ORDERS**
O'Reilly Verlag
Balthasarstr. 81
D-50670 Köln
Germany
Telephone: 49-221-973160-91
Fax: 49-221-973160-8
Email: anfragen@oreilly.de (inquiries)
Email: order@oreilly.de (orders)

## CANADA (FRENCH LANGUAGE BOOKS)

Les Éditions Flammarion ltée
375, Avenue Laurier Ouest
Montréal (Québec) H2V 2K3
Tel: 00-1-514-277-8807
Fax: 00-1-514-278-2085
Email: info@flammarion.qc.ca

## HONG KONG

City Discount Subscription Service, Ltd.
Unit D, 3rd Floor, Yan's Tower
27 Wong Chuk Hang Road
Aberdeen, Hong Kong
Tel: 852-2580-3539
Fax: 852-2580-6463
Email: citydis@ppn.com.hk

## KOREA

Hanbit Media, Inc.
Sonyoung Bldg. 202
Yeksam-dong 736-36
Kangnam-ku
Seoul, Korea
Tel: 822-554-9610
Fax: 822-556-0363
Email: hant93@chollian.dacom.co.kr

## PHILIPPINES

Mutual Books, Inc.
429-D Shaw Boulevard
Mandaluyong City, Metro
Manila, Philippines
Tel: 632-725-7538
Fax: 632-721-3056
Email: mbikikog@mnl.sequel.net

## TAIWAN

O'Reilly Taiwan
No. 3, Lane 131
Hang-Chow South Road
Section 1, Taipei, Taiwan
Tel: 886-2-23968990
Fax: 886-2-23968916
Email: benh@oreilly.com

## CHINA

O'Reilly Beijing
Room 2410
160, FuXingMenNeiDaJie
XiCheng District
Beijing, China PR 100031
Tel: 86-10-86631006
Fax: 86-10-86631007
Email: frederic@oreilly.com

## INDIA

Computer Bookshop (India) Pvt. Ltd.
190 Dr. D.N. Road, Fort
Bombay 400 001 India
Tel: 91-22-207-0989
Fax: 91-22-262-3551
Email: cbsbom@giasbm01.vsnl.net.in

## JAPAN

O'Reilly Japan, Inc.
Kiyoshige Building 2F
12-Bancho, Sanei-cho
Shinjuku-ku
Tokyo 160-0008 Japan
Tel: 81-3-3356-5227
Fax: 81-3-3356-5261
Email: japan@oreilly.com

## ALL OTHER ASIAN COUNTRIES

O'Reilly & Associates, Inc.
101 Morris Street
Sebastopol, CA 95472 USA
Tel: 707-829-0515
Fax: 707-829-0104
Email: order@oreilly.com

## AUSTRALIA

WoodsLane Pty., Ltd.
7/5 Vuko Place
Warriewood NSW 2102
Australia
Tel: 61-2-9970-5111
Fax: 61-2-9970-5002
Email: info@woodslane.com.au

## NEW ZEALAND

Woodslane New Zealand, Ltd.
21 Cooks Street (P.O. Box 575)
Waganui, New Zealand
Tel: 64-6-347-6543
Fax: 64-6-345-4840
Email: info@woodslane.com.au

## LATIN AMERICA

McGraw-Hill Interamericana
Editores, S.A. de C.V.
Cedro No. 512
Col. Atlampa
06450, Mexico, D.F.
Tel: 52-5-547-6777
Fax: 52-5-547-3336
Email: mcgraw-hill@infosel.net.mx

## O'REILLY®

TO ORDER: **800-998-9938** • **order@oreilly.com** • **http://www.oreilly.com/**
OUR PRODUCTS ARE AVAILABLE AT A BOOKSTORE OR SOFTWARE STORE NEAR YOU.
FOR INFORMATION: **800-998-9938** • **707-829-0515** • **info@oreilly.com**

O'Reilly & Associates, Inc.
101 Morris Street
Sebastopol, CA 95472-9902
1-800-998-9938

*Visit us online at:*
**http://www.ora.com/**
**orders@ora.com**

# O'REILLY WOULD LIKE TO HEAR FROM YOU

Which book did this card come from?

_____

Where did you buy this book?
- ❏ Bookstore
- ❏ Direct from O'Reilly
- ❏ Bundled with hardware/software
- ❏ Computer Store
- ❏ Class/seminar
- ❏ Other _____

What operating system do you use?
- ❏ UNIX
- ❏ Windows NT
- ❏ Macintosh
- ❏ PC(Windows/DOS)
- ❏ Other _____

What is your job description?
- ❏ System Administrator
- ❏ Network Administrator
- ❏ Web Developer
- ❏ Programmer
- ❏ Educator/Teacher
- ❏ Other _____

❏ Please send me O'Reilly's catalog, containing a complete listing of O'Reilly books and software.

Name _____  Company/Organization _____

Address _____

City _____  State _____  Zip/Postal Code _____  Country _____

Telephone _____  Internet or other email address (specify network) _____

Nineteenth century wood engraving
of a bear from the O'Reilly &
Associates Nutshell Handbook®
*Using & Managing UUCP.*

# BUSINESS REPLY MAIL
FIRST CLASS MAIL   PERMIT NO. 80   SEBASTOPOL, CA

*Postage will be paid by addressee*

### O'Reilly & Associates, Inc.
101 Morris Street
Sebastopol, CA  95472-9902